This book is due for return not later than the
last date stamped below, unless recalled sooner.

Urban Transport

Urban Transport

An Annotated International Bibliography

James McConville and John Sheldrake

MANSELL

London and Washington

First published 1997 by
Mansell Publishing Limited, *A Cassell Imprint*
Wellington House, 125 Strand, London WC2R 0BB, England
PO Box 605, Herndon, VA 20172

British Library Cataloguing in Publication Data
McConville, James, 1934–
    Urban Transport : an annotated international bibliography
    1. Urban transportation – Bibliography
    I. Title   II. Sheldrake, John, 1944–
    016.3'884

ISBN 0–7201–2335–6

Library of Congress Cataloging-in-Publication Data
McConville, J.
    Urban transport: an annotated international bibliography / James McConville and
John Sheldrake.
        p.   cm.
    Includes index.
    ISBN 0–7201–2335–6 (hard cover)
    1. Urban transportation — Bibliography.   I. Sheldrake, John. 1944– .   II. Title.
Z7164.U72M38   1997
[HE305]
016.3884 — dc20   96–32816
                                                                                  CIP

Typeset by York House Typographic Ltd, London
Printed and bound in Great Britain by Bookcraft (Bath) Ltd, Midsomer Norton, Somerset

Contents

Preface

Urbanisation is one of the defining characteristics of the modern world. Although urban centres did exist in antiquity, they were tiny in comparison to the cities of today. Athens, for example, only possessed a population of about 150,000 while Alexandria, the largest city in the ancient world, had around 700,000 inhabitants. These numbers were, however, quite exceptional and most towns in ancient, or for that matter medieval, times would have numbered a mere 1,500 to 2,000 people. Even a modest city of today such as Lille, Rabat or Dallas will have a population in excess of 1 million. It is also possible that a town which was once a free-standing settlement will have been absorbed into a conurbation or even become a megalopolis. Greater London has a population of almost 6.5 million, Paris and its environs 9 million, Tokyo 11 million, Cairo 14 million and Mexico City an estimated 17 million. These massive urban agglomerations pose huge transportation problems. The rise of road transport, both passenger and freight, has literally choked metropolitan streets and city populations alike. Supertrams, rapid transit systems and light railways are now being constructed throughout the world in an attempt to provide viable alternatives to automobiles and buses for passenger movement. Policy makers are grappling with the problems of environmental pollution, the desire for economic efficiency, issues of public safety and matters of public finance. These are some of the issues which provide the context for this bibliography.

There is a self-evident need for more research into the subject of urban transport in order that all concerned may be better informed of the risks and advantages of present policies and future plans. Accessing relevant information sources and literature is of course an essential but often time-consuming task, especially when undertaking academic or business research. Furthermore, while the search may often produce information relevant to the immediate problem, it may nevertheless fail to stimulate wider and perhaps more pertinent approaches. This bibliography is intended to facilitate literature searches for those engaged in the practice and study of urban transport. To date there has been no comprehensive bibliography for urban transport. This volume attempts to fill this gap by bringing together a vast amount of material relevant to both academics and practitioners in the field of urban transport at large. It is hoped that this work will serve to generate increased cross-fertilisation between academic researchers and those operating in 'the real world'.

In preparing this bibliography, we have chosen to define urban transport by its purpose. That is: the movement of people and materials through, or within, the environs of towns and cities. This definition has been applied irrespective of mode and encompasses commercial, public, private, pedestrian and cycle traffic. The volume thus provides a compilation of economic, social, political and legal – as well as developmental – literature relating to the urban transport sector. Operational issues and the underlying technology of urban transport, including most aspects of vehicle design and manufacture, are included only in so far as they affect wider institutional and resource allocation considerations. Although the work does not claim to be definitive, it is nevertheless comprehensive. A central guiding principle of compilation has been to include significant contributions to the subject published in English since 1970, although certain seminal works published prior to that date have also been cited. Indeed, given the vast quantity of literature dealing with the historical development of urban transport, entries on this topic are more or less limited to those concerning developments since the 1880s.

As can be seen from the list of contents, this volume covers an enormous range of literature. Although a certain amount of prioritisation and interpretation is inevitable in any process of compilation, the work is not calculated to be of a selective, indicative or normative character. Entries therefore appear alphabetically within categories. The contents are divided into 14 major categories, each of which is further divided into sections, and may be regarded as self-contained for the purpose of identifying areas of interest. Most entries are annotated in order to assist users in accessing the materials most relevant to their needs. It has not, however, been possible to read all the material included, and theses published before the mid-1980s are not annotated. Although there are no cross references, users of the bibliography are referred not only to the table of contents but to the two indices; that is, authors' name and subject.

Finally, although the bibliography has been prepared in the United Kingdom, it nevertheless aims to provide a broadly international perspective.

Professor James McConville
Director
Centre for International Transport Management
London Guildhall University

Dr John Sheldrake
Reader
Department of Politics and Modern History
London Guildhall University

June 1996

Acknowledgements

In the course of compiling this volume we have received support and assistance from many friends and colleagues to whom we would like to express our thanks. The work formed part of the extensive research programme of the London Guildhall University Centre for International Transport Management which was established with funding from the London School of Foreign Trade – the educational charity. We are grateful for their generous support. Similarly, the venture could not have been sustained without the ready support of Dr Iwan Morgan, Head of the University's Department of Politics and Modern History. Self-evidently, compilation of such a work would have been impossible without the provision of library services and the collaboration of other institutions. In particular, we are grateful for the help of Carole Symes and Philip Pothen of our own Moorgate library, Helen Berry of the Chartered Institute of Transport library and Kay Tregaskis of the University of Derby library. Our work has been greatly facilitated by the use of computer technology and we would like to thank the London Guildhall University's Computer Centre staff and particularly the Applications officer, Ronnie Capaldi. We are also grateful for the help of Carol Reoch and Leslie McKinnon, our research assistants during the early phase of the project. Finally, we would like to thank Ian Barraclough who, in his role as research assistant throughout the project, not only played a prominent part in data collection and final production but also made numerous editorial suggestions. Having said all of this, we naturally take full responsibility for all the errors, omissions and shortcomings from which the work may suffer. Our hope is that this volume will stimulate the further study of, and research into, urban transport.

Abbreviations

AA	Automobile Association
ADB	Asian Development Bank
AFC	Automatic fare collection
AGT	Automated guideway transit
AMA	Association of Metropolitan Authorities
APT	Advanced passenger train
BAA	British Airports Authority
BIFA	British International Freight Association
BR	British Rail
CBD	Central business district (New York, USA)
CBI	Confederation of British Industry
CEDA	Committee for Economic Development Australia
CES	Census of employment (USA)
CIPFA	Chartered Institute of Public Finance and Accountancy
CIT	Chartered Institute of Transport
COBA	Cost benefit analysis
COBS	Continuous on-bus survey
CPRE	Council for the Protection of Rural England
CPT	Confederation of Passenger Transport
D of E	Department of the Environment
D of T	Department of Transport
DATAR	French organisation for regional development
DD	Double-deck vehicle
DG IV	Directorate General IV
DOT	Department of Transportation (USA)
DRIVE	Dedicated Road Infrastructure Vehicle Safety in Europe

DTI	Department of Trade and Industry
ETC	Employee transportation co-ordinators
EC	European Community
ECMT	European Conference of Ministers of Transport
ETB	Electronic trolley buses
EU	European Union
FES	Family expenditure surveys
FHWA	Federal Highway Administration (USA)
FTA	Freight Transport Association
GATT	General Agreement on Tariffs and Trade
GIDS	General intelligent driver support
GLC	Greater London Council
GLTS	Greater London transport survey
GWR	Great Western Railway
HGV	Heavy goods vehicle (this term has been replaced by LGV, see below)
HMSO	Her Majesty's Stationery Office (Ltd)
ITF	International Transport Workers' Federation
ILO	International Labour Organisation
IVHS	Intelligent vehicle highway system
ICE	Institute of Civil Engineers
IFF	Institute of Freight Forwarders
IHT	Institution of Highways and Transportation
INRETS	Institute for Research on Transport and Traffic Safety (France)
IOTA	Institute of Transport Administration
IRT	Integrated Road Transport
IRTE	Institute of Road Transport Engineers
ISTEA	Intermodal Surface Transport Efficiency Act 1991 (USA)
LATA	London motorway action group
LGV	Large goods vehicle (replaced the term HGV)
LILT	Leeds Integrated Land Use Transport Model
LRT	London Rail Transport

LRTL	Light Railways Transport League
LT	London Transport
LUL	London Underground Limited
MAP	Market analysis project
NBC	National bill company
NTS	National travel surveys
ODA	Overseas Development Administration
OECD	Organization for Economic Co-operation and Development (OCDE or OESO)
OMO	One-man operation
P & R	'Park and Ride'
PLB	Public light buses (Hong Kong)
PROMETHEUS	Programme for European Traffic with Highest Efficiency and Unprecedented Safety
PRT	Personal rapid transit
PSERC	Public Sector Economic Research Centre
PSV	Public service vehicle
PTA	Passenger Transport Authority
PTE	Passenger Transport Executive
PTP	Public transport plan
PTRAC	Planning and Transport Research Advisory Council
PVR	Peak vehicle requirement
RATP	Régie autonome des transports parisiens
RGS	Route guidance systems
RHA	Road Haulage Association
RHDTC	Road Haulage and Distribution Training Council
RSA	Royal Society for the Encouragement of Arts, Sciences and Manufactures (Royal Society of Arts)
RSG	Rate support grant
RTA	Road Transport Association
RTAs	Road traffic accidents
RTAC	Road Transport Association of Canada
SADCC	South Africa Development Co-ordination Conference
SAPTCO	Saudi Arabian Public Transport Company
SBS	Singapore Bus Service

SSRC	Social Service Research Council
SD	Single-deck vehicle
SSB	Swiss State Railways
STA	State Transport Authority (South Australia)
STC	Sistema de transporte colectivo (Mexico Metro)
SUBTE	Buenos Aires underground system
TPP	Transport policies and programme
TREWSURB	Metropolitan rail mass transit system (Brazil)
TRRL	Transport and Road Research Laboratory (DTI)
TSG	Transport supplementary grant
TSM	Transport system management
UES	Urban Employment Service (Bureau of the census, USA)
UITP	Union internationale des transports publics
UMOT	United mechanism of travel
UN	United Nations
UPT	Urban transport planning
UTP	L'Union des transports publics (France)
WHO	World Health Organization

1   Reference Books

Bibliographies

1 **Alpert, Mary** and **Lesley, Lewis.** *The Role of Public Transport in New Towns with Reference to Runcorn, Skelmersdale and Telford: a bibliography.* Liverpool: Liverpool Polytechnic, 1979. 476 pp.

Entries classified under eight main headings according to subject matter, with an additional section on sources of information. Annotations presented for a number of the references and an index of authors is included.

2 **Bannister, David** and **Pickup, Laurie.** *Urban Transport and Planning: a bibliography with abstracts.* London: Mansell, 1989. 354 pp.

Bibliography of urban transport, and planning policy and practice since 1980. Contains around 600 records and is divided into seven major sections covering the urban and transport context; policy and planning in transport; social issues; travel modes; methods and evaluation; area studies; and bibliographies and research registers.

3 **Black, W. R.** and **Horton, Frank E.** *A Bibliography of Selected Research on Networks and Urban Transportation Relevant to Current Transportation Geography Research.* Evanston, IL: Northwestern University, 1968. 47 pp.

An annotated bibliography comprising a selection of publications relating to the field of urban transportation and geography.

4 **Department of Transport.** *Cycling Bibliography.* Traffic advisory leaflet no. 5/93. London: Department of Transport, June 1993. 6 pp.

5 **Department of Transport.** *Traffic Calming Bibliography.* London: Department of Transport, August 1993.

6 **Longo, Joseph.** *Urban Transportation: a guide to Canadian resources.* Illinois: Council of Planning Librarians, 1974. 23 pp.

Contains a selection of Canadian articles relating to the field of urban transportation.

7 Merger, Michele. Transport History in France: a bibliographical review. Manchester: *Journal of Transport History,* Vol. 8(2), September 1987, 177–201.

Examines the most important publications which have extended knowledge of French transport in the spheres of roads, waterways and railways.

8 National Technical Information Service. *Bus Transit Planning and Operations.* Virginia: National Technical Information Service, 1972. 69 pp.

Bibliography comprising 483 entries relating to the development and operation of bus transit systems in the United States.

9 Northwestern University Transportation Center. *Bus Transit Planning and Operations.* Evanston, IL: Northwestern University, 1972. 64 pp.

Annotated bibliography containing materials relating to the planning and operation of bus systems.

10 Royles, M. *Literature Review of Short Trips.* Project Report No. 104. Crowthorne: Transport and Road Research Laboratory, 1995. 24 pp.

Encyclopedias; dictionaries; glossaries

11 Allan, Ian. *The Little Red Book 1987: Road Passenger Transport Directory for the British Isles and Western Europe.* London : Ian Allan, 1987. 256 pp.

12 Bushell, Chris (ed.). *Jane's Urban Transport Systems.* 14th ed. (1995–96). Coulsdon, Surrey: Jane's Information Group, 1995. 680 pp.

Encyclopedic reference book on urban transport for 1995–96.

13 Crow, Geoffrey (ed.). *Encyclopedia of Transportation.* London: Reference International, 1977. 261 pp.

Integrated illustrated encyclopedia of transportation covering all aspects of land, sea and air transport from both a historical and a modern technological perspective. Deals with the general technical terms, and with the scientific principles which relate directly to the field and covers achievements and products of engineering and science that make particular modes of transport possible.

14 Elms, Charles P. (ed.). *Dictionary of Public Transport.* Düsseldorf: Alba Buchverlag, 1981.

Provides a dictionary of public transport with translations of terms and definitions in English, French and German.

15 Giacone, Linda; Heine, Erika; Lange, Elisabeth and **Jackson, Lynn.** *Dictionary of Public Transport.* Washington, DC: Lea Transportation Research Corporation, 1981.

Technical dictionary composed within the framework of an international transit handbook and compendium in three main sections cross-referenced to each other. The first contains English terms alphabetically with German and French translations. In the second, German terms are referenced with English and French translations. The third section displays French terminology with German and English translations.

16 Gray, Benita H. (ed.). *Urban Public Transportation Glossary.* Washington, DC: Transportation Research Board, 1989. 74 pp.

Contains selected terms relating to urban public transportation planning and operations, with definitions.

17 Hibbs, John. *Glossary of Economic and Related Terms for the Use of Students on Transport Courses.* Chatham: Roadmaster Publishing, 1993. 39 pp.

Intended to help students and managers to achieve competence in using economic terms. Each entry begins with a brief definition. Where possible examples are related to various modes of transport.

18 Hussain, Khalifa Afzal. *New Concepts and Terminologies in Modern Transport Systems.* Karachi: Transport Consultant Corporation, 1990. 136 pp.

Aims to serve as a reference book to aid the understanding of new concepts in the principal modes of transport including highways, railways, aviation and maritime.

19 Kaye, David. *The Pocket Encyclopaedia of Buses and Trolleybuses: before 1919.* London: Blandford Press, 1972. 149 pp.

Commencing with the carrier's wagon on the roads of Elizabethan England and continuing up to the years of the First World War when the spate of early bus company formations suffered a temporary halt. Illustrated.

20 Kaye, David. *The Pocket Encyclopaedia of Buses and Trolleybuses: 1919 to 1945.* London: Blandford Press, 1970. 191 pp.

Covers the period when the bus and the trolley bus broke away from the designs of the horse bus and the tramcar and began to emerge as two distinct vehicles in their own right.

21 Logie, Gordon. *Glossary of Transport.* Amsterdam: Elsevier, 1980. 296 pp.

International planning glossary published in a six-language edition, covering private transport, roads, road traffic, parking and road vehicles in English, French, Italian, Dutch, German and Swedish.

22 Lowe, David. *Dictionary of Transport Terms and Abbreviations.* Surrey: Fairplay Publications, 1991. 115 pp.

Aims to identify terms and abbreviations associated with road transport operation and also to provide explanations in simple language of what they mean, whom they represent or the legal definition.

Handbooks

23 Bayman, Bob and **Connor, Piers.** *The Underground Official Handbook.* Middlesex: Capital Transport Publishing, 1994. 96 pp.

Attempts to provide a guide which answers many of the questions often asked about London's underground – how the system works, how the equipment operates and the historical background.

24 Blonk, W. A. G. (ed.). *Transport and Regional Development: an international handbook.* Farnborough: Saxon House, 1979. 338 pp.

Divided into three parts; part one adopts a theoretical approach and covers aspects of transport and regional policy, such as public obligations in transport and their impact on underdeveloped regions. Part two provides a country by country analysis which aims at identifying the contribution of transport to the development of backward regions. Part three covers the problem of transport and regional policy in the European Community and the area covered by the Council of Europe.

25 Central Office of Information. *Inland Transport in Britain.* London: HMSO, 1977. 19 pp.

Pamphlet outlining a number of developments in the various parts of the inland transport system including roads (road transport and road haulage), railways and inland waterways. Also describes the organisation and administration of each sector.

26 Downs, D. E. *Understanding the Freight Business.* 4th ed. Surrey: Micro Freight UK, 1992. 236 pp.

Covers international movement of freight shipments from point of origin to destination. Mainly concerned with shipping but with reference to rail and road transport.

27 Greater London Council. *Transport Facts and Figures.* 2nd ed. London: Greater London Council, 1980. 30 pp.

Series of maps and diagrams presenting basic facts about London's transportation systems.

28 Hudson, Mike. *Way Ahead: the bicycle warrior's handbook.* London: Friends of the Earth, 1978. 59 pp.

Campaign manual for the use of groups and individuals interested in attempting to persuade local authorities and other organisations to make provisions to encourage the use of bicycles.

29 Jonchay, Yvan du. *The Handbook of World Transport.* London: Macmillan, 1978. 146 pp.

Inland transport such as pipelines, river traffic, railways and roads are discussed as well as two major modes of international transport, namely maritime and aviation. Contains three case studies: a history of oil and the search for new reserves; the oil crisis and the future of electricity; uranium and new energy sources.

30 Lay, M. G. *Handbook of Road Technology.* Volume 2: Traffic and Transport. New York: Gordon and Breach Science Publishers, 1986. 712 pp.

Offers insights into road operating environments including driver behaviour, traffic flow, lighting and maintenance; and assesses the costs, economics, and environmental impact of road use.

31 Lowe, David. *The European Bus and Coach Handbook 1995.* London: Kogan Page, 1995. 215 pp.

Comprehensive guide to all aspects of the road passenger transport industry. Contains practical information, key facts and useful addresses.

32 Lowe, David. *The Transport Manager's and Operator's Handbook 1995.* 25th ed. London: Kogan Page, 1995, 550 pp.

Reference work, updated annually, contains a comprehensive coverage of road transport legislation.

33 Lowe, David. *The Transport and Distribution Manager's Guide to 1992.* London: Kogan Page, 1989. 206 pp.

Looks at the European transport market and the legal and business implications of the single European market.

34 Ritchie, A. J. *Accounting in the Passenger Service Vehicle Industry.* London: Chartered Institute of Management Accountants, 1986. 51 pp.

Provides a guide to accounting in the passenger service vehicle industry.

Statistics and research

35 Department of Transport. *Journey Times Survey 1994: inner and outer London.* Transport statistics report. London: Department of Transport, 1995. 40 pp.

36 Department of Transport. *Road Accidents Great Britain 1994: the casualty report.* London: Department of Transport, 1995. 167 pp.

37 Department of Transport. *Vehicle Speeds in Great Britain.* Statistics Bulletin No. 95/32. London: Department of Transport, June 1995. 26 pp.
A statistical bulletin of vehicle speeds in Great Britain.

38 Department of Transport. *Transport Statistics for London 1980–1990: Transport Statistics Report.* London: HMSO, 1991. 45 pp.
Looks at the demographic and economic activity and the transport infrastructure. Argues that the most significant development in this decade was the completion of the M25 in 1986.

39 Department of Transport. *Transport Statistics Great Britain: 1994 edition.* London: HMSO, 1994. 236 pp.
Official source of information covering all aspects of transport for the decade 1984 to 1994.

40 Department of Transport. *Transport Statistics for London 1994: Transport Statistics Report.* London: HMSO, 1994. 45 pp.
Looks at the population and employment and travel patterns, and the major developments since 1983, including cycle routes, rail, air, and the docklands.

41 Department of Transport. *Traffic Speeds in Central and Outer London: 1993–94: Transport Statistics Report.* London: HMSO, 1995. 10 pp.
New surveys of traffic speeds in central and outer London have found average speeds of just under 11 mph throughout the working day in the central area, and between 17.5 mph in the morning peak and just under 23 mph in the off-peak in outer London. Together with results from the 1992 survey of inner London, these figures represent an interruption to the downward trend in speeds that has been evident since this series of surveys began in 1968.

42 Department of Transport. *Transport Statistics Great Britain: 1979–1989.* London: HMSO, 1993. 227 pp.

16th edition of Transport Statistics Great Britain. The content and format are basically the same as in other issues. However, there are some new and amended statistical tables which take into account recent developments within the Department of Transport.

43 Department of Transport. *Transport Statistics Great Britain: 1991* edition. London: HMSO, 1991. 302 pp.

17th edition of Transport Statistics Great Britain, although similar in content to previous editions, takes into account some new and amended statistical tables and charts which reflect recent developments within the Department of Transport.

44 Department of Transport. *Transport Statistics Great Britain: 1993* edition. London: HMSO, 1993. 227 pp.

19th edition of Transport Statistics Great Britain brings together a comprehensive range of statistical data designed to assist informed discussion of transport developments and policies.

45 Greater London Transport. *External Cordon and Screen Line Survey Technical Manual.* Greater London Transportation Survey: Volume V. London: Greater London Transport, 1974. 178 pp.

46 International Road Transport Union. *World Transport Data.* Geneva: International Road Transport Union, 1973. 261 pp.

Bilingual (English/French) transport reference compendium which allows comparisons to be made between statistical data relative to the world of transport generally and to that of road transport in particular.

47 Johnson, F. *The Transport of Goods by Road in Great Britain 1984: Annual Report on the continuing survey of road goods transport: Statistics bulletin* (85) 23. London: Department of Transport, 1985.

Report analyses the freight activity and vehicle kilometres done on public roads in the UK by goods vehicles greater than 3.5 tonnes gross vehicle weight (GVW), and 1525 kgs unladen (ULW), registered in Great Britain.

48 Rogers, Lee H. *International Statistical Handbook of Urban Public Transport.* Brussels: International Union of Public Transport, 1975. 387 pp.

Handbook of statistics relating to urban transport activities worldwide.

49 United Nations. *1990 Annual Bulletin of Transport Statistics for Europe.* New York: United Nations, 1990. 281 pp.

Provides basic data on transport and related trends in European countries, Canada and the United States of America. Purely statistical in character, the bulletin covers the rail, road and inland waterway sectors including freight.

Yearbooks and annual reports

50 Booth, Gavin (ed.). *Buses Annual 1984.* London: Ian Allan, 1983. 128 pp.

51 Booth, Gavin (ed.). *Buses Annual 1985.* London: Ian Allan, 1983. 128 pp.

52 Booth, Gavin. *Classic Bus Yearbook 1995.* London: Ian Allan, 1995. 128 pp.

53 Brown, Stuart J. *Buses Yearbook 1996.* London: Ian Allan, 1995. 128 pp.

54 Commission of the European Communities. *Observation of Transport Markets: Europa Transport: Annual Report 1987.* Brussels: Commission of the European Communities, 1988. 126 pp.

Statistical information on international intra-community transport of goods collected under 'Market Observation System'. Focuses on road, inland waterway, rail and combined modes of transport.

55 Commission of the European Communities. *Observation of Transport Markets: Europa Transport: Annual Report 1988.* Paris: Organisation for Economic Co-operation and Development, 1990. 134 pp.

Statistical information on international intra-community transport of goods collected under the 'Market Observation System'. Focuses on road, inland waterway, rail and combined modes of transport.

56 Commission of the European Communities. *Observation of Transport Markets: Europa Transport: Annual Report 1989.* Paris : Organisation for Economic Co-operation and Development, 1992. 114 pp.

Statistical information on international intra-community, transport of goods collected under the 'Market Observation system'. Focuses on road, inland waterway, rail and combined modes of transport.

57 Gretton, John and **Harrison, Anthony** (eds). *Transport UK 1985: an economic, social and policy audit.* Berks: Policy Journals, 1985. 120 pp.

Critical appraisal of all aspects of transport provision, operation and use within the four countries of the United Kingdom, the starting point being the relevant government spending programme and the Department of Transport. Both the sectors are considered and the interactions of these with other government programmes and other aspects of the total UK economy are comprehensively examined and critically appraised.

58 Hughes, Murray (ed.). *Developing Metros 1990: a Railway Gazette Yearbook: Metros, Trams, Light rail, Commuter rail.* Sussex: Reed Business Publishing, 1990. 86 pp.

Annual collection of special features and reports. International. Includes an item, 'London: Managing Engineering Better.'

59 Hughes, Murray (ed.). *Developing Metros 1992: a Railway Gazette Year Book: Light rail, Trams, Metros, Suburban.* Sussex: Reed Business Publishing, 1992. 83 pp.

Annual publication incorporating special features and reports. International. Includes an item, 'London offers Guidelines to other Metros.'

60 Keeler, Theodore E. (ed.). *Research in Transportation Economics: a research annual: Volume 1 1983.* Greenwich, CT: JAI Press, 1983.

Includes three papers on urban transportation: impacts of higher petroleum prices on transportation patterns and urban development, bus priority and congestion pricing on urban expressways, and pareto-optimal urban transportation equilibria.

61 TAS Partnership (ed.). *Rapid Transit Monitor 1993.* Preston : Transport Advisory Service, 1993. 159 pp.

2 Textbooks and Standard Works

General

62 Ballou, Ronald H. *Business Logistics Management.* 3rd ed. Englewood Cliffs, NJ: Prentice Hall, 1992. 688 pp.

63 Bardi, Edward J., Cavinato, Joseph L. and **Coyle, John J.** *Transportation.* St Paul, MN: West Publishing, 1982. 520 pp.
Adds some new topics not usually found in basic transportation texts, many of which are in the area of management. In addition, such topics as urban transportation (freight and passenger), international transportation, and transportation equipment, receive attention.

64 Bell, G., Bowen, P. and **Fawcett, P.** *The Business of Transport.* Plymouth: Macdonald and Evans, 1984. 344 pp.
After an introductory chapter on the transport industry, each mode of transport is studied in five separate chapters written in a common format which allows inter-modal comparisons to be made. Latter half of the book synthesises the earlier chapters and considers in turn, inter-modal transport, economic and financial aspects, policy and planning, the role of government, transport institutions and trade unions.

65 Delaney, R. E. and **Woellner, G. W.** (eds). *Elements of Transport.* 3rd ed. Sydney: Butterworths, 1974. 211 pp.
Covers all the elementary aspects of movement plus the complex economic issues of ownership, costs, monopoly and competition as well as detailing the principal features of transport; each mode is dealt with individually. Particular characteristics of road, rail, water, air and pipe-line transport; their spheres of operations, and the advantages and limitations in the way in which they are used and the unit of transport they provide are all clearly established.

66 European Conference of Ministers of Transport. *Transport and the Challenge of Structural Change: introductory reports and summary of the discussion.* Eighth International Symposium on Theory and Practice in Transport Economics, Istanbul, 1979. Paris: Organisation for Economic Co-operation and Development, 1980. 539 pp.

Investigates long-term trends in the world economy and developments in the transport field and looks at changing patterns of economic activity, trade and freight transport. Papers are also presented on the subject of behavioural changes and decentralisation and regional environment (passengers and freight) together with a general introduction and a summary of the discussion.

67 European Conference of Ministers of Transport. *Resources for Tomorrow's Transport: introductory reports and summary of discussions.* 11th International Symposium on Theory and Practice in Transport Economics. Paris: Organisation for Economic Co-operation and Development, 1989. 524 pp.

Divided into five sections: the main European links, maintenance and renewal of infrastructures, financing of transport system operations, quality of life and social costs, logistics and information technologies. Finally, a conference summary and conclusions are given.

68 European Conference of Ministers of Transport. *Transport Growth in Question.* 12th International Symposium on Theory and Practice in Transport Economics. Paris: Organisation for Economic Co-operation and Development, 1993. 653 pp.

Divided into five sections; demographic structure and social behaviour, economic trends and transport specialisation, infrastructure capacity and network access, impact of new technologies on efficiency and safety, environment, global and local effects. Finally, a conference summary and conclusions are given.

69 Faris, Martin T. and **Sampson, Roy J.** *Domestic Tranportation: practice, theory and policy.* 4th ed. Boston, MA: Houghton Mifflin, 1979. 518 pp.

Introductory text which deploys an applied and theoretical approach. The basic modes of transport are viewed as a whole rather than separately and the traditional areas of transportation such as economics, physical distribution and traffic management are also investigated on a broad basis.

70 Faulks, R. W. *Elements of Transport.* London: Ian Allan, 1965. 200 pp.

Elementary introduction to the study of transport as a whole; a general groundwork designed to provide an overall grasp of the fundamentals, primarily for new entrants into the industry and new students of the discipline.

71 Faulks, R. W. *Urban and Rural Transport.* London: Ian Allan, 1981. 188 pp.

Goes beyond 'the bus' to trolley-buses, trams and rapid transit. Covers traffic side of business in considerable depth.

72 Faulks, Rex W. *Principles of Transport.* 4th ed. London: McGraw-Hill, 1990. 190 pp.

Standard basic text book for transport students. Attempts to relate theory to reality and this is supported by inclusion of case studies. Looks at the transport systems of the world including transport infrastructure.

73 Fullerton, Brian. *The Development of British Transport Networks.* Oxford: Oxford University Press, 1975. 59 pp.

Description and analysis are combined in this account of how British transport systems penetrated the living space of the island and improved accessibility for its inhabitants. Emphasises the constraints imposed upon transport development by the physical landscape of Britain and discusses the effects of private actions, public attitudes, and government planning on the actual shape of the transport system.

74 Gubbins, Edmund J. *Managing Transport Operations.* London: Kogan Page, 1988.

Examination of the interaction between economic, social and technical aspects underpinning the transport system with chapter 9 concentrating on an examination of urban transport.

75 Hazard, John L. *Transportation Management Economics Policy.* Centreville, MD: Cornell Maritime Press, 1977. 597 pp.

Synthesis of transportation management, economics and policy which draws upon a number of underlying fields and disciplines, primarily economics, engineering, and legal and policy studies. The functional approach supplies the integrative thread which ties the work together. The scope of this work is broad and encompasses all principal passenger and freight modes, rail-road, and highway. Also examines issues such as urban transportation and urban inter-modal problems.

76 Hibbs, John. *An Introduction to Transport Studies.* 2nd ed. London: Kogan Page, 1988. 110 pp.

Aims to provide an informal overview of the transport industry. Chapters include: why study transport?, the approaches to transport, the function of transport, the control of transport, men and management, careers in transport, and an appendix on suggested further reading.

77 Hoyle, B. S. (ed.). *Transport and Development.* New York: Barnes and Noble, 1973. 230 pp.

Selection of contributions published on the role of transport in the economic and social advancement of the less-developed countries. Emphasis is on material from tropical Africa and Latin America, but reference is also made to during its formative 'developing' period. Based on economic theory and on spatial analysis, together with discussions on the role of specific transport modes, especially roads, railways and seaports.

78 Maltby, D. and **White, H. P.** *Transport in the United Kingdom.* London: Macmillan, 1982. 207 pp.

The four themes which run throughout this interdisciplinary text include the pervasive nature of transport activity; whether transport should be dealt with as a total system; the concept of the life-cycle for any transport mode in socio-economic and technological terms and, finally, the relative roles of the private and public sectors in transport activity.

79 Manheim, Marvin L. *Fundamentals of Transportation Systems Analysis: basic concepts.* Volume 1. Cambridge, MA: MIT Press, 1979. 658 pp.

Claims that transportation systems analysis is a multidisciplinary field which draws on engineering, economics, operations research, political science, psychology, management and other disciplines.

80 McCullagh, Patrick. *Transportation in Modern Britain.* 2nd ed. Oxford: Oxford University Press, 1971. 64 pp.

Brief overview of transportation on Britain which covers the railways; the container revolution; roads; ports; the transmission of energy; hovercraft and inland waterways; and air transportation.

81 Munby, Denys (ed.). *Transport: selected readings.* Harmondsworth: Penguin Books, 1970. 333 pp.

Collection of many individual and varied studies linked to the common theme of 'transport' and split into the following four broad areas: consumers' surplus and pricing; costs and prices; traffic and cities; and project appraisal.

82 Nijkamp, Peter. *Europe on the Move.* Aldershot: Avebury, 1993. 350 pp.

Four-part European-orientated analysis concentrating consecutively on mega-trends in European communications and transport activity, impacts of informatics and logistics, transport policy issues and the question of modelling spatial interactive behaviour.

83 Rallis, Tom. *City Transport: in developed and developing countries.* London: Macmillan, 1988. 202 pp.

Provides an overview of city transport research as made by architects, engineers, economists and administrators and makes an attempt to classify cities in time and space. Various models are used to compare and evaluate city transport in Cairo, Calcutta, Copenhagen, London, Los Angeles, Rio de Janeiro and Singapore.

84 Scott Hellewell, D. (ed.). *Public Transport in the Commercial World.* Welwyn: Construction Industry Conference Centre, April 1994. 108 pp.

Proceedings of a conference held in Nottingham in April 1994.

85 Steward-David, David. *The Theory and Practice of Transport.* London: Heinemann, 1980. 182 pp.

Explains both the theory and practice of transport operations. Examines the purpose of transport activities and the ways in which efficient transport can improve standards of living. Looks at the nature of different modes of transport suitability. Discusses financial aspects of private and public sector transport.

86 Taff, Charles A. *Commercial Motor Transportation.* 5th ed. Centreville, MD: Cornell Maritime Press, 1975. 576 pp.

Textbook designed for courses in motor transportation and carrier management; and as a reference guide for more general courses in transportation, physical distribution, logistics, and traffic management. Competitive aspects of the government provided rail passenger service of Amtrak and some of the implications are also covered.

87 White, Peter. *Public Transport.* 2nd ed. London: UCL Press, 1995. 240 pp.

General textbook that serves as an introduction to all modes of public transport. Topics covered include: organisation and control of transport in Britain; the role of public transport; the technology of bus and coach systems; urban railways and rapid transit systems; network planning; costing and cost-allocation methods; pricing in theory and practice; impacts of national transport policy; policy in the long run; rural public transport and intercity public transport.

88 Whitelegg, John. *Urban Transport.* London: Macmillan, 1985. 49 pp.

Examines some of the problems related to transport in cities. Stresses the social implications of the technological developments in transport which are accompanying the current restructuring of many urban areas in the developed world.

Economics

89 Abouchar, Alan. *Transportation Economics and Public Policy: with urban extensions.* New York: John Wiley and Sons, 1977. 326 pp.

Attempts to integrate the three main aspects of public sector transportation analysis and decision-making: price theory and policy, cost theory and measurement, and investment choice; and to develop policy guidelines on the basis of welfare maximising principles and real world complexities and constraints. Empirical examples and case studies are provided to illustrate applications and to suggest ways to bridge the gap between everyday data limitations and the theory and concepts presented.

90 Adler, Hans A. *Economic Appraisal of Transport Projects: a manual with case studies.* Baltimore, MD: Johns Hopkins University Press, 1987. 235 pp.

Provides a practical introduction to the economic appraisal of transport projects in developing countries. Key topics are accident reduction, traffic forecasting, time savings and transport sector planning. Intended as a primer on the application of cost-benefit analysis of transport investments.

91 Beesley, M. E. *Urban Transport: studies in economic policy.* London: Butterworth, 1973. 413 pp.

The function of this book is to provide, in easily available form, articles appearing between 1962 and 1972 which were scattered and often in sources inaccessible to the reader, and to comment on developments since the articles were first published. Uses a practical approach with the emphasis on getting usable results in order to assist policy makers to appraise critically the consequences of adopting new forms of analysis when abandoning older patterns of organisation of urban transport.

92 Bell, G., Blackledge, D. A. and **Bowen, P.** *The Economics and Planning of Transport.* London: Heinemann, 1983. 248 pp.

Basic economic theory is introduced covering supply and demand, pricing policy and investment appraisal. Transport problems such as urban congestion and its concomitant, rural isolation, are discussed in relation to planning and subsidy policies. Finally, the programmes and experiences of the British Isles are placed in a wider international context.

93 Button, K. J. *The Economics of Urban Transport.* Farnborough: Saxon House, 1977. 181 pp.

Study analysing the developments and changes in urban transport. Aims to explain the causes and consequences of recent trends with the particular intention of providing an overview of the economics of urban transport. Set against a background of the main urban transport debates together with an historical impact review of transport on urban land usage over the last century, the main problems which have resulted are investigated.

94 Button, K. J. and **Pearman, A. D.** *Applied Transport Economics: a practical case studies approach.* London: Gordon and Breach Science Publishers, 1985. 146 pp.

Practical guide which demonstrates how economic theories can successfully be applied to transport problems. Offers detailed case studies on a wide range of transport questions relating to urban congestion. Railway investment, inter-urban road provision and shipping cartels are also looked at.

95 Button, Kenneth. *Transport Economics.* 2nd ed. Cambridge: Cambridge University Press, 1993. 269 pp.

Economic analysis of transport issues dealing with the regulation of transport markets. Examines in general terms the many aspects of the demand for, and supply of, transport, including the various methods of government intervention needed to ensure that social and environmental criteria are met.

96 Cole, Stuart. *Applied Transport Economics.* London: Kogan Page, 1987. 318 pp.

Provides an insight into the field of transport economics and explains the range of techniques involved. Begins by considering the practical application of economic theories, and then develops each concept to the level of theory required. Elasticity of demand is examined and further chapters look at costing and pricing. Contains a series of case studies which place transport in the wider economic context.

97 Dalvi, M., Stubbs, P. C., Tyson, W. J. and **Carter, Charles** (eds). *Transport Economics.* London: Allen and Unwin, 1980. 216 pp.

Synthesis of theoretical and empirical material used to explain elements of transport economics. Includes basic material such as supply and demand, pricing and investment at a level accessible to non-specialists. The needs of more advanced students are met in chapters on passenger transport demand models and spatial equilibrium models.

98 Daughety, Andrew F. *Analytical Studies in Transport Economics.* Cambridge: Cambridge University Press, 1985. 253 pp.

Collection of research papers concerned with the application of economic theory and analytical techniques to current issues in transportation economics. Provides an introduction to analytical transport economics followed by a section on technology and demand and a section on equilibrium pricing and market behaviour.

99 Foster, C. D. *The Transport Problem.* London: Croom Helm, 1975. 340 pp.

Introduction to the principles of transport economics examining the economic objectives of road and rail, pricing and investment criteria, competition and coordination of transport policy.

100 Frankena, Mark W. *Urban Transport Economics.* Toronto: Butterworths, 1979. 141 pp.

Monograph which presents a survey of urban transportation economics and deploys data from various studies which have taken place in Canada.

101 Glaister, Stephen. *Fundamentals of Transport Economics.* Oxford: Basil Blackwell, 1981. 194 pp.

Guide for students into applying simple, quantitative tools to solve real problems in transport economics. Urban transport is covered theoretically under such fields as queues, car ownership, discrete choices and travel demand. Regulation, pricing and welfare economics are also examined.

102 Gwilliam, K. M. and **Mackie, P. J.** *Economics and Transport Policy.* London: Allen and Unwin, 1975. 390 pp.

Discussion of the developments of transport policy in the UK against a background of economic theory. Comprises a comprehensive review of transport policy in both urban and inter-urban situations from an economic perspective.

103 Harrison, A. J. *The Economics of Transport Appraisal.* London: Croom Helm, 1974. 293 pp.

Comprehensive review of the techniques involved in applying economic concepts to the appraisal of transport policies.

104 Heertje, Arnold and **Polak, Jacob.** *European Transport Economics.* Oxford: Basil Blackwell, 1993. 310 pp.

Presents the main theoretical and practical issues that transport raises for all modern economies. Topics include travel demand, transport markets and supply, the external effects of transport and the role of government.

105 Hendrickson, Chris and **Wohl, Martin.** *Transportation Investment and Pricing Principles.* New York: John Wiley and Sons, 1984.

Introductory text on the theory of transport pricing, financing, and investment planning.

106 Hensher, David A. (ed.). *Urban Transport Economics.* Cambridge: Cambridge University Press, 1977. 277 pp.

Provides a frame of reference for identifying key issues in urban transport economics.

107 Kain, J. F., Meyer, J. R. and **Wohl, M.** *The Urban Transportation Problem.* Cambridge, MA: Harvard University Press, 1965. 527 pp.

Economic analysis of the urban travel and transportation problem which summarises various proposed solutions. In particular this study looks at changes in the technology of urban transportation, the changing pattern of land use within metropolitan areas and trip-making behaviour.

108 Kanafani, Adib. *Transportation Demand Analysis.* New York: McGraw-Hill, 1983. 320 pp.

A textbook of transportation demand analysis. Chapter four focuses on urban passenger travel demand.

109 Kneafsey, James T. *Transportation Economic Analysis.* Lexington, MA: Lexington Books, 1975. 418 pp.

Aims to limit the broad scope of transport economics with its imprecise boundaries in order to concentrate on a field of analysis which includes domestic transportation within the continental United States. Examines the operation and facilities of urban transport, including passenger and intercity travel, as well as freight movements across North America.

110 Kneafsey, James T. *The Economics of the Transportation Firm.* Lexington, MA: Lexington Books, 1974. 132 pp.

A study of the firms comprising the transportation industries in the United States focusing on the industrial organisational aspects of the largest transportation firms. Specifically examines the market structures of motor trucking, railroad and airline industries and includes selected urban transportation statistics for 1970.

111 Mohring, Herbert. *Transport Economics.* Massachusetts: Ballinger Publishing, 1976. 174 pp.

Examines the economics of congestion, travel time evaluation, peak-load and related cost allocation problems, transportation benefit/cost analysis, scale economies and pricing problems.

112 Nash, C. A. *Economics of Public Transport.* London: Longman, 1982. 194 pp.

Using detailed applications, the book seeks to demonstrate the usefulness of applying economic analysis to problems such as fare structures and levels, service planning and investment decisions. Concentrates on road and rail based systems which form the bulk of urban public transport systems throughout the world.

113 National Bureau of Economic Research. *Transportation Economics: a conference of the Universities–National Bureau Committee for economic research.* New York: National Bureau of Economic Research, 1965. 464 pp.

114 Norton, Hugh S. *Modern Transportation Economics.* 2nd ed. Ohio: Charles E. Merrill, 1971. 470 pp.

Focuses on an aggregate view of the means and purposes of transport including cost-output relations and pricing, the basis and framework of public control, application of public control and finally problems and prospects for the future.

115 Prest, Alan R. *Transport Economics in Developing Countries.* New York: Praeger, 1969.

Emphasises the significance of correct pricing of roads and railways to ensure transport coordination.

116 Sharp, C. H. *Transport Economics.* London: Macmillan, 1973. 80 pp.

Identifies the basic economic problems of transport in Britain. Provides an introductory coverage of the methods of measuring the output of transport services and the relative importance of the different modes of transport.

117 Small, Kenneth A. *Urban Transportation Economics: Fundamentals of Pure and Applied Economics Series.* Switzerland: Harwood Academic, 1992. 185 pp.

Reviews the contribution that economics can make to the analysis of urban transportation, placing heavy emphasis on highway transportation and formal models in this area. Discusses travel demand, covering aggregate models; disaggregate or behavioural models; logit models for mode choice and trip scheduling choice on the journey to work; and theoretical and empirical analyses of the monetary valuation of the travel-time savings brought about by transportation improvements.

118 Thomson, J. M. *Modern Transport Economics.* Harmondsworth: Penguin Books, 1974. 282 pp.

Examines the economics of transport and the problems involved in attempting to achieve a satisfactory balance between supply and demand. Also discusses how these problems might be overcome.

Geography

119 Bamford, C. G. and **Robinson, H.** *Geography of Transport.* Plymouth: Macdonald and Evans, 1978. 430 pp.

Deals with the geography of transport in four sections. First, the general principles and modes of transport are introduced and discussed. Second, international transport systems are considered on a regional basis. Third, the problems of urban and rural transport are examined. Finally, the role of transport in regional development and tourism growth is covered. Chapters on transport planning and policy are also provided.

120 Daniels, P. W. and **Warnes, A. M.** *Movement in Cities: spatial perspectives on urban transport and travel.* London: Methuen, 1980. 393 pp.

Looks at the spatial aspects of transport in cities and describes and analyses urban travel in terms of purpose, distance and frequency of journeys and modes and routes used. Concentrates on British towns with references to the USA and Australia.

121 Gauthier, Howard L. and **Taaffe, Edward J.** *Geography of Transportation.* Englewood Cliffs, NJ: Prentice Hall, 1973. 226 pp.

Survey of some ways in which geographers have approached the study of transportation. Deals with how geographers view a transportation system and how transport systems have been analysed.

122 Hanson, Susan (ed.). *The Geography of Urban Transportation.* New York: Guilford Press, 1986. 424 pp.

Collection of essays addressing urban transportation from a geographic perspective. Divided into three parts: part one gives an overview of urban transportation; part two describes urban transportation in empirical terms and presents the technical methods by which urban travel is analysed and predicted; the final part concerns itself with urban transport policy.

123 Hoyle, B. S. and **Knowles, R. D.** (eds). *Modern Transport Geography.* London: Belhaven Press, 1992. 276 pp.

Based on geographical theory and focused on contemporary issues. The topics covered include an analysis of the relationship between transport and economic development. The twin trends of transport deregulation and privatisation are also assessed. Urban transport patterns are examined along with the distinctive problems of inter-urban transport and of rural accessibility and isolation.

124 Hurst, Michael (ed.). *Transportation Geography: comments and readings.* New York: McGraw-Hill, 1974. 528 pp.

The general framework of this text is provided by reports issued by Northwestern University in the early 1960s and the book's division into networks, flows, nodes, and interrelationships comes from the breakdown used in those reports. Transportation systems are examined as firmly entrenched structures in the economic milieu.

125 Kansky, K. *Structure of Transportation Networks: relationships between network geometry and regional characteristics.* Chicago, IL: Department of Geography, University of Chicago, 1965. 154 pp.

Study of transportation networks stressing that the structure of the transportation network cannot be divorced from the geographic characteristics of that area.

126 Morrison, Alastair. *Traffic Study as Quantitative Field Work.* Teaching Geography No.14. Sheffield: The Geographical Association, 1970. 27 pp.

127 Robinson, Roger. *Ways to Move: the geography of networks and accessibility.* Massachusetts: Cambridge University Press, 1977. 90 pp.

Uses many examples and exercises taken from a variety of situations in order to develop general ideas and techniques which can be applied to studies of transportation and communication in any area. Many of the practical examples come from the UK, particularly the Midlands.

128 Senior, M. L. and **White, H. P.** *Transport Geography.* London: Longman, 1983. 224 pp.

Introduction to transport studies from a geographical perspective which in particular traces the evolution of transport patterns and their interaction with other human activities. Divided into three main sections: the first examines basic factors in transport development with chapters exploring past decision making; the second deals with the spatial qualities of transport patterns, and the final section deals with the quantitative aspects of transport geography.

129 Stutz, Frederick P. *Social Aspects of Interaction and Transportation.* Washington, DC: Association of American Geographers, 1976. 74 pp.

Resource paper designed to fill gaps which existed in text material for urban and transportation geography courses.

130 Tolley, Rodney and **Turton, Brian.** *Transport Systems, Policy and Planning: a geographical approach.* Harlow: Longman Scientific and Technical, 1995. 402 pp.

Provides a review of the major spatial aspects of transport systems throughout the world, together with a detailed analysis of transport problems arising in urban and rural areas, and an evaluation of the principal social, environmental and policy issues generated by contemporary transport systems.

History

131 Abell, P. H. *Transport and Industry in Greater Manchester.* South Yorkshire: P. H. Abell, 1978. 84 pp.

Examines the part played by the transport system in the industrialisation of Manchester.

132 Aldcroft, D. H. and **Dyos, H. J.** *British Transport: an economic survey from the seventeenth century to the twentieth.* Leicester: Leicester University Press, 1969. 473 pp.

Study of the origins and development of modern British transport. Deals specifically with the history and traffic of British roads, rivers, ports, canals, railways, urban streets, motor transport and airways. Considers the growth of the transport system in economic as well as social and technological terms.

133 Aldcroft, Derek H. *British Transport Since 1914: an economic history*. Newton Abbot: David and Charles, 1975. 336 pp.

Survey of developments in the principal sectors of British transport since 1914. Attention is focused particularly on trends since the First World War and the problems created out of technological improvement and structural change are examined. The size of the transport sector in the economy is noted as well as the changing structural format of transport services.

134 Aldcroft, Derek H. and **Freeman, Michael J.** *Transport in Victorian Britain*. Manchester: Manchester University Press, 1988. 310 pp.

Account of developments in transport from around 1840 to 1914. Urban transport is analysed and the way in which steam, both on land and at sea, transformed economic and geographical relationships is considered.

135 Aldcroft, Derek H. and **Freeman, Michael J.** *Transport in the Industrial Revolution*. Manchester: Journal of Transport History, 1983. 237 pp.

Presents a collection of writings on different aspects of transport in the eighteenth and nineteenth century. Topics include the Turnpike Road System, river navigation in England, and the finance of canal building.

136 Aldcroft, Derek H. *Studies in British Transport History 1870–1970*. Newton Abbot: David and Charles, 1974. 309 pp.

Attempts to provide an understanding of some of the neglected areas of transport history over the last century. Each chapter is written with the idea of answering questions with reference to the economic aspects of transport. Examines the factors which determined the demand for passenger transport in Britain since the Second World War.

137 Bagwell, Philip S. *The Transport Revolution from 1770*. London: Batsford, 1974. 460 pp.

Historical analysis of transport since the industrial revolution including inland navigation, roads, railways, coastal shipping, air and motor transportation.

138 Bagwell, Philip S. *The Transport Revolution: 1770–1985*. London: Routledge, 1988. 474 pp.

Describes the development of transport in Britain.

139 Barker, T. C. and **Robbins, Michael.** *A History of London Transport: Volume 1 – The nineteenth century*. London: Allen and Unwin, 1963. 411 pp.

Details the origins of the world's largest urban passenger transport systems together with the growth of London until 1900.

140 Barker, T. C. and **Robbins, Michael.** *A History of London Transport: Volume 2 – The 20th century to 1970.* London: Allen and Unwin, 1974. 554 pp.

Details the development of London's transport system during the first seventy years of the present century.

141 Barker, T. C. and **Savage, C. I.** *An Economic History of Transport in Britain.* 3rd ed. London: Hutchinson University Library, 1974. 280 pp.

Substantially re-written edition of Savage's standard work. Places greater emphasis on eighteenth-century developments than the original and also deals more comprehensively with road transport.

142 Bonavia, Michael R. *The Nationalisation of British Transport: the early history of the British Transport Commission, 1948–1953.* London: Macmillan, 1987. 192 pp.

Examines the attempt by the Labour Government of 1945–51 to create a publicly owned and integrated transport system for Britain.

143 Boughey, Joseph. *Hadfield's British Canals.* Stroud: Allan Sutton, 1994. 343 pp.

Revised and expanded eighth edition of Charles Hadfield's standard work. Provides an account of the impact of canals on, and within, urban areas.

144 Butt, John. Achievement and Prospect: transport history in the 1970's and 1980's. Manchester: *Journal of Transport History,* Vol. 2 (1), March 1981, 1–24.

Reviews the increase and change in emphasis of academic activity in the field of transport history. Specialist literature produced in the 1970s is examined mode by mode. A section is included on urban development and transport.

145 Chaloner, W. H. and **Ratcliffe, Barrie M.** (eds). *Trade and Transport: essays in economic history in honour of T. S. William.* Manchester: Manchester University Press, 1977. 293 pp.

Volume of essays covering a wide span of industrial and commercial activity in Britain from the Cumbrian iron industry in the seventeenth century to Scottish exports in the twentieth.

146 Charlesworth, George. *A History of the Transport and Road Research Laboratory 1933–1983.* Aldershot: Avebury, 1987. 267 pp.

Examines how the Transport and Road Research Laboratory, from its small beginnings as an experimental outstation of the Ministry of Transport Roads Department, and later as the Road Research Laboratory in the Department of Scientific Industrial Research, has come to play a significant role in the development of road transport, both nationally and internationally.

147 Cheape, Charles W. *Moving the Masses: Urban Public Transport in New York, Boston and Philadelphia.* Cambridge, MA: Harvard University Press, 1980. 292 pp.

An account of the transition from horse to mechanical traction in three of the four largest conurbations in the USA. Demonstrates that in these large American cities public transport implementation did not proceed as quickly as the American electric tramway mileage totals of the 1890s suggest.

148 Gordon, Anne. *To Move with the Times: the story of transport and travel in Scotland.* Aberdeen: Aberdeen University Press, 1988. 248 pp.

Historical survey of the social effects of transport, or indeed the lack of it, on the daily lives of people in Scotland.

149 Humphries, Steve and **Weightman, Gavin.** *The Making of Modern London 1815–1914.* London: Sidgwick and Jackson, 1983. 176 pp.

Illustrated account of the nineteenth-century development of London, including its transport networks.

150 Hunter, D. L. G. *Edinburgh's Transport.* Yorkshire: Advertiser Press, 1964. 398 pp.

151 Jackman, W. T. *The Development of Transportation in Modern England.* London: Frank Cass, 1962. 820 pp.

Comprehensive historical text dealing with the development of roads, river navigation, canals, railways, steam navigation and postal history.

152 Jackson, Alan A. *Semi-Detached London: suburban development, life and transport, 1900–1939.* 2nd ed. Didcot: Wild Swan Publications, 1991. 278 pp.

Survey of the great suburban expansion of London during the first forty years of the twentieth century. Includes an important chapter on the provision of transport infrastructure for the suburbs.

153 Jones, D. *Urban Transit Policy: an economic and political history.* New Jersey: Sole, 1985.

Examines the mass transit industry in the United States of America in the period

1902 to 1982 with its growth and integration with federal and state governments.

154 Klapper, Charles F. *Roads and Rails of London 1900–1933.* London: Ian Allan, 1976. 191 pp.

Evolution of the era of independent bus and tram companies, horse-drawn goods vehicles and steam trains. Illustrated.

155 Piggott, Stuart. *The Earliest Wheeled Transport: from the Atlantic Coast to the Caspian Sea.* London: Thames and Hudson, 1983. 272 pp.

Account of the earliest wheeled transport in Europe which is traced back to around 3000 BC. Study of comparative technology which raises questions of social order, culture and economy.

156 Pratt, Edwin. A. *A History of Inland Transport and Communication.* Newton Abbot: David and Charles, 1970. 532 pp.

Reprint of Pratt's 1912 text which examines transport from the earliest roads, down through the river and the canal era to the electrically operated railways of 1911. Chapters deal with such issues as transport and its environment, roads and the Church, early trading conditions and the turnpike system.

157 Ransom, P. J. G. *The Archaeology of the Transport Revolution 1750–1850.* Surrey: World's Work, 1984. 208 pp.

Historical survey of transport from the mid-eighteenth century to the mid-nineteenth century.

158 Savage, C. I. *Inland Transport: History of the Second World War.* London: HMSO, 1957. 678 pp.

Describes the efforts of the Ministry of War Transport to close the gap between the supply of transport resources and the demands made upon them – efforts which had their technical, administrative and political as well as economic aspects. Outlines the chief inland transport developments in Britain from 1914 to 1939 before describing the performance of this transport and evaluating how it coped against heavy German bombing and port diversion.

159 Savage, Christopher I. *An Economic History of Transport.* 3rd ed. London: Hutchinson University Library, 1966.

Economic history of transport up until the Second World War with emphasis placed on developments in the nineteenth and twentieth centuries. Attempts to provide an understanding of transport and of current problems of transport policy through an interpretation of the economic development of the transport industries and of the growth of state control over them.

160 Schaeffer, K. H. and **Sclar, E.** *Access for All: transportation and urban growth.* Harmondsworth: Penguin Books, 1975. 182 pp.

An historical analysis of the development of transport in cities, suggesting that the growth of private motor transport has resulted in the growth and dispersion of urban areas, leading to an overall loss of access with accompanying economic problems.

161 Sherrington, C. E. R. *100 Years of Inland Transport 1830–1933.* London: Frank Cass, 1969. 376 pp.

Survey focusing on the Railway Age in Britain and how this affected the postal service and electric telegraph. There are also sections on the history of the horse omnibus, tramways and bicycles. Concludes with a very full consideration both of the impact of motor transport on the railway industry and of the problems of transport co-ordination which occupied the Royal Commission on Transport from 1928.

162 Symons, Leslie and **White, Colin.** *Russian Transport: an historical and geographical survey.* London: G. Bell and Sons, 1975. 192 pp.

Examines the salient features of the transport systems of the Russian empire and the Soviet Union, rather than providing a comprehensive account of the development of all the systems. Each transport medium and its development is dealt with by a specialist in that field.

163 Turnbull, Gerard L. *Traffic and Transport.* London: Allen and Unwin, 1979. 196 pp.

Traces the growth of Britain's inland transport services, chiefly goods traffic by road, canal and railway from the early seventeenth century to the eve of nationalisation in 1947 and focuses on the history of Pickfords, long a member of the transport industry.

164 Yago, Glenn. *The Decline of Transit: urban transportation in German and US cities 1900–1970.* Cambridge: Cambridge University Press, 1984. 293 pp.

Examines in detail the social, political, and technological forces that shaped the cities and their transportation systems in the twentieth century. Compares the United States and West Germany looking at the factors that transformed urban life and offers an explanation of past urban and economic policy failures.

Politics and policy

165 Altshuler, Alan; Pucher, John R. and **Womack, James P.** *The Urban Transportation System: politics and policy innovation.* Cambridge, MA: MIT Press, 1979. 558 pp.

Divided into two parts, part one reviews the post-war history of American urban transportation policy and advances a set of propositions about how to rank potential innovations with reference to political feasibility. Part two examines the criteria by which critics and defenders of the urban transportation system seem to evaluate it. Problems looked at in detail are: energy, air quality, safety, equity, congestion and land use and urban development.

166 Banister, David and **Button, Kenneth** (eds). *Transport in a Free Market Economy.* London: Macmillan, 1991. 255 pp.

Considers the situation in North America and makes comparisons with Europe.

167 Burke, Catherine G. *Innovation and Public Policy: the case of personal rapid transit.* Lexington, MA: D. C. Heath, 1979. 401 pp.

Presents a theoretical framework in which the processes of technological innovation are linked with political processes. A review of the history and development of urban transportation problems with proposed alternative solutions is given. The case of personal rapid transit is then examined. The successes and failures as experienced in four US cities are contrasted with experiences of England, France, Germany and Japan.

168 Button, K. J. and **Gillingwater, D.** *Future Transport Policy.* London: Croom Helm, 1986. 230 pp.

Discussion on a world-wide basis of the issues involved in transport policy. Examines how policies have evolved, what factors affect present decision-making and the trends likely to prevail in the future. Includes consideration of those contentious areas which so often hit the headlines such as urban transport and international airline deregulation.

169 Button, Kenneth and **Pitfield, David.** *Transport Deregulation: an international movement.* London: Macmillan, 1991. 211 pp.

Looks at devolution of transport policy in Europe; transport regulation in Switzerland, and transport regulation, deregulation and regulatory reform in Australia. Includes a section on modal studies which contains a chapter on the bus industry in the UK, USA and Australia.

170 Colcord, Frank C. and **Altshuler, Alan.** Urban Transportation and Political Ideology: Sweden and the United States. In *Current Issues in Transportation Policy.* Lexington, MA: Lexington Books, 1980.

Argues that transportation decisions are in fact ideological in character, representing differing notions of the proper role of government and the proper distribution of the costs and benefits of government programmes among social groups. Argues that societies with different dominant ideologies resolve comparable controversies in consistent and different ways.

171 Cornehls, James V. and **Taebel, Delbert A.** *The Political Economy of Urban Transportation.* New York: Kennikat Press, 1977. 218 pp.

Provides an analysis of the urban transportation crisis in America. Examines the ideology of the political and economic decision-making process that affects transportation policy and the ability of the urban transportation system to respond to change. Broader issues of social policy, urban design, citizen reaction and the impact of the transportation system on minorities are also explored.

172 European Conference of Ministers of Transport. *Resources for Tomorrow's Transport.* Introductory Remarks and Summary of Discussions. Brussels: European Conference of Ministers of Transport, 1988. 524 pp.

Attempts to clarify what resources will be needed by the transport systems of the future. Looks at the main European links, the maintenance and renewal of infrastructures, the financing of transport system operations, the quality of life and social costs, and logistics and information technologies.

173 Garbutt, Paul E. *London Transport and the Politicians.* London: Ian Allan, 1985. 128 pp.

Examines the transport policy of the Greater London Council in an attempt to determine how much political control is necessary.

174 Germane, Gayton E. *Transport Policy Issues for the 1980s.* London: Addison-Wesley Publishing, 1983. 503 pp.

Intended to give students experience of analysing complex economic and political problems and to broaden understanding of a variety of economic and transportation problems which will remain for many years.

175 Giannopoulos, G. and **Gillespie, A.** (eds). *Transport and Communications Innovation in Europe.* London: Belhaven Press, 1993. 369 pp.

Focuses on the convergence of the previously separate realms of telecommunications and transport. Also looks at the implications of innovation in transport and communications for the spatial organisation of economy and society.

176 Gwilliam, K. M. and **Chapman, Brian** (eds). *Transport and Public Policy.* London: Allen and Unwin, 1970. 259 pp.

Assessment of the role of government and its agencies in the transport sector.

177 Lande, Richard. *National Transportation Policy.* Toronto: Butterworths, 1992. 217 pp.

Aims to evaluate aspects of Canada's national transportation policy, concentrating on surface transportation. An analysis is offered of the way transportation policy is formulated in Canada.

178 Levinson, Herbert S. and **Weant, Robert A.** *Urban Transportation: perspectives and prospects.* Connecticut: Eno Foundation for Transportation, 1982. 414 pp.

Compendium of articles concerned with the planning, management and financing of urban transportation systems.

179 McConville, James and **Sheldrake, John** (eds). *Transport in Transition: aspects of British and European experience.* Aldershot: Avebury, 1995. 182 pp.

Collection of essays dealing with various aspects of transport policy including ideology, political control and Europeanisation.

180 O'Sullivan, Patrick. *Transport Policy: an interdisciplinary approach.* London: Batsford, 1980. 313 pp.

Examines transport using an interdisciplinary approach encompassing the viewpoints of political economists and theoreticians, historians, engineers, planning analysts and geographers.

181 Plowden, William. *The Motor Car and Politics 1896–1970.* London: Bodley Head, 1971. 468 pp.

Focuses on changing attitudes towards private motoring, as revealed in the press, Cabinet discussions, departmental files, public enquiries and parliamentary debates. Examines the interactions of Westminster, Whitehall and public opinion in the light of changing attitudes.

182 Purdy, H. L. *Transport Competition and Public Policy in Canada.* Vancouver: University of British Columbia Press, 1972. 327 pp.

Examination of the forces of intermodal competition as they relate to the inter-city transport picture. Features an introduction to the various modes of transportation and the competitive inter-relationships that exist among them. Also features an analysis of the considerable inequality in public treatment of the intermodal competitors, based on a comparison of government subsidy programmes; and an appraisal of how public regulation of rates and services has affected intermodal competition.

183 Sargent, J. R. *British Transport Policy.* Oxford: Clarendon Press, 1958. 163 pp.

Looks specifically at the Transport Act of 1953, but is also concerned with the specific issue of efficiency in transport and how it can be improved in Britain.

184 Sheldrake, John. *Modern Local Government.* Aldershot: Dartmouth, 1992. 108 pp.

Provides an account of the rise and relative decline of local government in England and Wales with an emphasis on urban developments. Contains a substantial chapter on local government and urban passenger transport.

185 Smerk, George M. *Federal Urban Mass Transportation Programs and Policy.* Lexington, MA: Lexington Books, 1980.

Discussion of the development of the urban transportation programmes of the federal government.

186 Starkie, David. *The Motorway Age: road and traffic policies in post-war Britain.* Oxford: Pergamon Press, 1982. 175 pp.

Provides insight into 'why' and 'how' government road and traffic policies change. Questions how cities cope with the rising tide of traffic, especially in relation to the abandonment of plans for urban motorways.

187 Wistrich, Enid. *The Politics of Transport.* London: Longman, 1983. 185 pp.

Overview of the long-term trends and developments in transport policy and in the principal operating systems since 1945. Investigates the guiding ideologies of the professionals, policy-makers and politicians involved. Policy issues are considered from two perspectives: pressure group and political party stances and an analysis of the policy options. Issues examined include environmental matters, conflict over lorry loads and the question of transport subsidy.

188 Zwerling, Stephen. *Mass Transit and the Politics of Technology.* London: Praeger Publishers, 1974. 159 pp.

Study of the political consequences of technological choice. A substantial portion of the work deals with two public transit systems in the San Francisco Bay area, though the underlying theme is to deal with politics in relation to technological change.

Planning and engineering

189 Adams, John. *Transport Planning: vision and practice.* London: Routledge and Kegan Paul, 1981.

Systematic and detailed critique of the contemporary practice of transport planning.

190 Ampt, Elizabeth S., Meyburg, Arnim H. and **Richardson, Anthony J.** *Survey Methods for Transport Planning.* Melbourne: Eucalyptus Press, 1995. 459 pp.

191 Ampt, E. S., Brog, W. and **Richardson, A. J.** *New Survey Methods in Transport: 2nd International Conference.* Utrecht: VNU Science Press, 1985. 377 pp.

Compilation of survey techniques employed in the broad field of transport planning.

192 Banister, David and **Hall, Peter.** *Transport and Public Policy Planning.* London: Mansell, 1981. 455 pp.

Preview of transport policy and planning from a broad social science perspective. Seeks to give an up-to-date summary of the research which has been, and is being, carried out into transport and public policy making.

193 Barber, Gerald; Holtzclaw, Gary D. and **O'Sullivan, Patrick.** *Transport Network Planning.* London: Croom Helm, 1979. 187 pp.

A study synthesising the policy, philosophical and technical issues involved in transport planning.

194 Bennet, D. W. and **Ogden, K. W.** *Traffic Engineering Practice.* 3rd ed. Victoria: Department of Civil Engineering, 1984. 474 pp.

Includes sections on traffic management planning, traffic control systems, design for public transport, the use of simulation techniques in traffic analysis, and cost-effectiveness evaluation of traffic proposals.

195 Black, Alan. *Urban Mass Transportation Planning.* New York: McGraw-Hill, 1995. 411 pp.

Provides a general textbook written for an American audience on urban mass transportation. Emphasises policy issues with a minimum of technical material, thus requiring little mathematical knowledge.

196 Blanchard, Benjamin S. *Logistics Engineering and Management.* 4th ed. Englewood Cliffs, NJ: Prentice Hall, 1992. 556 pp.

197 Boer, E. de. *Transport Sociology: social aspects of transport planning.* Oxford: Pergamon Press, 1986. 235 pp.

Collection of international literature on the acute social problems implicit in transport planning. These range from social disintegration to political, safety and behavioural issues. Covers both theoretical and practical considerations.

198 Bridger, G. A. and **Winpenny, J. T.** *Planning Development Projects.* London: Overseas Development Administration, 1983.

Practical guide to project appraisal.

199 Bruton, Michael J. *Introduction to Transportation Planning.* 3rd ed. London: UCL Press, 1992. 288 pp.

Places the issue of transport within a broad social context, relating it to demographic, socio-economic, political and environmental considerations. Contains a chapter on computers in transportation planning and the most commonly used software packages.

200 Creighton, Roger L. *Urban Transportation Planning.* Champaign, IL: University of Illinois Press, 1970. 375 pp.

General work on overall planning methods for transportation in cities. Divided into two parts: part one deals with basic problems and policy issues of transportation, travel, land use and transportation facilities. Part two follows the major steps of the transportation planning process.

201 Cresswell, Roy (ed.). *Passenger Transport and the Environment: the integration of public passenger transport with the urban environment.* London: Leonard Hill, 1977. 299 pp.

Overview of public transport in the urban setting with contributions from the different branches of planning, technology and design involved. Covers aspects of the subject ranging from the overall structure of towns to individual transport design.

202 Cullingworth, J. B. *Town and Country Planning in Britain.* 10th ed. London: Unwin Hyman, 1988. 408 pp.

Contains a chapter on planning for traffic.

203 Gray, George E. and **Hoel, Lester A.** (eds). *Public Transportation: planning operations and management.* Englewood Cliffs, NJ: Prentice Hall, 1979. 749 pp.

Covers the historical development of public transportation; systems and technologies; planning public transportation systems; managing and operating public transit systems; policy considerations; and, finally, considers likely future developments.

204 Hakkert, A. S.; Link, Dan; Rihmann, S. and **Shaul, P. Ben** (eds). *Traffic, Transportation and Urban Planning.* Volume 1. London: George Godwin, 1981. 245 pp.

Contains edited versions of 24 papers originally presented at an international conference in Tel Aviv in 1978 of the Institute of Transportation Engineers, the Association of Engineers and Architects and the International Technical Cooperation Centre.

205 Hakkert, A. S.; Link, Dan; Rihmann, S. and **Shaul, P. Ben** (eds). *Traffic, Transportation and Urban Planning.* Volume 2. London: George Godwin, 1981. 268 pp.

Contains edited versions of 22 papers originally presented at an international conference in 1978 in Tel Aviv of the Institute of Transportation Engineers, the Association of Engineers and Architects and the International Technical Cooperation Centre.

206 Hall, Peter. *London 2001.* London: Unwin Hyman, 1989. 226 pp.

Examines the long-term strategic planning of London. Contains a chapter on London's transport.

207 Hobbs, F. D. *Traffic Planning and Engineering.* 2nd ed. Oxford: Pergamon Press, 1979. 543 pp.

Comprehensive analysis of traffic studies including administration and planning in traffic engineering, traffic and environmental management and traffic stream capacity. Also deals with the road user, the vehicle and the road, street lighting and signs and road markings, together with accidents and road safety.

208 Homburger, Wolfgang S. and **Kell, James H.** *Fundamentals of Traffic Engineering.* 12th ed. Berkeley, CA: Institute of Transportation Studies, University of California, 1988.

Covers the fundamentals of traffic engineering in the context of California.

209 Hutchins, John G. B. *Transport and the Environment.* London: Elek Books, 1970. 106 pp.

Argues that economic activity, centralised in the railway age, is now becoming decentralised again in the present multimodal transport age. Surveys the long term effects of revolutionary changes in transportation, including the location of industry, systems of trading, geographical living patterns and patterns of leisure.

210 Hutchinson, B. G. *Principles of Urban Transport Systems Planning.* Washington, DC: Scripta Books, 1974. 444 pp.

Analysis of the processes involved in urban transport strategic planning within a systems type framework. Techniques employed to estimate travel demands which are likely to be created by a given land use arrangement are also reviewed.

211 Institute of Civil Engineers. *Transport for Society: proceedings of the conference organised by the Institution of Civil Engineers, 11–13 November 1975.* London: Institute of Civil Engineers, 1976. 175 pp.

212 Kresge, David T. and **Roberts, Paul O.** *Techniques of Transport Planning.* Volume 2. Washington, DC: Brookings Institution, 1971. 571 pp.

Study of transportation planning in developing countries. Covers systems analysis and simulation models.

213 Lane, Robert; Powell, Timothy J. and **Prestwood-Smith, Paul.** *Analytical Transport Planning.* London: Gerald Duckworth, 1971. 283 pp.

Attempts to explain the conventional method of analytical transport planning and to show its limitations. Main elements of the process are described from survey, analysis and model building to forecast and evaluation.

214 Meyer, John R. and **Straszheim, Mahlon R.** *Techniques of Transport Planning.* Volume 1. Washington, DC: Brookings Institution, 1971. 571 pp.

Study of transportation planning in developing countries. Covers pricing and project evaluation.

215 Plowden, Stephen. *Taming Traffic.* London: André Deutsch, 1980. 221 pp.

Critique of the principles and methods of analysis which underline the traditional approach to urban transport planning based on the indiscriminate use and provision of roads and of the massive studies which seem to lend them support. Offers an alternative approach, although the discussions of alternatives is not extensive.

216 Simpson, Barry J. *Urban Public Transport Today.* London: E. and F.N. Spon, 1994. 222 pp.

Addresses the issue of how local public transport might meet the demands made upon it and how it can be made into a viable alternative to the private car.

217 Simpson, Barry J. *Planning and Public Transport in Great Britain, France and West Germany.* Harlow: Longman Scientific and Technical, 1987.

Study of the inter-relationships between urban development and public transport. The legislative contexts in which planning and transport are embodied are outlined.

218 Thomas, David. *London's Green Belt.* London: Faber and Faber, 1970.

219 Trench, Sylvia and **Taner, Oc** (eds). *Current Issues in Planning.* Volume 2. Aldershot: Avebury, 1995. 304 pp.

Divided into five parts: parts one and two are specifically concerned with urban transport. Part one addresses urban congestion and pollution and whether or not road pricing is the solution. Part two addresses traffic calming theory and practice. Part three contains an essay on the London experience of transport. Part four contains an essay on transport investment using the example of light railway. Part five concerns itself with environmental planning.

220 Vuchic, Vukan R. *Urban Public Transportation: systems and technology.* Englewood Cliffs, NJ: Prentice Hall, 1981. 673 pp.

Presentation of definitions, descriptions and analyses of transit systems and technology including the development of transit and its impact on urban development in different countries. Main emphasis of the work is placed on a systematic description of the basic concepts, terms, and relationships, physical systems and their predominantly engineering aspects. A number of new definitions and classificiations are also explained.

221 Weiner, Edward. *Urban Transportation Planning in the United States: an historical overview.* New York: Praeger, 1987. 122 pp.

Covers the evolution of urban transportation planning from early developments in highway planning in the 1930s, to the Federal Aid Highway Act in 1962, to the contemporary emphasis on reducing the role played by the Federal government in local decision making. Addresses environmental and legislative issues in addition to describing the technology and planning techniques that have evolved over the past fifty years.

222 Wells, G. R. *Comprehensive Transport Planning.* London: Charles Griffin, 1975. 147 pp.

General introduction to the comprehensive transport planning process. Claims that transport planning cannot be considered in isolation from other factors. Argues that the interaction of all means of movement and the effects of restraint upon the overall movement pattern must be considered.

223 Wells, G. R. *Traffic Engineering: an introduction.* London: Charles Griffin, 1970. 157 pp.

Appreciation of social priorities and concerns which involve all local authorities, a range of industries and every road user.

224 White, Peter (ed.). *Public Transport: its planning, management and operation.* 3rd ed. London: UCL Press, 1995. 230 pp.

Provides a general introduction to all modes of public transport. Current technology is reviewed together with network planning techniques and the relationship between public transport systems and urban structure. Costing and pricing techniques are also discussed. British transport policy is reviewed with particular reference to the effects of deregulation and restructuring during the 1980s. Long-run policy issues are also examined.

3 General

General

225 Ardekani, Siamak A. and **Hobeika, Antoine G.** Logistics Problems in the Aftermath of the 1985 Mexico City Earthquake. Westport, CT: *Transportation Quarterly*, Vol. 42(1), January 1988, 107–124.

Describes the state of the transportation services immediately after the 1985 earthquake and discusses the role of the transportation system in the events following the quake. The major problems faced in the management of the transportation system pertaining to the overall emergency operations and restoration of normality are identified. Transportation related areas discussed are: the street and highway network; traffic devices and control; mass transit; emergency vehicles and crowd management.

226 Armstrong-Wright, A. *Public Transport in Third World Cities.* State of the Art Review no. 10. Crowthorne: Transport and Road Research Laboratory, 1993. 115 pp.

227 Armstrong-Wright, Alan. *Urban Transit Systems: guidelines for examining options.* World Bank Technical Paper Number 52. Washington, DC: The World Bank, 1986. 77 pp.

Compares the characteristics and costs of the main types of urban transit system, including buses, trains, light rail, rapid rail and suburban rail systems. Offers a simple and quick screening process to avoid costly detailed examination of inappropriate solutions and to focus attention on systems most likely to meet the particular needs of a city. Asserts the need for careful consideration of all the implications of new transit systems before firm commitments are made to any system in particular.

228 Asher, Norman J., Boyd, J. Hayden and **Wetzler, Elliot S.** Non-Technological Innovation in Urban Transit: a comparison of some alternatives. London: *Journal of Urban Economics*, Vol. 5(1), January 1978, 1–20.

Transit alternatives, including conventional technology used in innovative ways, are compared on the basis of full costs (capital and operating costs plus user time costs).

229 Asmervik, Sigmund. *Transportation of Man: the hierarchical relationship between transport demand, distance and speed.* Trondheim: Institute of City and Regional Planning, Technical University of Norway, 1970. 207 pp.

Seeks to develop criteria for improved transportation facilities, including minimising the amount of unwanted travel.

230 Asteris, Michael and **Green, Peter** (eds). *Contemporary Transport Trends.* Aldershot: Avebury, 1992. 279 pp.

Series of essays including topics ranging from road, rail, sea and air transport, on the domestic and international fronts. Emphasis is on the period since the late 1950s. Includes consideration of environmental and technological trends.

231 Baker, Laurie; Harper, John; Mouland, David and **Williamson, Annette.** *Transport Trends in Camden.* London: London Borough of Camden, 1988. 67 pp.

Transport trends are considered for road traffic, buses, the Underground, British Rail, bicycles and motor cycles, accidents and lorries.

232 Bayliss, David. One Billion New City Dwellers: how will they travel? Amsterdam: *Transportation,* Vol. 10, 1981, 311–343.

Considers the growth of cities until the millennium and the changing demand for urban travel, and analyses the many forms of urban transport, their development and use.

233 Brucati, Patricia S. Co-operation in Chaos. Washington, DC: *Mass Transit,* November/December 1989, 16–17.

Looks at a city faced with utter devastation after a 7.0 earthquake which forced many people to rely heavily on their mass transportation systems to transport them to safety, shelters and their homes.

234 Bruttomesso, R. and **Mingardi, E.** Integration of Waterborne Transport in Public Transport. Brussels: *Public Transport International,* Vol. 43(5), September 1995, 9–13.

Deals with the different aspects of waterborne transport in Venice, Sydney and Vancouver.

235 Buchanan, Colin. *London Traffic Inquiry.* London: London Motorists' Association, 1977. 67 pp.

Inquiry concerning the policies and proposals of the GLC for the regulation of traffic and parking and their impact on inner-city life and the industrial and commercial prosperity of the capital.

236 Camarena-Luhrs, Margarita. Urban Transport in Emergency Conditions: effect of the earthquakes of September 1985 on the movement of people and merchandise in Mexico City. Mexico: *Revista Mexicana de Sociología*, 1986. Vol. 48(2), Apr–June, 249–262.

Examines how urban transport played an absolutely crucial role in the movement of people during a time of crisis. Distruption of all forms of transport, not particularly well organised during normal times, is looked at in detail. Considers preventative action in the event of any similar future crisis.

237 City Transport. Lausanne: a public transport showcase. Surrey: *City Transport*, March/May, 1987, 43–45.

Report on a congress and exhibition bringing together transport operators and suppliers.

238 European Conference of Ministers of Transport. *Impact of the Structure and Extent of Urban Development on the Choice of Modes of Transport: the case of medium size conurbations.* ECMT Round Table 28. Paris: Organisation for Economic Co-operation and Development, 1975. 60 pp.

239 European Conference of Ministers of Transport. *Benefits of Different Transport Modes.* Report of the ninety-third round table on transport economics. Paris: Organisation for Economic Co-operation and Development, 1994. 101 pp.

Considers the benefits of different modes of transport. Includes reports from Germany and the Netherlands and a summary of the round table debate.

240 Genzel, M. Public Transport, the Challenge. Brussels: *Public Transport International*, Vol. 44(4), July 1995, 12–14.

Presentation of the Union Internationale des Transports Publics (UITP) Congress and an overview of the different ideas about public transport.

241 Goetz, A. R. Air Passenger Transportation and Growth in the U.S. Urban System, 1950–1987. Lexington, KY: *Growth and Change*, Vol. 23(2), Spring 1992, 217–238.

242 Group Planning Office, London Regional Transport. *Traffic Trends Since 1970: an analysis of London bus and underground travel trends (1970–1985).* Economic Research Report R266. London: London Regional Transport, 1987. 43 pp.

Report refining the estimates of the sensitivity of London Regional Transport traffic to factors such as fares and ticketing policy, service level and quality, and external economic and social trends.

243 Gunston, Bill. *Transport: problems and prospects.* London: Thames and Hudson, 1972. 216 pp.

Considers growth points and new developments for the future and suggests priorities for overcoming the problems while enjoying the utility which technology promises.

244 Haefele, Edwin T. (ed.). *Transportation and National Goals.* Washington, DC: Brookings Institution, 1969.

Series of essays by authors such as Mason (India), Weisshoff (Colombia), Hughes (Malaysia), and Owen (transport and food).

245 Heraty, Margaret (ed.). *Urban Transport in Developing Countries: lessons in innovation.* London: PTRC Education and Research Services, 1991. 284 pp.

Collection of edited versions of papers taken from six years of PTRC annual meetings. Divided into seven sections, it looks at: international overviews, planning and policy making, regulation and management, bus systems and practical operations, light rail transit and metros, and energy aspects of public transport.

246 Heraty, Margaret J. (ed.). *Developing World Transport.* Hong Kong: Grosvenor Press International, 1990. 304 pp.

Provides an overview of transport modes and a selection of articles on specific technical developments or case studies from developing countries. Contains nine articles specifically on urban passenger transport. Topics include: bus provision in developing world cities; paratransit in Hong Kong; bicycles in large cities in China; the Cairo metro; the performance and ownership of bus services in India, and criteria for the choice of light rail systems.

247 Heraty, Margaret J. (ed.). *Developing World Land Transport.* Hong Kong: Grosvenor Press International, 1987. 512 pp.

Collection of articles which provide an overview of land transportation in the developing world. Includes sections on traffic management and transport planning, road passenger transport operations, public transport planning and policy, and education and training for transport. Also includes an article on non-motorised transport.

248 Hillbom, B. and **Savary, Y.** *42nd International Congress: Montreal 1977.* International Commission on Prospective Study of Public Transport. Brussels: International Union of Public Transport, 1977. 9 pp.

Contains a paper, on proposals for prospective approaches to public transport problems, which examines changes in the environment of public transport and provides recommendations regarding town planning and public transport. Also investigates technological developments.

249 Independent Commission on Transport. *Changing Directions: the report of the Independent Commission on Transport.* London: Coronet Books, 1974. 365 pp.

Bishop Hugh Montefiore set up a commission to investigate Britain's transport, with Stephen Plowden as Executive Secretary. This is the report of that commission.

250 Joseph, A. E. *Traffic Studies of an Urban Network.* Birmingham: University of Birmingham (MSc Thesis), 1970.

251 Lieb, Robert C. *Transportation: the domestic system.* Virginia: Reston Publishing Company, 1978. 436 pp.

Primary focus of this book is intercity transportation, but attention is also devoted to transportation systems in metropolitan areas. Examines the industry structure of transportation, the role of government in transportation, and the significance and role of transportation within society.

252 London Transport. *Urban Public Transport: towards 2000.* Conference Report. London: London Transport, 1983. 154 pp.

Papers from London Transport's Golden Jubilee three-day conference held in September 1983. Key issues discussed were future developments in planning and organisation of transport, finance and marketing and the operation and technical development. Reports of the discussions that took place at the syndicate meetings are included.

253 Murray, James J. *Urban and Regional Ground Transportation: surveys and readings.* North Carolina: Planning Transport Associates, 1973. 472 pp.

Compilation of forty-four papers which look at various aspects of urban transport such as technology and design, planning, economics and human factors.

254 Nash, C. A. *Public Versus Private Transport.* London: Macmillan, 1976. 95 pp.

Comparison of the economic and environmental characteristics of public and private transport modes including a review of the potential for modifying modal split in each of the main sectors of the transport market.

255 Odunmbaku, Abiodun Olatunji. *An Evaluation of Transit Systems for a Rapidly Growing City in a Developing Country.* Philadelphia, PA: University of Pennsylvania (PhD Thesis), 1988. 219 pp.

Analyses trends and policies regarding development of public and private transport in large cities of developing countries. Suggests a comprehensive methodology for selection of transit modes with special attention to the needs of the developing countries. Quantitative and qualitative elements are included. The developed methodology was applied to a major corridor in Lagos, Nigeria which is typical for conditions found in rapidly growing Third World cities.

256 Owen, Wilfred. *Transportation and World Development.* London: Hutchinson, 1987. 156 pp.

Examines the problems and the potential of transportation on a global scale. Focuses on the vital role which transport plays in meeting the world's food requirements. Also looks at its effect on expanding industry and trade, improving access to schools, jobs, services, opportunities for joint business and virtually every aspect of social and economic progress from an urban to a global scale.

257 Peake, S. *Transport in Transition.* London: Earthscan, 1994.

Explores the idea of economic growth being correlated with traffic growth. Draws on the lessons learnt from the 1973 oil crisis that energy and economic growth did not necessarily have a mutual relationship. This has important implications for the control of the impact of the car on the environment, in that economic activity could be sustained or increased while reducing mass movement in the economy.

258 Plowman, E. Grosvenor (ed.). *Co-ordinated Transportation.* Centreville, MD: Cornell Maritime Press, 1968. 320 pp.

Presents the dimensions and potentials of coordination, its demand and supply characteristics and requirements, its economic and legal environment, institutional barriers, and the impacts of new cargo handling methods and of applied research. Pioneering work on the subject of coordinated transportation and containerisation as it affects all forms of transportation.

259 River Thames Working Group. *A Report into Transport on the River Thames.* London: River Thames Working Group, 1995. 86 pp.

260 Robinson, David. Transport Moves into the Limelight. London: *Transport*, Vol. 6, June, 1985, 17–20.

Transport in all aspects came under scrutiny for a week in March 1985 during the second of three symposia linked to the Expo '86, held in Vancouver. Provides a report on the conference and the event which had transport and communication as its main theme.

261 Scudamore, C. N. J. *Transport Problems.* Oxford: Pergamon Press, 1976. 56 pp.

Methods and problems of the various types of transport including road, rail, sea and air are dealt with separately. Includes an investigation into what is wrong with roads in Britain and looks at the problems of traffic in towns.

262 Sharp, Clifford. *The Problem of Transport.* Oxford: Pergamon Press, 1965. 202 pp.

Discussion of significant aspects of transportation such as the measurement of costs and their relation to charges; the organisation of transport in Britain; methods of controlling road transport by licensing in Britain, the USA and other European countries; the importance of speed, comfort and other 'qualities' of transport services; the nature of the demand for goods transport; problems arising from congestion on urban roads; and some special problems in transport for underdeveloped countries.

263 Tyson, W. J. Public Transport 'Hidden Treasure'. Brussels: *Public Transport International*, Vol. 43(3), May 1994, 35–36.

Provides an overview of the wide range of benefits public transport gives to both users and non-users.

264 Vickrey, W. Reaching an Economic Balance Between Mass Transit and Provision for Individual Automobile Traffic. Vancouver: *Logistics and Transportation Review*, Vol. 30(1), March 1994, 3–19.

265 Webster, F. V. *Urban Passenger Transport: some recent trends and prospects.* TRRL Laboratory Report 771. Crowthorne: Transport and Road Research Laboratory, 1977. 37 pp.

Discusses the travel habits of people and their adaptability to situations in which they find themselves. Examines past trends in transport usage and factors which affect usage, notably the quality of service and fare levels.

266 White, Dan. The City's View of Public Transport. London: *Proceedings of the Chartered Institute of Transport*, Vol. 4(1), 1995, 35–44.

267 Wohl, Martin. *Urban Transportation in Perspective.* Massachusetts: Ballinger Publishing, 1975. 160 pp.

Survey detailing many problems related to urban transportation including regulation, pollution, safety, minority groups and many others.

Commuting

268 Abane, A. M. *Work Travel in Ghana: the case of Accra.* Southampton: University of Southampton (PhD Thesis), 1992.

Attempts to analyse and explain the travel behaviour of workers in the city of

Accra, Ghana. The specific objective was to analyse how individual workers perceive and articulate their travel behaviour in response to the availability, cost and performance of the various transport systems used for work travel in the city.

269 Abdel Nasser, K. G. *Factors Affecting the Choice of Mode for the Journey to Work.* London: Imperial College of Science and Technology (PhD Thesis), 1980.

270 Alfa, Attahiru Sule. Departure Rate and Route Assignment of Commuter Traffic During Peak Period. Oxford: *Transportation Research*, Vol. 23B(5), October 1989, 337–344.

Presents an incremental heuristic model for estimating the departure rate of commuters in a network. Undertanding of the relation between the commuters' departure time from home and their desired arrival times at their destination, it is hoped, will assist the traffic planner in assessment of the effect of varying work start times on traffic congestion. Seeks to improve the understanding of how commuters respond to changes in the transport systems such as changes in roadway capacity.

271 Cervero, Robert. *American Suburban Centers – The Land Use-Transportation Link.* London: Unwin Hyman, 1989.

Focuses on land use and transport links. Argues that a fundamental change is taking place in cities with the dispersion of jobs and the development of extended commuting patterns. Suggests that traffic will be the dominant issue around which the battle to halt suburban growth will revolve. Gives an empirical analysis from fifty-seven US suburban employment centres on land use, employment and travel patterns.

272 Chakraborti, S. C. *Some Commuting Trends from Outer Metropolitan Areas of London, with Particular Reference to Rushmoor District in Hampshire.* Salford: University of Salford (MSc Thesis), 1983.

273 Crocker, T. J. C. *A Study of the Journey-to-Work in Three Free-Standing Cities.* London: City University (M.Phil Thesis), 1985.

Retrieves data from central and local Government traffic surveys which relate specifically to journey-to-work in cities or towns of sufficient size to be considered as free-standing by rural encirclement. The data are analysed statistically and compared where possible with earlier data. Seeks to provide the basis for further research on a comparison of the characteristics of the journey to work and the changes which have taken place over time due to changing social conditions.

274 Cubukgil, Adil and **Miller, Eric J.** Occupational Status and the

Journey-to-Work. Amsterdam: *Transportation*, Vol. 11, 1982, 251–276.

Claims that the importance of occupational status as an explanatory variable in the determination of work trip commuting flows has not been well studied in the literature. Addresses this issue by means of an empirical investigation of commuting patterns in the Toronto Census Metropolitan Area using 1971 census data.

275 Daniels, P. W. *Office Location and the Journey to Work: a comparative study of five urban areas.* Aldershot: Gower, 1980. 174 pp.

Presents the findings of a research project comparing the journey to work and residential location behaviour of employees in several decentralised offices grouped in five urban areas of varying size and location.

276 Das, Mira. *Travel to Work in Britain: a selective review.* TRRL Laboratory Report 849. Crowthorne: Transport and Road Research Laboratory, 1978. 36 pp.

Presents information about the changing pattern of the work journey in Britain. Transport surveys from 1950 are reviewed together with the 1975/76 National Travel Survey.

277 Dryden, K. *Travel Patterns of Office Employees in Central Croydon.* London: Polytechnic of Central London, 1991. 81 pp.

278 Dubin, R. Commuting Patterns and Firm Decentralization. Madison, WI: *Land Economics.* Vol. 67(1), February 1991, 15–29.

Claims that individuals with greater residential and job mobility will have shorter commutes.

279 Dunne, John Paul. Commuting Mode Choice in New Towns: a case study of Livingston. Harlow: *Scottish Journal of Political Economy*, February 1984. Vol. 31(1), 60–71.

Presents a study of mode choice for the journey to work within Livingston New Town, using a multinomial logit model. The transport orientated development of the town, which has walking as a feasible alternative to car and bus, provides an interesting object of study with implications for future transport planning in more orthodox urban structures. Overall, the results imply that commuting mode choice is determined by factors other than the levels of service of the available modes.

280 European Foundation for the Improvement of Living and Working Conditions. *Commuter Transport: experiences in participation, a consolidated report.* Paris: Organisation for Economic Co-operation and Development, 1986. 125 pp.

Aims to evaluate the role that participatory processes might play in securing more balanced and democratic decision-making in the sphere of commuter transport and in enhancing the quality, convenience and efficiency of such transport. Based on research conducted in Denmark, France, Ireland, Italy and Britain.

281 Fae, M. I. *Explaining Developments in Commuting Patterns to Central London During the 1980's.* Leeds: University of Leeds (PhD Thesis), 1993.

Attempts to identify and understand the key factors involved in the changing patterns of commuting into Central London during the period 1981–1989, in particular through a case study of Kent.

282 Garner, Barry J., Taaffe, Edward J. and **Yeates, Maurice H.** *The Peripheral Journey to Work: a geographic consideration.* Evanston, IL: Northwestern University Press, 1963. 125 pp.

Attention is focused on one changing component of the aggregate metropolitan traffic flow, the journey-to-work to employment centres at the periphery of the city. As manufacturing continues to decentralise, the peripheral journey-to-work is becoming a more important component of the internal circulation system. Claims that better understanding of the emerging character of peripheral laboursheds should provide some insight into the processes which change the spatial structure of cities.

283 Graindor, E. Home Working: a second competitor for public transport. Brussels: *Public Transport International*, Vol. 43(3), May 1994, 46–47.

Examines the potential incursions which the development of teleworking could make into the public transport market.

284 Hall, Peter and **Sammons, Roger.** Urban Structure and Modal Split in the Journey to Work. Glasgow: *Urban Studies Journal*, Vol. 14(1), February 1977, 1–11.

Investigates relationships between modal split for the journey to work and patterns of social and economic activity in large urban areas. Small zone data from six major land-use transportation studies were used as a basis for a systematic comparative analysis of these relationships. Three of these studies were British and three American. Standard correlation and regression programmes were employed on a wide range of data using three different models.

285 Hamed, Mohammad M. and **Mannering, Fred L.** Commuter Welfare Approach to High Occupancy Vehicle Lane Evaluation: an exploratory analysis. Oxford: *Transportation Research*, Vol. 24A(5), September 1990, 371–379.

Focuses on high occupancy vehicle lanes, which have become a popular method of addressing the problem of urban traffic congestion. Demonstrates a theoretically consistent and defensible approach of high occupancy vehicle lane evaluation based on consumer welfare theory. Potential suitability of this welfare approach is illustrated in the context of a dynamic traffic equilibrium model.

286 Hamilton, Bruce W. Wasteful Commuting. Chicago, IL: *Journal of Political Economy*, Vol. 90(5), October 1982, 1035–1051.

Examines the ability of the monocentric models to predict the mean length of commutation in urban areas. Compares actual mean commute with that which is predicted by monocentric models and finds that actual commuting distance is about eight times greater than that predicted by the model. The volume of commuting is calculated that would result if people chose their houses and jobs at random, making no effort to economise on commuting. This overpredicts actual commuting by about 25 per cent.

287 Hanson, Susan. The Importance of the Multi-Purpose Journey to Work in Urban Travel Behaviour. Amsterdam: *Transportation*, Vol. 9, 1980, 229–248.

Examines the journey to work as a multiple-purpose trip (home-to-home circuit). Using disaggregate travel diary data collected over 35 consecutive days, the study shows the importance of the multi-purpose work trip in the overall travel pattern of the urban household. Also examines the nature of these work-induced travel linkages and finds that many types of urban establishment depend heavily upon stops made in connection with the work trip.

288 Hardwick, P. A. Journey to Work Patterns in Salisbury, Rhodesia: the Contrast between Africans and Europeans. London: *Journal of Transport Economics and Policy*, Vol. 8(2), May 1974, 180–191.

289 Hensher, David A. The Value of Commuter Travel Time Savings: empirical estimation using an alternative valuation method. London: *Journal of Transport Economics and Policy*, Vol. 10(2), May 1976, 167–176.

A model is presented for the evaluation of travel time saved in relation to income, trip length and the amount of time saved.

290 Hutchinson, B. G. Structural Changes in Commuting in the Toronto Region 1971–1981. London: *Transport Reviews*, Vol. 6(4), October–December 1986, 311–329.

Changes in the commuting structure of Toronto CMA are examined using 1971–1981 census journey-to-work data. Important changes in household structure, employment base and associated location decisions have in turn created significant changes in commuting structure.

291 Khaw Keng Hong. *Further Development in the Continuous Modelling of Commuter Travel Patterns in Cities.* London: University College London (PhD Thesis), 1979.

292 Markham, J. and **O'Farrell, P. N.** *The Journey to Work: a behavioural analysis.* Oxford: Pergamon Press, 1975. 288 pp.

293 Maunder, D. A. C. and **Mbara, T. C.** Sudden Impact? London: *Global Transport*, Vol. 3, Summer 1995, 43–47.

Deals with the consequences of initiating urban commuter omnibus services.

294 McCarthy, Patrick S. Residential Location and the Journey to Work: an empirical analysis. London: *Journal of Transport Economics and Policy*, Vol. 11(2), May 1977, 169–184.

A mail canvas of 2,078 people who had recently moved into the San Francisco Bay Area indicates that residential location is a significant factor in determining individual choice of mode for the journey to work.

295 McKay, R. V. Commuting Patterns of Inner-City Residents. Washington, DC: *Monthly Labour Review*, Vol. 96(11), November 1973, 43–48.

Describes transportation of residents of selected low income areas of six major U.S. cities to suburban jobs in terms of location of work (inside or outside the city), and means of getting to work, occupations, and earnings. Data derived from the Bureau of the Census' Urban Employment Survey (UES), 1968–69, and the Census Employment Survey (CES), 1970–71, obtained from special household interviews.

296 Miron, John R. Centrifugal Relocation and Back-Commuting from the Metropolitan Fringe. London: *Journal of Transport Economics and Policy*, Vol. 16(3), September 1982, 239–258.

People who have recently moved to the outlying parts of a city are more likely than other residents to commute to or towards the city centre to work. Commuting flows in Toronto are disaggregated on the basis of duration and previous place of residence.

297 Mitchell, H. Time for a Break with the Past: cars, roads and pollution. *Public Policy Review*, Vol. 3(4), 1995, 72–76.

Looks at the ways in which commuter travel can be reduced by increasing the amount of working from home which includes speculation on the future of electronic networking and teleworking. Uses evidence from Australia and the USA.

298 Mogridge, M. J. H. Changing Spatial Patterns in the Journey to

Work: a comparison of the 1966 and 1971 Census Data in London. Glasgow: *Urban Studies Journal*, Vol. 16, 1979, 179–190.

The 1966 and 1971 census journey-to-work data for London analysed by traffic zone of origin and destination.

299 Nilles, Jack M. Telecommuting and Urban Sprawl: mitigator or incitor? Amsterdam: *Transportation*, Vol. 18, 1991, 411–432.

There is some evidence to the effect that as cities become increasingly congested new housing starts occur at greater distances from urban centres while jobs tend to remain centre-concentrated or develop in other suburbs. In either case, mean commute distances tend to increase. Telecommuting is seen as a means of increasing the jobs-housing balance in urban areas by enhancing the ability to move work to, or closer to, the workers' residences rather than requiring workers to commute to work daily.

300 Nilles, Jack, M. Traffic Reduction by Telecommuting: a status review and selected bibliography. Oxford: *Transportation Research*, Vol. 22A(4), 1988, 301–317.

Telecommuting is defined as a subset of teleworking. Two main forms of telecommuting (home and regional centre) are described. The means by which these forms of telecommuting may alter urban transportation patterns are outlined, followed by a review of the empirical evidence to date on the impacts and usefulness of telecommuting.

301 Obeiro, S. V. O. *Public Transport and the Peak Hour in Nairobi.* Cardiff: University of Cardiff (PhD Thesis), 1992.

Focuses on how to solve traffic congestion and inadequate public transport services especially at the journey-to-work peak period. Establishes that the cheapest and most effective means of providing public transport service would be through the participation of the private sector, including the use of small-size paratransit vehicles. Claims that this would necessitate a proper planning framework.

302 Olayemi, O. A. *Workplace and Residence: an analysis of commuting in metropolitan Lagos and its implications for regional planning.* London: London School of Economics and Political Science (PhD Thesis), 1977.

303 Pickup, L. and **Town, S. W.** *A European Study of Commuting and its Consequences.* Crowthorne: Transport and Road Research Laboratory, 1984. 210 pp.

Travel demand and its effect on transport planning is looked at from a Community-wide perspective with the aim of presenting an overview and a critical appraisal of the research literature on commuting. A compilation of statistics on existing travel to work patterns as a background to the literature together with an outline of various policies which affect travel to work is concluded by a look at gaps in present knowledge and areas for further research.

304 Pratsch, Lew W. Reducing Commuter Traffic Congestion. Westport, CT: *Transportation Quarterly*, Vol. 40(4), October 1986, 591–600.

Explores how the number of commuters transported each day through highway and rail systems can be increased.

305 Rasheed, R. A. *A Study of Travel to University.* Glasgow: University of Strathclyde (MSc Thesis), 1978.

306 Smith, B. H. Anxiety as a Cost of Commuting to Work. London: *Journal of Urban Economics*, Vol. 29(2), March 1991, 260–266.

Examines the impact of the psychological costs incurred in commuting to and from work. Proposed measures of psychological costs are presented and tested against the backdrop of empirical evidence for Columbus, Ohio. Empirical results suggest that the psychological costs associated with today's models of transportation militate against adoption of alternative means of getting to work – walking and bicycling.

307 Smyth, A. W. *Decision-Making and Modal Choice by Commuters in the Belfast Region.* Belfast: Queen's University (PhD Thesis), 1982.

308 Stucker, James P. Transport Improvements, Commuting Costs, and Residential Location. London: *Journal of Urban Economics*, Vol. 2(2), April 1975, 123–143.

Develops a theoretical framework for evaluating one of the long-run or secondary effects of a transport improvement. Model of residential location is manipulated to derive an estimating equation relating changes in the households' preferred location. When estimated for a particular transport situation the major finding is the importance of the price effect.

309 Sturt, A. R. *Spatial Aspects of Commuting to Central London, 1951–66.* London: London School of Economics and Political Science (PhD Thesis), 1977.

310 Thomson, J. Michael. *Great Cities and Their Traffic.* Harmondsworth: Penguin Books, 1977. 344 pp.

A study of the transport problems, policies and plans of the world's greatest metropolises.

311 Torchinsky, Raymon Lev. *Individual Choice Behaviour and Urban Commuting.* Vancouver: University of British Columbia, 1987.

Develops a simulation approach to commuting modelling, based on the explicit characterisation of the inter-relationship between urban location and inter-action in terms of labour market processes.

312 Urban Transport International. Copenhagen: focus on the Danish capital. London: *Urban Transport International*, Vol. 1, 1993, 16–21.

An examination of urban commuter railways in Copenhagen, in particular the renewal of the S-Tog fleet of suburban trains, is analysed in the light of the effects of private operators who are taking over bus services in the capital. Also, light rail is considered as an option for an airport link.

313 Vickerman, R. W. Urban and Regional Change, Migration and Commuting: the dynamics of workplace, residence and transport choice. Glasgow: *Urban Studies Journal*, Vol. 21(1), February 1984, 15–30.

A key factor in the spatial structure of metropolitan areas is the relationship between workplace and residential location. This is particularly critical in any attempt to model the changes in structure which result from intra-metropolitan moves of employment and households. Aims to provide a more satisfactory framework for understanding the dynamics of these changes. Empirical evidence is presented for the London area based on a wide range of data.

314 Voith, R. The Long-Run Elasticity of Demand for Commuter Rail Transportation. London: *Journal of Urban Economics*, Vol. 30(3), 360–372.

315 Westcott, D. Employment and Commuting Patterns: a residential analysis. London: *Monetary Labour Review*, Vol. 102(7), July 1979, 3–9.

Describes some characteristics of persons living in central cities, suburbs, and non-metropolitan areas. By most economic measures, it is found that suburban residents appear better off than their central city or non-metropolitan counterparts.

316 Wilson, F. R. *Journey to Work – Modal Split.* London: Maclaren and Sons, 1967. 270 pp.

Study carried out in the Department of Transportation and Environmental Planning, the University of Birmingham. Covers the problems associated with the choice of travel mode related to the individual on a work trip in an urban area. The product is a mathematical model based on a limited number of definable measurable factors which are capable of evaluating the level of use of public transport for the work trip.

317 Wong, Y. S. O. *An Empirical Study of Attitude and Mode Choice Behaviour of Car Commuters in Hong Kong.* London: University College London (M.Phil Thesis), 1980.

318 Zuckerman, S. *Patterns of Commuting in Hertfordshire: a methodological study.* London: University College London (PhD Thesis), 1977.

Labour, management and organisations

319 Allal, Moise and **Edmonds, G. A.** *Manual on the Planning of Labour-Intensive Road Construction.* Geneva: International Labour Office, 1977.

Manual for the planning, evaluation, and design of road projects, with emphasis on labour-intensive technology.

320 Anderson, Eric E. and **Talley, Wayne K.** An Urban Transit Firm Providing Transit, Paratransit and Contracted-Out Services: a cost analysis. London: *Journal of Transport Economics and Policy*, Vol. 20(3), September 1986, 353–368.

Public transit firms may be able to reduce operating deficits by providing paratransit and contracted-out services. Contracting out can induce employees and their unions, fearful of job losses, to accept changes in working agreements which reduce costs.

321 Baldwin, Nicholas. The International Transport Workers' Federation Archive. Manchester: *Journal of Transport History*, Vol. 7(1), March 1986, 61–66.

Examines the holdings of the International Transport Workers' Federation archive. The ITF has been one of the largest and most active of the international trade secretariats of affiliated multi-national unions in particular fields of employment.

322 Barton, Mark. Not So New New York. Peterborough: *Coach and Bus Week*, Issue 163, April 1995, 30–31.

Describes the organisation of the publicly owned Metropolitan Transportation Authority, which runs most of New York's buses and all of its underground and suburban rail services.

323 Brooks, Dennis. *Race and Labour in London Transport.* London: Oxford University Press, 1975. 389 pp.

Provides the first comprehensive and thorough study of the impact of a considerable proportion of coloured immigrant workers on a large organisation in Britain. Also one of the very few sociological works on public transport so far published. Examines traditions, values and tasks, both of London Transport as a whole and at the level of the individual work group. Provides detailed studies of Central Buses, the Railway Operating Department, the Permanent Way Department, recruitment and training.

324 Collins, Michael F. and **Pharoah, Timothy M.** *Transport Organisation in a Great City: the case of London.* London: Allen and Unwin, 1974. 660 pp.

Examines the problems confronting the public transport system in Greater London and considers the measures required to overcome them. A brief historical introduction is followed by a description of the responsibilities and powers relating to passenger transport of London Transport, British Rail, Metropolitan Police, the Greater London Council and the London Boroughs.

325 Costantino, James. Overcoming Institutional Barriers to IVHS. Virginia: *Transportation Quarterly*, Vol. 47(4), October 1993, 3–13.

Looks at institutional constraints, local government involvement and the standards required for a national Intelligent Vehicle Highway System.

326 Cotton, W. A. *The Management of British Railways by the Railway Executive, 1945–51.* Sheffield: University of Sheffield (PhD Thesis), 1985.

327 Deakin, B. M. and **Seward, T.** *Productivity in Transport: a study of employment, capital, output, productivity and technical change.* Cambridge: Cambridge University Press, 1969. 248 pp.

An empirical study of productivity in six sectors of public transport and communication in the UK: railways, public road passenger transport, road haulage contracting, sea transport, port and inland waterways, air transport and postal services.

328 Diandas, J. *Sri Lanka Transport Sector Study.* Colombo: Friedrich-Ebert-Stiftung, 1983. 338 pp.

Prepared with the intention of assisting trade unions with the evaluation of data and information about the transport sector, its orientation is towards the role that the workforce plays in the sector. All aspects of transport are covered, including a section on non-motorised transport and the impact of transport on the environment.

329 European Conference of Ministers of Transport. *Employment in Transport: quantitative and qualitative evolution, substitution possibilities.* Report of the seventy-third round table on transport economics. Paris: Organisation for Economic Co-operation and Development, 1987. 122 pp.

Contains three papers one of which concentrates on urban transport, and looks at major trends, trends in productivity and consideration of solutions. Includes a summary of the Round Table debate.

330 Fouracre, P. R., Kwakye, E. A., Okyere, J. N. and **Silcock, D. T.** Public Transport in Ghanaian cities – a case of union power. London: *Transport Reviews*, Vol. 14(1), January–March 1994, 45–61.

Examines the performance and development of urban public transport in Ghana. An explanation is sought of the role of unions and how the attempts of Government to develop its own public transport organisation have failed. Public transport development options that the Government is now considering attempt to make the best use of the unions' capabilities, while reducing dependence on union powers.

331 Giuliano, Genevieve and **Wachs, Martin.** Employee Transportation Coordinators: a new profession in Southern California. Westport, CT: *Transportation Quarterly*, Vol. 46(3), 1992, 411–427.

Describes the employee transportation coordinators (ETCs) of Los Angeles, providing data on their gender, ethnicity, age and educational background. Also documents their preparation training, how they were selected, and how much working time is devoted to ETC assignments, as well as the views of ETCs regarding relative effectiveness of their programmes.

332 Goldstein, Harvey A. and **Luger, Michael I.** Federal Labor Protections and the Privatization of Public Transit. New York: *Journal of Policy Analysis and Management*, Vol. 8(2), Spring 1989, 229–250.

Article concludes that labour protections contained in the Urban Mass Transportation Act are costly to local transit management, but do not significantly impede the contracting out of those services, as some government officials claim. Conclusions and recommendations are based on tabular presentations and discrete choice analysis of data from a survey of transit managers.

333 Greater London Transport. *Greater London Transportation Survey:* Volume 9: Structure Report. London: Greater London Transport, 1974. 53 pp.

Discusses the form of organisation, management, and setting up of survey company, London Movements Surveys Ltd.

334 Gwilliam, K. M. Institutions and Objectives in Transport Policy. London: *Journal of Transport Economics and Policy*, Vol. 13(1), January 1979, 11–27.

Examines conflicts in the transport sector between: EEC and UK; central government and nationalised industries; central and local government; local government and transport operators. Concludes that continual reappraisal is necessary to ensure that institutional arrangements and operational objectives are consistent with political reality.

335 Hamer, Mick. Centralising London's Transport. London: *Transport*, Vol. 3, September/October, 1982, 7–9.

The plan to set up a metropolitan transport authority to control transport in London has received widespread support, but despite this acclaim, the proposal contains both possibilities and problems. This article reviews both.

336 Hatry, Harry P. and **Winnie, Richard E.** *Measuring the Effectiveness of Local Government Services: transportation.* Washington, DC: Urban Institute, 1972. 84 pp.

A suggestion of measures for the promotion of effectiveness of transportation serving municipalities, urban counties and metropolitan agencies whose population exceeds 50,000 people. Major roles of urban transport are discussed, and measures proposed for the improvement of local transportation systems which can be applied to various modes of transport.

337 Holding, David; Holding, Patricia and **Wileman, Robert.** *Managing People in Road Transport.* Kingston-upon-Thames: Croner Publications, 1992. 212 pp.

Looks at the road transport industry and its people; managing communication; recruitment; the structure of industrial relations; pay and benefits; patterns of work; employer and employee legal relationship; handling a dispute; and mergers and acquisitions.

338 Jenkins, Deborah. Sources for Transport History in the CBI Predecessor Archive. Manchester: *Journal of Transport History*, Vol. 4(1), March 1983, 77–81.

Describes the work of the three distinct employers' organisations which fused in 1965 to form the Confederation of British Industry (CBI). Cataloguing of the predecessor archive of the CBI turned up documents relevant to twentieth-century transport from the Federation of British Industries, the British Employers' Confederation and the National Association of British Manufacturers.

340 Naylor, J. B. *Institutional Constraints on the Urban Transport System.* Liverpool: University of Liverpool (MA Thesis), 1977.

341 Nigerian Institute of Transport Technology. *Proceedings of the National Workshop on Training Needs of the Nigerian Transport Sector.* Zaria: Nigerian Institute of Transport Technology, 1989. 114 pp.

342 O'Neill, Peter. The Role of Public Authorities. Amsterdam: *Transportation*, Vol. 17(3), 1990, 313–328.

Discusses the role of public authorities in the field of travel information.

343 Sheldrake, John. *The Origins of Public Sector Industrial Relations.* Aldershot: Avebury, 1988. 98 pp.

Traces the development of industrial relations in the public utilities, including tramways, from the turn of the century to the eve of the Second World War.

344 Tomazinis, Anthony R. *Productivity, Efficiency, and Quality in Urban Transportation Systems.* Lexington, MA: Lexington Books, 1975. 237 pp.

Investigation of personnel needs of urban mass transit systems.

345 Topp, Hartmut H. Mutual Cooperation in Public Transit. Westport, CT: *Transportation Quarterly*, Vol. 44(2), April 1990, 303–316.

Describes the system of 'transport communities' in the former West Germany. Transit cooperatives and transit federations cooperated to produce improvements in terms of coordinated schedules, combined networks, and unified fares.

346 Topp, Hartmut H. Cooperation in Transit Delivery in West German Metropolitan Areas. Amsterdam: *Transportation*, Vol. 15, 1989, 279–295.

German transit federations during the 1970s succeeded in significantly increasing ridership, while during the 1980s patronage either remained steady or declined. Yet transit federations showed much better performance than did public transport in general. In terms of costs, no public transit organisation in Germany is able to break even. Concludes that hidden subsidies for automobile traffic are higher than anticipated because of environmental damage and the high social cost of traffic accidents.

347 Webster, A. M. *Interest Groups, Professions and Public Policy Change: the case of Paris transport 1968–1976.* London: London School of Economics and Political Science (PhD Thesis), 1990.

Examines theories of policy change by applying them to the specific problem of understanding a striking and apparently contradictory shift in Paris Transport policy in the early 1970s.

348 Wolley, Susan. *The First Seventy Years: a history of the Chartered Institute of Transport.* London: Chartered Institute of Transport, 1992. 230 pp.

Reviews the development of the Institute as an educational and examining body since 1919.

Law

349 Dale, Iain. Government: a look at the coming Parliamentary session's legislation affecting transport. *Transport Law and Practice*, Vol. 1(5), 1993/94, 43.

Policy issues following Railways Act 1993, the deregulation and Contracting Out Bill 1994 and the Channel Tunnel Rail Link.

350 Durkin, Joe; Lane, Peter and **Peto, Monica.** *Blackstone's Guide to the Transport and Works Act 1992: planning for infrastructure development.* London: Blackstone Press, 1992. 184 pp.

Provides a guide to the Transport and Works Act 1992, which in itself was a 'rationalising' act designed to rectify problems which have been identified in existing systems or institutions. Covers the background of the Act, the new authorisation system and orders, the obtaining of planning permission, procedures in Scotland, schemes of 'national significance', harbours, inland waterways, tramways and rail crossings. Includes safety on transport systems and the control of drink and drugs.

351 Hackett, Michael. Transport and Works Act 1992: part 1. *Sveriges Juristforbund*, Vol. 137(9), 1993, 220–221.

Procedures for making and objecting to orders made under the Transport and Works Act 1992.

352 Haynes, Rebecca. Free Movement of Goods. Paris: *International Trade Law and Practice*, Vol. 1(1), 1995, S4.

Criminal Proceedings Against Van Schaik. Case C55/93(ECJ). A case comment which looks at whether Treaty provisions of EEC law precluded legislation by Member States requiring test certificates for vehicles registered in a state to be issued by garages of that state. Considers the free movement of services, motor vehicles and EEC law and road safety.

353 Maltby, Nick. Multimodal Transport and EC Competition Law. Colchester: *Lloyd's Maritime and Commercial Law Quarterly*, Vol. 1(February), 1993, 79–87.

Council Regulation 1017/68 applying rules of competition to transport by rail, road and inland waterway; Council regulation 4056/86 laying down detailed rules for the application of Arts 85 and 86 of the Treaty to maritime transport.

354 Pawley, Andrew. VAT on Transport? *Transport Law and Practice*, Vol. 3(1), 1995, 86–87.

Covers common policies, EEC law, public transport and the prospects of extending VAT.

355 Robinson, Mark. Development in EC Competition Law in the Field of Transport. *Lawyers' Edition,* Spring 1993, 10–11.

Article portraying the views of Jonathan Faull, head of DG IV Transport Unit.

356 Smith, Herbert. *Transport and Works Act 1992.* London: In-House Library, February 1993. 31 pp.

New procedure for authorising major infrastructure construction projects by Ministerial Order.

357 Terry, George. Keeping Transport on the Right Side of the Law. London: *Transport,* Vol. 3, March/April, 1983, 13–14.

Sir George Terry, Chief Constable of Sussex, discusses the relationship between the police and road transport.

358 Vine, Christopher. Part 1 of the Transport and Works Act 1992. *Journal of Planning Law,* January 1993, 3–12.

Discusses new procedures to authorise transport and other works to replace previous private Bill methods.

Transport management

359 Barker, William G. A Transit Management Strategy for the 1990s. Westport, CT: *Transportation Quarterly,* Vol. 46(4), 1992, 529–540.

Key trends affecting the transit industry's future are discussed, including energy and environmental concerns, land development and urban growth, demographics and the workforce, social ills, computers and communication technology, and economics and the automobile industry. Recommendations are made for a strategy that can be used by transit managers to meet challenges of the 1990s.

360 Bassett, R. G. *Road Transport Management and Accounting.* London: Heinemann, 1974. 188 pp.

Considers how to plan and control a transport company or department and make it profitable.

361 Bly, P. H. Managing Public Transport: commercial profitability and social service. Oxford: *Transportation Research,* Vol. 21A(2), March 1987, 109–125.

Examines the range of objectives of public transport policy and the difficulties of ensuring maximum efficiency and effectiveness given the scale of subsidies and poorly defined goals. Discusses management information and operating strategies in relation both to commercial considerations and to satisfying social objectives. The context is the expected changes following the deregulation of stage bus services in the UK.

362 Farahmand-Razavi, Arman. The Role of International Consultants in Developing Countries. Oxford: *Transport Policy*, Vol. 1(2), March 1994, 117–123.

Presents results of an examination of the development of the urban transportation planning and policy making process in the city of Tehran between 1960 and 1990.

363 Fielding, Gordon J. *Managing Public Transit Strategically: a comprehensive approach to strengthening service and monitoring performance.* San Francisco, CA: Jossey-Bass, 1987. 270 pp.

Provides advice, and constructive proposals, on how to expand and improve public transportation services, while controlling costs.

364 Gargett, Adrian and **Wallis, Ian.** Transit Service Performance Assessment in Adelaide. London: *Transport Reviews*, Vol. 9(1), January–March 1989, 75–92.

Examines the need for management information.

365 Gentile, Pierluigi. Information Requirements and Needs for Public Transport Companies Management. Brussels: *Public Transport International*, Vol. 41(2), May 1992, 76–92.

Looks at the types of information which companies and local or national governments would need in order to manage and control their business, and how to identify techniques for obtaining information. In English, with French and German translations.

366 Hyman, William A. Pavement, Bridge, Safety and Congestion Management Systems: A Need for a Clear Federal Vision. Virginia: *Transportation Quarterly*, Vol. 47(2), April 1993, 151–165.

Examines issues that concern the implementation of the Intermodal Surface Transportation Efficiency Act of 1991, which requires all US States and metropolitan planning organisations in larger urbanised areas to implement six management systems. These systems pertain to 1) pavements; 2) bridges; 3) safety; 4) congestion; 5) intermodal transportation facilities and systems; and 6) public transportation facilities and equipment.

367 Jackson, Michael C. and **Keys, Paul.** *Managing Transport Systems: a cybernetic perspective.* Aldershot: Gower, 1985. 191 pp.

Compilation of papers presented and discussed in a series of seminars held at Hull University. Sets out to describe some important issues in the management of transport systems and to interpret these from within cybernetic frameworks. Potential of the cybernetic approach for analysing the management of transport systems is illustrated. In relation to urban transport, the management aspects of the Tyne and Wear Metro are thoroughly examined.

368 *No Entry.*

369 Lohrmann, Klaus-Dieter. Transport System Management with Priority for Public Transport. Brussels: *Public Transport International*, Vol. 43(4), July 1994, 47–49.

Claims that today's modern transport management system requires closer cooperation between transport carriers.

370 Lowe, David. *How to Become a Transport Manager.* Surrey: Fairplay Publications, 1989. 60 pp.

A practical guide for the preparation and steps needed to become a transport manager.

371 Mendedez, Aurelio. *Estimating Capital and Operating Costs in Urban Transportation Planning.* Westport, CT: Praeger, 1993. 187 pp.

Presents a framework for the cost-estimating process that acknowledges the interplay among the different actors involved.

372 Murphy, G. J. *The West Midlands Road Transport Industry.* Birmingham: Aston University (PhD Thesis), 1989.

Seeks to identify those elements of management practice which characterise firms in the West Midlands road transport industry with the aim of establishing the contents of what might be termed a management policy portfolio for growth.

373 Organisation for Economic Co-operation and Development. *Integrated Urban Traffic Management.* Paris: Organisation for Economic Co-operation and Development, 1978. 70 pp.

Report considering how individual traffic control measures in urban areas can be co-ordinated and integrated into a total management system. After a brief description of the background to modern traffic engineering the report develops a definition and sets the objectives of integrated urban traffic management.

374 Organisation for Economic Co-operation and Development. *Urban Public Transport: evaluation of performance: Road Research.* Paris: Organisation for Economic Co-operation and Development, 1980. 76 pp.

Study of evaluation methods and performance indicators designed to help decision makers and public transport managers assess the options and strategies for urban transport operation and investment.

375 Orski, C. Kenneth. Employee Trip Reduction Programs: an evaluation. Virginia: *Transportation Quarterly*, Vol. 47(4), October 1993, 327–341.

376 Orski, C. Kenneth. Can Management of Travel Demand Help Solve Our Growing Traffic Congestion and Air Pollution Problems? Westport, CT: *Transportation Quarterly*, Vol. 44(4), October 1990, 483–498.

Reviews the technique of demand management. Argues that it faces the difficulty of affecting travel behaviour in the face of circumstances that favour the continuing use of the car.

377 Ryden, Tom K. (ed.). *Managing Urban Transportation with Limited Resources.* New York: American Society of Civil Engineers, 1983.

A collection of papers originally presented at a two-day symposium in 1983 on Managing Urban Transportation with Limited Resources. Papers describe specific projects, revenue generation techniques and agency management approaches designed and implemented in response to a fiscal crisis in urban transportation.

378 Wachs, Martin. Regulating Traffic By Controlling Land Use: the southern California experience. Amsterdam: *Transportation*, Vol. 16(3), 1990, 241–256.

Critically examines several transportation growth management strategies in Los Angeles. Los Angeles' emphasis in transportation planning shifted from facility construction to transportation system management and the control of land use with the goal of slowing the growth in traffic congestion. Concludes that though these policies were well intentioned, they might not lead to the intended consequences.

379 Woodward, Frank H. *Managing the Transport Services Function.* 2nd ed. Aldershot: Gower, 1977. 321 pp.

Examines the management, organisation and administration of those responsible for the movement of people and goods. Specifically the movement of freight and that of personnel are analysed individually as are management objectives and financial controls.

4   Finance and Markets (General)

Deregulation and privatisation

380 Amsler, Yves. New Public-Private Relationship. Brussels: *Public Transport International*, Vol. 42(3), October 1993, 42–46.

Relates the evolution in the last five years of the share of risks and responsibilities between public authorities and private partners through urban mass transit projects franchising.

381 Bates, Malcolm. Crisis or Opportunity. London: *Transport*, Vol. 8, December, 1987, 235–236.

Questions whether or not the many changes occurring in local councils and the public utilities are appropriate. Also examines public transport and its problems.

382 Bell, Philip and **Cloke, Paul** (eds). *Deregulation and Transport: market forces in the modern world.* London: David Fulton, 1990. 208 pp.

Collection of edited papers with two broad objectives: The first relates to transport in the wider context of New Right governments and a policy agenda for state activity which clearly reflects a shift in relations between public and private sectors. The second focuses on transport per se and aims to provide evidence of the contexts, policies and practical outcomes of deregulatory measures.

383 Berechman, J. *Public Transit Economics and Deregulation Policy.* Amsterdam: Elsevier, 1993.

384 Bramall, Stephen. Government: the beginning of the end for the DTP? *Transport Law and Practice*, Vol. 1(7), 1994, 59–60.

Claims that recent reforms of transport policy encouraging involvement of private sector will reduce the need for control by civil servants.

385 Colston, Donald. Switching from Public to Commercial Service.

Brussels: *Public Transport International*, Vol. 42(3), October 1993, 38–41.

Relates the experience of the West Midlands Passenger Transport Executive, which has been turned in a short space of time from a publicly-owned company to a private one, with an intermediate stage as a private company within the public sector.

386 Darbera, Richard. Deregulation of Urban Transport in Chile: what have we learned in the decade 1979–1989? London: *Transport Reviews*, Vol. 13(1), January–March 1993, 45–59.

Chile is the only example in the world where access to the urban bus transport market is totally free, and where the government does not exercise any control over the fares. Ten years after the progressive implementation it is possible to draw conclusions, relevant for developing countries where bus-transport is the main mode of transport for 60–90 per cent of urban travellers, and where inadequate regulation and poor enforcement are generally blamed for the chaotic transport conditions.

387 Douglas, Neil J. *A Welfare Assessment of Transport Deregulation.* Aldershot: Gower, 1987. 349 pp.

Study which assesses deregulation in terms of its effect on market structure, fares, service quality and costs using data provided by nationalised express coach operators. Argues that travellers benefited from deregulation and their benefits were found to more than offset a reduction in operator profit. Claims that deregulation has produced a net social welfare gain in the long distance travel market.

388 European Conference of Ministers of Transport. *The Role of the State in a Deregulated Transport Market.* Report of the eighty-third Round Table on transport economics. Paris: Organisation for Economic Co-operation and Development, 1991. 141 pp.

Proceedings of a conference held in Paris in 1989 which sought to define the role of government in a deregulated transport market. Includes reports from Germany, the UK and Japan.

389 Fielding, Gordon J. and **Johnston, Douglas C.** Restructuring Land Transport in New Zealand. London: *Transport Reviews*, Vol. 12(4), October–December 1992, 271–289.

Restructuring of governmental activities in New Zealand calls for public enterprises to operate in competitive environments. This has created problems for highways and urban passenger transport. New roles have been legislated for regional agencies and local governments: they are expected to either privatise service delivery or create public corporations to maintain highways and operate passenger transport.

390 Fuller, John W. (ed.). *Regulation and Competition in Transportation: selected works of James C. Nelson.* Columbia: University of Columbia, Center for Transportation Studies, 1983. 441 pp.

Selection of the writings of James C. Nelson which incorporates his belief in the necessity for free competition and the positive advocacy of considered methods of deregulation in the transport industry.

391 Gwilliam, Ken; Gretton, John; Harrison, Anthony and **O'Leary, Laura** (eds). Deregulation, Commercialisation, and Privatisation: transport under the Conservatives, 1979–1987. Berkshire: *Policy Journals*, 1987, 7–19.

Paper which assesses how far the Government has pursued the three policies of deregulation, commercialisation and privatisation. Looks at domestic surface transport, namely rail, express bus, stage bus and taxis.

392 Haritos, Z. J. Public Transport Enterprises in Transition. Amsterdam: *Transportation*, Vol. 14(2), 1987, 193–207.

Reviews the literature on public enterprise and draws on the Canadian experience. Discusses the rationale for and concept of public enterprise and focuses on two reform proposals, accountability and privatisation.

393 Hedemann, Janice M. and **Leick, Janet D.** Contracting Private Transit Operators. Westport, CT: *Transportation Quarterly*, Vol. 41(3), July 1987, 427–438.

Reports on the experiences of Johnson County, Kansas in contracting out public transit services to private operators.

394 O'Conner, Robert. Going Private. Washington, DC: *Mass Transit*, November/December, 1991, 30–31.

Looks at the privatisation strategy for transport in Britain and how it was implemented under the Thatcher government.

395 Pashigian, B. P. Consequences and Causes of Public Ownership of Urban Transit Facilities. Chicago, IL: *Journal of Political Economy*, Vol. 84(6), December 1976, 1239–1259.

Examines the reasons for the shift from private to public ownership of urban transit facilities. Regulation theory suggests this shift is due to the increasing severity of regulation, while the declining market and externalities hypotheses suggest that increases in automobile ownership is the reason for reduced profits and public ownership. Regression results indicate profit margins of privately owned systems are higher when regulation is by a state rather than a local agency.

396 Roschlau, Michael W. Nationalisation or Privatisation: policy and prospects for public transport in Southeast Asia. Oxford: *Transportation Research*, Vol. 23A(6), November 1989, 413–424.

Investigates why despite private urban transit delivering a very high standard of service and making few demands on public resources, there is still a continued interest in government regulation, state ownership and foreign involvement. Claims that government aspirations to gain political status by building prestigious projects plus the desire for a more Western image and the need for more control over the industry lie behind this movement towards more state intervention.

397 Roth, Gabriel and **Wynne, George G.** *Free Enterprise Urban Transportation: learning from abroad.* Washington, DC: Council for International Urban Liaison, 1982. 72 pp.

Looks at privately-owned profitable modes of public transportation in Africa, Asia and parts of Latin America and puts the case for an alternative free enterprise-sponsored transportation system in the United States.

398 Transport Committee of the House of Commons. *The Consequences of Bus Deregulation.* Vol. 1. Report and Minutes of Proceedings. London: HMSO, 1995. 60 pp.

399 Transport Committee of the House of Commons. *The Consequences of Bus Deregulation.* Vol. 2. Minutes of Evidence. London: HMSO, 1995. 172 pp.

400 Veljanovski, Cento (ed.). *Privatisation and Competition: a market prospectus.* London: Institute of Economic Affairs, 1989. 239 pp.

Examines the interplay between privatisation, competition and regulation and attempts to identify the trade-offs, tensions and consequences of the sacrifice of market forces and competitive pressures in Britain's privatisation programme. Contains two papers on transport, one which looks at privatisation and competition in road passenger transport and one which looks at competition within British Rail.

401 Vitharana, A. J. *The Influence of Competition and Regulation on the Development of Modern Transportation: a comparison of the laws and policies of the United States with those of her 'major' trading partners.* Southampton: University of Southampton (PhD Thesis), 1982.

402 White, Peter. Public Transport: privatisation and investment. Oxford: *Transport Policy*, Vol. 1(3), June 1994, 184–194.

Recent British experience in privatisation and investment within the public transport sector is considered. Alternative approaches to rail privatisation are examined. Privatisation within the bus industry is reviewed, with stress on the danger of high prices secured for some companies placing subsequent pressure on profits and the ability to finance investment. Criteria for investment appraisal in public transport infrastructure are also examined, stressing the need for a more comprehensive approach.

Fares and pricing

403 Abe, M. A. Reciprocal Consumption Externalities in Urban Transportation: problems of optimal tolls and investment. Wisconsin: *Economic Studies Quarterly*, Vol. 29(3), December 1978, 248–258.

Discusses the importance of money price and time price in choice of travel modes, automobile or bus, also the optimal allocation of commuters between the two travel modes under reciprocal externalities between them in terms of both money cost and time cost. Governmental policies to achieve the optimal flow of traffic are discussed.

404 Abe, Masatoshi A. Distributional Equity and Optimal Pricing of Urban Transport. London: *Journal of Transport Economics and Policy*, Vol. 9(2), May 1975, 178–185.

Claims that equity requires pricing to depart from marginal cost, and that a bus subsidy is justified on distributional grounds even more than for Paretian efficiency.

405 Abkowitz, Mark and **Driscoll, Mary K.** Automatic Fare Collection in Transit: a synthesis of current practice. London: *Transport Reviews*, Vol. 7(1), January–March 1987, 53–63.

Article presents a synthesis of several sources of information pertaining to AFC operations, including a discussion on system requirements, the advantages and disadvantages of system operation, reliability and maintainability.

406 Baum, H. F. Free Public Transport. London: *Journal of Transport Economics and Policy*, Vol. 7(1), January 1973, 3–19.

Survey of transport studies in Germany and elsewhere concludes that advocates of free public transport have overestimated the possible diversion from private cars, and underestimated the cost. Reviews opinion surveys and empirical demand studies, and claims that motorists' impressions of trip costs are misleading. Concluding section discusses possible effects of free public transport on efficiency and on the redistribution of income.

407 Bly, P. H. and **Oldfield, R. H.** *Relationships Between Public Transport Subsidies and Fares Service Costs and Productivity.* TRRL

Research Report 24. Crowthorne: Transport and Road Research Laboratory, 1985. 27 pp.

Report describing the analysis of the effects of urban public transport operating subsidies prepared for the European Conference of Ministers of Transport in 1979.

408 Bohley, P. Free Transit in Metropolitan Areas. Germany: *Kyklos*, Vol. 21(1), 1973, 113–142.

Evaluates free transit on economic and ecological grounds.

409 Boyd, Colin; Martini, Christine; Rickard, John and **Russell, Allen.** Fare Evasion and Non-Compliance: a simple model. London: *Journal of Transport Economics and Policy*, Vol. 23(2), May 1989, 189–198.

To improve labour productivity and reduce ticket issuing costs many European transport operators have introduced various honour fare collection systems which incorporate spot-check or random ticket inspection. The increased opportunity for fare evasion in such honour systems forces consideration of the appropriate level of ticket inspection. Discusses a general model of non-compliance.

410 Carbajo, Jose C. The Economics of Travel Passes: non-uniform Pricing in Transport. London: *Journal of Transport Economics and Policy*, Vol. 22(2), May 1988, 153–174.

A framework is identified to examine different non-uniform price schemes implemented by transport operators such as travelcard plus ordinary ticket, railcard plus full fare, or multiple-ride ticket plus cash fare. Optimal pricing rules for these schemes are derived emphasising the informational requirements about the distribution of consumers, in terms of their trip behaviour, necessary to implement them.

411 Cervero, Robert. Time-of-day Transit Pricing: comparative US and international experiences. London: *Transport Reviews*, Vol. 6(4), October-December 1986, 347–364.

Examines ridership, financial and efficiency impacts associated with time-of-day pricing, also highlights innovative approaches to implementing fare differentials in the US, compared to those in other countries. Concludes that useful lessons can be gained by sharing policy insights from experiments with differential transit pricing in both the US and elsewhere.

412 Department of the Environment: Transport and Road Research Laboratory. *Symposium on Public Transport Fare Structure: papers and discussion.* TRRL Supplementary Report 27 UC. Crowthorne: Transport and Road Research Laboratory, 1974. 196 pp.

Symposium dealt with fares systems and their role in policy and the central problem of elasticity of travel demand as expressed by public response to changes in fare levels.

413 Dheerasinghe, K. G. *An Evaluation of British Rail's Fare Policy.* Leeds: University of Leeds (MA Thesis), 1982.

414 Domencich, Thomas A. and **Kraft, Gerald.** *Free Transit.* Lexington, MA: Lexington Books, 1970. 104 pp.

Based on a Boston case study, this analysis of free transit services considers the effects of free transit participation and its associated costs, passenger responsiveness to changes in travel time and costs and an assessment of the effectiveness of free transit overall.

415 Doxsey, Lawrence B. Demand for Unlimited Use Transit Passes. London: *Journal of Transport Economics and Policy,* Vol. 18(1), January 1984.

Claims that monthly transit passes result in lost revenue for operators.

416 Duke, Barry. Getting Smarter. London: *London Lines,* Winter 1995, 1–4.

Article attempts to analyse the demands that will be placed on a new, multimodal 'smart' ticketing system which London Transport plans to develop over the next few years.

417 Duke, Barry. A Fare Comparison. London: *London Lines,* Winter 1995, 17–19.

Public transport fares in London are roughly on par with a broad range of those in other major cities, despite the fact that London Transport is the only transport authority which receives no operating subsidy. Article analyses the results of a study by the London Research Centre which compares metropolitan transport fares.

418 Filho, Romulo Dante Orrico and **Simoes, Raul de Bonis de Almeida.** The Travel Voucher. Westport, CT: *Transportation Quarterly,* Vol. 45(3), July 1991, 469–476.

Discusses the use of the travel voucher in Brazil to reduce user travel costs. Explores its background, significance and limitations.

419 Focas, C. *Fares Compared: an international comparison of public transport fares.* London: London Research Centre, September 1994. 6 pp.

420 Gibson, J. G. A Rational Alternative Fare Structure for British Rail's

London and South East Commuter Passengers. London: *Journal of Transport Economics and Policy*, Vol. 15(3), September 1981, 269–276.

Author derives an alternative fare structure based on two premises: First, the total cost associated with a particular train journey is met by the sum of the fares and secondly, that no passenger pays a different rate from that of a fellow passenger at any instant in the journey.

421 Gilbert, Christopher L. and **Jalilian, Hossein.** The Demand for Travel and for Travelcards on London Regional Transport. London: *Journal of Transport Economics and Policy*, Vol. 25(1), January 1991, 3–31.

Joint model for the demand for travel and the demand for travelcards on the London Regional Transport network. Confirms previous findings that underground travel is inelastically demanded while the demand for bus travel is elastic.

422 Glaister, S. Generalised Consumer Surplus and Public Transport Pricing. London: *Economic Journal*, Vol. 84(336), December 1974, 849–867.

Relationships between economic welfare and various versions of consumer surplus are discussed and the welfare interpretation of the generalisation appropriate to the case of multiple price changes is established.

423 Glaister, S. Transport Pricing Policies and Efficient Urban Growth. Lausanne: *Journal of Public Economics*, Vol. 5(1/2), January–February 1976, 103–117.

Urban growth is assumed to depend on the balance between advantages of urban employment and the costs of public and private transport. With constant money prices or average cost pricing of buses (free competition) growth is towards a small congested city, with a period of urban decay when congestion and all travel costs are increasing, although the city is shrinking. Marginal social cost pricing of both modes removes this dynamic inefficiency and leads to much larger cities with faster transport services.

424 Glaister, S. and **Lewis, D.** An Integrated Fares Policy for Transport in London. Lausanne: *Journal of Public Economics*, Vol. 9(3), June 1978, 341–355.

A common but disputed justification for public transport subsidy is that lower fares will encourage transfer from private vehicles, alleviating the congestion externality. A quantitive method is developed to judge the validity of this 'second best pricing' argument, and it is applied to the best available evidence on peak and off-peak bus, rail and private car models in Greater London.

425 Goh, Jeffrey. Railway Ticketing. *Utilities Law Review*, Vol. 6(2), 1995, 67–69.

Rail regulator issues policy statement on ticketing for passenger services following consultation exercise completed in April 1995.

426 Grey, Alexander. *Urban Fares Policy.* Farnborough: Saxon House, 1975. 156 pp.

An exploration of a number of issues concerned with how public transport services in towns should be charged for.

427 Hart, Martin and **Wanless, David.** Automatic Ticketing on London Underground. London: *Transport Reviews*, Vol. 9(4), October–December 1989, 361–370.

Describes the history of ticket and issuing machines on the London Underground, as well as discussing development and project management tasks.

428 Heseltine, P. M. *Pre-Paid Ticketing in Public Transport Fares Policy.* Plymouth: Plymouth Polytechnic (M.Phil Thesis), 1988.

An investigation of the impact of Plymouth Citybus's pre-paid ticket scheme on fares revenue.

429 Howells, C. *Public Transport and the Power Game: a case study of South Yorkshire's fares policy.* Sheffield: University of Sheffield (PhD Thesis), 1990.

Examines the structure of relationships between central and local government.

430 Kirkpatrick, C. H. *Public Sector Transport Pricing in Developing Countries.* London: Planning and Transport Research and Computation, 1975.

Emphasises the importance of the relationship between transport pricing and investment decisions.

431 Kons, W. New Forms of Ticketing. Brussels: *Public Transport International*, Vol. 43(3), May 1994, 44–45.

Describes how Düsseldorf, in order to reduce road traffic and maintain ridership, introduced a new ticketing system.

432 Kooreman, Peter. Fare Evasion as a Result of Expected Utility Maximisation: some empirical support. London: *Journal of Transport Economics and Policy*, Vol. 27(1), January 1993, 69–74.

Provides some empirical support for the hypothesis that passengers behave as expected utility maximisers.

433 Kraus, M. Discomfort Externalities and Marginal Cost Transit Fares. London: *Journal of Urban Economics*, Vol. 29(2), March 1991, 249–259.

434 Laconte, Pierre. *Automatic Fare Collection in Public Transport.* Brussels: International Union of Public Transport, 1990. 503 pp.

Collection of articles designed to present developments in automatic fare collection; the respective advantages of 'strip' card and 'chip' card; functional requirements of operators; experiences with advanced ticketing systems in Asia, North America and Europe; data modelling and collection. Articles are presented in English, French and German.

435 Li, Si-Ming and **Wong, Fiona C. L.** The Effectiveness of Differential Pricing on Route Choice: the case of the mass transit railway of Hong Kong. Dordrecht: *Transportation*, Vol. 21(3), 1994, 307–324.

Attempts to analyse the effectiveness of a differential pricing policy in diverting passengers from an overcrowded section of Hong Kong's railway to a less heavily utilised route.

436 Lloyd, J. E. *Some Aspects of the Purchase and Use of 'Travelcard' Tickets in Urban Public Transport.* Newcastle Upon Tyne: University of Newcastle Upon Tyne (PhD Thesis), 1991.

Examines the factors that decide the purchasing and use of travelcard tickets.

437 Mogridge, M. J. H. *Study of Effects of Fare Increases and Road Improvements on Journey Speeds in London.* London: Greater London Council, 1986. 49 pp.

438 Nelson, James R. (ed.). *Criteria for Transport Pricing.* Centreville, MD: Cornell Maritime Press, 1972. 320 pp.

For some time there has been increasing interest and debate in regard to the criteria in transportation pricing among the carrier industries and in the government, both in Europe and the Americas. As a result, twenty transportation scholars from Europe and the Americas presented papers to the International Symposium on Transportation Pricing, at The American University, Washington DC. The papers here have been edited and represent thinking in regard to this problem dealing with all phases of transport.

439 O'Reilly, Deirdre M. *Concessionary Fare Schemes in Great Britain.* TRRL Research Report 165. Crowthorne: Transport and Road Research Laboratory, 1988. 37 pp.

Aims to provide a descriptive summary of the variety of concessionary fare schemes provided by District, Borough and County Councils and Passenger Transport Executives.

440 Oram, Richard L. Deep Discount Fares: building transit productivity with innovative pricing. Westport, CT: *Transportation Quarterly*, Vol. 44(3), July 1990, 419–440.

Describes 'deep discount fares', which are seen as a means to reverse the negative relationship between fare level and ridership.

441 Organisation for Economic Co-operation and Development. *Co-ordinated Urban Transport Pricing: road transport research.* Paris: Organisation for Economic Co-operation and Development, 1985. 151 pp.

Reviews co-ordinated pricing concepts and practice in OECD Member countries as a tool to improve the performance and quality of urban transport.

442 Price Commission. *London Transport Executive – Increase in Passenger Fares.* London: HMSO, 1978. 75 pp.

Report on the investigations by the Price Commission under Section 4 or 5 of the Price Commission Act 1977 looking at increasing public passenger fares for the administrative area of Greater London.

443 Pun, C. L. *Urban Public Passenger Transport Service and Fare Levels.* London: University College London (M.Phil Thesis), 1979.

444 Rat, J. W. The Public Transport Ticket for Students. Brussels: *Public Transport International*, Vol. 43(3), May 1994, 24–29.

In order to avoid the complex administrative task of giving students a grant to cover travel costs, the Dutch government has instituted a student pass. Article reviews the implications of this scheme.

445 Robinson, David. Joint Efforts. London: *Urban Transport International*, September/October 1988, 14–15.

The Singapore metro has linked up with two local bus companies to provide integrated ticketing. Article reviews Singapore's experience in creating a unified fares structure for its urban transport network.

446 Shon, E. Y. *Evaluation of Public Transport Fare Integration in London.* Leeds: University of Leeds (PhD Thesis), 1989.

Public transport integration has conventionally been thought to increase economic efficiency, particularly where railways are well developed. Study investigates the cost/benefit changes in terms of passengers, operators and externalities of alternative levels of public transport fare integration in London.

447 Train, Kenneth. The Salt Lake City Experiment with Short Term

Elimination of Transit Fares. Amsterdam: *Transportation*, Vol. 10(2), 1981, 185–199.

The Utah Transit Authority eliminated off-peak transit fares for the month of October, 1979. The purpose was to increase ridership in the long term. Article evaluates the short-term and long-term effects of this temporary fare elimination.

448 Wan, W. M. W. I. *Fare Policies: a tool for improving the financial performance of Malayan Railway.* Birmingham: Aston University (PhD Thesis), 1990.

Focuses on the improvement of Malayan Railway revenue performance through a fare policies approach utilising the elasticity of demand concept. Examines relationships between changing fares and changing demand, using the concept of elasticity.

449 White, Peter R. 'Travelcard' Tickets in Urban Transport. London: *Journal of Transport Economics and Policy*, Vol. 15(1), January 1981, 17–34.

Regional intermodal season tickets have grown rapidly in importance, especially in Western Europe. Article claims that after introduction at a low price, moderate increases in price have little effect on sales, and there are important benefits.

450 Yearsley, Ian. Smartcards Add Revenue to Fares. Brussels: *Public Transport International*, Vol. 41, February 1993, 98–106.

Examines the use of a contactless smartcard fare collection system in Greater Manchester.

451 York, I. *Passenger Reactions to Present and Alternative Travelcard Schemes.* Crowthorne: Transport and Road Research Laboratory, 1995. 44 pp.

Investment and finance

452 Alcaly, R. E. Transportation and Urban Land Values: a review of the theoretical literature. Madison, WI: *Land Economics*, Vol. 52(1), February 1976, 42–53.

Concerned primarily with the relationship between transportation costs and urban land values. Begins, however, by placing that discussion within a general consideration of the role and importance of transport costs in the formation of cities. This is followed by an analysis and critique of the theoretical literature linking transport developments and urban land values.

453 Ashworth, Stephen. Travelling Hopefully: highway proposals and private sector investment. *Parliamentary Reports*, Vol. 4(4), 1994, 125–128.

Examines the conflict between the approach adopted by courts to developers' offers of planning benefits involving road schemes and Government policies to encourage private financing of infrastructure.

454 Baum, W. C. and **Tolbert, S. M.** *Investing in Development.* New York: Oxford University Press, 1985.

Presents the lessons of World Bank experience in financing development projects. Chapter 11 deals with transport projects.

455 Bradbury, Katharine L., Moss, Philip and **Slavet, Joseph S.** *Financing State-Local Services.* Lexington, MA: Lexington Books, 1975. 176 pp.

Examination of the provision of community services in the Boston area. The study includes urban transportation and assesses alternative methods of financing. Recommendations are made for the transfer of financing to the State.

456 Brandwein, Robert and **Sheldon, Nancy W.** *The Economic and Social Impact of Investments in Public Transit.* Lexington, MA: Lexington Books, 1973. 170 pp.

Study designed to provide data and guidelines on public transit in order to assist government decision makers in the design of policies and the allocation of capital investment for urban transportation.

457 Button, K. J. and **Pearman, A. D.** (eds). *The Practice of Transport Investment Appraisal.* Aldershot: Gower, 1983.

Essays by transport planners and economists on the application, rather than the theory, of project appraisal.

458 Button, Kenneth and **Rietveld, Piet.** Financing Urban Transport Projects in Europe. Amsterdam: *Transportation*, Vol. 20(3), 1993, 251–265.

Examines the specific nature of urban transport financing in Europe.

459 Cohen, Benjamin I. *Capital Budgeting for Transportation in Under-Developed Countries.* Harvard discussion paper 39. Cambridge, MA: Harvard University Press, 1966.

460 Farrell, Sheila (ed.). *Financing Transport Infrastructure.* London: PTRC Education and Research Services, 1994. 216 pp.

Selection of papers aiming to present the issues of private financing arrangements: private concessions, public toll roads, private-public partnerships, the capture of land development benefits and community fund raising by targeted local taxation. Draws on experience from Western and Eastern Europe, Southeast Asia and the United States.

461 Fowkes, A., Hopkinson, P. and **May, A.** *The Development of a Common Investment Appraisal for Urban Transport Projects.* Leeds: University of Leeds, Institute for Transport Studies, December 1991. 78 pp.

462 Fromm, Gary (ed.). *Transport Investment and Economic Development.* Washington, DC: Brookings Institution.
Series of essays on various aspects of transportation economics.

463 Grieco, M. *Transport Investment and Economic Development.* Aldershot: Avebury, 1993.

464 Grieco, Margaret. *The Impact of Transport Investment Projects upon the Inner City: a literature review.* Aldershot: Avebury, 1994. 194 pp.
Report prepared for the Inner Cities Directorate of the Department of the Environment, 1987. Questioned, on the basis of a comprehensive review of the existing literature, the extent to which urban transport investment projects could be viewed as either generating economic development or resolving the problem of congestion.

465 Halcrow Fox. *Research into Pricing and Financing of Urban Transport: final report.* London: Halcrow Fox, 1995. 173 pp.
Results of an investigation considering the potential for employing pricing policies to manipulate demand away from private car use to public transport services. Report looks at the impact of five policies which include congestion charging, increasing subsidies for public transport, increase of charges for fuel or on parking, and higher taxes on car ownership.

466 Haritos, Z. Transport Costs and Revenues in Canada. London: *Journal of Transport Economics and Policy*, Vol. 9(1), January 1995, 16–33.

467 Hoare, Anthony G. Transport Investment and the Political Pork Barrel: a review and the case of Nelson, New Zealand. London: *Transport Reviews*, Vol. 12(2), 133–151.
One perspective on the allocation of transport investments by public authorities is offered by the so-called 'pork barrel' model, whereby politicians and political

parties allocate public investment spatially in such a way as to gain electoral support from localities so benefited. Introduces this model. Discusses its attractions and problems in the case of the transport sector. Reviews a modest number of published examples of this approach, before considering railway investment in Nelson.

468 Howard, David F. Funding Transport Expenditure in the UK. Brussels: *Public Transport International*, Vol. 43(2), March 1994, 35–36.

Describes the mechanisms for local transport investments in the United Kingdom over the last twenty-five years.

469 Hutchinson, B. G. An Approach to the Economic Evaluation of Urban Transportation Investments. *Highway Research Record*, Vol. 31(4), 1970, 72–86.

Attempts to deal not only with the economic efficiency of urban transportation, but also with distributional and associated environmental effects.

470 Kelvin, A. *Effectiveness of Capital Investment Decision Making, Case Study of National Transportation in Zaire.* Cardiff: University of Wales, University College Cardiff (PhD Thesis), 1994.

471 Lenski, William; Voccia, Joseph and **Wheeler, Linda M.** Financial Resource Needs of Public Transportation Systems. Westport, CT: *Transportation Quarterly*, Vol. 43(4), October 1989, 527–548.

Studies three transit categories; systems serving urbanised areas over 200,000 in population; systems serving urbanised areas of 50,000 to 200,000; and specialised and rural transit systems. Gives an analysis of the difference between estimated capital investment costs and projected available capital funding for each transportation system category. Data are drawn from the Illinois Department of Transportation.

472 Local Transport Today. Package Approach: flexible finance for urban transport strategies. London: *Local Transport Today*, July, 1990, 10–11.

Considers possible changes in local transport investment.

473 Martinez, F. J. *The Impact of Urban Transport Investment on Land Development and Land Values.* Leeds: University of Leeds (PhD Thesis), 1991.

Focuses on the impact of urban transport projects on the use and value of land. Addresses itself to who finally acquires the benefits of transport projects, or to what extent direct benefits are capitalised into land in the form of land rent or prices and, secondly, to what extent transport projects generate local urban development.

474 Ogden, K. W. Road Cost Recovery in Australia. London: *Transport Reviews*, Vol. 8(2), April–June 1988, 101–123.

Addresses the question of road cost recovery in the Australian context. Reviews some of the major issues and emphasises the inherent problems (both theoretical and practical), in resolving these issues.

475 Organisation for Economic Co-operation and Development. *Managing and Financing Urban Services.* Paris: Organisation for Economic Co-operation and Development, 1987. 94 pp.

Report which examines the decentralisation of urban services including transport. Looks at how to encourage the provision of services by the private sector and by non-profit-making organisations; and how to raise new sources of finance – including user charges – for urban services.

476 Pettengill, Robert and **Uppal, J. S.** *Can Cities Survive?* New York: St. Martin's Press, 1974. 166 pp.

Presentation of comparative studies of city expenditures, revenue, and the gaps between expenditure and revenue which serve to highlight some urban fiscal problems. The unequal relationship between cities and suburbs is identified and explored, with some possible solutions suggested.

477 Porter, Alan L. Transit Funding: implications of federal aid strategies. Amsterdam: *Transportation*, Vol. 10(1), 1981, 3–22.

Federal funding strategies greatly affect investment in urban transportation facilities in the United States. Analyses the implications of varying federal aid matching requirements, structuring aid programmes as categorical or block grants, and allocating funds on a discretionary basis or according to formula.

478 Robinson, David. Ways to Pay: IMTA hears of the various options for funding public transport projects. London: *Urban Transport International*, July/August 1988, 22–23.

Alongside the surge of interest in building urban transit systems, both in developed and developing countries, the competition to fund, construct, manage and supply equipment has also grown. Article aims to reveal the many different options which are being considered for funding public transport projects.

479 Roe, Michael. *Evaluation Methodologies for Transport Investment.* Aldershot: Avebury, 1987. 302 pp.

Provides an introduction to the evaluation problem and the context for highway evaluation. A case study of the West Midlands is considered and the implications given for transport evaluation.

480 Schaevitz, Robert. Transit in the 1990s: private industry financing of major capital projects. Washington, DC: *Mass Transit*, July/August 1988, 8–14.

Article which attempts to forecast the role which privatisation will play in bringing about new transit systems.

481 Transport Committee of the House of Commons. *The Government's Expenditure Plans for Transport 1986–87 to 1988–89.* 3rd Report. London: HMSO, 1986. 95 pp.

482 Transport Committee of the House of Commons. *The Government's Expenditure Plans for Transport: 1991–92 to 1993–94.* 5th Report. London: HMSO, 1991. 57 pp.

483 Vickerman, R. W. *Pricing and Investment in Urban Infrastructure.* Oxford: Phillip Allan, 1984.

Contains four sub-sections including an introduction to urban infrastructure, optimal pricing, the optimal city, transport problems and policies and housing problems and policies.

484 White, Peter R. Allocation of Funds to Public Transport Investment and Operating Support. Amsterdam: *Transportation*, Vol. 7, 1978, 225–242.

Reviews the present levels of operating support to, and public investment in, public transport systems in Western Europe. Urban bus, tram and rail services are included and estimates made for total support in Britain, Sweden, Germany, the Netherlands and France. To make comparisons meaningful, these are shown in relation to GDP and traffic carried.

Markets and marketing

485 Bamford, C. G., Carrick, R. J., Hay, A. M. and **MacDonald, R.** The Use of Association Analysis in Market Segmentation for Public Transport: a case study of bus passengers in West Yorkshire, UK. Amsterdam: *Transportation*, Vol. 14, 1987, 21–32.

Demonstrates that association analysis is capable of identifying important and distinctive segments and that, unlike certain other techniques of segment identification, enables the researcher to define these segments in terms of the variables used. Further, the results of the study exhibit the crucial characteristics of an effective segmentation as identified by Kotler, i.e., measurability, accessibility and substantiality.

486 Barnes, Chris. *Successful Marketing for the Transport Operator: a practical guide.* London: Kogan Page, 1989. 165 pp.

Examines the concept of marketing; marketing theory and the search for new opportunities; researching the transport market; creating a transport product; case studies in transport product differentiation; pricing and placing transport products; promotion and the transport service.

487 Bates, John W. and Lawrence, Dewel J. Transit Marketing: a strategic approach. Westport, CT: *Transportation Quarterly*, Vol. 40(4), October 1986, 549–558.

Describes the development and weaknesses of modern transit marketing and provides recommendations for improvement in the principal marketing areas of product development, pricing, promotion and evaluation.

488 Bateson, John E. G., Day, George S., Lewin, Gordon and Lovelock, Christopher H. *Marketing Public Transit: a strategic approach.* New York: Praeger, 1987.

Looks at the role of marketing, once considered inappropriate for the public sector, in assisting the design, structure, operation and promotion of public transportation.

489 Cooke, Peter N. C. *Transport Marketing.* Bradford: MCB University Press, 1989. 35 pp.

Examines a wide range of transport topics and how each can be effectively marketed.

490 European Conference of Ministers of Transport. *Marketing and Service Quality in Public Transport.* Paris: Organisation for Economic Co-operation and Development, 1993. 193 pp.

Proceedings of a conference held in Paris in December 1991. Compares the developments throughout Europe in the marketing and service quality of public transport within the context of mounting deficits experienced by public transport operators. Contributions from Germany, Spain, France and Sweden. A summary of the Round Table debate is included.

491 European Conference of Ministers of Transport. *Promotion of Urban Public Transport.* Paris: Organisation for Economic Co-operation and Development, 1973. 85 pp.

Examines the 'normal' measures taken in implementation of a general policy for the organisation of traffic within a given built-up area; also looks at the 'promotional experiments' of which have the object of showing what might be done in the future.

492 Frumkin-Rosengaus, Michelle. *Increasing Transit Ridership Through a Targeted Transit Marketing Approach.* Princeton, NJ: Princeton University (PhD Thesis), 1987. 126 pp.

Concentrates on commuters as the target market segment, analysing their response to transit marketing at the place of employment. Two marketing theories are tested. The first is a Peer Pressure Theory proposing that it is more effective for a marketing campaign to target areas of existing high ridership. The second is a Utilitarian Theory suggesting that marketing campaigns will have an effect regardless of the area's previous ridership trends.

493 Guillossou, Maudez. Marketing and Urban Public Transport. Brussels: *Public Transport International*, Vol. 43(4), July 1994, 44–46.

Suggests that the type of marketing used in association with urban transport combines different elements.

494 Hargreaves, John. A New Way to Sell Public Transport. London: *Transport*, Vol. 9, March, 1988, 119–121.

Offers suggestions for encouraging the greater use of public transport.

495 Hibbs, John. *Transport without Politics...? a study of the scope for competitive markets in road, rail and air.* London: Institute of Economic Affairs, 1982. 95 pp.

496 Hovell, Peter J., Jones, William H. and **Moran, Alan J.** *The Management of Urban Public Transport: a marketing perspective.* Farnborough: Saxon House, 1975. 263 pp.

The urban environment and the competitive position of public transport, together with the managerial response of urban public transport, are investigated from a marketing perspective in order to try to establish a more competitive system.

497 Mathieu, Y. Quality and Expectancy. Brussels: *Public Transport International*, Vol. 44(4), July 1995, 15–16.

Brief presentation about actions aiming at improving the quality of service of public transport.

498 Plowden, Stephen. *Transport Reform: changing the rules.* London: Policy Studies Institute, 1985. 249 pp.

Aims to describe in detail the failings of the market economy in respect to transport, from the point of view of users, and what changes in law and taxes could reduce these failings. Concentrates on road transport. Also looks at the prospects for rationalising the use of cars. The relationship between central and local government is examined.

499 Urban Transport International. Markets Link for 1992. London: *Urban Transport International*, December 1988/January 1989, 3–4.

Autobus RAI, Amsterdam, shows how bus builders are reaching across the frontiers.

500 Wijsenbeek, Siep. A Reflection of Quality: operators must make the most of image. London: *Urban Transport International*, September/ October 1988, 23–25.

Continuous advances in the design of the private passenger car have not been matched in the public transport sector. Article argues that the glamour and appeal which public transport once had, has now been lost. Claims that good design has to be one of the principal means for re-establishing pride in public transport and restoring its image.

501 Wragg, David W. *Publicity and Customer Relations in Transport Management.* Aldershot: Gower, 1981. 144 pp.

An introduction to the subject of publicity and customer relations in transport management. Attempts to explain the role of public relations and the relationship with such associated disciplines as advertising and staff relations.

Subsidy

502 *No Entry.*

503 Bayliss, David; Gretton, John; Harrison, Anthony and **O'Leary, Laura.** *Transport Subsidy Costs and Benefits: the case of London Transport, in Transport UK: an economic, social and policy audit.* Berkshire: Policy Journals, 1987.

One argument in favour of subsidising public transport is that lower fares may divert people away from their cars, thus benefiting the transport system as a whole. Research done within London Transport between 1981 and 1982 – when fares on bus and underground services were revised, both upwards and downwards in quick succession – demonstrates the value of this argument.

504 Bly, P. H., Pounds, Susan and **Webster, F. V.** Effects of Subsidies on Urban Public Transport. Amsterdam: *Transportation*, Vol. 9, 1980, 311–331.

Study in which eighteen countries took part, concerned with the aims of subsidy, the sources and conditions attached to subsidy, trends in subsidies and the effect of subsidies on patronage, fares, service levels, costs and productivity.

505 Bly, P. H. and **Oldfield, R. H.** The Effects of Public Transport Subsidies on Demand and Supply. Oxford: *Transportation Research*, Vol. 20A(6), November 1986, 415–427.

Reports the result of a statistical analysis of cross-sectional and longitudinal public transport operating statistics from sixteen countries aimed at identifying the relationships between subsidy on the one hand, and fares, service, passengers, unit costs and output per employee on the other.

506 Bly, P. H., Pounds, Susan and **Webster, F. V.** *Subsidisation of Urban Public Transport.* TRRL Supplementary Report 541. Crowthorne: Transport and Road Research Laboratory, 1980. 43 pp.

Investigates the impact of subsidy in attempting to shift car drivers to public transport.

507 Bristow, A. L. *The Distributional Impact of Subsidies in Urban Public Transport.* Newcastle Upon Tyne: University of Newcastle Upon Tyne (PhD Thesis), 1991.

Focuses on the impact of urban public transport subsidy on the distribution of income.

508 Crampton, G. R. *The Subsidisation of Public Passenger Transportation in Greater London and the English Metropolitan Counties.* Discussion Paper in Urban Reading: University of Reading, 1982. 19 pp.

Discussion of the role of local government in subsidising bus and rail transportation within its area. Deals with the controversy over the subsidising of public passenger transportation by the GLC and the other Metropolitan Counties. Set within the context of relevant theoretical issues, and with reference to the development over the period 1972–1982 of subsidies from local taxation to passenger transportation.

509 Department of Transport. *Public Transport Subsidy in Cities.* London: HMSO, 1982. 10 pp.

White Paper which looks at the role of public transport subsidy, proposed legislation, guidance figures and the relationship between the guidance and targets for local authority current expenditure. Also looks at getting better value for money and goes on to outline the framework for the future with proposals designed to achieve better transport in some of the UK's major cities.

510 Dodgson, J. S. Benefits of Changes in Urban Public Transport Subsidies in the Major Australian Cities. Sydney: *Economic Record*, Vol. 62(177), June 1986, 224–35.

Considers the economic efficiency benefits of urban public transport subsidies and presents estimates of the marginal benefits of fare and service level changes in the main Australian cities.

511 Else, Peter K. Optimal Pricing and Subsidies for Scheduled Transport Services. London: *Journal of Transport Economics and Policy*, Vol. 19(3), September 1985, 263–280.

Suggests that optimum subsidies could possibly be as high as 60 per cent of an operator's costs.

512 Else, Peter K. Criteria for Local Transport Subsidies. London: *Transport Reviews*, Vol. 12(4), October–December 1992, 291–309.

Examines the impact of government subsidies and regulation.

513 Evans, Andrew. Equalising Grants for Public Transport Subsidy. London: *Journal of Transport Economics and Policy*, Vol. 19(2), May 1985, 105–138.

Investigates equalising grants for public transport, using a county-level economic model of bus services and data for 36 English counties. Concludes that if the equalisation principle were adopted, almost all central grants would go to rural areas. This would not preclude public transport subsidy in urban areas, but it would be financed by local, not central, taxation.

514 Frankena, Mark W. The Efficiency of Public Transport Objectives and Subsidy Formulas. London: *Journal of Transport Economics and Policy*, Vol. 17(1), January 1983, 67–77.

515 Frankena, Mark W. The Effects of Alternative Urban Transit Subsidy Formulas. Lausanne: *Journal of Public Economics*, Vol. 15(3), June 1981, 337–348.

Demonstrates that for a given cost to the taxpayer, the effects of a transit subsidy depend on the subsidy formula, the objective function of the transit firm, and the transit demand function.

516 Frankena, Mark. Income Distributional Effects of Urban Transit Subsidies. London: *Journal of Transport Economics and Policy*, Vol. 7(3), September 1973, 215–230.

Subsidies to urban public transport in Canada are financed from general municipal, general provincial revenues, profits on other routes or on public utilities. Concludes that the net effect is often regressive, and that low-income groups do not benefit.

517 Gollin, Anthony E. A. and **Guria, Jagadish C.** Net Tax Incidence for Urban Public Transit Subsidies in New Zealand. Amsterdam: *Transportation*, Vol. 13(4), 1986, 319–328.

Examines the impact of policy changes in the funding of New Zealand public transit modes.

518 Goodwin, P. B., Bailey, J. M., Brisbourne, R. H., Clarke, M. I., Donnison, J. R., Render, T. E. and **Whiteley, G. K.** *Subsidised Public*

Transport and the Demand for Travel: the South Yorkshire example. Aldershot: Gower, 1983. 234 pp.

Investigation into the effects of a policy using subsidy to hold down public transport fares and maintain services.

519 Guria, J. C., Kirby, J. M and Willis, R. P. Impact of a Transit Subsidy Policy Change on a New Zealand Region. London: *Transport Reviews*, Vol. 5(3), July–September 1985, 193–206.

Analyses the impacts on a particular region of a recent policy change regarding public transit subsidy in New Zealand, under which the contributions of local authorities are increased from 0 to 50 per cent of net direct expenditures. The options open to the community are examined and their effects on regional income, future development and social equitability are analysed. Also illustrates the cost effectiveness of a natural monopoly under increased accountability.

520 Hirschman, Ira; Markstedt, Anders and Pucher, John. Impacts of Subsidies on the Costs of Urban Public Transport. London: *Journal of Transport Economics and Policy*, Vol. 17(2), May 1983, 155–176.

Reviews nationwide (US) trends in subsidies, compares them with changes in productivity and cost indices, and uses multiple regression analysis on a pooled cross-section sample of 77 transit systems in 1979, and 135 systems in 1980. Recommendations are made for revisions.

521 Jackson, Raymond. Optimal Subsidies for Public Transit. London: *Journal of Transport Economics and Policy*, Vol. 9(1), January 1975, 3–15.

Presents a model for determining optimal fare subsidies, and optimal subsidies for increasing transit speed. No significant improvement is apparent unless marginal social cost per car passenger mile is 80 per cent above private cost in the highway sector.

522 Leicestershire County Council. *Transport Policies and Programme: 1976/1977: including submission for transport supplementary grant.* Leicester: The County Council, 1975. 128 pp.

Sets out policies and proposals on transport for the County of Leicestershire.

523 Oram, Richard L. The Role of Subsidy Policies in Modernizing the Structure of the Bus Transit Industry. Amsterdam: *Transportation*, Vol. 9, 1980, 333–353.

Claims that full reliance on conventional forms of bus transit for peak hour needs reduces industry productivity and creates major new subsidy requirements. Restructuring of transit is therefore needed to enable paratransit integration and other innovations than can improve efficiency. Discusses the industry's long-term neglect of efficiency and describes subsidy policies that would promote necessary changes.

524 Pickrell, Don H. Rising Deficits and the Uses of Transit Subsidies in the United States. London: *Journal of Transport Economics and Policy*, Vol. 19(3), September 1985, 281–298.

Claims that increases in subsidies to transit in recent years have been absorbed by increased costs, expanded services, and reductions in real fares, rather than compensating for real demand. Argues that increased availability may itself be a cause of increased costs and deficits.

525 Pucher, John. Urban Public Transport Subsidies in Western Europe and North America. Westport, CT: *Transportation Quarterly*, Vol. 42 (3), July 1988, 377–402.

Examines the urban transportation trends throughout the seventies and eighties. Looks at the variations in the philosophy of subsidisation; the variations in levels of subsidy; the outcomes of transit policies; the impact of subsidy policy on transit costs and productivity; impacts of subsidy policy on service and ridership and other factors influencing transit outcomes.

526 Tyson, J. A. A Critique of Road Passenger Transport Subsidy Policies. Manchester: *Manchester School of Economic Studies*, Vol. 40(4), December 1972, 397–417.

Analyses the implications for resource allocation within the passenger transport sector of the system of subsidies given to finance deficits on bus services in the UK. Argues that as these are based on the existence and amount of financial deficits they are unlikely to alter significantly the efficiency of resource allocation.

527 Viton, Philip A. Eliciting Transit Services. Peace Dale, RI: *Journal of Regional Science*, Vol. 22(1), February 1982, 57–71.

Examines in detail two subsidy policies: one based on the mileage provided by the carrier, the other depending on its success in attracting riders. Numerical estimates of the minimal supply-side transit subsidies needed to elicit services are obtained for a wide variety of market layouts; whether such programmes are likely to be worthwhile is also discussed.

528 Withana, R. *Grants Policy to Nationalised Industries, with Special Reference to London Transport.* Birmingham: University of Birmingham (M. Comm. Thesis), 1971.

5 Policy and Planning

General policy

529 Agop, D. N. *Factors Affecting Modal Split Between Public and Private Transportation in Leicester.* Bradford: University of Bradford (MSc Thesis), 1973.

530 Altshuler, Alan (ed.). *Current Issues in Transportation Policy.* Lexington, MA: Lexington Books, 1979. 205 pp.

Collection of papers covering many facets of urban transport in the United States, including transport and the environment; urban highway investment and the political economy of fiscal retrenchment; federal urban mass transportation programmes and policy; equity issues in urban transportation; urban transportation planning in transition; and urban transportation and political ideology.

531 Armstrong-Wright, Alan. *Urban Transport: a World Bank Policy Study.* Washington, DC: The International Bank for Reconstruction and Development, 1986. 61 pp.

Sets out the current views of the World Bank on urban transport and the bank's approach to future lending in this sector to developing countries. Recognises the vital role that urban transport plays in the urban development process.

532 Beesley, M. E. and **Gwilliam, K. M.** Transport Policy in the United Kingdom: a critique of the 1977 white paper. London: *Journal of Transport Economics and Policy*, Vol. 11(3), September 1977, 209–223.

Describes the recent white paper as a 'pretentious failure' to secure allocational efficiency between road and rail.

533 Bly, P. H., Dasgupta, M., Johnson, R. H., Paulley, N. and **Webster, F. V.** *Changing Patterns of Urban Travel.* Paris: Organisation for Economic Co-operation and Development, 1985. 80 pp.

Report into the way cities have been changing over the years and the implications of such changes in relation to population and employment on transport and travel. Trends and reasons for changes in public transport are then analysed in a global context.

534 Bramall, Stephen. Department of Transport Reorganises. *Transport Law and Practice*, Vol. 2(2), 1994, 10–11.

Critique of the reorganisation of the Department of Transport and a look at the likely consquences.

535 Cleary, J., Hamilton, K., Hanna, J. and **Roberts, J.** (eds). *Travel Sickness: the need for a sustainable transport policy for Britain.* London: Lawrence and Wishart, 1992. 358 pp.

Collection of papers arguing that a sustainable transport policy could best be achieved by adopting 'quality-of-life' objectives for transport. This proposition is developed within the context of an integrated transport policy. Includes criticism of individual modes of transport and proposes solutions. A single government department combining land-use and transport planning with devolvement to regional or local authorities is favoured.

536 Department of Transport: Scottish Development Department: Welsh Office. *Transport Policy.* London: HMSO, 1977. 76 pp.

Examines the objectives in transport policy together with the role of government and local planning and choice. Transport in towns is assessed as well as transport in rural areas. Inter-urban passenger transport is also investigated. Freight, the public sector and roads are also covered. Implications for public expenditure are examined with a review of consultation and policy making prior to a summary of decisions taken.

537 Dickins, Ian; Mabbott, Roger; Pirie, Madsen; Sinclair, Clive and **Telford-Beasley, John.** *Traffic in the City.* London: Adam Smith Institute, 1989. 32 pp.

Five papers by the above authors entitled 'Buses in the Future'; 'The Role of the Riverbus'; 'Light Rail Transit – Prospects for the Future'; 'Traffic in the City' and 'Avoiding Chaos in the Twenty-First Century'.

538 Due, J. F. Urban Mass Transit Policy: a review article. Champaign, IL: *Quarterly Review of Economics and Business*, Vol. 16(1), Spring 1976, 93–105.

Review article looks at four publications; George Smerk's 'Urban Mass Transportation – a dozen years of Federal Policy', which provides a summary of federal policy with an evaluation. George Hilton's 'Federal Transit Subsidies', a severe criticism of federal policies. The Urban Institute's 'Para-Transit', a review of various alternatives to conventional transit. Finally, a Senate Judiciary Committee report discusses whether General Motors sought to destroy the transit industry.

539 Dunn, James A. *Miles to Go: European and American Transportation Policies.* London: Massachusetts Institute of Technology Press, 1981. 202 pp.

Gives a comparative analysis of transportation policies in the United States, France, West Germany and Britain. Also provides a comparison between European and American experience of the automobile.

540 European Conference of Ministers of Transport. *Structural Changes in Population and Impact on Passenger Transport.* Report of the eighty-eighth round table on transport economics. Paris: Organisation for Economic Co-operation and Development, 1992. 158 pp.

Proceedings of a seminar held in Paris in 1991 which sought to determine the scale of the changes in the structure of population and the various ways in which public transport can respond. Includes contributions from France, Germany and the United Kingdom and a summary of the round table debate.

541 Filion, P. *Transport Policies in London, 1965–1980: a study of political conflict and social injustice.* Kent: Kent University (PhD Thesis), 1983.

542 Gomez-Ibanez, Jose A. and **Meyer, John R.** *Autos Transit and Cities.* Cambridge, MA: Harvard University Press, 1981. 360 pp.

Discussion of mass transportation and a critical examination of government policies aimed at improving its effectiveness. Conventional transport is discussed together with van pooling, dial-a-ride and taxis. Proposals are offered for means to improve transportation and to make it more cost effective. The automobile's impact on land use, energy, and air pollution is considered. The problems experienced by minority groups in relation to transport are also looked at.

543 Greater London Council. *Transport Policies and Programme 1986–1987.* London: Greater London Council, 1985. 105 pp.

Looks at the modes of transport and expenditure, traffic management and parking control, and construction and maintenance of highways required to provide an adequate transport service for London.

544 Hamilton, Neil W. and **Hamilton, Peter R.** *Governance of Public Enterprise: a case study of urban mass transit.* Lexington, MA: Lexington Books, 1981. 152 pp.

Focuses on urban mass transit and its form as public enterprise, a structure which many Americans forget exists within the US. Looks at the problems of the legal structure and policy formation, and the development of a transit corporation model.

545 Institute for Public Policy Research and Transport 2000. *All Change: a new transport policy for Britain.* London: Institute for Public Policy Research, 1992. 30 pp.

546 Lane, Peter. Transport and Works Orders: the story so far. *Transport Law and Practice*, Vol. 1(3), 1993, 23–24.

Notes the slow start to the new system of ministerial orders for transport projects replacing Private Bill procedures.

547 London Regional Transport. *Statement of Strategy: June 1985.* England: S. W. Sharman, 1986. 23 pp.

548 May, A. D. Integrated Transport Strategies: a new approach to urban transport policy formulation in the UK. London: *Transport Reviews*, Vol. 11(3), July–September 1991, 223–247.

Reviews the background to Integrated Transport Strategy studies, evaluation approaches adopted, policy instruments considered, and the analytical methods developed for the studies. Focuses on urban areas within the UK.

549 Miller, David R. (ed.). *Urban Transportation Policy: new perspectives.* Lexington, MA: D. C. Heath, 1972. 209 pp.

Volume of ten papers (plus a concluding chapter), most of which were prepared for the Urban Transportation Policy Seminar held at Syracuse University in the Spring of 1970, reporting a variety of perspectives on urban transport sections: 1) policy and the 'urban transportation problem'; 2) policy and specific urban transport programmes; 3) policy and other aspects of urban growth and development; and 4) a concluding section considering some new developments in policy planning.

550 Morrison, Doug. Gummer's Crusade for Quality. London: *Estates Gazette*, No.9445, 1994, 58–59.

Interview with Environment Secretary, John Gummer, which looks at the details of his campaign to revitalise British town centres.

551 National Consumer Council. *Ways and Means: a consumer view of local public transport policy.* London: National Consumer Council, 1983. 48 pp.

Report based on a survey of local public transport policies.

552 Nijkamp, Peter; Reichman, Shalom and **Wegener, Michael** (eds). *Euromobile: transport communications and mobility in Europe: a cross-national comparative overview.* Aldershot: Avebury, 1990. 413 pp.

Brings together information from nineteen countries to serve as a source of reference on trends, analyses and policies in the field of transportation, communications and mobility.

553 Ochojna, A. D. The Influence of Local and National Politics on the Development of Urban Passenger Transport in Britain 1850–1900. Manchester: *Journal of Transport History*, Vol. 4(3), February 1978, 125–146.

Looks at the growth of the city and the conflict caused by the physical constraints imposed on the size of the town by the maximum commuting distance that people were prepared to travel.

554 Peel, Malcolm. *Making Tracks for the Future: towards a national transport policy.* Corby: British Institute of Management, 1992. 49 pp.

Summary of the British Institute of Management's members' views on transport in Britain. Provides a critique of post-war policies, particularly those of the previous decade. Reviews the problems that make policy formulation in transport especially difficult and summarises the key issues in this area.

555 PTRC. *Integrated Urban Planning and Transport Policies?: the Cambridge conference on urban transport policy.* London: PTRC Education and Research Services, 1993. 140 pp.

Proceedings of conference held in June 1993.

556 Pucher, John. Urban Passenger Transport in the United States and Europe: a comparative analysis of public policies. London: *Transport Reviews*, Vol. 15(3), July–August 1995, 211–227.

Focuses on the roles and impacts of the public sector as these have varied by country and over time.

557 Pucher, John. A Comparative Analysis of Policies and Travel and Behaviour in the Soviet Union, Eastern and Western Europe, and North America. Westport, CT: *Transportation Quarterly*, Vol. 44(3), July 1990, 441–466.

Compares urban transportation systems in the former Soviet Union with its almost exclusive reliance on public transport and that of the United States with its almost exclusive reliance on the automobile.

558 Samuels, Alec. Planning and Transportation: transportation and planning. Chichester: *Local Government Review*, Vol. 157(21), 1993, 401–414.

Article detailing important policy considerations for planners working in the transport sector.

559 Shaw, Stephen J. *Transport: strategy and policy.* Oxford: Basil Blackwell, 1993. 258 pp.

Examines business strategies of passenger and freight carriers in road, rail, sea and air transport, in an increasingly competitive and commercial market.

560 Sherlock, Harley. *Cities Are Good for Us.* London: Transport 2000, 1990. 99 pp.

Argues that better public transport combined with physical and financial restraint on cars in city centres is the solution to traffic congestion.

561 Smith, Geoffrey. Vitality and Viability of Town Centres. Occasional Paper No.22. *Journal of Planning Law,* December 1994, 91–106.

Examines government planning policy on out of town shopping centre development from the 1960s.

562 Sturt, Alan. Taking the Integrated Route. London: *Transport,* Vol. 12, May/June, 1991, 73–75.

Claims that British transport policy is in crisis and that mounting road, rail and air congestion serve as daily evidence of the consequences of the failure to develop effective transport policies and infrastructure investment plans. Examines how the Netherlands is addressing similar problems.

563 Turton, B. J. (ed.). *Public Issues in Transport.* Keele: Keele University Transport Geography Study Group, 1983. 156 pp.

Looks into the relationship between public policy and transport provision during a decade which witnessed fundamental reforms in local government structure and a succession of Acts and White Papers concerned with passenger and goods movement.

564 Wachs, Martin. Transportation Policy in the Eighties. Amsterdam: *Transportation,* Vol. 6, 1977, 103–120.

Urban transportation policy during the 1970s was characterised by attempts to deal with four major problems: environmental issues, inequalities in mobility, accommodating public transport demands and the rise of public transport costs. Claims that policies designed to solve one of them have often intensified others.

565 White, Peter. Transport Policies: a critical review. London: *Transport,* Vol. 1, March/April 1980, 7–8.

Claims that political debate on transport matters prior to May 1979 was in general less heated, and seemingly less dogmatic, than on many other issues.

566 Whitelegg, John. *Transport for a Sustainable Future: the case for Europe.* London: Belhaven Press, 1993. 174 pp.

Sets the policy debate within widest possible framework of economic, social and environmental issues in Europe.

General planning

567 Al-Sarraj, A. H. A. *Trip Generation, Modal Choice and Traffic Assignment in Urban Transportation Planning.* Glasgow: University of Strathclyde (PhD Thesis), 1978.

568 American Association of State Highway and Transportation Officials. *Design of Urban Highways and Arterial Streets.* Washington, DC: American Association of State Highway and Transportation Officials, 1973. 740 pp.

Emphasises the importance of planning in the total highway programme and the necessity for coordination between planning and engineering in the location and design of highways.

569 Anderson, D. L. *Strategic Development of Transport Systems: a study of the physical constraints on planning processes.* Birmingham: Aston University (PhD Thesis), 1989.

Argues that the scale of infrastructure investment is the most important type of constraint on the processes of transportation planning and claims that adequate appraisal of such constraints may be best achieved by evaluation more closely aligned to policy objectives.

570 Bannister, D. *Transport Planning.* London: E. and F.N. Spon, 1994. 247 pp.

An historical account of the evolution of transport planning; its strengths and weaknesses, and likely future development. Examples are taken from Europe and the USA.

571 Barnard, Louise. Co-ordinated Policies for Planning and Transport. *Constitutional Law*, Vol. 5(2), 1994, 65–68.

PPG13 outlines Government approach to changing travel patterns and reducing traffic via the planning system.

572 Baron, Paul. The Impact of Transport on the Social and Economic Development in Less-Developed Countries. *Transport Policy and Decision Making*, Vol. 1, 1980, 47–53.

Suggests that since transport is an important, but not the only, requirement for development, transport planning should be part of a comprehensive approach towards regional and urban development.

573 Bennett, R. and **Elmberg, G. M.** *Priority for Surface Public Trans-*

port: 42nd International Congress. Montreal 1977. Brussels: International Union of Public Transport, 1978. 20 pp.

Report prepared for the International Commission on traffic and urban planning. Concerns itself with how public transport priorities are arrived at and applied in various parts of the world and their subsequent effect on public transport and other traffic.

574 Bly, P. H. and **Webster, F. V.** *Public Transport and the Planning of Residential Areas.* TRRL Supplementary Report 510. Crowthorne: Transport and Road Research Laboratory, 1979. 17 pp.

Considers the various components of the 'generalised cost' of making a public transport journey. Reviews modelling approaches which have been used to examine trade-off situations.

575 Boyce, David E., Day, Norman D. and **McDonald, Chris.** *Metropolitan Plan Making: an analysis of experience with the preparation and evaluation of alternative land use and transportation plans.* Monograph Series Number Four. Pennsylvania: Regional Science Research Institute, 1970. 474 pp.

576 Costa, A. *The Organisation of Urban Public Transport Systems in Western European Metropolitan Areas.* Loughborough: University of Loughborough, 1995. 27 pp.

577 Cresswell, Roy (ed.). *Urban Planning and Public Transport.* London: Construction Press, 1979. 172 pp.

Based on the conference 'Urban Planning and Public Transport' held at the University of Nottingham, 1979.

578 Dimitriou, Harry T. *Urban Transport Planning: a developmental approach.* London: Routledge, 1992.

An outline and critique of the Urban Transport Planning (UTP) process from its inception in the mid-1950s in the USA and its subsequent application to other industrialised nations. Examines the effectiveness of transferring the UTP process to developing countries and argues for a more appropriate approach. Based on research and interviews with planners and academics in the USA and developing countries.

579 Dimitriou, Harry T. (ed.). *Transport Planning for Third World Cities.* London: Routledge, 1990. 432 pp.

Twelve papers provide a contextual account of third world city transport problems; review the state-of-the-art of urban transport planning; and explore directions and techniques for future action. Papers focus on transport and third world city development and the transport problems of third world cities; the inadequacies of urban public transport systems; the role of non-motorised urban travel; the evolution of the urban transport planning process and its application to third world cities.

580 Edwards, Martin and **Martin, John.** Planning Notes. London: *Estates Gazette*, No.9320, 1993, 120–121.

A review of the new draft PPG13 – Planning Policy Guidance on Transport.

581 Feilden, G. B. R., Wickens, A. H. and **Yates, I. R.** *Passenger Transport After 2000 AD.* London: E. and F.N. Spon, 1995. 259 pp.

Proceedings of one of a series of discussion meetings convened by the Royal Society with the aim of reviewing the ways in which human needs and national expectations can be served by technological developments in the 21st century. Looks at the issues and problems facing transport planners in the 21st century. Presents a North American and European perspective.

582 Flyvbjerg, Bent; Kahr, Kjeld; Peter, Bo Persen and **Johs, Vive-Petersen.** Evaluation of Public Transport: method for application in open planning. Amsterdam: *Transportation*, Vol. 13(1), 1986, 13–23.

Discusses a method to evaluate scheduled, fixed-route public transport.

583 Grant, John. *The Politics of Urban Transport Planning: an analysis of transportation policy formulation in three UK County Boroughs between 1947 and 1974.* London: Earth Resources Research, 1977. 164 pp.

584 Hanna, Judith. Will the Public Accept it? Involving the community in transport planning. London: *Local Transport Today*, February, 1993, 12–13.

585 Hart, D. A. *Strategic Planning in London: the rise and fall of the Primary Road Network: Urban and Regional Planning Series, Volume 12.* Oxford: Pergamon Press, 1976. 237 pp.

London's post-war planning strategy was an attempt to construct a system of urban motorways. Examines the policy assumptions that underlay initial design of the road system and claims that it was a symbol of a wider concept of urban order.

586 Hart, T. Transport, the Urban Pattern and Regional Change. Harlow: *Urban Studies*, Vol. 29(3–4), May 1992, 483–503.

587 Hass-Klau, Carmen. *The Pedestrian and City Traffic.* London: Belhaven Press, 1990. 277 pp.

Reviews the urban planning responses to motor transport in British, American and German cities.

588 Henderson, Irwin; Hillman, Mayer and **Whalley, Anne.** *Transport Realities and Planning Policy: studies on friction and freedom in daily travel.* London: Political and Economic Planning, 1976. 196 pp.

Focuses on personal travel as determined by a person's role in society and by travel preferences. Methods of travel examined include walking, the use of the private car, public transport and the bicycle, all of which are available in different degrees to different people. Looks at how these methods interact with each other and with the characteristics of different areas.

589 Hills, Peter J. The Car Versus Public Transport. Occasional Paper No.22. *Journal of Planning Law*, December 1994, 63–72.

Examines transport planning principles to reduce need to travel by car under PPG 13 and the likely future interaction between public and private modes of transport.

590 Houel, B. J. *National Transportation Planning in Developing Countries.* Berkeley, CA: University of California, 1979.

Critical review of the methodologies used in transport sector planning, based primarily on nine case studies of transport undertaken between 1962 and 1975.

591 Institute of Transportation Engineers: Association of Engineers and Architects: International Technical Co-operation Centre. *Traffic, Transportation and Urban Planning.* London: George Godwin, 1981.

Proceedings of an international conference of the Institute of Transportation Engineers, the Association of Engineers and Architects and the International Technical Co-operation Centre, held in Tel Aviv in 1978. Edited versions of forty-six papers covers the theme of 'the integration of traffic and transportation planning in urban planning'.

592 Kanafani, Adid and **Sperling, Dan.** *National Transportation Planning.* The Hague: Martinus Nijhoff, 1982.

Presents a detailed methodology and procedure for conducting a national transportation plan. Includes an extensive bibliography.

593 Kendall, Sarita. *Comparative Planning Data and Transportation Characteristics of Major Cities.* London: Greater London Council, 1972. 70 pp.

Presents a view of demographic, socio-economic and transportation characteristics and of transport investment and facilities for a selection of major cities in the UK, Europe, North America and elsewhere. Statistical data is presented in a tabulated form and comparisons are made wherever practicable. A useful bibliography is also provided.

594 Lassave, P. and Offner, J. M. Urban Transport: changes in expertise in France in the 1970s and 1980s. London: *Transport Reviews,* Vol. 9(2), April–June 1989, 119–134.

Analysing changes in the professional environment of experts in urban transport throws light on the evolution and aims of planning in France. The theory of democratic, decentralised and contractual planning which took shape during the 1970s was institutionalised in the 1980s in the form of the Urban Travel Plans. However, this took place in the context of deregulation and illustrates the ambiguous environment of the experts.

595 MacRae, John. PPG 13: sustaining its crusade. London: *Estates Gazette,* No.9439, 1994, 94–96.

Role of PPG 13 on Transport and Regional Planning Guidance in the Government's campaign against out of town development.

596 Mahayni, R. G. Reorienting Transportation Planning Rationale in Developing Countries. Westport, CT: *Traffic Quarterly,* Vol. 31(2), 1977, 351–365.

Claims that planning should consider transport as an integrated system rather than as an aggregation of projects and modes.

597 Neff, Charlotte and Wilson, Tay. *The Social Dimension in Transportation Assessment.* Aldershot: Gower, 1983. 339 pp.

Discusses planners and their approach to transportation planning; the social indicators used for transport planning; citizen participation; futurology and technology assessment; the social implications of transport cuts, introducing a workers' bus service and using social information for decision making.

598 Nijkamp, Peter and Reichman, S. (eds). *Transportation Planning in a Changing World.* Aldershot: Gower, 1987. 340 pp.

Proceedings of a series of three international workshops on transportation, sponsored by the European Science Foundation in 1984–1985.

599 Organisation for Economic Co-operation and Development. *The Urban Transportation Planning Process.* Paris: Organisation for Economic Co-operation and Development, 1971.

Contains a report and bibliography of a conference held under the auspices of the OECD to discuss urban transportation planning processes.

600 Poister, Theodore H. *Performance Monitoring.* Lexington, MA: D. C. Heath, 1983. 231 pp.

Presents a general approach to developing a performance monitoring system that is applicable to any programme area and then illustrates its application in one major transportation agency, the Pennsylvania Department of Transportation.

601 Rosen, Nils T. I. A Critique of 'The City Traffic Network'. London: George Godwin, *International Forum Series*, Vol. 2, 1981. pp. 137–154.

Argues that competition is necessary if we want to save money, energy and raw materials.

602 Schofer, Joseph L. and **Stopher, Peter R.** Specifications for a New Long-Range Urban Transportation Planning Process. Amsterdam: *Transportation*, Vol. 8, 1979, 199–218.

Asserts the continuing need for a long-range component to urban transport planning, citing particularly the relationships between short- and long-range planning and the dangers of a single-minded concentration on short-range planning. Some of the specific requirements and capabilities of a new procedure are described, and existing procedures are compared against these.

603 Simpson, Barry J. *City Centre Planning and Public Transport: case studies from Britain, West Germany and France.* Andover: Van Nostrand Reinhold, 1988. 204 pp.

Provides an examination of public transport policies in several cities in Britain, West Germany and France in order to represent a range of solutions to common transport problems. Looks at the role of light transit systems. Discusses the principles, legislation and practice of physical planning in city centres.

604 Sloan, Allan K. *Citizen Participation in Transportation Planning: the Boston experience.* Massachusetts: Ballinger Publishing, 1974. 180 pp.

Examines citizen participation and the way it influences changes in basic public policy. Based on the decision by the Governor of Massachusetts in 1970 to declare a moratorium on the construction of interstate highways.

605 Starkie, D. N. M. *Transportation Planning, Policy and Analysis.* Oxford: Pergamon Press, 1976. 147 pp.

Integrates the analytical aspects and the policy aspects of transportation planning.

606 Stovell, Rick. Planners' Notes. *Public Week*, Vol. 48(1), 1994, 33–35.

Examines the provisions of planning policy guidance notes PPG13 and PPG6 on reducing the use of cars and the encouragement of town centre shopping developments.

607 Sutton, J. C. Organization and Planning of Ambulance Transport Services in England and Wales. London: *Transport Reviews*, Vol. 10(2), April–June 1990, 149–170.

Ambulances are the largest special needs operator in England and Wales: the organisation of the ambulance service is described from a number of perspectives, historical, institutional, and managerial.

608 Thomson, J. Michael. *Toward Better Urban Transport Planning in Developing Countries: World Bank Staff Working Papers Number 600.* Washington, DC: The International Bank for Reconstruction and Development, 1983. 105 pp.

Describes the defects in transport planning and the various approaches that have been adopted in order to find solutions, but which have had limited success. Includes a discussion on the deficiencies and problems of the 'Big Plan' approach to transport planning with specific reference to developing countries and the causes of planning failure.

609 Transport and Road Research Laboratory. *The Demand for Public Transport.* Crowthorne: Transport and Road Research Laboratory, 1980. 329 pp.

Attempts to distil the very large body of information available on the many different factors which affect the demand for public transport and to draw conclusions which have a direct applicability to transport planning.

610 *No Entry.*

611 Truelove, Paul. *Decision Making in Transport Planning.* London: Longman, 1992. 184 pp.

Discusses UK transport policy and planning with examples and contemporary experiences from both central and local authority decision making. Provides a critical assessment of planning procedures and the wider institutional framework in which they are set.

612 W. S. Atkins and Partners. *Transportation Study: Harlow.* Surrey: W. S. Atkins and Partners, 1971. 66 pp.

613 White, Peter R. *Planning for Public Transport.* London: Hutchinson, 1976. 224 pp.

Concise account of public transport systems in Britain along with suggestions for improvement. Basic principles of bus operation, urban railways, rapid transit systems and principles of pricing are all discussed.

614 Winfield, Richard. *Public Transport Plans and All That.* Cardiff: Welsh Consumer Council, 1981. 36 pp.

Designed to alert consumers to their rights in the preparation of annual public transport plans and to assist them in exercising those rights. Provides a description of the way the system works and what it seeks to achieve.

European Union policy

615 Abbati, Carlo Degli. *Transport and European Integration.* Paris: Organisation for Economic Co-operation and Development, 1987. 229 pp.

Defines the general question of the organisation of transport at European level. Deals specifically with transport rates and conditions, the monitoring of transport supply, harmonisation of conditions of competition and infrastructure problems. Also discusses the European Community's external transport relations.

616 Banister, D. and **Berechman, J.** (eds). *Transport in a Unified Europe: policies and challenges.* Amsterdam: Elsevier, 1993.

617 Bayliss, B. T. Transport in the European Communities. London: *Journal of Transport Economics and Policy.* Vol. 13(1), January 1979, 28–43.

Reviews the development of transport policy within the European Community since 1958 and suggests reasons for lack of progress in a number of key policy areas.

618 Bendixson, Terence. *Transport in the Nineties: the shaping of Europe.* London: Surveyors Publications, 1989. 53 pp.

A report about the institutional changes and the investment required to create a transport infrastructure that is European in scale.

619 Bowers, Chris. Balancing Transport and Environmental Needs Leaves EC in a Policy Quandary. London: *Local Transport Today,* January, 1993, 12–13.

In December of 1992, the European Community published its long awaited White Paper on the future of the Community's transport policy. Article reviews the White Paper and claims that it takes a cautious approach, with concerns about subsidiarity, the needs of industry, and environmental protection hard to reconcile.

620 Commission of the European Communities. *Communication of the Commission to the Council on the Development of the Common Transport Policy: Objectives and Programme: Bulletin of the European Communities: Supplement 16/73.* Paris: Organisation for Economic Co-operation and Development, 1973. 24 pp.

621 Commission of the European Communities. *The Future Development of the Common Transport Policy: a global approach to the construction of a community framework for sustainable mobility.* Paris: Organisation for Economic Co-operation and Development, 1993. 72 pp.

622 Cresswell, R. W. and **Young, A. P.** (eds). *The Urban Transport Future: a contribution to the Council of Europe's European Campaign for Urban Renaissance.* London: Construction Press, 1982. 202 pp.

623 Delaney, K. PROMETHEUS: making the best of what we've got. *Public Policy Review,* Vol. 3(4), 1995, 70–71.

PROMETHEUS (Programme for European Traffic with Highest Efficiency and Unprecedented Safety), as part of the European Commission's DRIVE programme, looks at the possibilities of integrating synergies from major car and commercial vehicle manufacturers, scientific institutes and electronics engineers, in order to develop a co-ordinated approach to in-vehicle and road-side information systems using the latest technologies.

624 Erdmenger, Jurgen. *The European Community Transport Policy: towards a common transport policy.* Aldershot: Gower, 1983. 155 pp.

Describes the efforts of the European Communities institutions to work towards a common transport policy in the period 1973–82.

625 European Community. *The European Communities Transport Policy.* Paris: Organisation for Economic Co-operation and Development, 1981. 37 pp.

Facts and figures are presented which illustrate the importance of transport and the need to integrate it into the European Community.

626 European Parliament. *Community Policy on Transport Infrastructures: research and documentation papers/series regional policy and transport 16.* Paris: Organisation for Economic Co-operation and Development, 1991. 33 pp.

627 Frazer, Tim and **Holmes, Peter.** Self-Restraint: cars, complaints and the Commission. *Environmental and Planning Law,* Vol. 1(1), 1995, 85–95.

Looks at the relationship between competition and commercial policies considered in the decision which challenged the European Union's refusal to investigate complaints made by a consumer interest group.

628 Frohnmeyer, A. Transport Systems in the Future. Amsterdam: *Transportation,* Vol. 14(2), 1980, 159–165.

Reviews the major features of the transport policy of the European Community. Assesses the likely characteristics of future transport supply, identifying the particular competing developments in road and air transport which would affect the success of investments in high speed rail projects such as that proposed between Amsterdam, Groningen and Hamburg.

629 Graaf, G. de and **Nieuwenhuis, D. K.** EC Legislation in the Field of Public Contracts. Brussels: *Public Transport International*, Vol. 42(4), November/December 1993, 39–42.

Indicates the ways in which European Community legislation on public contracts relating to public transport will generally affect the members of the Union Internationale des Transports Publics (UITP).

630 Grieco, Margaret and **Jones, Peter** (eds). *Transport Technology in an Integrating Europe: the development of European transport policy.* Aldershot: Avebury, 1996. 180 pp.

Investigation into the barriers to and opportunities for the development of pan-European technologies and pan-European transport policies.

631 Hamilton, Kerry. *Transport Policy: Spicers European Policy Reports.* London: Routledge, 1990. 79 pp.

Examines the evolution, current problems, and future directions of transport policy in the European Community. Briefly discusses the role, institutions and legislation of the EC. Provides an introduction to EC transport problems and discusses the Common Transport Policy of the EC. Examines the implications of EC transport policy and provides summaries of specific treaty articles that guide the Common Transport Policy. Presents summaries of key documents relating to the development of transport policy.

632 Hand, C. C. *A Critical Interpretation of the Transport Infrastructure Policy of the European Economic Community.* Reading: University of Reading (M.Phil Thesis), 1985.

Examines a policy proposal by the European Economic Community to intervene in the planning and provision of transport infrastructure.

633 Institute of Civil Engineers. *European Transport.* London: Thomas Telford, 1987. 155 pp.

Proceedings of a conference organised by the Institution of Civil Engineers and held in London on 1 October 1986. European transport policy and other developments in transport are discussed and four main streams of progress are identified: change, technological advances, growth and investment.

634 Jennings, A. Infrastructure Pricing and the EEC Common Transport Policy: the case of roads and commercial vehicles. London: *Journal of Transport Economics and Policy*, Vol. 10(2), May 1976, 177–195.

EEC proposals for harmonisation of commercial vehicle taxation would require all the proceeds to be spent on the roads, and no regard is paid to congestion and other elements of marginal social cost.

635 Kinnock, Neil. Urban Public Transport and the European Commission. Brussels: *Public Transport International*, Vol. 44(4), July 1995, 9–11.

An outline of the position of the European Commission and its projects concerning urban public transport.

636 Kiriazidis, Theo. *European Transport: problems and policies.* Aldershot: Avebury, 1994. 127 pp.

An analysis of the European Union and its attempts to integrate member states' transport sectors following the Single European Act 1986. Aims to identify and evaluate barriers to integration and critically examines European Community transport policy.

637 Kok, Coraline. Political Agreement on Road Transport Taxation. Amsterdam: *European Taxation*, Vol. 33(8), 1993, 26–27.

Council of Ministers Agreement of 19th June 1993 on the question of diesel excise duties, vehicle taxes and tolls.

638 Markham, John. Public Service Contracts for Rail, Road, and Inland Waterway Services. Brussels: *Public Transport International*, Vol. 41, February 1993, 64–67.

Description of the new Council regulation (EEC) aimed at improving the relationship between member States and their Public Transport undertakings.

639 Muller-Hellmann, A. Overview of Current EC-Developments and Regulations of Concern to Public Transport. Brussels: *Public Transport International*, Vol. 43(1), January 1994, 39–42.

Overview of the different European Community directives related to public transport.

640 Pease, Jack. DRIVE: more than the mysticism of just a clever acronym? London : *Local Transport Today*, August 1991, 10–11.

Widely quoted, but little understood, the European Community's DRIVE programme is now moving into its second phase. Article attempts to unravel the details behind the project and looks at the justification for investing so much money in a project which some argue will never reap any real economic benefits.

641 Public Transport International. Essential Links in Europe. Brussels: *Public Transport International*, Vol. 41, February 1993, 48–53.

Argues that the European Community is only interested in the high-speed network, whereas links between urban passenger transport systems are vital if overall speeds are to be maintained throughout a journey.

642 Quidort, Michel and **Richard, Jean-Paul.** Europe's Impact on Public Transport. Brussels: *Public Transport International*, Vol. 41, February 1993, 54–63.

Although the Treaty of Rome makes no explicit provision for Community responsibility in the urban transport field, each Directorate General is already carrying out some work on an urban scale within the framework of its responsibility.

643 Reynolds, Charles. Up Yours, Delors? London: *Proceedings of the Chartered Institute of Transport*, Vol. 1(3), Summer 1992, 37–48.

Looks at the requirements for completing the single market within the European Community in transport. Shipping, aviation, road haulage, and bus and coaches are discussed. Its implementation and implications for the United Kingdom are also examined.

644 Sawyer, David. Common Transport Policy within the European Union. *European Business Brief*, Vol. 3(10), 1993, 7–10.

CEC White paper on transport policy stresses concept of sustainable mobility.

645 Scherer, Peter. Completion of the Single European Market and the Transport of Goods: recent developments. *Utilities Law Review*, Vol. 4(1), 1993, 25–30.

With a focus on Germany, this article looks at recent development in the completion of the Single European Market, in particular, the regulations on quota restrictions, professional qualifications, cabotage and tariffs in the road haulage sector and other recently applied measures applying to other transport sections.

646 Simmons and Simmons. Commission Fine Annulled. *Practical Law for Companies*, Vol. 6(6), 1995, 47.

647 Stasinopoulas, Dinos. The External Dimension of the Common Transport Policy. *Transport Law and Practice*, Vol. 1(9), 1994, 76–79.

Considers the relationship between the EC and non-Member States concerning a broad range of transport issues.

648 Thomson, Ian. Bibliographic Snapshot: the transport policy of the European Community. *European Access*, No.5, 1993, 36–41.

649 Vanderelst, Alain and **Wijckmans, Frank.** The EC Commission's Draft Regulation on Motor Vehicle Distribution: alea iacta est? *European Competition Law Review*, Vol. 16(4), 1995, 225–236.

Considering the legislation of the Commission Regulation on the application of Art. 85(3) of the Treaty to certain categories of motor vehicle distribution and service agreements (Draft), looks at the provisions on exclusivity and territorial protection, non-complete obligation, selectivity and measures to improve quality of distribution network.

650 Vougias, S. Transport and Environmental Policies in the EC. London: *Transport Reviews*, Vol. 12(3), September-December 1992, 219–236.

Deals with the complex relationship between transport and the environment and describes and discusses the relevant policies adopted by the EC. Major transport related environmental impacts are briefly analysed and analytical data regarding traffic and infrastructure statistics for all EC countries are presented, in order to better understand the trends and prospects for the year 2000.

651 Whitelegg, John. *Transport Policy in the EEC.* London: Routledge, 1988. 233 pp.

Explains the structure of transport in Europe and places in context the relevant importance of different modes.

652 Williams, Karen. The Way Ahead: road transport in the EU. *European Business Law Review*, Vol. 6(11), 1994, 81–83.

Claims that European Union road haulage policy must be defined in terms of infrastructure requirements and balancing modes of transport against social and environmental impact.

Theory

653 Adler, Hans A. *Sector and Project Planning in Transportation.* World Bank occasional paper 4. Baltimore, MD: Johns Hopkins University Press, 1967.

Deals with the preparation of a transport sector programmes and project appraisal.

654 Anderson, Edward J. *Transit Systems Theory.* Lexington, MA: Lexington Books, 1978. 340 pp.

Examines many forms of urban transit while emphasising its network characteristics. Focuses heavily on automated transit systems.

655 Annen, J. J. *Urban Transport planning: an appraisal of recent approaches in Britain.* Edinburgh: University of Edinburgh (M.Phil Thesis), 1977.

656 Ayad, H. and **Oppenlander, J. C.** Simplified Transportation System Planning. London: George Godwin, *International Forum Series*, Vol. 1, 1981, 77–90.

Attempts to develop a rational concept for the design and evaluation of urban transportation systems.

657 Barringer, Robert L. and **Sagner, James S.** Toward Criteria in the Development of Urban Transportation Systems. Amsterdam: *Transportation*, Vol. 7, 1978, 87–96.

Describes the efforts of the European Communities institutions to work towards a common transport policy in the period 1973–82.

658 Bayliss, Brian. *Planning and Control in the Transport Sector.* Aldershot: Gower, 1981. 202 pp.

Deals with policy areas from the standpoint of national transport planning. Issues covered are: energy policy, counter-cyclical policy, regional policy, designated lorry routes, subsidies, quantity and quality control in road haulage and transport policy in the European Community.

659 Ben-Akiva, Moshe. Policy-Sensitive and Policy-Responsive Transportation Planning. London: George Godwin, *International Forum Series*, Vol. 1, 1981, 91–104.

Reviews recent developments and new approaches representing significant improvements and broadening of capabilities in the methods and procedures available for transportation planning.

660 Benwell, M. *The Derivation of Social Performance Measures in Transport Planning and Managment.* Cranfield: Cranfield Institute of Technology (PhD Thesis), 1983.

661 Bonsall, Peter; Dalvi, Quasim and **Hills, Peter J.** *Urban Transportation Planning: Current Themes and Future Prospects.* Tunbridge Wells: Abacus Press, 1977. 386 pp.

Edited papers originally presented at a conference on Urban Transport Planning held at the University of Leeds in 1976.

662 Bourdrez, Jan A., Klaassen, Leo H. and **Volmuller, Jacques.** *Transport and Reurbanisation.* Aldershot: Gower, 1981. 214 pp.

Attempt to relate the functioning of the transport system in an urban area to that area's structural development.

663 Brown, Richard J. The Role of Transportation Planning in the

Management of the Total Urban System. London: George Godwin, *International Forum Series*, Vol. 1, 1981, 29–38.

Theory and management of urban systems are discussed, essential steps in the planning process are identified in the context of the urban system, and an organisational structure is proposed for effective improvements in urban travel conditions.

664 Burns, Robert E. Transport Planning: selection of analytical techniques. Bath: *Journal of Transport Economics and Policy*, Vol. 3(3), 1969, 306–321.

Discusses several major approaches to transport planning, such as the bottleneck approach, project analysis, linear programming, integer programming, and simulation models, and their applicability to a developing country such as Pakistan.

665 Campisi, D. An Empirical Study of Interregional Transportation Plans. Rome: *International Journal of Transport Economics*, Vol. 18(1), February 1991, 31–46.

666 Chazoul, K. N. *Transportation Planning: an assessment study of the sensitivity of planning variables.* Glasgow: University of Strathclyde (MSc Thesis), 1971.

667 Dargay, G. and **Stokes, G.** *What is a Sustainable Transport Policy?* Oxford: Oxford University, Transport Studies Unit, 1993. 13 pp.

Paper presented to the PTRC Summer Annual Meeting held in Manchester in 1993.

668 Department of the Environment: Transport and Road Research Laboratory. *Moving People in Cities: a conference held at the TRRL, Crowthorne, 5 and 6 April 1973.* TRRL Supplementary Report 6 UC. Crowthorne: Transport and Road Research Laboratory, 1974. 169 pp.

669 DeSalvo, Joseph S. (ed.). *Perspectives on Regional Transportation Planning.* Lexington, MA: Lexington Books, 1973. 441 pp.

Provides an analysis of the efficacy of transportation planning at the regional level.

670 Dickey, John W. *Metropolitan Transportation Planning.* Washington, DC: Scripta Books, 1975.

Emphasises the transportation planning process from problem identification to operation. Also provides an interdisciplinary background to transportation planning.

671 Dimitriou, H. T. *A Development Approach to Urban Transport Planning.* Aldershot: Avebury, 1995.

672 Emerson, E. C. *A Systems Approach to Caribbean Transport Planning.* Birmingham: Aston University (MSc Thesis), 1971.

673 Evans, S. P. *Some Applications of Mathematical Optimisation Theory in Transport Planning.* London: University College London (PhD Thesis), 1976.

674 Fernandez, J. Enrique. Optimum Dynamic Investment Policies for Capacity in Transport Facilities. London: *Journal of Transport Economics and Policy*, Vol. 17(3), September 1985, 267–284.

675 Foster, C. D. *A Policy for Transport.* London: The Nuffield Foundation, 1977.
Collection of articles on public policy, mobility, subsidies and the environment.

676 Foster, R. G. *Urban Transport Planning in Developing Countries.* Reading: University of Reading (PhD Thesis), 1984.

677 Freeman Fox and Associates. *The Alternative Transportation Systems: Nottingham and environs transportation study.* Volume 1. London: Freeman Fox and Associates, 1976. 375 pp.
Describes the development and evaluation of three alternative transportation strategies for the improvement of transport in the Greater Nottingham area.

678 Gakenheimer, Ralph; Meyer, Michael and **Altshuler, Alan** (eds). *Urban Transportation Planning in Transition: The Sources and prospects of TSM, in Current Issues in Transportation Policy.* Lexington, MA: Lexington Books, 1980.
During the mid-1970s, conservation emerged as a central theme of urban policy with a resultant shift in the field of transportation toward planning that is service-orientated. The outcome was transportation system management (TSM). Chapter 9 looks at TSM's potential.

679 Goodwin, P. *Some Effects of Public Transport Policy.* Oxford: Oxford University, Transport Studies Unit, 1992. 12 pp.

680 Goodwin, P. *New Transport Policies – What Can Go Wrong?* Oxford: Oxford University, Transport Studies Unit, 1993. 10 pp.

681 Grant, J. A. *An Analysis of Urban Transportation Planning and Policy Making in Three County Boroughs, 1947–1974.* Reading: University of Reading (PhD Thesis), 1977.

682 Grieco, M. *Transport Policy and Urban Integration.* Oxford: Oxford University, Transport Studies Unit, 1992. 7 pp.

683 Hammerton, S. K. *Public Transport and Town Planning: an investigation into trips from the home in Teesside, with special reference to fluctuations in demand.* Leeds: University of Leeds (PhD Thesis), 1976.

684 Hartgen, David T. Getting Transportation Well-Being Out of the Capitalist Engine. Westport, CT: *Transportation Quarterly*, Vol. 45(4), October 1991, 599–610.

Looks back from 2010 at the actions taken in the 1990s to resolve transportation problems. Assumes that government subsidies will be minimal and that the capitalist free enterprise system will be the dominant economic system for transportation.

685 Hellewell, D. Scott. Towards the Year 2000: transport for our cities. London: *Proceedings of the Chartered Institute of Transport*, Vol. 1 (2), Winter 1991, 13–31.

Paper presented for the Arnold Stone Lecture, Yorkshire Section (CIT) in December 1991. Concerns itself with a forward look to the end of the century and prospects for transport. Argues that the market approach to transport policy has led to an inability to match supply with demand, without restraints on existing traffic and/or major expenditure on public transport. Proposes that investment to improve public transport must precede measures to curtail car usage.

686 Jones, P. M. *A New Approach to Understanding Travel Behaviour and its Implications for Transportation Planning.* London: Imperial College of Science and Technology (PhD Thesis), 1983.

687 Kamp, J. B. van der and **Polak, J. B.** *Changes in the Field of Transport: essays on the progress of theory in relation to policy making, in honour of Prof. Tissot van Patot.* The Hague: Martinus Nijhoff, 1980. 216 pp.

Collection of essays which attempt to identify changes in the nature of the subject matter of transport economics, in the methods of the subject, and in the interaction of theory, policy and decision-making. Highlights the development of a multi-disciplinary approach to transport economics and the central role taken by an explicit consideration of spatial phenomena.

688 Kawakami, Shogo. A Method of Evaluating Urban Transportation Planning. London: George Godwin, *International Forum Series*, Vol. 1, 1981, 183–190.

Develops a methodology for the evaluation of urban transportation planning based on the concept of relative value or utility and disutility.

689 Kay, G. B. *The Urban Transport Problem: a systematic approach to the determination of policy.* Dublin: Trinity College Dublin (MSc Thesis), 1984.

690 Knowles, R. D. (ed.). *Transport Policy and Urban Development: methodology and evaluation.* Salford: University of Salford, Transport Geography Study Group, 1989. 178 pp.

Collection of papers including 'Assessing and modelling the impact of road transport informatics technology on the road transport environment in Europe'; 'Transport policy and urban rank: a model for the optimisation of transport infrastructures'; and 'Urban public transport policy in Thatcher's Britain'.

691 Kraft, Walter. Can Mass Transit Cope with the Dispersion of Downtown? Washington, DC: *Mass Transit*, April 1988, 51–53.

For years planners, politicians, engineers and developers have grappled with traffic congestion in city centres. Article claims that the problem was brought about by a range of causes including high numbers of commuters, insufficient parking, poorly timed traffic signals, ineffectively policed curb restriction and inadequate roadways.

692 Langley, C. J. Adverse Impacts of the Washington Beltway on Residential Property Values. Madison, WI: *Land Economics*, Vol. 51(1), February 1976, 54–65.

Results of this study supports the hypothesis that adverse effects of the Washington Beltway upon the quality of life in the adjacent residential community are reflected in property sales values.

693 Lindquist, Peter Stanley. *Traffic Zones Reconsidered: a geographical examination of zonal restructuring for system-wide mass transit ridership forecasting.* Milwaukee: University of Wisconsin (PhD Thesis), 1988. 244 pp.

Attempts to restructure the zone system to account for passenger accessibility in system wide transit ridership forecasts.

694 Lumsden, I. G. C. *The Case for a Reappraisal of Urban Transport Planning.* Edinburgh: Heriot-Watt University (MSc Thesis), 1977.

695 Martin, Brian V. and **Warden, Charles N.** *Transportation Planning* *in Developing Countries.* Washington, DC: Brookings Institution, 1965.

Emphasises the value of systems analysis in project appraisal.

696 May, A. *Integrated Transport Strategies: a review of recent developments in the UK.* Leeds: University of Leeds, Institute for Transport Studies, April 1992. 11 pp.

697 May, A. D. and **Roberts, M.** The Design of Integrated Transport Strategies. Oxford: *Transport Policy*, Vol. 2(2), April 1995, 97–105.

Integrated transport strategies use a combination of infrastructure, management and pricing measures to achieve better performance against transport policy objectives. This principle is incorporated in the UK DoT's Package Approach, but little guidance is available on strategy design. A range of measures are tested, a shortlist generated, and packages developed focusing on three sources of synergy: complementarity, financial support and public acceptability.

698 Meyer, Michael D. and **Miller, Eric J.** *Urban Transportation Planning: a decision orientated approach.* New York: McGraw-Hill, 1984.

Attempts to provide an understanding of the link between urban transportation planning and the decision making processes that such planning is designed to support. Divided into four parts, part one provides a general background to urban transportation; part two gives an overview of decision making in the urban transportation environment and discusses data management and diagnosis; part three looks at analysis techniques and part four assesses programme and project implementation.

699 Moyes, A. (ed.). *Companies, Regions and Transport Change.* Aberystwyth: Transport Geography Study Group, University of Wales, 1991. 166 pp.

Collection of papers including an article on the congested road network and the changing nature of public transport.

700 Naroff, J. L. Decentralisation and the Demand for Gasoline. Madison, WI: *Land Economics*, Vol. 56(2), May 1980, 169–180.

Aims to determine the impact of urban structure on the demand for fuel. Demonstrates that both population and employment dispersal have greatly influenced fuel demand in urban areas.

701 Organisation for Economic Co-operation and Development. *Transport Requirements for Urban Communities: planning for personal travel.* Paris: Organisation for Economic Co-operation and Development, 1977. 91 pp.

Considers some of the problems involved in the methodology of transport planning as applied to personal travel requirements. Reviews issues facing transport planners and looks at the ways in which the transport planning process has evolved to deal with these issues.

702 Peedle, T. J. *An Analysis of Transport Appraisal and Decision Making in Strathclyde Region.* Glasgow: University of Strathclyde (MSc Thesis), 1991.

Attempts to analyse the method of appraisal and the decision making process relating to both roads and public transport in the Strathclyde Region.

703 Pickering, G. G. *Modal Split in Urban Transportation Planning.* Salford: University of Salford (PhD Thesis), 1971.

704 Pouliquen, L. Y. *Risk Analysis in Project Appraisal.* World Bank staff occasional paper 11. Washington, DC: World Bank, 1970.

Applies formal risk analysis techniques primarily to transport and public utility projects.

705 Puvanachandran, V. M. *The Viability of British Urban Transport Planning in the Post-Buchanan Period: a systematic study.* Warwick: University of Warwick (PhD Thesis), 1982.

706 Roe, M. S. *Priority Evaluation in Transportation Policies and Programmes.* Birmingham: Aston University (PhD Thesis), 1983.

707 Rundle, C. J. *A Framework for the Integrated Analysis of Transport Policy.* Manchester: University of Manchester (MSc Thesis), 1992.

Focuses upon transport policy and the requirements for its appraisal in terms of its environmental, social and economic impact.

708 Terzis, G. C. *The Longitudinal Method: an application to public transport policies in London.* London: University College London (PhD Thesis), 1988.

709 Vandu-Chikolo, I. P. *Comparative Study of Transportation Investment Planning in Developing Countries.* Sheffield: University of Sheffield (PhD Thesis), 1985.

Comparative study of the transportation planning processes in Great Britain, Malaysia, Nigeria and Upper Volta.

710 Want, H. F. *A Generalised Aggregation Methodology in Transport Planning.* Cambridge: Cambridge University (MSc Thesis), 1983.

711 Westwell, A. R. *Public Transport Policy in Conurbations in Britain.* Keele: Keele University (PhD Thesis), 1991.

Aims to research the content of public transport policy and to construct a means of assessing the effectiveness of declared transport policy together with the establishment of a procedure for its formulation. Main period of concentration after tracing the development of public transport policy is 1968 to 1985.

712 Wilson, L. W. *A Study of Comprehensive Traffic Planning Techniques in Small Towns.* Salford: University of Salford (MSc Thesis), 1971.

713 Zertali, M. *A Critical Approach to the Urban Transport Planning Process.* Bradford: University of Bradford (MSc Thesis), 1979.

Infrastructure

714 Assad, Arjang; Ball, Michael; Bodin, Lawrence; Golden, Bruce and **Spielber, Frank.** Garage Location for an Urban Mass Transit System. Baltimore, MD: *Transportation Science*, Vol. 18(1), February 1994, 56–75.

Discusses a model for the problem of locating garages in an urban mass transit system and the associated assignment of vehicles to garages for background and peak services of transit lines.

715 Barham, P., Oxley, P. and **Shaw, T.** *Design Guidelines for Public Transport Infrastructure: technical report.* Crowthorne: Transport and Road Research Laboratory, 1994. 136 pp.

716 Bayliss, David. Public Transport Infrastructure in Europe. London: *Proceedings of the Chartered Institute of Transport*, Vol. 1(3), Summer 1992, 3–28.

Paper presented to the American Public Transit Association's Annual General Meeting, Houston, 1990. Sets out to describe current developments, issues and plans being laid to maintain, upgrade and extend Europe's public transport infrastructure. Comparisons are made between Europe and North America and the differences identified.

717 Bell, Margaret C. Passenger Transport Interchange: car, bus and train. London: George Godwin, *International Forum Series*, Vol. 2, 1981, 63–73.

Critical review of over one hundred reports on passenger transport interchange has led to the formulation of criteria for successful interchange. Research findings of various investigators throughout the world are compared and contrasted to gain an understanding of the role of interchange in a journey and the stages of a journey in which interchange occurs. The need for careful interchange design and planning is discussed with relation to available resources for urban transportation systems.

718 Black, John A. and **Esguerra, George D.** Implementation Measures for Land-Use and Transport Infrastructure Projects. Nagoya, Japan: *Regional Development Dialogue*, Vol. 13(3), Autumn 1992, 164–167.

Examines the sources of funding for urban transport infrastructure projects. Case studies from Asia are used as examples which show that developing countries have problems generating sufficient revenues in their metropolises to fund change.

719 Carr, Stephen and **Ashely, Myer.** *City Signs and Lights: a policy study.* Cambridge, MA: Massachusetts Institute of Technology Press, 1973. 272 pp.

Results of a project designed to analyse the presentation of information on signs for motorists and pedestrians. Various proposals for improvement of transport information are offered.

720 Confederation of British Industry. *Missing Links: settling national transport priorities: a CBI discussion document.* London: Confederation of British Industry, 1995. 43 pp.

Examines the UK's transport infrastructure and identifies the key strengths and weaknesses in European transport experience to show a possible way forward for UK transport policy.

721 Coopers and Lybrand Deloitte. *London World City: a research project.* London: HMSO, 1991. 236 pp.

The London Planning Advisory Committee commissioned this research to investigate London's future competitiveness as a world city, and how this can be sustained and enhanced. Transport is examined briefly in the chapter on enabling infrastructure.

722 Dupree, Harry. *Urban Transportation: the new town solution.* Aldershot: Gower, 1987. 267 pp.

Examines ways in which present and future transportation needs have been catered for in the new towns of Great Britain. Traces the history of the towns through the planning and construction stages in the context of transportation.

723 *No Entry.*

724 European Conference of Ministers of Transport. *Transport Infra-*

structure in Central and Eastern Europe: selection criteria and funding. Paris: Organisation for Economic Co-operation and Development, 1995. 140 pp.

Analyses the sources of funding and examines the modernising and maintenance of current schemes and likely investments for new transport schemes. Also establishes the regulatory criteria for service, environmental, technical, and safety standards which will be required for transport infrastructure investment on priority transport routes within Europe.

725 European Conference of Ministers of Transport. *Pricing the Use of Infrastructure.* ECMT Round Table 7. Paris: Organisation for Economic Co-operation and Development, 1971. 97 pp.

726 European Conference of Ministers of Transport. *Environment and Transport Infrastructures.* Report of the seventy-ninth round table on transport economics. Paris: Organisation for Economic Co-operation and Development, 1989. 157 pp.

Examines environmental studies carried out when infrastructures are being built and indicates how the findings can be incorporated in the decision-making process, for example, by final choice of route, measuring degrees of disamenity, threshold values, and the assignment of a monetary value to effects.

727 Greater London Council Steering Group. *East London River Crossing Study: studies volume.* London: Greater London Council, 1975. 113 pp.

728 Greater London Council Steering Group. *East London River Crossing Study: report of the steering group.* London: Greater London Council, 1975. 32 pp.

729 Hall, Peter and **Hass-Klau, Carmen.** Time for a Fresh Look. London: *Transport*, Vol. 8, December, 1987, 250–253.

Attempts to outline the trend in new urban transport projects.

730 Helm, Dieter and **Thompson, David.** Privatised Transport Infrastructure and Incentives to Invest. London: *Journal of Transport Economics and Policy*, Vol. 25(3), September 1991, 231–247.

Examines incentives to invest in transport infrastructure under public and privatised ownership. Argues that methods used to regulate the UK's nationalised industries up to the late 1970s provided inadequate constraint on industries' investment plans but that changes in regulation, introduced after 1978, provided more effective incentives.

731 Kenworthy, Jeffrey and **Newman, Peter W. G.** Transport and Urban

Form in Thirty Two of the World's Principal Cities. London: *Transport Reviews*, Vol. 11(3), July–October 1991, 249–272.

Study of 32 major world cities claims that there are very clear relationships between transport and urban form. Suggests that economic factors, such as income and petrol prices, are less important than the direct policy instruments of the transport planner and urban planner, such as the relative provision of infrastructure for automobiles and rapid transit, or the density of population and jobs.

732 Maggi, Ricco; Masser, Ian; Nijkamp, Peter and **Vleugel, Jaap.** *Missing Transport Networks in Europe.* Aldershot: Avebury, 1994. 224 pp.

Offers a novel approach to European infrastructure by focusing attention on missing networks. Examines various European case studies in order to trace the critical success factors for efficient and effective transport policy. Concludes with strategic recommendations on European transport and telecommunications policy.

733 Nwogu, T. S. *Some Aspects of Transport Planning in British New Towns.* Salford: University of Salford (MSc Thesis), 1980.

734 Oort, Conrad J. *Criteria for Investment in the Infrastucture of Inland Transport.* Munich: European Conference of Ministries of Transport, 1967.

Introduction to the cost-benefit analysis of transport projects.

735 Organisation for Economic Co-operation and Development. *Infrastructure Policies for the 1990s.* Paris: Organisation for Economic Co-operation and Development, 1993. 91 pp.

Assesses the current state of infrastructures and public investment patterns in OECD countries and certain dynamic non-member economies, and suggests likely future trends. Examines those policy options able to improve the efficiency of infrastructural provision, and reviews the problem of decision making and planning for major infrastructure projects.

736 Phillips, Robert J. Infrastructure: risk. *Transport Law and Practice*, Vol. 2(4), 1994, 31–32.

Examines allocation of risk in private sector involvement in transport infrastructure.

737 Potter, S. *Transport and New Towns: Volume One: The historical development of transportation planning for new communities.* Milton Keynes: Open University, New Towns Study Unit, 1976. 63 pp.

Describes the first two garden cities, i.e. Letchworth and Welwyn Garden City, together with the land use and road network principles utilised. Provides an account of the ideas of Ebenezer Howard, the pioneer of garden cities.

738 Potter, S. *Transport and New Towns: Volume Two: The transport assumptions underlying the design of Britain's new towns. 1946–1976.* Milton Keynes: Open University, New Towns Study Unit, 1976. 208 pp.

Describes the first new towns built in the UK between 1946 and 1950, i.e. Stevenage, Crawley, Cwmbran, Harlow and Aycliffe. Looks at the influence of the Buchanan Report, 'Traffic in Towns', on transport planning in new towns. Also examines the development of public transport priority in new towns and the importance given to pedestrians and cyclists in the planning of new towns. Discusses the principles of design and the application of those principles in the light of eighty years' experience.

739 Potter, S. *Transport and New Towns: Volume Three: Conflicts and Externalities in New Town Transport Plans.* Milton Keynes: Open University, New Towns Study Unit, 1977. 158 pp.

Examines the nature and inter-relationship of the major external costs and benefits arising under different transport policies in the planning of a new town. Discusses the often conflicting requirements of the three major forms of transport, i.e. car, public transport, walking and cycling. Considers three possible alternative land use/transport designs for a theoretical new town of 100,000.

740 Puvanachandran, V. M. Factors Influencing the Provision of Urban Transport Infrastructure. Amsterdam: *Transportation*, Vol. 13(3), 1986, 295–317.

Discusses the impact of frequent political interruptions on the implementation of transport plans.

741 Runkel, M. Interchanges in Public Transport. Brussels: *Public Transport International*, Vol. 43(5), September 1995, 32–36.

Describes the development and the location of interchanges and presents various examples of interchanges in public transport.

742 Schuler, R. E. Transportation and Telecommunications Networks: planning urban infrastructure for the 21st century. Harlow: *Urban Studies*, Vol. 29(2), April 1992, 297–310.

743 Stokes, G. *The Role of Public Transport Interchange in Improving Public Transport.* Oxford: Oxford University Press, 1994. 13 pp.

Paper presented to the European Transport Forum held in September 1994.

744 United States Department of Transportation. *Comparative Costs of Urban Transportation Systems.* USA: Department of Transportation, 1978. 100 pp.

Overview of typical time and monetary resources required to provide transportation service by various contemporary modes in large urbanised areas.

745 Urban Transport International. Transit Finance. London: *Urban Transport International,* May/June 1988, 29–30.

Investigation into how the government of the United States might aid urban infrastructure renewal.

746 Vickerman, Roger W. Transport Infrastructure and Region Building in the European Community. Oxford: *Journal of Common Market Studies,* Vol. 32(1), 1994, 1–24.

Exposes the gap between non-spatial and macroeconomic understanding of the role of infrastructure in the European Union's approach to community wide infrastructure.

Land use

747 Barra, Tomas de la. *Integrated Land Use and Transport Modelling: Decision Chains and Hierarchies.* Cambridge: Cambridge University Press, 1989. 179 pp.

Proposes a general and consistent theoretical framework for land use and transport analysis.

748 Black, J. A. and **Blunden, W. R.** *The Land-Use/Transport System.* 2nd ed. Sydney: Pergamon Press, 1984. 250 pp.

Examines the concepts of land-use and transport systems.

749 Bly, P. H., Paulley, N. J. and **Webster, F. V.** (eds). *Urban Land-Use and Transport Interaction: policies and models: Report of the International Study Group on Land-Use/Transport Interaction.* Aldershot: Avebury, 1988. 520 pp.

Results of a study group set up to compare and contrast interactive land-use/transport models.

750 City and County of Kingston Upon Hull. *Kingston Upon Hull and Nearby Areas: land use/transportation study.* Volume 1. Edinburgh: Freeman Fox, Wilbur Smith and Associates, 1969. 254 pp.

751 City and County of Kingston Upon Hull. *Kingston Upon Hull and*

Nearby Areas: land use/transportation study. Volume 2. Edinburgh: Freeman Fox, Wilbur Smith and Associates, 1972. 95 pp.

752 Clayton, P. D. *Some Aspects of the Contribution of Economics to Land-Use and Transportation Planning.* Salford: University of Salford (MSc Thesis), 1977.

753 Freeman, A. J. *Land Use and Traffic Generation in a Central Business District.* Southampton: University of Southampton (M.Phil Thesis), 1970.

754 Freilich, Robert H. and **White, S. Mark.** The Interaction of Land Use Planning and Transportation Management. Oxford: *Transport Policy*, Vol. 1(2), March 1994, 101–115.
Examines the new legal frameworks, ordinances, financial structures and planning case law that have developed in the USA as a result of growing concern over traffic growth, congestion and environmental damage.

755 Goldberg, M. A. An Evaluation of the Interaction Between Urban Transport and Land Use Systems. Madison, WI: *Land Economics*, Vol. 48(4), August 1972, 338–346.
Suggests an alternative approach to evaluation techniques grounded in modern urban land economics and relating elasticities of demand for land and transport improvements.

756 Kraus, M. Land Use in a Circular City. San Diego, CA: *Journal of Economic Theory*, Vol. 8(4), August 1974, 440–457.
Examines the optimal allocation of urban land to transportation.

757 Kumar, Ram Krishna. *An Interactive Model of Strategic Land Use-Transport Planning: a case study of the greater Toronto area.* Waterloo, Ont.: University of Waterloo (PhD), 1987.
Develops a microcomputer-based urban activity model.

758 Levinson, Herbert S. The 21st Century Metropolis: a land-use and transportation perspective. London: George Godwin, *International Forum Series*, Vol. 1, 1981, 15–22.
Examines the 21st-century American city in the context of current trends and public policy options. Demonstrates how various land development strategies, social programmes, transportation technologies and energy supplies will affect urban forms, life-styles and mobility. Describes the steps needed to bring about major changes in existing development patterns and trends and presents various

futures in the form of scenarios for twenty-five- , fifty- and seventy-five-year planning horizons.

759 Lichfield, Nathaniel. Transport and Land-Use Planning. London: George Godwin, *International Forum Series*, Vol. 1, 1981, 1–14.

Examines the nature of land-use planning and the role of transportation within it. Demonstrates how traffic and transportation planning has evolved in its relationships with land-use planning.

760 Mackett, R. L. LILT and MEPLAN: a comparative analysis of land-use and transport policies for Leeds. London: *Transport Reviews*, Vol. 11(2), April–June 1991, 131–154.

Describes the comparative analysis of the application of the Leeds Integrated Land-Use Transport model (LILT) and the MEPLAN model of Marcial Echenique & Partners to the city of Leeds.

761 Maltby, D. *The Problems of Traffic Generation by an Industrial Land Use.* Salford: University of Salford (PhD Thesis), 1971.

762 Mogridge, M. J. H. Transport, Land Use and Energy Interaction. Glasgow: *Urban Studies Journal*, Vol. 22(6), December 1985, 481–492.

Analysis of data from London and Paris, using directly comparable methods of expressing all results in terms of distance from the centre.

763 Neuburger, H. User Benefit in the Evaluation of Transport and Land Use Plans. London: *Journal of Transport Economics and Policy*, Vol. 5(1), January 1971, 52–75.

764 Orosei, J. U. *Some Aspects of Land Use: urban transport problems in Greater Lagos.* Salford: University of Salford (MSc Thesis), 1978.

765 Owens, Susan. From 'Predict and Provide' to 'Predict and Prevent'?: pricing and planning in transport policy. Oxford: *Transport Policy*, Vol. 2(1), January 1995, 43–49.

Explores policy instruments which are central to the new approach – 'getting the price right' and influencing travel patterns through land use planning. Suggests that the concept of the 'right' price is problematic, that land use measures are necessary but not sufficient and that neither pricing nor planning policies are likely, in isolation, to have sufficient effect across the range of environmental impacts of transport.

766 Paulley, N. J. and **Webster, F. V.** An International Study on Land-

Use and Transport Interaction. London: *Transport Reviews*, Vol. 10(4), October–December 1990, 287–308.

Briefly describes the first phase of a study in which nine models from seven countries were subjected to a rigorous set of tests covering a variety of policies. The second phase of the study was conducted in which some models were applied to several cities each so that the differences due to the particular characteristics of the cities could be identified. The setting up of the second phase is given in this paper, but not the results.

767 Pederson, E. O. *Transport in Crisis.* Oxford: Pergamon Press, 1980. 87 pp.

Study concentrating on some aspects of transportation in cities, emphasising the relationships between transportation and land uses in urban areas. Offers an historical perspective and contrasts wealthy nations with developing countries.

768 *No Entry.*

769 Pushkarev, Boris S. and **Zupan, Jeffrey M.** *Public Transportation and Land Use Policy.* London: Indiana University Press, 1977. 241 pp.

Reviews various transport issues which combine to make a case for revitalising public transportation through making changes in land use policy. The relationships developed are used to illustrate the suitability of different urban densities to eight types of transportation: the taxicab, dial-a-bus, local bus, express bus, light rail, light guideway transit, rapid transit and commuter rail.

770 Stokes, G. *Long Term Effects of Current Trends in Transport on Land Use in Great Britain.* Oxford: Oxford University, Transport Studies Unit, 1992. 13 pp.

771 Transport and Road Research Laboratory. *Land Use and Transport Planning.* Current topics in transport no. 16. Crowthorne: Transport and Road Research Laboratory, February 1993. 46 pp.

772 Transportation Planning Associates. *Monmouthshire Land Use: transportation study: main report.* Birmingham: Transportation Planning Associates, 1973. 76 pp.

773 Tulley, Graeme. Land Use and Transport Policy: confusion reigns. *Parliamentary Reports*, Vol. 4(2), 1994, 52–54.

Claims that inconsistencies in government policy are demonstrated by guidance in PPG6 on town centres and retailing and PPG13 on transport.

774 **Young, W.** Land Use: transport interaction 1969–1989. Victoria: *Australian Road Research*, Vol. 20(1), March 1990.

Addresses some of the issues and developments in the land-use transport interaction that took place in the two decades from 1969 to 1989. Describes some of the developments and causes and considers urban policy changes and the likely impacts of the information revolution.

Routing and scheduling

775 **Akcelik, R.** *Traffic Signal and Route Control in Urban Areas.* Leeds: University of Leeds (PhD Thesis), 1973.

776 **Al-Asam, A. A. H.** *Heuristic Methods for the Solution of some Variations of the Vehicle Routing Problem.* Birmingham: University of Birmingham (PhD Thesis), 1977.

777 **Assad, A. A.** and **Golden, B. L.** (eds). *Vehicle Routing: Methods and Studies.* Amsterdam: North Holland, 1988. 479 pp.

Collection of papers addressing the issue of vehicle routing problems. Divided into five parts: part one gives an overview, part two looks at algorithmic techniques for vehicle routing, part three discusses models for complex routing environments, part four provides examples of practical applications and part five looks at the development of vehicle routing systems.

778 **Ballou, Ronald H.** and **Bott, Kevin.** Research Perspectives in Vehicle Routing and Scheduling. Oxford: *Transportation Research*, Vol. 20A(3), May 1986, 239–243.

Classifies and appraises the developing methodology concerned with the problems of vehicle routing and scheduling. Identifies restrictions and extensions that should ideally be incorporated into a generalised vehicle routing and scheduling methodology.

779 **Benshoof, J. A.** *The Route Selection Process.* Newcastle Upon Tyne: University of Newcastle Upon Tyne (MSc Thesis), 1970.

780 **Bonsall, Peter.** The Influence of Route Guidance Advice on Route Choice in Urban Networks. Dordrecht: *Transportation*, Vol. 19(1), 1992, 1–23.

Reviews current knowledge of route choice processes and claims a mismatch between this knowledge and the route choice assumptions embedded in the most widely used assignment models.

781 **Boyce, David E.** Route Guidance Systems for Improving Urban

Travel and Location Choices. Oxford: *Transportation Research*, Vol. 22A(4), 1988, 275–281.

Reviews the technology of navigation systems for private vehicles, and explores the information and prediction requirements for the computer models required to implement such a system.

782 Kawashima, Hironao; Takahashi, Riichi; Tsuji, Hiroyoshi and **Yamamoto, Yoshitsugu.** A Stochastic Approach for Estimating the Effectiveness of a Route Guidance System and its Related Parameters. Baltimore, MD: *Transportation Science*, Vol. 19(4), November 1985, 333–351.

Develops mathematical models for estimating the effectiveness of a route guidance system in which the control strategy is to guide vehicles toward the shortest travel time routes.

783 Kirby, Ronald F. Involving Private Route Associations in Public Transit. Westport, CT: *Transportation Quarterly*, Vol. 41(3), July 1987, 411–426.

Considers the role of route associations of private operators in the provision of urban public transportation within the United States.

784 Li, L. Y. O. *Vehicle Routeing for Winter Gritting.* Lancaster: University of Lancaster (MSc Thesis), 1992.

Addresses the question of designing routes for gritters which will minimise costs.

785 Macbriar, I. D. *Some Fundamental Characteristics of those Measures Used for Scheduled Passenger Services in Towns.* Newcastle Upon Tyne: University of Newcastle Upon Tyne (PhD Thesis), 1977.

786 Manington, P. D. *Mathematical and Heuristic Approaches to Road Transport Scheduling.* Leeds: University of Leeds (PhD Thesis), 1977.

787 Ratcliffe, E. P. *A Comparison of Drivers' Route Choice Criteria and those Used in Current Assignment Processes.* Newcastle Upon Tyne: University of Newcastle Upon Tyne (PhD Thesis), 1971.

788 Rhee, Jong-Ho. *Vehicle Routing and Scheduling Strategies for Demand Responsive Transportation Systems.* Newark, DE: University of Delaware (PhD Thesis), 1987. 177 pp.

789 Skelton, E. *Route Planning.* London: Thomas Telford, 1987. pp. 27–39.

Claims that the engineering aspects of route planning cannot be considered in isolation from the transport planning aspects summarised in the typical objectives and features of an urban railway.

790 Small, K. A. Trip Scheduling in Urban Transportation Analysis. Nashville, TN: *American Economic Review*, Vol. 82(2), May 1992, 482–486.

791 *No Entry.*

792 Vliet, Dirck van and **Vuren, Tom van.** *Route Choice and Signal Control: the potential for integrated route guidance.* Aldershot : Avebury, 1992. 222 pp.

Formal statement of the problems of interaction between signal control and traffic assignment. The main control policies are discussed against a background of cost functions and their influence on solution methods. Analyses signal control in an integrated route guidance context and provides recommendations for practical use of the iterative assignment control procedures and the various signal control policies in an integrated environment.

793 Waters, C. D. J. *Solution Procedures for Vehicle Scheduling Problems.* Glasgow: University of Strathclyde (PhD Thesis), 1986.

The role of the physical distribution is examined and associated costs estimated. The importance of efficient vehicle routes is emphasised and examined in relation to the formalised 'Vehicle Scheduling Problem'. Available solution procedures are examined and the need for reliable heuristics identified.

794 Wren, Anthony (ed.). *Computer Scheduling of Public Transport: urban passenger vehicle and crew scheduling.* (Papers based upon presentations at the International Workshop held at the University of Leeds, 16–18 July, 1980.) Oxford: North-Holland Publishing, 1981. 359 pp.

The use of computers in scheduling buses and their crews is reviewed, drawing on sources used at a previous workshop in Chicago together with material presented to the 1980 International Workshop held at the University of Leeds. The review deals largely with methodology as opposed to implementation, though comments are made on the status of systems discussed and the report concludes with a summary on the overall position with regard to implementation.

6 Regional Studies and Development

General

795 Armstrong-Wright, Alan. *Public Transport in Third World Cities.* London: HMSO, 1993. 110 pp.

Highlights the vital role played by public transport in Third World cities. Aims to provide background information for researchers, and to provide information for Third World authorities interested in the approaches adopted to solve urban transport problems by other developing cities. Review is based on bus services, light rail transit and metros embracing 65 cities.

796 Diez-Palma, A. *Project Evaluation Techniques in the Transport Sector in Underdeveloped Countries.* Manchester: University of Manchester (MA Thesis), 1979.

797 Godard, X. *The International Dimension of Valuing Metros in Developing Countries.* Paper from the proceedings of 'Rail Mass Transit for Developing Countries' organised by the Institution of Civil Engineers. London: Thomas Telford, 1990, 69–77.

As part of the work undertaken at the French Institute for Research on Transport and Traffic Safety on metros in developing countries, the paper examines the consequences, in terms of project valuation, of interventions by industrialised countries offering metro technology.

798 Institute of Civil Engineers. *Moving People in Tomorrow's World.* London: Thomas Telford, 1987. 171 pp.

Proceedings of a conference organised by the Institution of Civil Engineers, held in London in 1986. Divided into five parts, it gives an overview of public transport operations in the Third World, looks at metropolitan railways, public transport by road, light rail and trams and finally political and financial considerations.

799 Lago, Armando M. *Cost Functions for Intercity Transportation Systems in Underdeveloped Countries: a model of optimum technology.* Cambridge, MA: Harvard University (PhD Thesis), 1966.

United Kingdom

800 Bartle, M. H. *An Analysis of Public Transport Needs in South-West Shropshire.* Salford: University of Salford (MSc Thesis), 1981.

801 Bayliss, David; Lichfield, Nathaniel; Ridley, Tony; Travers, Tony and **Glaister, Stephen** (eds). *Transport Options for London.* London: London School of Economics and Political Science, 1991. 216 pp.

Examines the progress of London's transport system during the past thirty years. Questions of ownership and subsidy are discussed as are pricing and various ways of funding capital investment.

802 Bell, Sandra and **Hurdle, David.** *All Aboard! Attractive Public Transport for London.* London: London Boroughs Association, 1993. 71 pp.

Raises numerous concerns, including inadequate funding, insecure passenger environments, and the future of the popular concessionary travel scheme for the elderly and Travelcard. Also makes recommendations to central government, public transport operators and London's local authorities.

803 Bibby, Peter. *The Croydon Corridor: study of transport in a corridor through South London.* London: London Centre for Transport Planning, 1986. 50 pp.

Transport study of a corridor running south from Central London to the former GLC boundary and the M25. Compares the use of cars and public transport in the Croydon Corridor with that of other world cities and reviews various methods used in those cities to reduce congestion on the roads and improve public transport.

804 Bibby, Peter. *Croydon Corridor Two: study of transport in a corridor through South London.* London: London Centre for Transport Planning, 1987. 46 pp.

Study of the way people travel during the morning peak period, in a corridor running south from Central London to the former GLC boundary. Investigates how many people are using cars when they could easily travel by British Rail mainline and examines some of the factors which influence their choice. Argues that reducing rail fares would encourage certain car drivers to transfer to train. The effect of company car subsidies is investigated. Concludes that 25 per cent of car traffic at peak time is unnecessary.

805 Bradley, Morris and **Thompson, Stephen.** *Getting There: a survey of everyday journeys in an urban area.* Glasgow: Scottish Consumer Council, 1981. 68 pp.

Report on a survey to compare the conditions in which people in three selected communities in the Glasgow area make their various daily journeys.

806 Buchan, Keith. *Wheels of Fortune: strategies for transport integra-tion in the South East.* Stevenage: South East Economic Development Strategy, 1990. 142 pp.

Sets out a new framework for transport planning in the South East.

807 Buchanan, Malcolm; Bursey, Nicholas; Lewis, Kingsley; Mullen, Paul and **Tzedakis, Alexander.** *Transport Planning for Greater Lon-don.* Farnborough: Saxon House, 1980. 315 pp.

Reviews transport policies in Greater London and attempts to distinguish between those that are effective from those that are not. Argues for a thorough appraisal of all policy options and a more consistent application of those selected.

808 Chadwick De Leuw O hEocha. *City of Edinburgh: A review of the Public Transport Elements of the Recommended Plan: Final Report: February 1975.* Edinburgh: Chadwick De Leuw O hEocha, 1975. 129 pp.

Report of a study of transportation problems in Edinburgh carried out between 1968 and 1972.

809 City of Coventry Council. *The Report of the Study Group on the Preliminary Phase of the Coventry Transportation Study: report on phase one, 1968.* Coventry: City of Coventry Council, 1968.

Report of a study undertaken by Coventry City Council, concerned with the implications of high car ownership, resolved in 1966 to embark on an overall transport plan for the city. Considers such issues as the usage of private and public transport; road networks; traffic management; car parking and the effects of land use.

810 City of Coventry Council. *Coventry Transportation Study Report on Phase Two: the final analysis: part two: the background.* Coventry: City of Coventry Council, December 1972.

Part two of a report covering the main phase of the work of the City of Coventry Transportation Study Group. The objectives of the study are set out in The Report on Phase One, 1968.

811 City of Coventry Council. *Coventry Transportation Study Report on Phase One: the technical report: part one.* Coventry: City of Coventry Council, 1973.

Provides the technical background to the City of Coventry transportation study. The objectives of the study are set out in the report on 'Phase One', 1968.

812 Confederation of British Industry. *Transport in London – The*

Business Response: London Transport Task Force survey results January 1994. London: Confederation of British Industry, 1994. 16 pp.

813 Constable, M. *Objectives and Achievement in London Transport.* Bath: University of Bath (MSc Thesis), 1974.

814 Department of Transport. *Public Transport in London.* London: HMSO, 1983. 9 pp.

815 Docklands Joint Committee. *The Docklands Spine: Tube, Bus or Tram?: a working paper for consultation 3.* London: Docklands Development Team, 1975. 30 pp.

Examines the case for an east-west link as the basis of the Docklands public transport system and reviews the forms that such a link might take. All possibilities – bus, boat, tram, train – are considered.

816 Dunne, J. P. *Mode Choice in New Towns: a case study of Livingston.* Edinburgh: University of Edinburgh (PhD Thesis), 1982.

817 Eveleigh, S. *Transport and Industry within the District of Chiltern, Buckinghamshire: an analysis.* Salford: University of Salford (MSc Thesis), 1982.

818 Fisher, Mark and **Rogers, Richard.** *A New London.* Harmondsworth: Penguin Books, 1992. 255 pp.

Concerned with the planning and design of London to help overcome its decline in infrastructure, overcrowding and polarisation between rich and poor. Although not specifically examined, transport is nevertheless discussed in the context of the problems of London.

819 Freeman Fox and Associates. *Grangemouth/Falkirk Growth Area Road Study.* Edinburgh: Freeman Fox, Wilbur Smith and Associates, 1972. 121 pp.

820 Freeman Fox and Associates. *The Swindon Transportation Study: final report.* London: Freeman Fox and Associates, 1986. 168 pp.

Report on the work carried out by the Swindon Transportation Study team in formulating recommended transport proposals for 1986.

821 Gardner, K. E. and **May, A. D.** Transport Policy for London in 2001: the case for an integrated approach. Amsterdam: *Transportation,* Vol. 16(3), 1990, 257–277.

Reports the results of a series of studies conducted to enable the London Planning Advisory Committee to provide advice on strategic transport policy for London.

822 Glaister, S. (ed.). *Transport Options for London.* Greater London papers no. 18. London: London School of Economics and Political Science, 1991. 224 pp.

823 Greater London Council: SCPR: Transmark. *Survey Operation Report.* Greater London Transport Survey Vol. VIII. London: Greater London Council, 1976. 199 pp.

Detailed examination of the principal points of the survey method designed specifically to analyse travel behaviour in an urban area by residents in private households.

824 Greater London Council. *Transport Policies and Programme 1975–1980.* London: Greater London Council, 1974. 68 pp.

825 Greater London Council. *Transport Policies and Programme 1980–1985.* London: Greater London Council, 1979. 130 pp.

Looks at modes of transport and expenditure, traffic management and parking control, construction and maintenance of highways.

826 Greater London Council. *Transport Policies and Programme 1982–1984.* London: Greater London Council, 1981. 92 pp.

827 Greater London Council. *Greater London Transportation Survey 81: transport data for London.* London: Greater London Council, 1985. 229 pp.

Results of the Greater London Transportation Survey of 1981.

828 Greater London Council. *Transport Policies and Programme 1979–1984.* London: Greater London Council, 1978. 113 pp.

Looks at modes of transport and expenditure, traffic management and parking control, construction and maintenance of highways.

829 Greater London Council. *Transport Policies and Programme 1981–1984.* London: Greater London Council, 1980. 78 pp.

830 Greater London Council. *Transport Policies and Programme 1977 – 1982.* London: Greater London Council, 1976.

831 Greater London Council. *The Three Year Plan for London Transport: as modified by the Greater London Council.* 1984–1987. London: Greater London Council, 1983.

832 Heys, John S. and **Kreppel, Alan.** Quality Transport for the New Planning Environment, the West Glamorgan Experience. London: *Proceedings of the Chartered Institute of Transport,* Vol. 4(3), 1995, 47–56.
Describes traffic policies and management in West Glamorgan.

833 Ipswich County Borough Council: East Suffolk County Council. *Structure Plan for the Ipswich Sub-Region: report of the survey.* Ipswich: Ipswich County Borough Council, 1973. 110 pp.

834 Jamieson Mackay and Partners. *Transportation Study Bath Area: report of surveys.* Bristol: Jamieson Mackay and Partners, 1976. 85 pp.

835 Jamieson Mackay and Partners. *Transportation Study Bath Area: final report.* Bristol: Jamieson Mackay and Partners, 1976. 117 pp.

836 Kadhim, M. B. A. H. *A Study of Some Aspects of Urban Transport Problems in Chester.* Manchester: University of Manchester (PhD Thesis), 1980.

837 Kenwood, A. G. Transport Capital Formation and Economic growth on Teeside, 1820–1850. Manchester: *Journal of Transport History,* Vol. 2(2), September 1981, 53–71.
Examines the pattern of investment activity associated with the growth of the Teeside economy during the second quarter of the nineteenth century when transport innovations and improvements played a critical role.

838 Local Transport Today. Birmingham's Bid for Balanced Transport. London: *Local Transport Today,* March 1990, 10–11.

839 London Transport. *Statement of Strategy 1994–1997.* London: London Transport, 1995. 50 pp.

840 Merseyside Passenger Transport Authority and Executive. *A Transport Plan for Merseyside: a joint report.* Liverpool: Merseyside Passenger Transport Authority and Executive, 1972. 158 pp.

841 Metropolitan Transport Research Unit. *West London Transport*

Study Stage 2: new transport options for West London. London: West London Roadwatch, 1989. 106 pp.

842 Mitchell, T. C. *The Reorganisation of Public transport: the case for a Passenger Transport Authority in the Lothian region.* Edinburgh: Heriot-Watt University (MSc Thesis), 1977.

843 Prentice, Richard. *Transport Planning Solutions for Central Swansea: the views of the public.* Fieldwork Report. Swansea: University of Swansea, 1990. 30 pp.

844 Prestwood-Smith, P. and **Smith, J. E. R.** *Greater London Transport Survey: initial results.* Research Report No. 18: London: Greater London Council, 1974. 24 pp.

Undertaken in 1971, as a background to policy for London transport planning authorities, the report covers demand, change in travel behaviour, and trends and projections.

845 Robertson, J. *A Case Study of Public Transport in Harris.* Aberdeen: Aberdeen University (PhD Thesis), 1982. 165 pp.

846 Sharp, Clifford. *Problems of Urban Passenger Transport.* Leicester: Leicester University Press, 1967.

Leicester based case study is used to illustrate and discuss the problems of urban passenger transport in the UK.

847 Taylor, C. *A Realistic Plan for London Transport.* London: Bow Publications, 1982.

Recommendations of an interim policy for London Transport which claims to balance the needs of London Transport users with those of rate payers.

848 Thomson, J. Michael. *Transport Strategy in London.* London: London Motorway Action Group, 1971. 299 pp.

Evidence presented at the Public Inquiry into the Greater London Development Plan. Considered as a sequel to 'Motorways in London', published by LATA (London motorway action group) in October 1969.

849 Tight, M. P. *The Changing Role and Value of London's Public Transport.* London: University College London (PhD Thesis), 1982.

850 Transport Committee of the House of Commons. *Fifth Report from the Transport Committee: Session 1981–1982: Transport in London:*

together with the proceedings of the committee, minutes of evidence and appendices: Vol. I. London: HMSO, 1982. 163 pp.

Purpose is to describe and assess the main problems confronting London's transport system and to identify problems which, by common consent, would be the subject of priority action by the public authorities concerned. Also, examines, and where necessary considers changes in the policy making, financing, legislative and organisational arrangements which are the main direct responsibilities of Parliament in this field.

851 Transport Committee of the House of Commons. *Transport in London.* Fifth Report from the Transport Committee Session 1981–82 together with the proceedings of the committee, minutes of evidence and appendices. Vol. III. London: HMSO, 1982. 379 pp.

852 Tuckwell, R. M. *Traffic and Transport Problems of Westmorland.* Salford: University of Salford (MSc Thesis), 1972.

853 Tyneside Passenger Transport Executive. *Public Transport on Tyneside: a plan for the people.* Newcastle Upon Tyne: Tyneside Passenger Transport Authority, 1973. 143 pp.

Report on the maintenance, integration and development of public transport in the Tyneside area at the conclusion of the operation of Tyneside Passenger Transport Executive.

854 Wilson, D. G. *Transport Policy, Integration and Deregulation: greater Glasgow and Tyneside: a comparative analysis.* Glasgow: University of Strathclyde (M.Phil Thesis), 1988.

855 Wragg, Richard. *A Study of the Passenger Transport Needs of Urban Wales.* Aberystwyth: Welsh Council, 1977. 283 pp.

Western Europe

856 Anderson, Bjorn. A Survey of the Swiss Public Transport System and Policy. London: *Transport Reviews*, Vol. 13(1), January–March 1993, 61–81.

Surveys Swiss public transport structure and policy. The regulatory regime is explained with the division between the two operators working under federal monopoly – the State Railways and the postbuses – and the rest of the system. Federal government's emphasis on introducing cheap public transport fares on environmental grounds through the federal transport measures and the use of cheap fares in urban areas are discussed.

857 Apel, D. and **Pharoah, T.** *Transport Concepts in European Cities.* Aldershot: Avebury, 1995. 307 pp.

Selection of detailed case studies of ten European cities' transport policies. Examines the possibilities for reducing dependence on the private car in favour of more environmentally compatible modes of transport.

858 Bieber, Alain; Massot, Marie-Helene and **Orfeuil, Jean-Pierre.** Prospects for Daily Urban Mobility. London: *Transport Reviews*, Vol. 14(4), October–December 1994, 321–339.

Seeks to define a basis for the prospect of mobility in large conurbations. Provides cross section comparisons between countries as regards land use and related mobility schemes. Includes comparative exercise used to build very different images of three possible futures for French conurbations: Saint Simonian (modernist); Rhenan (conservative); Californian (post-modernist).

859 Bruins, B. J. and **Kaper, G. A.** Urban Planning: the influence of traffic and transport in The Hague. Brussels: *Public Transport International*, Vol. 43(2), March 1994, 39–41.

Outlines the relationship between urban transport and the future development of the Hague.

860 Croc, Michel. Planning and Management in an Expanding City. Surrey: *City Transport*, December 1986/ February 1987, 32–33.

Examines Marseilles's programme of public transport expansion and development.

861 Dale, Iain. Trans European Network. *Transport Law and Practice*, Vol. 2(2), 1994, 15.

Highlights the apparent shortcomings in the British Government's approach to opportunities offered by Trans-European Networks in the transport sector.

862 Dunn, James A. Co-ordination of Urban Transit Services: the German model. Amsterdam: *Transportation*, Vol. 9, 1980, 33–43.

Discusses the operation of the Hamburg Transit Federation and considers a number of factors which have created a favourable climate for the development of public transportation in Germany.

863 European Conference of Ministers of Transport. *Benefits of Different Transport Modes: report of the ninety-third round table on transport economics.* Paris: Organisation for Economic Co-operation and Development, 1994. 101 pp.

Papers presented at the European Conference of Ministers of Transport held in 1992. Considers different modes of transport and their respective contributions to economic growth, regional development, social relations and mobility. Contains detailed papers on Germany and the Netherlands and a summary of discussions.

864 European Conference of Ministers of Transport. *The Regionalisation of Transport and Regional Planning in Practice: an examination based on case studies.* ECMT Strasbourg Seminar, December 1983. Introductory reports and summaries of the discussions. Paris: Organisation for Economic Co-operation and Development, 1984. 199 pp.

Attempts to lay the foundations of European co-operation in regional planning and thereby influence regional planning in Europe.

865 European Conference of Ministers of Transport. *Prospects for East–West European Transport: international seminar, Paris 6th – 7th December 1990.* Paris: Organisation for Economic Co-operation and Development, 1991. 561 pp.

Considers the consequences for transport of closer East–West relations since the demise of the Communist Bloc in 1989. Contains a section on the development prospects for passenger transport between East and West. Includes structural data on the East European states and a scenario for transport development.

866 European Conference of Ministers of Transport. *Research Relevant to Trends in Transport over the Coming Decade.* Round Table 75. Paris: Organisation for Economic Co-operation and Development, 1987. 57 pp.

Presents an overview of key transport issues in Europe. The Round Table was based on fifty interviews with transport specialists. Topics covered include deregulation and decision-making processes with comments on environment, energy finance in the transport sector, demand and supply.

867 European Parliament. *Transport as a Bottleneck to Economic Growth in Ireland: research and documentation papers/series regional policy and transport 14.* Paris: Organisation for Economic Co-operation and Development, 1991. 33 pp.

868 Faber, Wim. Berlin's Transport Unification: how two operators are welding together their separate systems. London: *Urban Transport International*, August/September, 1990, 28–31.

869 Goldsack, Paul. France: trends in urban transport. Washington, DC: *Mass Transit*, May 1988, 8–12.

Examines the ways in which transport operators in France are dealing with funding shortages.

870 Goldsack, Paul. Italy: a mass transit bonanza. Washington, DC: *Mass Transit*, January/February 1987, 8–11.

Reviews the state of progress of mass transit in Italy and the possibilities for further investment.

871 Jansen, Gijsbertus R. M. and **Vuren, Tom van.** Travel Patterns in Dutch Metropolitan Cities: the importance of external trips. Amsterdam: *Transportation*, Vol. 15, 1989, 317–336.

Analyses decentralisation of population and employment in four Dutch urban areas (Amsterdam, Rotterdam, The Hague and Utrecht) over the last 20 years. Claims that suburbanisation, plus greater car ownership has increased the number of external trips related to the metropolitan cities enormously.

872 Kreibich, K. The Successful Transportation System and the Regional Planning Problem: an evaluation of the Munich rapid transit system in the context of urban and regional planning policy. Amsterdam: *Transportation*, Vol. 7, 1978, 137–145.

The development of the Munich Rapid Transit System, coupled with the growth of the Munich region, has had a major effect on the spatial structure of the region. The radial form of the rapid transit system has led to an outward movement of higher income families and a strengthening of the service function of the city to the cost of local centres. Although the rapid transit system has reduced congestion, it has encouraged the development of an urban structure incompatible with state or regional objectives.

873 Lauer, Andre. Development of Urban Transport Systems. Brussels: *Public Transport International*, Vol. 43(3), May 1994, 48–52.

Provides an overview of the development of urban transport systems in France since the Second World War.

874 Mass Transit. Update on Italy. Washington, DC: *Mass Transit*, October 1988, 8–19.

Examines the state of urban transport in mainland Italy and the islands of Sardinia and Sicily. Focuses on the cities of Turin, Genoa, Naples, Rome and Milan.

875 Maubois, R. Urban Transport in France. Brussels: *Public Transport International*, Vol. 44(2), 1995, 46–47.

876 Perrin, J. P. The RATP and Transport Development in the Ile-de-France. Brussels: *Public Transport International*, Vol. 44(2), 1995, 48–50.

Describes the Régie autonome des transports parisiens, its history, its present situation and its prospects for the future.

877 Peterson, B. E. Traffic Infrastructure in the Stockholm Region.

Brussels: *Public Transport International*, Vol. 42(2), July 1993, 50–54.

878 Saitz, Hermann H. Erfurt City and Traffic: an example of transport policy and planning in the German Democratic Republic. London: *Transport Reviews*, Vol. 8(1), January–March 1988, 1–17.

879 Sheldrake, John and **Webb, Paul.** *State and Market: aspects of modern European development.* Aldershot: Dartmouth, 1993. 178 pp.

Provides an account of recent economic developments in Europe, including the trend towards privatisation. Contains a chapter on the de-regulation of road passenger transport in the United Kingdom.

880 Soupault, T. Urban Public Transport in France. Brussels: *Public Transport International*, Vol. 44(2), 1995, 50–55.

Examines the public transport company – L'Union des Transports Publics – and also offers an overall perspective of the varied elements affecting urban public transport in France.

881 Tjon a Ten, John F. Amsterdam: the city and the municipal transport company. Brussels: *Public Transport International*, Vol. 43(4), July 1994, 36–38.

Describes the different transport modes and light rail projects of Amsterdam.

882 Wood, Chris. Copenhagen Plans for the New Century. London: *Urban Transport International*, Issue 1, 1993, 16–19.

883 Yearsley, Ian. Integration in the Randstand. London: *Urban Transport International*, December 1988/January 1989, 14–15.

Examines the ways in which two Dutch cities proposed to link their suburban services together with a light railway network.

Central and Eastern Europe; Middle East

884 Abalkhail, A. H. O. *Socio-economic Impacts of Transportation and Planning Design for Saudi Arabian Cities.* Glasgow: University of Strathclyde (PhD Thesis), 1992.

Considers the socio-economic impacts of the development of modern transportation in Saudi Arabian urban areas, and attempts to develop guidelines for future planning to minimise damaging impacts.

885 Abdulaal, J. A. M. *Public Transport in Saudi Arabian Cities.* Cardiff: University of Cardiff (PhD Thesis), 1991.

Focuses on the demand and economic performance of the first scheduled bus system under the management and operation of the Saudi Arabian Public Transport Company introduced in 1979.

886 Al-Mehairi, J. M. *The Role of Transportation Networks in the Development and Integration of the Seven Emirates Forming the United Arab Emirates, with Special Reference to Dubai.* Durham: Durham University (PhD Thesis), 1993.

887 Al-Rawas, M. A. S. *Urban Transportation Problems in the Muscat Area, Sultanate of Oman.* Salford: University of Salford (PhD Thesis), 1993.

888 Ambler, John; Shaw, Denis J. B. and **Symons, Leslie** (eds). *Soviet and East European Transport Problems.* London: Croom Helm, 1985. 260 pp.

Examines the transport systems of the Soviet Union and Eastern Europe. Looks at the different modes of transport and the problems faced by each.

889 Coombe, R. D. Urban Transport Policy Development: two case studies in the Middle East. London: *Transport Reviews,* Vol. 5(2), July–September 1985, 165–188.

Two major transport studies of predominantly urban areas in the Middle East (Amman-Jordan and Bahrain) have provided the opportunity to compare and contrast the transport characteristics of, and medium term transport policies for, the two areas. Examines the social and economic backgrounds of Amman, Jordan and Bahrain and reviews their transport systems and the organisations responsible for them.

890 Gospoarcja, Izba. Principal Problems of Public Transport in Poland. Brussels: *Public Transport International,* Vol. 41, February 1993, 42–47.

Since 1990, urban public transport is no longer the property of the State, but of the municipalities. Because of the economic situation, these municipalities find it difficult to finance public transport.

891 Grava, Sigurd. The Planned Metro of Riga: is it necessary or even desirable? Westport, CT: *Transportation Quarterly,* Vol. 43(3), July 1989, 451–472.

892 Hunter, Holland. *Soviet Transport Experience: its lessons for other countries.* Washington DC: Brookings Institution, 1968.

893 Janic, Milan. The Transport System of Slovenia: problems and perspectives. London: *Transport Reviews*, Vol. 14(3), July–September 1994, 269–285.

Slovenia became a new independent state in Central Europe in 1991/92. Article outlines the nature of its transport system consisting of rail, road, port, marine, and air. Details the physical and institutional characteristics of the system, looks at the relationships beween demand and supply of transport services during the years before independence and discusses problems confronting policy makers.

894 Jenkins, Ian A. All Change: new directions for the road transport industries of Russia, Ukraine, Kazakhstan and Belarus. London: *Transport Reviews*, Vol. 14(4), October–December 1994, 289–320.

Describes the present situation of the road transport industries in four republics of the CIS which are embarking on economic reform programmes. Conclusions are drawn about the extent and direction of change required.

895 Lesley, Lewis. Assessment of an Eastern European City's Public Transport System. Oxford: *Transportation Research*, Vol. 23A(2), March 1989, 129–137.

Examines public transport services in Budapest. Concludes that the proposed investment in a metro system will not maintain public transport's competitive position in the face of rising car ownership and that other measures and investments might be more effective.

896 Lijewski, Teofil. Transport in Warsaw. London: *Transport Reviews*, Vol. 7(2), April–June 1987, 95–98.

A city burnt to the ground during World War II and reconstructed from its ruins, Warsaw experienced a changed road network and modernised system of transport. However, the design was not far-sighted enough. Article claims that immense amount of travel is generated by the inappropriate distribution of residences, places of work and services, and also by the low fares on public transport, subsidised by the state and working more as a social service.

897 Link, Dan. Preferential Treatment for Public Transport in Jerusalem. London: George Godwin, *International Forum Series*, Vol. 2, 1981, 105–112.

In the summer of 1978 a busway was opened in Jerusalem along the main arterial connecting the western suburbs of the city with downtown. Highlights certain aspects of the busway in an attempt to determine the results of the project and to evaluate its degree of success. The series of events leading to its opening, including both support and objection to the busway concept, are described. Possible lessons to be learned from the short history of the project are also discussed.

898 Mackett, Roger. Transport Planning and Operation in a Changing Economic and Political Environment: the case of Hungary. London: *Transport Reviews*, Vol. 12(1), January–March 1992, 77–96.

Hungary is in a period of major political and economic transition. Article presents a review of the implications of these changes for the transport sector for the country as a whole and for the capital Budapest, in particular. Analysis is carried out in terms of the growth of the private sector in transport, levels of investment, the implications for the transport user, and the performance of the transport system.

899 Mekki, Z. A. *Transportation Problems in the City of Makkah Outside the Period of Hajj.* Durham: Durham University (PhD Thesis), 1988.

900 Mieczkowski, Bogdan. *Transportation in Eastern Europe: empirical findings.* New York: Columbia University Press, 1978. 221 pp.

Review of transportation in Eastern Europe which looks at geographic and economic determinants of transport, factors which impact on national planning, statistical growth of transport in Eastern Europe since World War II, the costs of transportation and a review of the international aspects of global and inter-Comecon co-operation and investment.

901 Mieczkowski, Bogdan (ed.). *East European Transport: regions and modes.* The Hague: Martinus Nijhoff Publishers, 1980. 353 pp.

Focuses on the development of transportation and the integration of the Comecon transport systems. Also looks at the effects of new technology and includes an econometric model of freight transport.

902 Pucher, John. The Road to Ruin? impacts of economic shock therapy on urban transport in Poland. Oxford: *Transport Policy*, Vol. 2(1), January 1995, 5–13.

Radical economic reforms in Poland since 1990 have had important impacts on transport. Increased political and economic freedom, access to Western consumer markets, reduction in government subsidies, increases in public transport fares and service cut-backs has led to huge shift to automobile use. Article argues that leaving transport to the private market seems certain to end in excessive car use and such deteriorating public transport systems that irreversible damage would be done to Polish cities.

903 Pucher, John. The Transport Revolution in Central Europe. Virginia: *Transportation Quarterly*, Vol. 47(4), October 1993, 97–113.

Examines urban transport both before and after Communist control. Specifically focuses on urban transport changes in Czechoslovakia, Hungary and Eastern Germany.

904 Pucher, John. The Challenge to Public Transport in Central Europe.

Brussels: *Public Transport International*, Vol. 41, February 1993, 28–41.

The political and economic revolutions in Central Europe in 1989 and 1990 have produced fundamental changes, which significantly affect transportation. Article examines urban transport trends in Czechoslovakia, Hungary, and the former East Germany.

905 Quidort, Michel. Controlling Structural Change. Brussels: *Public Transport International*, Vol. 41, February 1993, 12–15.

Article looks at how East European Countries face internal difficulties and external problems which pose questions to the survival and development of public transport.

906 Roe, Michael. Transport Planning in Hungary: a case study of Pecs. London: *Transport Reviews*, Vol. 10(3), July–September 1990, 229–243.

Analyses the situation in Hungary as a whole, before focusing on the city of Pecs and its relation to national transport planning, includes detailed case studies drawn from local and regional road networks; the growth of car ownership; development of rail services; local buses; and growth of local taxi services. Compares the problems of Pecs with those of urban areas elsewhere in Europe and emphasises particular difficulties faced by East European planners.

907 Roe, Michael. Transport Policy in Eastern Europe: a case study of Hungary. Amsterdam: *Transportation*, Vol. 16(4), 1990, 343–359.

Analyses the development of transport policy making in Eastern Europe from the 1950s and describes the role of the CMEA in determining national developments in Poland, Romania, East Germany, Czechoslovakia, Hungary and Bulgaria. The planning system as operated in the Eastern Bloc is described, followed by a case study of Hungarian policy making with respect to the transport sector.

908 Ryder, Andrew. Polish Transit in the New World. Washington, DC: *Mass Transit*, July/August, 1992, 40–41.

After 45 years of communist rule, Poland's municipal transportation systems face a difficult situation. Buses and streetcars are the mainstays of Polish urban transit, although a few cities have trolleybuses, and a metro is being constructed in Warsaw. Article addresses itself to the problems of a newly capitalistic country as it tries to deal with massive urban transport problems.

909 Saad-Yeser, M. A. *Transport and Development in the Yemen Arab Republic.* Swansea: University of Swansea (PhD Thesis), 1991.

910 Tournai, Carton V. de. Can the Cities of Eastern Europe Learn from Our Mistakes? Brussels: *Public Transport International*, Vol. 41, February 1993, 16–27.

The Cities of Eastern Europe are on the threshold of major urban transformations and they tend to look to the West for inspiration. However, in many ways, these cities have enormous potential, particularly in transport development. Article focuses on St. Petersburg.

911 Urban Transport International. Assignment in Istanbul: planning public transport in a city with paratransit, ferries, taxis, buses and LRT. London: *Urban Transport International*, December 1988/ January 1989, 20–21.

912 White, Paul M. *Planning of Urban Transport Systems in the Soviet Union.* Birmingham: University of Birmingham, Centre for Urban and Regional Studies, November 1978. 36 pp.

Review of Soviet and Western literature on urban transport planning in the USSR. Notes the emergence of the classic conflict between the desire to retain a dense, cheap, public transport system and the desire to relax the constraints on individual car ownership.

North America

913 Ardekani, Siamak A. Transportation Operations Following the 1989 Loma Prieta Earthquake. Westport, CT: *Transportation Quarterly*, Vol. 46(2), April 1992, 219–233.

Describes transportation activities in the Bay area following the 1989 California earthquake. Reviews the organisation and activities of the Emergency Operations Centers. Addresses data collection and processing, traffic management and operational improvement projects; emergency transit and ferry operations; and command centre operations. Recommendations are made for the establishment of multi-agency Transportation Operation Centers to coordinate post-earthquake actions.

914 Baldassare, Mark. Transportation in Suburbia: trends in attitudes, behaviours and policy preferences in Orange County, California. Amsterdam: *Transportation*, Vol. 18, 1991, 207–222.

Analyses transportation attitudes, behaviours and policy preferences in a suburban region. Focuses on Orange County which has experienced rapid growth and industrialisation in recent decades.

915 Benz, Gregory P.; Leventer, Wendy; Nichols, Foster and Porter, Benjamin D. West Side Manhattan Transitway Study. Paper presented at the National Conference on 'Light Rail Transit: new system successes at affordable prices'. Washington, DC: Transportation Research Board, National Research Council, 1989, 269–285.

In response to the current and anticipated changes in the type and intensity of land use activities on Manhattan's West Side, the New York City Department of City Planning has conducted a West Side Transitway Study to ensure that adequate transportation services are in place to serve the new workers, residents and visitors. Article reports on the operation, rehabilitation and upgrading of New York City's existing transportation systems.

916 Biehler, Allen D. *Exclusive Busways Versus Light Rail Transit.* Paper presented at the National Conference on 'Light Rail Transit: new system successes at affordable prices'. Washington, DC: Transportation Research Board, National Research Council, 1989, 89–97.

Busways can offer clear advantages over light rail in many transit corridors. Article compares Pittsburgh's exclusive busways with light rail there and in four other cities, Buffalo, Portland, Sacramento, and San Diego.

917 Campion, Douglas R. and **Wischmeyer, Oliver W.** *Infrastructure Rehabilitation and Technology Sharing in Bringing LRT to St. Louis.* Paper presented at the National Conference on 'Light Rail Transit: new system successes at affordable prices'. Washington, DC: Transportation Research Board, National Research Council, 1989, 201–224.

Metropolitan St.Louis, after 19 years of planning, is developing a dual-mode, cost-effective public transportation system integrating light rail technology with a vastly improved regional bus network. Article provides a comprehensive review.

918 Carr, G. W. and **Topp, R. M.** *Toronto's Harbourfront Line: LRT in reserved right-of-way as a local transit alternative.* Paper presented at the National Conference on 'Light Rail Transit: new system successes at affordable prices'. Washington, DC: Transportation Research Board, National Research Council, 1989, 544–560.

Recent LRT developments in North America are demonstrating the success of LRT as a high-capacity transit mode linking the suburbs with the downtown. Article examines a somewhat different application of LRT technology planned for the city of Toronto: that of an upgraded local transit service operating within the downtown area but generally unaffected by downtown traffic conditions.

919 Carrington, Burr. Iron Belt Rail Renews. Washington, DC: *Mass Transit*, June 1988, 6–14.

Several rust belt cities clung to their beleaguered streetcar systems; now they are demonstrating that renewed investment in urban light rail has the potential to bring about dramatic ridership increases. Article looks at the effects in Pittsburgh, Cleveland, Buffalo and Philadelphia.

920 Cervero, Robert. Urban Transit in Canada: integration and innovation at its best. Westport, CT: *Transportation Quarterly*, Vol. 40(3), July 1986, 293–316.

Looks at Canada's experience of attracting people onto urban transport and away from cars. Argues that speed and reliability were considered two of the major factors in determining a preference for public transport away from the automobile.

921 Cervero, Robert. Transit-Based Housing in California: evidence on ridership impacts. Oxford: *Transport Policy*, Vol. 1(3), June 1994, 174–183.

Clustering of housing development around railway stations holds promise not only for increasing transit ridership, but also for yielding important environmental and social benefits. Article examines evidence on the degree to which existing housing complexes near railway stations in California have encouraged transit usage.

922 City Transport. Light Rail Comes to Silicon Valley. Surrey: *City Transport*, Vol. 2(4), December 1987/February 1988, 29.

Examines the opening of a light rail transit in Santa Clara County in the United States.

923 Curry, Martha and **Onibokun, Adepoju G.** An Ideology of Citizen Participation: the metropolitan Seattle transit case study. Washington, DC: *Public Administration Review*, Vol. 36, May–June 1976, 269–277.

924 Damm, David; Lerman, Steven R.; Lerner-Lam, Eva and **Young, Jeffrey.** Response of Urban Real Estate Values in anticipation of the Washington Metro. London: *Journal of Transport Economics and Policy*, Vol. 14(3), September 1980, 315–337.

The anticipated construction of the metro line in Washington, DC increased values of some properties and decreased those of others. Article considers some implications of proposals to tax the benefits.

925 Davy, Greg. Moving Pictures! London: *Global Transport*, Vol. 3, Summer 1995, 28–36.

Los Angeles has finally constructed a subway system. Article surveys some of the structural problems involved in the construction of the subway in the attempt to make it safe enough to withstand earthquakes.

926 Dickins, Ian. *Rapid Transit and Land Use in North America.* Birmingham: Birmingham Polytechnic, Department of Planning and Landscape, 1987. 19 pp.

Examines American and Canadian experience in using rapid transit as a means to alter urban development patterns and as a catalyst for urban and physical regeneration. Makes a number of recommendations on how the results might be recreated in the UK.

927 Ellis, Clifford A., Harf, Alfred H., Kirkyla, Viktoras A., Luton, Jerome M. and **Robins, Martin E.** *Integrating Light Rail Transit into Development Projects on the Hudson River Waterfront.* Paper presented at the National Conference on 'Light Rail Transit: new system successes at affordable prices'. Washington, DC: Transportation Research Board, National Research Council, 1989, 121–134.

The New Jersey Department of Transportation, in conjunction with NJ Transit, recently completed a conceptual engineering study for a combined bus/light rail transit system on the Hudson River waterfront. Article details the process used to define the appropriate easement envelopes and negotiate transit easements with developers.

928 Fletcher, Joseph M. Choosing the Right Modes for Miami's Public Transport. Surrey: *City Transport*, December 1986/February 1987, 38–41.

Explains the planning which led to Miami's integrated system of rail rapid transit, automated people mover and buses.

929 Gratwick, John. *Canadian Transportation: origins, perspectives and prospects.* Tantallon: John Gratwick, 1993. 155 pp.

Traces the evolution of Canadian transportation from its beginnings to the present day, and its prospects for the future.

930 Hebert, Ray. Regional Transportation. Washington, DC: *Mass Transit*, Vol. 46, September 1987, 46–51.

Few cities can boast such a diversity of public transportation as San Francisco. It includes heavy rail trains, light rail streetcars, trackless trolleys, standard buses, carpools, vanpools and, of course, the city's inimitable cable cars. Article looks at some of the problems generated by the various different modes of transportation.

931 Kapinos, Thomas S. Attitudes Towards Mass Transit. Washington, DC: *Mass Transit*, April 1989, 10–16.

New York City's car congestion problem exemplifies how bad a central business district's traffic problem can be and how necessary mass transit is to the smooth movement of people in a major city. Article describes how the New York Port Authority and the Metropolitan Transportation Authority joined forces to study the problems and propose some solutions.

932 Kemp, Roger L. *America's Cities: problems and prospects.* Aldershot: Avebury, 1995. 208 pp.

Examination of the contemporary problems facing the cities of the United States. Covers the problems of urban transport, design and planning.

933 Kitchen, H. Urban Transit Provision in Ontario: a public/private sector cost comparison. Newbury Park, CA: *Public Finance Quarterly*, Vol. 20(1), January 1992, 114–128.

934 Levinson, Herbert S. Transportation Policy and Development in New York City Area. Westport, CT: *Transportation Quarterly*, Vol. 46(3), July 1992, 361–381.

Describes the history of New York City regions's transportation systems; notes changing patterns of travel demand; identifies public policy responses; and suggests a regional transport strategy for the 21st century.

935 Northwestern University Transportation Center. *Public Transportation in the Chicago Region: present performance and future potential.* Research Report. Chicago, IL: Northwestern University, 1973. 27 pp.

936 Poulton, Michael. Replanning the Residential Street System in Vancouver. London: George Godwin, *International Forum Series*, Vol. 2, 1981, 197–208.

Report on the development and application of a general model used to establish an optimal strategy for the replanning of existing residential access and secondary arterial street systems. Attempts to determine and apply the general principles of road layout and traffic control that should be pursued so as to improve the residential environment systematically and at minimum cost to road users.

937 Pucher, John. Public Transport Developments: Canada vs. The United States. Virginia: *Transportation Quarterly*, Vol. 47(4), October 1993, 65–78.

Compares taxation and parking policies within the US and Canada, and also looks at coordination of land-use and transportation.

938 Pucher, John. Urban Public Transport in the United States: recent development and policy perspectives. Brussels: *Public Transport International*, Vol. 42(3), October 1993, 12–25.

After thirty years of sharp decline from 1945 to 1975, public transport in the United States has succeeded at improving the quality of its service and stabilising ridership levels over the past two decades. Article examines recent trends in public transport supply and demand in North American cities.

939 Smith, Michael. Canada. Washington, DC: *Mass Transit*, June 1987, 6–8.

Article looks at the way in which Canada's urban mass transit companies are expanding plants, building light rail systems, experimenting with alternative technologies and installing state-of-the-art automated vehicle control systems.

940 Stein, Martin. Regional Impacts of National Transport Systems on Population and Travel. London: *Journal of Transport Economics and Policy*, Vol. 9(3), September 1995, 255–267.

Demand for travel is generated by changes in population and income and increased mobility, as well as by projects such as the Interstate highway system. Article compares various estimates for the regions of the United States.

941 Tober, Ronald J. Trolleybus Tunnels to Relieve City Congestion. Surrey: *City Transport*, March/May, 1987, 46–48.

Seattle's director of transit, Ronald J. Tober, describes the project now under way to provide a central area tunnel link operated by dual mode trolleybuses but with long-term provision for light rail.

942 Viton, Philip A. How Big Should Transit Be? evidence of the benefits of reorganisation from the San Francisco Bay Area. Amsterdam: *Transportation*, Vol. 20(1), 1993, 35–57.

Examines whether the many public urban transit providers in the San Francisco Bay Area could realise cost economies by consolidating into larger systems.

943 Williams, Ernest W. (ed.). *The Future of American Transportation.* Englewood Cliffs, NJ: Prentice Hall, 1971. 211 pp.

Seven of America's most prominent transportation experts, among them George W. Wilson, Lyle C. Fitch, and John L. Weller, examine the transportation problems which threaten the economic, social and political life of the United States; including over-crowded subway systems; late commuter trains; hectic air travel; and slow freight deliveries. Problems revealed include inadequate federal legislation, impractical planning, and actual misappropriation of public funds.

944 Zakaria, Thabet. Traffic Trends and Emerging Transportation Planning Issues in the Delaware Valley Region. Westport, CT: *Transportation Quarterly*, Vol. 40(2), April 1986, 171–188.

Describes changes in land-use patterns and the distribution of people and jobs in the Delaware Valley Region. Analyses the impact of these changes on the journey to work pattern and highway and transit volumes in the region.

Japan

945 Aoyama, Yoshitaka and **Kondo, Akio.** The Impact of Major Road Developments on the Spheres of Urban Influence of Japanese Cities. Amsterdam: *Transportation*, Vol. 20, 1993, 305–323.

Aims to measure the impact of major road developments on the spheres of urban influence of Japanese cities.

946 Bruhl, Friedemann and **Katakura, Msahiko.** Transport in Tokyo. London: *Transport Reviews*, Vol. 5(4), October–December 1985, 345–370.

Reviews the historical and geographical preconditions, as well as the population and economic development, which led to the unique and complex transport systems in Tokyo.

947 Hashimoto, Kotaro. Monitoring Road Traffic Congestion in Japan. London: *Transport Reviews*, Vol. 10(2), April–July 1990, 171–186.

Discusses the background to the attention that has recently been focused on traffic congestion in Japan, the current state of the problem, and the Construction Ministry's approach to the situation.

948 Jenkins, Ian A. Urban Public Transport in Japan. Amsterdam: *Transportation*, Vol. 8, 1979, 259–274.

Describes some general features of public transport provision in the urban areas of Japan (especially the large urban areas), and some specific features of an integrated transport system currently being developed in one such area.

949 Mizutani, Fumitoshi. *Japanese Urban Railways: a private-public comparison.* Aldershot: Avebury, 1994. 223 pp.

Quantitative analysis of Japan's private urban railways which aims to assess whether these are more efficient than their public counterparts.

950 Murata, Takahiro. Japan's Struggle for Traffic Accident Reduction. Oxford: *Transportation Research*, Vol. 23(1), 1989, 83–90.

Seeks to explain Japan's recent success in traffic accident reduction.

951 Nakajima, Yuji (ed.). *Problems of Transportation in Japan 2.* Tokyo: Institute of Transportation Economics, 1978. 88 pp.

Examination of various aspects of Japanese transportation from both a theoretical and a practical perspective. Includes discussion of the basic conditions for improvement in bus services; new trends in bus transportation; monorail and urban environmental problems; problems of monorail management; the dawn of the urban monorail age; and medium-sized guideway transportation systems.

952 Noguchi, Tomoki. Japan's Urban Transportation System in the Major Transport Spheres. Amsterdam: *Transportation*, Vol. 6, 1977, 171–189.

The urban areas in Japan have undergone rapid changes in the last two and a half decades. At the same time, the urban transportation system has been faced with numerous problems which need to be solved urgently. Article presents the development stage and problems in the three largest metropolitan areas, designated as transport spheres, in Japan.

953 Ohta, Katsutoshi. The Development of Japanese Transportation Policies in the Context of Regional Development. Oxford: *Transportation Research*, Vol. 23A(1), January 1989, 91–101.

Explains the development of post-war transportation policies in Japan, particularly how transportation infrastructure development planning is placed in the regional development context.

954 Yamamoto, Hirofumi (ed.). *Technological Innovation and Development of Transportation in Japan.* Tokyo: United Nations University Press, 1993. 296 pp.

Provides an account of the evolution of modern transport in Japan in the period 1867 to 1980. Details the development of roads, rail, river and coastal transport. Considers technology transfer from the West; domestic development; and the achievement of technological independence.

Asia, Australasia and Oceania

955 Abbas, T. *Problems of Urban Passenger Transport, with Special Reference to Karachi.* Edinburgh: Heriot-Watt University (MSc Thesis), 1972.

956 Abeles, Peter. An Antipodean View of Transport. London: *Transport*, Vol. 2, September/October, 1981, 23–26.

The Managing Director of Thomas Nationwide Transport looks at the unique transportation problems of Australia.

957 Ashley, Cedric. Testing Times for China's Roads. London: *Transport*, Vol. 7, October, 1986, 192–193.

As China's road transport industry develops, so its need for a test facility grows. Details the work of the UK's Motor Industry Research Association in the area.

958 Australian Transport and Distribution Management. CEDA Shows The Way Ahead. Sydney: *Australian Transport and Distribution Management*, April 1990, 3–9.

Provides an overview of the problems encountered in all modes of transport in Australia.

959 Barden, S. A. and **Runnacles, T. V.** Transport in a High-Density Urban Environment: the experience of Hong Kong. London: *Transport Reviews*, Vol. 6(3), July–September 1986, 219–258.

Traffic in Hong Kong has concentrated along particular corridors where its volume now exceeds road capacity. Development of an urban rail system has affected the economic stability of most public transport. Private motoring has increased rapidly and fiscal restraints have been imposed, generating a serious proposal for electronic road pricing. Links with China will end Hong Kong's relative isolation and present new transport planning challenges. Article reviews developments.

960 Barraclough, D. B. G. Mass Transit Railway: an increasingly vital part of Hong Kong's transport network. London: *Transport*, Vol. 5, September/October, 1984, 13–14.

A major factor in Hong Kong's viability and continuing growth is efficient transportation systems, whether for the carriage of goods or the movement of people. One such system is the Mass Transit Railway, the role of which is assessed.

961 Brown, Fred. Growth: the challenge for urban systems. London: *Transport*, Vol. 7, October 1986, 194–196.

The growth in travel and traffic demands in China has been nowhere more visible than in the rapidly developing urban regions, particularly Beijing, Shanghai, Guangzhou, Tianjin and the Special Economic Zones. Article reviews recent developments in urban transport.

962 Bultynck, Patrick. Asia: the rail takes over. Brussels: *Public Transport International*, Vol. 42(1), March–April 1993, 104–109.

Article claims that local and national authorities of several Asiatic countries realise that public transport is of top priority when it comes to urban development.

963 Burns, Robert E. Intercity Bus Transport in West Pakistan: entrepreneurs in an environment of uncertainty. London: *Journal of Transport Economics and Policy*, Vol. 5(3), September 1971, 314–343.

Claims that the West Pakistan bus industry is efficient, with low standards but low prices.

964 City Transport. Singapore's Public Transport Showcase. Surrey: *City Transport*, Vol. 2(2), June/August 1987, 6–7.

Review of a Singapore conference on the metro and its impact on public transport.

965 Clennell, Simon. Public Transport Prospects for Hong Kong. Brussels: *Public Transport International*, Vol. 42(1), March/April 1993, 110–118.

966 Dimitriou, Harry T. *A Developmental Approach to Urban*

Transport Planning: an Indonesian illustration. Aldershot: Avebury, 1995. 224 pp.

Investigation into the transport problems which many Asian cities are currently facing. Claims that many problems have arisen due to the application of inappropriate transport policy, planning and design. Suggests how to tackle the problems of urban transport with a 'developmental approach' and how this could be implemented in a fast-changing economy such as that in Indonesia.

967 Fouracre, Philip; Jacobs, Godfrey and **Maunder, David.** Matching Supply and Demand in India's Public Transport. London: *Transport*, Vol. 8, December, 1987, 241–243.

Indian cities offer a number of public transport options. Article provides comparisons of networks in three cities and includes a report of the work of the Transport Road and Research Laboratory Overseas Unit.

968 Gambhir, J. C. and **Narayan, Prakash.** Urban Transport Conditions in Delhi. Nagoya, Japan: *Regional Development Dialogue*, 13(3), Autumn 1992, 99–103.

Case study detailing the problems of the urban transportation system in Delhi and looks at ways in which improvements in public transport and the construction of a mass transit railway system might bring about significant improvements.

969 Gray, Mike G. Singapore: a track record to envy. London: *Transport*, Vol. 6, June 1985, 9.

Singapore, being a small island with only minimal natural resources, has to rely heavily on transport both internally and externally. Article argues that, by all standards, Singapore's track record is impressive.

970 Gray, Mike. A Land of Contrasts. London: *Transport*, Vol. 8, October 1987, 189–196.

Article reviews Singapore's transport network.

971 Hensher, David A. *The Transportation Sector in Australia: economic issues and challenges.* Oxford: Transport Policy, Vol. 1(1), October 1993, 49–67.

Discusses a number of initiatives undertaken in Australia to improve the efficiency of the transport sector, long recognised as one of the most inefficient links in the economic cycle of production, distribution and consumption. Deals with such issues as the so-called 'blind' commitment to light rail; road-user charges; safety and truck driving hours; and the future of transport in Australian cities.

972 Hidyat, Danis and **Priyohadi, Bambang S.** Problems and Issues in

Co-ordinating Urban Development Planning and Transportation in Jakarta Metropolitan Area. Nagoya, Japan: *Regional Development Dialogue*, 13(3), Autumn 1992, 111–117.

Investigates the associated problems of planning, transport and development in Jakarta, Indonesia. The development of the capital city is examined in the context of the development of the rest of Indonesia.

973 Howie, D. J. Traffic Engineering in Australia: a twenty year retrospective. Victoria: *Australian Road Research*, Vol. 20(1), March 1990, 30–35.

Considers the recent history of traffic engineering in Australia from a practitioner's point of view.

974 Islam, M. *Inter-Urban Bus Operation in Bangladesh: a comparative study of the efficiency of the public and the private bus sectors.* Cranfield: Cranfield Institute of Technology (PhD Thesis), 1978.

975 Joshi, P. M. *Transport Problems of Rapidly Developing Countries: the case of Bombay.* London: Bedford College (M.Phil Thesis), 1984.

976 Khanna, S. K., Sikdar, P. K. and **Umrigar, F. S.** Exploring the Scope of Private Participation for Urban Public Transport Supply in India. London: *Transport Reviews*, Vol. 9(2), April–June 1989, 135–146.

Examines the fortunes of India's publicly owned urban bus systems.

977 Kolsen, H. M. Transport Policy in Australia. The Role of the Inter-State Commission. London: *Journal of Transport Economics and Policy*, Vol. 20(2), May 1986, 275–282.

Examines the extent to which transport economics are able to influence transport policy in Australia.

978 Lee, E. S. W. Planning and Control of Paratransit Services in Hong Kong. London: *Transport Reviews*, Vol. 9(4), October–December 1989, 279–303.

As paratransit services, Hong Kong's taxis and public light buses carried some 30 per cent of the 9.7 million daily public transport boardings in Hong Kong in 1988. Article examines the introduction of planning and control mechanisms for these services.

979 Leinbach, Thomas. Transport Policies in Conflict: deregulation, subsidies, and regional development in Indonesia. Oxford: *Transportation Research*, Vol. 23A(6), November 1989, 467–475.

Set in the context of the expansion of the transport sector due to dramatic economic growth within Indonesia, this article presents an overview of several key issues including the inefficiency of the railway, the continued deregulation of the port system and subsidies within the transport system.

980 Melhuish, C. *A Potential Role for the ADB in Supporting Urban Transport.* Paper from the proceedings of 'Rail Mass Transit for Developing Countries' organised by the Institution of Civil Engineers. London: Thomas Telford, 1990, 353–360.

The Asian Development Bank is a multilateral development bank which assists in socio-economic development. Article provides an account of the Bank's growing interest in urban transport projects.

981 Munasinghe, T. G. I. B. *The Development and History of Transportation in Ceylon: a case study of roads and railways, 1800–1905.* London: London School of Economics and Political Science (PhD Thesis), 1972.

982 Naidu, G. *Rail and Road Transport in West Malaysia.* Oxford: Oxford University (B.Litt Thesis), 1972.

983 Nor, A. R. M. *Public Passenger Transport in Third World Cities: a case study of Kuala Lumpur, Peninsular Malaysia.* Keele: Keele University (M.A. Thesis), 1987.

Examines the problems of public passenger transport services in Third World cities using Kuala Lumpur, the Malaysian capital, as a case study.

984 Reza, A. *The Development of Local Transport in Bangladesh.* Leicester: University of Leicester (PhD Thesis), 1977.

985 Schabas, Michael. Quantitative Analysis of Rapid Transit Alignment Alternatives. Westport, CT: *Transportation Quarterly*, Vol. 42(3), July 1988, 403–416.

Examines the planning and design of a rapid transit system in Honolulu, a city squeezed in a narrow corridor between mountains and the sea, with few main roads and extreme traffic congestion.

986 Sharif, A. H. M. R. *Transport and Regional Development in Bangladesh: a geographical study.* Sheffield: University of Sheffield (PhD Thesis), 1986.

Investigates the relationships between development, transport networks and transport flows in a developing country using Bangladesh as a case study.

987 Shaw, Shih-Lung and **Williams, Jack F.** Role of Transportation in

Taiwan's Regional Development. Westport, CT: *Transportation Quarterly*, Vol. 45(2), April 1991, 271–298.

Examines the development of domestic transportation systems in Taiwan in terms of changes in spatial structures of transport networks and changes in flow distributions on these networks, focusing on inter-regional and inter-urban relationships between transport policy, economic growth and regional development.

988 Shengfu, Yang. New Innovations, Technical and Political. London: *Transport*, Vol. 7, October 1986, 189–191.

The development of China's extensive road network is a crucial part of modernising the country's transport infrastructure. Article examines the role of road transport and the measures being undertaken to improve the system.

989 Southern, R. J. *Road Transport in the New Guinea Highlands.* Bristol: University of Bristol (MSc Thesis), 1972.

990 Taylor, Michael A. P. The Performance of Urban Public Transport – an overview. London: *Transport Reviews*, Vol. 8(4), October–December 1988, 331–340.

Public transport in Australian cities has had broad political appeal and escalating financial support for more than a decade. However, there are now signs that political enthusiasm is waning. Article considers the current state-of-play and examines plans for the future of urban transport.

991 The World Bank. *China, the Transport Sector: Annex 6 to China, long-term development issues and options, a World Bank Country Study.* Washington DC: The World Bank, 1985. 122 pp.

Review of the state of the transport sector in China with proposals for future developments. Part one examines the major transport indicators and compares China's performance with international experience. Part two projects transport demand into the future and discusses its inter-relationship with other economic activities.

992 Toh, Rex (ed.). *Focus on Transportation.* Singapore: The Chartered Institute of Transport, 1976. 119 pp.

Review of various aspects of transport impacting upon Singapore including a look at trucking in Singapore and West Malaysia; measures to improve the urban transport system; and an evaluation of an area licensing scheme.

993 Transport. Helping to Keep Hong Kong on the Move. London: *Transport*, Vol. 9, May 1988, 237–240.

August 1988 witnessed the inauguration of Hong Kong's newest transport project, the Tuen Mun light rail transit system which will serve two large communities in the New Territories. Article outlines the development.

994 Wahab, I. *Urban Public Transport Policy for West Malaysia.* Cardiff: University of Wales (PhD Thesis), 1987.

Examination of the organisation and network system of road based public transport in West Malaysia.

995 Watson, P. L. *Singapore's Area License Scheme: results and lessons.* London: Planning and Transport Research and Computation, 1978.

Discussion of an effort to solve urban congestion problems by reducing the demand for transport through pricing and licensing, rather than by increasing the supply.

996 Weerasuriya, P. C. H. *The Development and Function of the Transport System in Ceylon: a network analysis.* Cambridge: University of Cambridge (PhD Thesis), 1973.

997 Wigan, M. R. Changes in the Transport Environment over Twenty Years. Victoria: *Australian Road Research*, Vol. 20(1), March 1990, 73–81.

Explores some of the changes in transport policy, research and implementation and the influence of the changing environment from the 1960s through to the 1980s. Considers the influence of the Monash Transport Group and its contributions to these changes both through direct involvement and the provision of graduates.

998 Woodward, Paul. Decide Now, Pay Later. London: *Transport*, Vol. 7, October 1986, 187–188.

China's seventh Five-Year Plan, which ran up until 1990, was one of the most significant periods in the country's development as a major economic power. Article claims that the Chinese have now recognised the vital importance of transport for maintaining strong economic growth.

999 Yearsley, Ian. An Asian Viewpoint. London: *Urban Transport International*, December 1988/January 1989, 5–6.

Examines South East Asia and the Pacific crescent where public transport competes for priority with everything from hospitals to drainage.

1000 Yee, Joseph. Directing the Traffic in Singapore. London: *Transport*, Vol. 6, October 1985, 7–8.

Singapore recognised very early after its independence in 1965 that, like all growing cities, it would have to grapple with increasing traffic problems. Building roads alone would not suffice, and the effective solution was a comprehensive set of policies formulated in land use and transportation development integrated into both private and public transport. Article assesses how well Singapore has performed.

Africa

1001 Abaynayaka, S. W. and **Hide, Henry.** *Some Vehicle Operating Cost Relationships for Developing Countries.* London: Planning and Transport Research and Computation, 1975.

Summary of the results of an investigation into vehicle operating costs in Kenya.

1002 Abaynayaka, S. W.; Hide, Henry; Sayer, I. and **Wyatt, R. J.** *The Kenya Road Transport Cost Study: research on vehicle operating costs.* TRRL report 672. Crowthorne: Transport and Road Research Laboratory, 1975.

Investigation into the effects of various road, vehicle and environmental parameters on vehicle operating costs.

1003 Adeniji, S. A. *Public Transport and Urban Development in Nigeria.* Cardiff: University of Wales (PhD Thesis), 1981.

1004 Banjo, G. A. *Travel Choice and Travel Time Savings in Developing Countries with Special Reference to Nigeria.* Liverpool: University of Liverpool (PhD Thesis), 1983.

1005 Bolade, Adeniyi 'Tunji. Transport in Metropolitan Lagos. London: *Transport Reviews*, Vol. 6(1), January–March 1986, 1–30.

Metropolitan Lagos is the fastest growing urban region in Nigeria, creating transport demand exceeding what the available transport infrastructures and services can cope with. Article claims that long term solutions lie in the promotion of mass transit; comprehensive traffic management; co-ordinated urban and transport planning; and administration of the metropolitan region.

1006 Drummond-Thompson, P. H. *The Development of Motor Transport in South-Western and Northern Nigeria, 1907–1937.* London: School of Oriental and African Studies (PhD Thesis), 1987.

Considers the growing involvement of Africans in motor transport enterprise in Nigeria during the 1920s and '30s together with the importance of the industry to the economy during a period of depression in overseas trade with Europe.

1007 Heggie, Ian G. Commercializing Africa's Roads: transforming the role of the public sector. London: *Transport Reviews*, Vol. 15(2), April–June 1995, 167–184.

Nearly a quarter of the capital invested in Sub-Saharan roads has been eroded through insufficient maintenance. Article claims that to restore roads and prevent further deterioration will require an annual expenditure of about $1.5 billion. Suggests that policy reforms need to focus on four areas: creating ownership and commitment; identifying a stable source of finance; clarifying who is responsible for what; and commercialising management of roads.

1008 Hofmeier, Rolf. *Transport and Economic Development in Tanzania (with particular reference to roads and road transport).* Munich: Weltforum Verlag, 1973. 363 pp.

Examines the specific case of Tanzania to show what contribution transport makes to the economic progress of a developing country. Study largely concentrates on road traffic, although this is treated with reference to the other parts of the transportation system.

1009 Ikya, S. G. (ed.). *Urban Passenger Transportation in Nigeria.* Ibadan: Heinemann Educational Books, 1993. 418 pp.

Collection of papers which focus on topical issues of urban transport policy, planning, operation and management. Divided into four parts it covers conceptual issues, empirical issues, infrastructural issues and planning and policy issues.

1010 Khezwana, Maria; Maunder, David and **Mbara, Tatenda.** The Effect of Institutional Changes on Stage Bus Performance in Harare, Zimbabwe. London: *Transport Reviews*, Vol. 14(2), April–June 1994, 151–165.

Examines the Zimbabwe government's decision (in 1988) to invest and participate directly in the provision of urban stage bus services in the country's major towns and cities. Assessment is made of the effects of the decision in terms of the operational and financial performance provided by Zimbabwe United Passenger Company in Harare.

1011 Kobe, Susumu. *Transport Problems in West Africa.* Paris: Organisation for Economic Co-operation and Development, 1967.

1012 Ogunremi, G. O. *Pre-Colonial Transport in Nigeria.* Birmingham: University of Birmingham (PhD Thesis), 1972.

1013 Omiunu, Francis. Towards a Transport Policy for the ECOWAS subregion. London: *Transport Reviews*, Vol. 7(4), October–December 1987, 327–340.

Examines transport policy development in a regional grouping of states in West Africa whose present transport policies reflect their differing colonial pasts.

1014 Reichman, Shalom (ed.). *Transportation and Urban Development in West Africa: a review*. In *Transport and Development: geographical readings*. London: Macmillan, 1973. Chapter 11.

Examines the interaction between the introduction of modern transport technology and urban growth.

1015 Stopher, Peter R. and **Wilmot, Chester G.** A Simplified Transportation Planning Process for South Africa. London: George Godwin, *International Forum Series*, Vol. 1, 1981, 201–208.

With the passing of the Urban Transport Act in 1977, it became compulsory in South Africa for metropolitan areas to carry out comprehensive urban transport planning to qualify for government funds for subsidies and transport investment. As a result it became necessary to develop a set of guidelines for urban transport planning within the metropolitan areas of South Africa. Article describes the process recommended by the National Institute for Transport and Road Research.

Central and South America

1016 Alouche, Peter. Public Transport Challenges in Latin America. Brussels: *Public Transport International*, Vol. 44(4), July 1995, 23–24.

Overview of cities and transport in Latin America and of the challenges which have to be overcome in that region.

1017 Camara, Richard. *Socio-Spatial Segregation and the Level of Service of Public Transport in Rio de Janeiro, Brazil*. London: University College London (PhD Thesis), 1991.

1018 Departamento de Planejamento de Trafego da Companhia do Metropolitano de São Paulo. *Brasil São Paulo Urban Transportation and Socioeconomic Data Fact Sheet*. Brazil: Companhia do Metropolitano de São Paulo Metro, 1976. 54 pp.

Presentation of urban transport statistics collected by governmental sources. Emphasis is given to information on transportation in São Paulo Metropolitan Area and its territorial sub-unities and is principally related to patterns of population trips and to characteristics of transportation systems.

1019 Dick, M. Urban Transportation in Latin America. Brussels: *Public Transport International*, Vol. 43(5), September 1995, 22–27.

Article deals with the issues and the options for urban transportation in Latin America.

1020 Gonzalez Gomez, O. and **Navarro Benitez, B.** *The Mexican Experience.* Paper from the proceedings of 'Rail Mass Transit for Developing Countries' organised by the Institution of Civil Engineers. London: Thomas Telford, 1990, 175–187.

In 1966 the Mexican government formally began studies for the construction of the first metro lines. The following year, an organisation was created for this mass transit system – Sistema de Transporte Colectivo. The Mexican Metro is probably the longest of the third world's metros and its network is as big as all the other Latin American metros put together. Article comprehensively reviews the Mexican Metro.

1021 Hall, Stephen; Rojas, Henry Malbran and **Zegras, Christopher.** Transportation and Energy in Santiago, Chile. Oxford: *Transport Policy*, Vol. 1(4), October 1994, 233–243.

Presents the current passenger transportation system and urban development trends in Santiago, Chile including institutional authority, vehicle fleets, modal splits, trip behaviour and emissions and energy consumption. Current responses by the city to date are discussed and measures for improving public transport, implementing travel demand management schemes, controlling sprawling land uses and reforming institutional structures are proposed.

1022 Hellewell, D. Scott. Public Transport – Brazilian Style. London: *Transport*, Vol. 5, March/April 1984, 12–13.

Of Brazil's 123 million population, 68 per cent live in urban areas. This urbanisation has occurred rapidly, rising from 31 per cent in 1940 to 45 per cent in 1960 and 68 per cent in 1980. Article examines the impact of this phenomenon on urban transportation.

1023 Henry, E. *The Metro Put to the Test in Latin America.* Paper from the proceedings of 'Rail Mass Transit for Developing Countries' organised by the Institution of Civil Engineers. London: Thomas Telford, 1990, 103–124.

Report on a research programme aimed at assessing the effects of metros on transport systems and urban structures in Latin America. This socio-economic assessment achieved in co-operation with local teams proceeded from four in-depth case studies completed by exploratory diagnoses of the other cases and an analysis of the decision making procedures of two systems in construction. The key notion discussed is the one of integration at the sector level and the town planning level.

1024 Hide, Henry. *Vehicle Operating Costs in the Caribbean.* TRRL laboratory report 1031. Crowthorne: Transport and Road Research Laboratory, 1982.

1025 International Union Association of Public Transport. Solving the Problems in Latin America. Brussels: *Public Transport International*, Vol. 41(2), May 1992, 14–33.

Describes the public transport systems of Latin America, an area that contains an enormous variety of terrain, and some of the world's most populous cities yet it's rural areas may have less than 5 inhabitants per square kilometre. Looks at urban bus operation, bus priorities, metros, suburban railways, light rail, bus manaufacture, railway manufacture and inter-urban bus terminals. Article in English, with French and German translations.

1026 Johnson, G. P. and **Steiner, H. M.** Evaluating Social Roads in Mexico. London: *Journal of Transport Economics and Policy*, Vol. 7(1), January 1973, 98–101.

Methods are presented for calculating investment priorities for roads on social rather than economic criteria.

1027 Koprich, Daniel Fernandez. The Modernization of Santiago's Public Transport: 1990–1992. London: *Transport Reviews*, Vol. 14(2), April–June 1994, 167–185.

Examines public transport deregulation in Chile.

1028 Lindau, L. A. and **Rosada, A. B. A.** *The Metropolitan Rail Mass Transit System of Porto Alegre.* Paper from the proceedings of 'Rail Mass Transit for Developing Countries' organised by the Institution of Civil Engineers. London: Thomas Telford, 1990, 145–158.

A suburban rail mass transit system was implemented in the metropolitan region of Porto Alegre, Brazil. Construction was funded by the World Bank and operation started in 1985. Several innovations at the political and institutional level were proposed but most of them are yet to be implemented. Level of service is high, fares tend to be lower than competing bus lines but patronage is lower than initial forecasts. Article provides an in-depth review of this metropolitan transport system.

1029 Montoya, Emilio Mujica. Transportation in the Metropolitan Area of Mexico City. Brussels: *Public Transport International*, Vol. 41(2), May 1992, 40–49.

Describes Mexico City's government enterprises: the metro, buses, their electric transportation system of trolleybuses and light rail. Also examines private provision including minibuses, vans and taxis. Finally, looks at private cars and the Goverment's method of dealing with environmental pollution. Article in English, with French and German translations.

1030 Sutherland, L. E. *Transport Planning in Mexico City.* London: University College London (M.Phil Thesis), 1979.

1031 Tobia, G. *Caracas Metro System: evolution and impact.* Paper from the proceedings of 'Rail Mass Transit for Developing Countries' organised by the Institution of Civil Engineers. London: Thomas Telford, 1990, 223–240.

Reviews the progress and shape of urban development in Caracas with the emphasis on urban transportation before the evolution of the metro system in order to ascertain the impact which the metro has had and continues to have on the city and its inhabitants.

1032 Wright, Charles L. Transport in Brasilia: the limits of aesthetics. London: *Transport Reviews*, Vol. 7(4), October–December 1987, 281–305.

Argues that most of the problems within the city proper are due to the excessive emphasis on facilitating car traffic to the disadvantage of buses and non-motorised traffic, while there are no local rail services. Claims that the regional transport problem stems from the location of the satellite cities from the Pilot Plan, forcing low-income bus riders to spend 3–4 hours daily in transit and up to 30 per cent of the minimum wage on the journey to work.

7 Roads

General

1033 Hamer, Mike. *Wheels within Wheels: a study of the road lobby.* London: Friends of the Earth, 1974. 57 pp.

1034 Hibbs, J. and **Roth, G.** *Tomorrow's Way: managing roads in a free society.* London: Adam Smith Institute, 1992. 37 pp.

An examination of the administration and ownership of public roads, the means of charging for their use and the criteria for investing in additional capacity. Reviews the history of roads funding in the UK and road vehicle taxation. Suggests two deficiencies in arrangements: average pricing and the consequent lack of direct market forces on investment decisions. Improvements to average pricing are proposed such as premiums for heavy vehicles; congestion charges; and pollution charges.

1035 Lenzi, G. *A Study of a Road Network.* Cambridge: University of Cambridge (MSc Thesis), 1976.

1036 Pease, Jack. The Midlands Motorways: massaging the heart of the highway system. London: *Local Transport Today*, July 1991, 10–11.

The West Midlands motorway system encapsulates virtually all the problems faced across Britain by urban traffic congestion including over-loaded inter-urban commuting, and the need for road access to help economic regeneration of certain areas. Article argues that it is therefore not surprising that the West Midlands is host to many novel schemes that aim to get the maximum use out of all available infrastructure.

1037 Wong, T. L. *A Study on the British Public Road Transport.* Glasgow: University of Strathclyde (MSc Thesis), 1985.

Focuses on three major themes: the state of the British bus and coach industry; the relation between the Government and public road transport; and the challenges that bus operators faced from the declining bus industry of the 1980s. A case study examines the commercial practice of Greater Manchester Transport.

History

1038 Barker, Theo. Towards an Historical Classification of Urban Transport Development Since the Later Eighteenth Century. Manchester: *Journal of Transport History*, Vol. 1(1), September 1980, 75–90.

Attempts to provide a framework within which public transport's contribution to urban growth is applied to particular places.

1039 Barker, Theo and **Gerhold, Dorian.** *The Rise and Rise of Road Transport, 1700–1990.* Basingstoke: Macmillan, 1993. 118 pp.

Addresses the neglect by historians of the growth of Britain's road transport system.

1040 Dunbar, Charles. *The Rise of Road Transport 1919–1939.* London: Ian Allan, 1981. 144 pp.

Guide to transport between the two world wars aims to reveal a revolution in inland transport during this era and argues that road began to supersede rail for all long distance movement.

1041 Evans, Penny (ed.). *Where Motor-Car is Master: how the Department of Transport became bewitched by roads.* London: Council for the Protection of Rural England, 1992. 72 pp.

Provides a history of the Department of Transport since 1919 which claims to explain their ambivalence to any form of transport other than the road. Argues that a major cultural and attitudinal shift is required to sensitise the Department to environmental issues. Claims that this will only occur when there are structural changes to the Department which disperse the 'roads mentality'.

1042 Hindley, Geoffrey. *A History of Roads.* London: Peter Davies, 1971. 158 pp.

Historical and international account of the creation and development of roads, the evolution of which has proven itself integral to the advancement of mankind.

1043 Phillips, A. D. M. and **Turton, B. J.** Staffordshire Turnpike Trusts and Traffic in the Early Nineteenth Century. Manchester: *Journal of Transport History*, Vol. 8(2), September 1987, 126–146.

1044 Silver, O. B. *The Development of the Fife Road System, 1700–1850.* St. Andrews: University of St. Andrews (PhD Thesis), 1985.

Explores the development of traffic and traffic systems during the first half of the eighteenth century in Fife as a result of the expansion of agricultural output and mineral exploitation in the area.

1045 St. Clair, David J. *The Motorization of American Cities.* New York: Praeger, 1986. 192 pp.

Documents the activities of groups and individuals who played the role of entrepreneurs in the successful promotion of urban highways and the related substitution of buses for streetcars in the United States since the 1920s. Examines the economics of public transit as it relates to the motorisation issue; considers evidence supporting the existence of a conspiracy to destroy transit through motorisation and describes industry tactics to promote an urban-orientated Interstate System.

1046 Suzuki, Peter T. Transportation Policies in a Medieval City. Westport, CT: *Transportation Quarterly*, Vol. 40(4), October 1986, 521–532.

Discusses the policies drawn up by Bruges, a historic medieval town in West Flanders, Belgium, to deal with the crisis epitomised by traffic gridlock.

1047 Todd, Kenneth. A History of Roundabouts in Britain. Westport, CT: *Transportation Quarterly*, Vol. 45(1), January 1991, 143–155.

Provides the history of the roundabout which was first proposed in 1897 but only officially adopted as a method of traffic control in the mid-1920s.

1048 Weiner, Edward. Urban Transportation Planning in the US: an historical overview. London: *Transport Reviews*, Vol. 5(1), January–March 1985, 19–48.

Claims that in planning for new major regional transport facilities, many urban areas neglected maintaining and upgrading other facilities.

1049 Williams, Herbert. *Stage Coaches in Wales.* South Glamorgan: Stewart Williams, 1977. 120 pp.

Traces the history of stage coaches and their complex organisation in Wales. Discusses the people who drove them and looks at the bitter rivalries between competing proprietors and the agitation for better roads.

Theory

1050 Abdul-Kareem, I. A. *Estimation of Benefits from Improvements to an Urban Road Network.* Glasgow: University of Strathclyde (MSc Thesis), 1977.

1051 Abelson, P. W. Quantification of Road User Costs: a comment with special reference to Thailand. London: *Journal of Transport Economics and Policy*, Vol. 7(1), January 1973, 80–97.

1052 Abu-Rahmeh, F. W. *Saturation Flow and Lost Time at Traffic Signals.* Sheffield: University of Sheffield (PhD Thesis), 1982.

1053 Al-Alawi, J. A. *Highway Offside Priority Roundabout Performance Using Computer Simulation.* Bradford: University of Bradford (PhD Thesis), 1981.

1054 Anandarup, Ray and **Tak, Herman G. van der.** *The Economic Benefits of Road Transport Projects.* World Bank Occasional Paper No.13. Baltimore, MD: Johns Hopkins University Press, 1971.

1055 Appa, Gautamkumar; Jarrett, David and **Wright, Christopher.** Conflict-Minimising Traffic Patterns: a graph-theoretic approach to efficient traffic circulation in urban areas. Oxford: *Transportation Research*, Vol. 23(2), 1989, 115–127.

Considers some idealised traffic networks and circulation systems which would serve to obviate some of the accidents and congestion that occur in city centres.

1056 Ardekani, Siamak and **Herman, Robert.** Characterizing Traffic Conditions in Urban Areas. Baltimore, MD: *Transportation Science*, Vol. 18(2), May 1984, 101–140.

A series of vehicular traffic experiments conducted in Austin, Texas, shows the reasonableness of the two assumptions in the two-fluid (moving and stopped vehicles) model of town traffic.

1057 Bonsall, Peter. The Generation Gap? London: *Local Transport Today*, August, 1989, 8–9.

The response by users to new road capacity, in particular trip generation, has become one of the key issues in the debate over catering for future traffic demand. Article attempts to explore new approaches to how such second-order consequences can be included in evaluation.

1058 Boyce, A. M. *The Effect of Vehicle Interactions on the Appraisal of Road Schemes in Developing Countries.* Southampton: University of Southampton (PhD Thesis), 1985.

Reviews the factors of importance concerning the costs and benefits of road improvement schemes and the methods of appraisal. Two computerised techniques were examined in detail, COBA and RTIM2.

1059 Braybrooke, David. *Traffic Congestion Goes Through the Issue-Machine: a case study in issue processing, illustrating a new approach.* London: Routledge and Kegan Paul, 1974. 62 pp.

1060 Buchan, I. *Vehicle Delay at a Fixed-Time Signal Intersection.* Glasgow: University of Strathclyde (MSc Thesis), 1970.

1061 Catling, Ian. System Convergence – The Potential for an Integrated Road Transport Environment. Amsterdam: *Transportation,* Vol. 17(3), 1990, 285–299.

Discusses the potential for co-ordinating developments in Road Transport Informatics in what could otherwise be a number of fragmented approaches, in order to approach what the DRIVE programme calls the 'Integrated Road Transport Environment'. Set within the context of European developments such as the PROMETHEUS and DRIVE research programmes it is nevertheless intended to encompass possible progress towards worldwide standardisation.

1062 Chrissikopoulos, V. *Aspects of Driver Behaviour in Main Road Traffic Streams.* London: Royal Holloway College (PhD Thesis), 1983.

1063 Danforth, Paul M. *Transport Control: a technology on the move.* London: Aldus Books, 1970. 192 pp.

Provides a review of problems affecting roads including congestion, automatic control systems, methods of improving traffic capacity, parking, road pricing and use of public transport. Observations are also made on pollution, noise and the use of electric vehicles.

1064 Darzentas, J. *Aspects of Decision Making by Drivers Entering Priority Traffic Streams: causes and effects.* London: Royal Holloway College (PhD Thesis), 1981.

1065 Dickinson, K. W. *Traffic Data Capture and Analysis Using Video Image Processing.* Sheffield: University of Sheffield (PhD Thesis), 1987.

Describes the development and evaluation, over a six year period, of an automatic video image processing system which was used to capture and analyse video pictures of road traffic. A number of potential applications for the use of automatic image analysis in the field of traffic monitoring and control are considered.

1066 Dutch, W. G. *The Capital Cost Aspects of the Environmental Impact of New Highways in Association with the New Design Technique of the Commercial Route Methodology.* Loughborough: University of Loughborough (PhD Thesis), 1989.

1067 El Shabrawy, M. M. A. *The Construction of Shortest Length and Efficient Transportation Networks.* Glasgow: University of Strathclyde (PhD Thesis), 1981.

1068 El Shawaly, S. A. A. *Queue Lengths and Delays at Oversaturated Traffic Signal Controlled Intersections.* Sheffield: University of Sheffield (PhD Thesis), 1986.

Attempts to compare the observed and estimated queue lengths and delays at fixed-time traffic signalised approaches during peak periods and the calibration of the theoretical formulae used in the study.

1069 Gartner, Nathan H. An Analytical Framework for Urban Traffic Management. London: George Godwin, *International Forum Series,* Vol. 2, 1981, 1–14.

Presents an analytical framework for multi-modal optimisation of the urban highway system and reports results of its application on a pilot basis.

1070 Golias, J. *Gap Acceptance, Delay and Capacity for Vehicles Crossing a Priority Stream.* London: University College London (PhD Thesis), 1981.

1071 Goodwin, P., Parkhurst, G. and **Stokes, G.** *Modifying Our Volume of Traffic: the primary route to sustainable transport.* Oxford: Oxford University, Transport Studies Unit, 1992. 81 pp.

1072 Grigg, P. J. *Simulation of Traffic Flows in a Network Using Conversational Techniques.* Manchester: University of Manchester Institute of Science and Technology (MSc Thesis), 1973.

1073 Hammer, Mick. *Getting Nowhere Fast.* London: Friends of the Earth, 1976. 90 pp.

Examines approaches to road transport including alternative passenger transport modes; the consequences of less movement, noise and pollution as well as the safety aspects of transportation.

1074 Hauer, E., Hurdle, V. F. and **Steuart, G. N.** (eds). *Proceedings of the Eighth International Symposium on Transportation and Traffic Theory.* 24–26 June, 1981, Toronto, Canada. Toronto: University of Toronto Press, 1981. 717 pp.

1075 Hayes, H. R. M. *Vehicle Interactions at Urban Intersections.* Birmingham: University of Birmingham (PhD Thesis), 1973.

1076 Heggie, Ian G. Economics and the Road Programme. London: *Journal of Transport Economics and Policy*, Vol. 13(1), January 1979, 52–67.

Criticises the bases on which trunk road schemes are evaluated by the Department of the Environment. Claims that traffic forecasts should relate car ownership to household characteristics rather than to the individual; small time savings should be ignored; and by-passes should be judged on their value to the environment and not only on financial cost/benefits.

1077 Heggie, Ian. Public Transport Problems Created by Ineffective Planning. London: *Transport*, Vol. 1, September/October 1980, 29–30.

The author, a special adviser to the Minister of Transport, sums up a resent Transport and Road Research Laboratory seminar which presented the results of the International Collaborative Study on the supply and demand problems of public transport.

1078 Herman, Robert and **Prigogine, Ilya.** *Kinetic Theory of Vehicular Traffic.* New York: Elsevier, 1971. 100 pp.

Uses an analogy between statistical physics and traffic to develop a viable theory for transportation and traffic. The theory of multiple-lane traffic flow is examined, in particular the prediction of the character of the traffic flow at arbitrary density in terms of driver behaviour in dilute, non-interacting traffic and the derivation of a kinetic equation to describe the space-time evolution of the velocity distribution of cars.

1079 Holden, David J. Wardrop's Third Principle: urban traffic congestion and traffic policy. London: *Journal of Transport Economics and Policy*, Vol. 23(3), September 1989, 239–262.

Argues that a dynamic statistical model is more appropriate than a static, micro-deterministic model for the study of urban transport equilibrium, and that seeking a behaviourally plausible interpretation of Mogridge's hypothesis leads inevitably in the direction of dynamic statistical equilibrium.

1080 Hope, Chris and **Peake, Stephen.** Sustainable Mobility in Context. Oxford: *Transport Policy*, Vol. 1(3), June 1994, 195–207.

Uncertainty surrounding the plausibility of predicted increases in traffic on the UK's roads highlights the need for an alternative to unconditional forecasting in transport planning. A scenario-based method, capable of dealing with this kind of uncertainty, is used to explore three alternative scenarios for the development of transport in the UK up to the year 2025.

1081 Humby, D. J. *Lane Occupancy as a Traffic Flow Parameter.* Sheffield: University of Sheffield (M.Eng Thesis), 1972.

1082 Hussain, A. M. *Evaluation of Area Traffic Control Schemes by*

Motor Vehicles' Fuel Consumption. Glasgow: University of Strath-clyde (PhD Thesis), 1979.

1083 Jadaan, K. S. R. *Relative Benefits of Disabled Vehicle Location and Aid Systems on Limited Access Highways.* Bradford: University of Bradford (PhD Thesis), 1977.

1084 Jefford, A. W. *Traffic Characteristics in Relation to Carriageway Edge-Lining.* Leeds: University of Leeds (PhD Thesis), 1977.

1085 Jonas, Pereira de Andrade. *The Performance of Urban Intersections in Brazil.* Southampton: University of Southampton (PhD Thesis), 1988.

Focuses on the prediction of delay and optimisation of the performance of urban intersections as they generally govern overall network capacity. A study was undertaken to calculate whether empirical studies from developed countries on factors which affect intersection capacity can be applied to Brazil. Concludes that Brazilian traffic characteristics are different from those elesewhere and therefore should be locally investigated.

1086 Jourdain, Susan. *Urban Intersection Control.* Sussex: The Book Guild, 1992. 234 pp.

Provides an examination of junction control devices including a detailed look at roundabouts. Includes a glossary and provides chapters on links and the roadway; priority intersections; roundabouts and gyratories; traffic signal controls; signal linking; bicycles and pedestrians; priority users; traffic congestion and choice of intersection.

1087 Khayer, Y. *Capacity and Delay at Roundabouts.* Glasgow: University of Glasgow (PhD Thesis), 1979.

1088 Kobayashi, Fumihiko. Improving Traffic Flow with a Route Guidance System. London: George Godwin, *International Forum Series*, Vol. 2, 1981, 25–32.

A pilot test of route guidance systems has been carried out in south-west Tokyo. Paper sumarises five sub-systems. A detailed explanation is also given of route guidance and the guidance algorithm based on the results of computer simulation. Paper also refers to the estimated cost and the possibility of improving the present traffic situation in the metropolitan area of Tokyo by introducing the route guidance system.

1089 Laurence, C. J. D. *Roundabout Capacity Prediction: a study of factors affecting roundabout capacity.* Sheffield: University of Sheffield (PhD Thesis), 1980.

1090 Leutzbach, Wilhelm. *Introduction to the Theory of Traffic Flow.* London: Springer Verlag, 1988. 204 pp.

Describes a coherent approach to the explanation of the movement of individual vehicles or groups of vehicles. English translation of a text originally published in German in 1972. An extended and totally revised edition.

1091 Linneker, B. J. and **Spence, N. A.** An Accessibility Analysis of the Impact of the M25 London Orbital Motorway on Britain. Cambridge: *Regional Studies*, Vol. 26(1), 1992, 31–47.

1092 Lo, P.-L. *A Method for Measuring the Efficiency with which Public Transport Systems Use Road-Space.* Warwick: University of Warwick (PhD Thesis), 1982.

1093 Local Transport Today. Traffic Rules OK? public backs road use regulations when they can understand them. London: *Local Transport Today*, October 1990, 12–13.

Survey of public perceptions of traffic regulations in urban areas which has revealed surprisingly strong support for tougher traffic laws.

1094 Mahmassani, M., Hani, S. and **Shen-Te Chen, Peter.** An Investigation of the Reliability of Real-Time Information for Route Choice Decisions in a Congested Traffic System. Amsterdam: *Transportation*, Vol. 20, 1993, 157–178.

Investigation into the reliability of information on prevailing trip times on the links of a network as a basis for route choice decisions by individual drivers. Considers a type of information strategy in which no attempt is made by some central controller to predict what the travel times on each link would be by the time it is reached by a driver that is presently at a given location. Study illustrates interactions between information reliability and user response.

1095 Miyagi, Toshihiko; Morisugi, Hisa and **Ohno, Eiji.** Benefit Incidence of Urban Ring Road: theory and case study of the Gifu Ring Road. Amsterdam: *Transportation*, Vol. 20, 1993, 285–303.

Aims at measuring the benefit incidence of each socio-economic sector in each zone by using a benefit measurement model and a simple socio-economic model, especially discussing the absentee landowners' share of the total benefit from the viewpoint of the degree of the city's openness. Case study deals with the ring road construction being undertaken in Gifu City, Japan.

1096 Mogridge, M. J. H. If London Is More Spread Out Than Paris, Why Don't Londoners Travel More Than Parisians? Amsterdam: *Transportation*, Vol. 13(1), 1986, 85–104.

Investigates the travel data for London and Paris in order to test theories about the relation of travel to land use, and about the influence of travel on the expansion of cities and especially about the changing relation between the central city, the inner core and the outer ring.

1097 Nash, C. and **Pearce D.** The Evaluation of Urban Motorway Schemes: a case study – Southampton. Abingdon: *Urban Studies*, Vol. 10(2), June 1973, 129–143.

An examination of the much-discussed systematic biases in urban motor-way evaluation, by looking at a particular case study – Southampton.

1098 Newell, G. F. *Traffic Flow on Transportation Networks.* London: Massachusetts Institute of Technology Press, 1980. 276 pp.

Examination of the advantages and limitations of network analysis applied to transportation problems.

1099 Palma, A. de A Game-Theoretic Approach to the Analysis of Simple Congested Networks. Nashville, TN: *American Economic Review*, Vol. 82(2), May 1992, 494–500.

1100 Pearman, A. D. *Road Network Optimisation: an examination of sub-optimal solutions to a spatial combinatorial problem.* Leeds: University of Leeds (PhD Thesis), 1978.

1101 Ray, Anandarup and **Tak, Herman G. van der.** *The Economic Benefits of Road Transport Projects.* Washington, DC: International Bank for Reconstruction and Development, 1971. 42 pp.

Within the context of developing the transport sector of developing countries this article explores one method for estimating benefits: the measure of social surplus. Simple versions of the social surplus method are discussed in detail to clarify the nature of the benefits covered by such measures.

1102 Reiss, R. A. Algorithm Development for Corridor Traffic Control. London: George Godwin, *International Forum Series*, Vol. 2, 1981, 33–47.

A traffic control algorithm has been developed which selects values of control variables to optimise traffic flow in a general inter-city corridor. Techniques from the field of network flow theory have been used and extended to find the optimal real-time assignment of traffic through a network. A corridor level control acts in a supervisory capacity, dynamically allocating traffic optimally among such corridor facilities as freeways, freeway-frontage road pairs, and signalised arterials.

1103 Reynolds, C. J. *Problems in Traffic Control at an Isolated Inter-section.* Manchester: University of Manchester (MSc Thesis), 1973.

1104 Robertson, D. I. *A Deterministic Method of Assigning Traffic to Multiple Routes of Known Cost.* TRRL Laboratory Report 757. Crowthorne: Transport and Road Research Laboratory, 1977. 21 pp.

A method is proposed for assigning road traffic to a network of urban streets. The objective is to predict the flows along alternative routes with the accuracy needed for the design of comprehensive urban traffic management schemes.

1105 Roth, Gabriel. *Roads in a Market Economy.* Aldershot: Avebury, 1996. 292 pp.

Makes the proposition that roads, as part of the 'command economy', exhibit typical command economy characteristics of congestion, chronic shortages of funds, and insensitivity to consumer demands. Proposes an alternative market economy framework, employing the concepts of ownership, market pricing and profitability for the commercial provision of roads on the model of telecommunications.

1106 Ruhm, K. *Traffic Data Acquisition and Analysis by Photogrammetric Methods.* London: City University (M.Phil Thesis), 1971.

1107 Schofield, Graham Paul. *Trip Chains in Peak and Off-Peak Travel by London Residents.* London: University College London (PhD Thesis), 1989. 516 pp.

1108 Seddon, P. A. *A Practical and Theoretical Study of the Dispersion of Platoons of Vehicles Leaving Traffic Signals.* Salford: University of Salford (PhD Thesis), 1971.

1109 Simhairi, N. Z. H. *Traffic Assignment and Network Analysis.* London: Royal Holloway College (PhD Thesis), 1987.

1110 Soberman, Richard M. *Transport Technology for Developing Regions.* Cambridge, MA: MIT Press, 1966.

Study of road transportation in Venezuela.

1111 Steenbrink, Peter A. *Optimization of Transport Networks.* London: John Wiley, 1974. 325 pp.

Theoretical aspects of the optimisation of transport networks. The second part focuses on the Dutch road network.

1112 Story, C. E. R. *A General Purpose Simulation of Road Traffic in a Network.* Birmingham: University of Birmingham (MSc Thesis), 1970.

1113 Taylor, M. A. P. and **Young, W.** *Traffic Analysis: new technology and new solutions.* Victoria: Hargreen Publishing Company, 1988. 353 pp.

Examines existing and new techniques and technologies for undertaking traffic surveys.

1114 Thornhill, F. L. *An Investigation into the Accuracy of Traffic Flow Estimation Using Distance Weighted Trend Analysis.* Glasgow: University of Strathclyde (MSc Thesis), 1983.

1115 Tyson, W. J. The Peak in Road Passenger Transport: an empirical study. London: *Journal of Transport Economics and Policy*, Vol. 6(1), January 1972, 77–84.

This study of one road passenger transport undertaking demonstrates that the long run marginal cost of the daily peak is greater than its long-run marginal revenue. Argues that raising fares at the peak and withdrawing services would involve social costs.

1116 Van As, S. C. *Traffic Signal Optimization: procedures and techniques.* Southampton: University of Southampton (PhD Thesis), 1979.

1117 Vaughan, B. C. *Original and Destination Matrices and Other Traffic Data from 35mm Photography.* Leeds: University of Leeds (PhD Thesis), 1981.

1118 Wooton Jeffreys Consultants: Department of Transport: Transport and Road Research Laboratory. *A Study to Show Patterns of Vehicle Use in the London area.* Supplementary Report to CR131: Contractor Report 131. Crowthorne: Transport and Road Research Laboratory, 1989. 8 pp.

Study directed specifically at the estimates of travel on motorways, including the M25, and on local roads contained in Report CR131, 'A Study to Show Patterns of Vehicle Use in the London Area'.

1119 Zlatoper, Thomas J. Regression Analysis of Time Series Data on Motor Vehicle Deaths in the United States. London: *Journal of Transport Economics and Policy*, Vol. 18(3), September 1984, 263–274.

Policy and planning

1120 As publisher. National Roads Plan May Lag Behind. *P.V.*, Vol. 13(1), 1993/94, 10–11.

Examines the effect of the National Roads Authority's control of the national road network from January 1994 and, in particular, the problems of the road improvement programme.

1121 Birch, Nigel and **Williams, Roger.** The Longer-term Implications of National Travel Forecasts and International Network Plans for Local Roads Policy: the case of Oxfordshire. Oxford: *Transport Policy*, Vol. 1(2), March 1994, 95–99.

Assessment of the effects on Oxfordshire of the Department of Transport's National Road Traffic Forecast and of the road improvements that would be involved in providing road capacity to accommodate unrestrained traffic demand. Argued that, in the long-term, the policy which supports improvements to the major routes in order to protect the minor roads, is not sustainable. Thus an integrated transport policy which would address traffic demand as well as road building is called for.

1122 Bovill, D. I. N., Heggie, I. G. and **Hine, J. L.** *A Guide to Transport Planning within the Roads Sector for Developing Countries.* London: Overseas Development Administration, 1978.

Survey which includes an extensive bibliography.

1123 Bramall, Stephen. Roads: the Highways Agency. *Transport Law and Practice*, Vol. 2(4), 1994, 28–29.

Looks at the Agency's uncertain role in the light of current debates on the future of the government's road transport policies.

1124 Burnham, Jane; Glaister, Stephen and **Travers, Tony.** *Transport Policy Making in Britain: with special reference to roads.* London: London School of Economics and Political Science, 1994. 188 pp.

Explores the formal structure of transport policy making. Claims that Whitehall and local government host a number of agencies with objectives, powers and duties which, at times, are in conflict. Notes also a push towards central control.

1125 Butler, Eamonn and **Roth, Gabriel.** *Private Road Ahead: ways of providing better roads sooner.* London: Adam Smith Institute, 1982. 32 pp.

Discusses the economic, social, environmental and fuel-saving significance of an efficient road system. Suggests new ways in which the road network could be improved without straining the public purse.

1126 European Conference of Ministers of Transport. *Tariff Policies for Urban Transport (other than Road Pricing).* ECMT Round Table

46. Paris: Organisation for Economic Co-operation and Development, 1980. 107 pp.

1127 Goodwin, Phil. Transport Policy and Road Inquiries: new proposals from the Royal Commission on Environmental Polution. Chichester: *Road Law*, Vol. 10(8), 1994, 504–508.

Argues that trunk road schemes should be considered as an intrinsic part of local authority structure plans.

1128 Hanna, Judith. Road Planning: what prospects for a fairer and less confrontational system? London: *Local Transport Today*, December 1992, 12–13.

Both those who support the need for road constuction, and objectors to road schemes argue that the current road planning system needs reform. Article attempts to address the questions of what is wrong with the present system, and what reforms are required.

1129 Hibbs, John. The True Cost of Planning: the lack of a market for transport land. Chichester: *Road Law*, Vol. 10(1), 1994, 2–4.

Examines the extent to which planning laws governing provision of roads contribute to accidents.

1130 Lane, Peter. Transport and the Environment: the impact of PPG13. *Transport Law and Practice*, Vol. 1(9), 1994, 74–75.

Details the policy change represented by revised planning guidance with the objective of reducing both journeys by road and reliance on private cars.

1131 Local Transport Today. Surrey Integrated Transport Plan Aims to Head Off Traffic Nightmare. London: *Local Transport Today*, December, 1990, 10–11.

In a bid to prevent Surrey turning into 'one big car park' the County Council is promoting what it believes to be a unique transport plan that looks beyond road building as a cure for all congestion.

1132 Mackie, Peter J. and **Simon, David.** Do Road Projects Benefit Industry? – a case study of the Humber Bridge. London: *Journal of Transport Economics and Policy*, Vol. 20(3), September 1986, 377–384.

Prime justification for the roads programme is to increase competitiveness by reducing transport costs. Roads tend to be improved incrementally except where estuaries are crossed. Case study of 52 regular commercial users of the new Humber Bridge demonstrates that operators adjusted by increasing vehicle utilisation, increasing market penetration, changing market areas serviced, and by internal rationalisation.

1133 Newbery, D. M. The Case for a Public Road Authority. Bath: *Journal of Transport Economics and Policy*, Vol. 28(3), September 1994, 235–253.

1134 Nilsson, Jan-Eric. Investment Decisions in a Public Bureaucracy: a case study of Swedish road planning practices. London: *Journal of Transport Economics and Policy*, Vol. 25(2), May 1991, 163–176.

Treats the problem of setting a socially relevant ranking of investment projects in the presence of budgetary restrictions and incomplete information. A road investment programme, settled under these conditions, is analysed using a binomial logit model.

1135 Salter, R. J. *Highway Traffic Analysis and Design.* 2nd ed. London: Macmillan, 1989. 374 pp.

Includes work on the fundamental principles of land use and transport planning methods and the subsequent appraisal of proposals. Reviews the analytical and practical aspects of highway traffic flow with sections discussing traffic noise generation; air pollution and the principles of road traffic restraint; and road pricing. Highway intersections are considered in detail with sections covering priority junctions; roundabouts; grade-separated junctions; and interchanges.

1136 Wells, Gordon. Highway and Transportation Planning in England. Amsterdam: *Transportation*, Vol. 8, 1979, 125–140.

Article presents an overview of highway and transportation planning in England. Covers the division of responsibilities between central and local government and the organisation of the Department of Transport together with the planning, financing and implementation of road schemes, both local and national. Brief review of transport legislation is also included.

1137 Younes, Bassem. Roads in Urban Areas: to build or not to build? London: *Transport Reviews*, Vol. 13(2), April–June 1993, 99–117.

Reports and reviews the findings of a research project recently completed at Imperial College, London. Examples of road building in urban areas in Britain, Germany and Sweden were examined to see whether these schemes met their stated objectives, with particular attention to re-distributing traffic and relieving traffic congestion.

Calming

1138 Association of District Councils. *Traffic Calming.* London: Association of District Councils, August 1994. 52 pp.

Collection of papers on traffic calming presented at seminars held in April and June of 1994.

1139 Boecker, G. and **Hass-Klau, C.** *Traffic Calming in Britain: the nationwide survey.* Brighton: Environmental and Transport Planning, July 1992. 439 pp.

1140 Brindle, R. E. Traffic Calming in Australia: a definition and commentary. Victoria: *Australian Road Research*, Vol. 21(2), June 1991, 37–55.

Addresses itself to the distinction between the theory and the practice of traffic calming programmes. Points out the nature of social and structural changes that would be required to achieve traffic calmed cities. Three levels of traffic calming are identified, and a distinction is made between physical or management measures on the one hand, and social or cultural characteristics on the other.

1141 Department of the Environment. *A Study of Some Methods of Traffic Restraint.* DOE Research Report 14. London: Department of the Environment, 1976. 128 pp.

Details a research study carried out between 1973 and 1975 aimed at providing an understanding of the several effects of restraint applied to a medium sized city and in particular to compare five alternative restraint systems.

1142 Devon County Council. *Traffic Calming Guidelines.* Devon: Devon County Council, 1991. 185 pp.

Illustrates ways in which traffic calming can be achieved. Divided into four sections: section one gives varying approaches to traffic calming, section two examines implementation of traffic calming, section three looks at specific measures and section four gives scheme examples.

1143 Garva, Sigurd. Traffic Calming – Can It Be Done in America? Virginia: *Transportation Quarterly*, Vol. 47(4), October 1993, 483–506.

Discusses the potential for traffic calming programmes in the USA given the resistance of Americans to constraints on the use of automobiles.

1144 Mackie, R. and **Windle, R.** *Survey on Public Acceptability of Traffic Calming Schemes.* Crowthorne: Transport and Road Research Laboratory, 1992. 50 pp.

1145 Moran, Mark. Dutch Show Courage to Calm Their Streets. London: *Local Transport Today*, May 1990, 10–11.

Taking cars out of the centres of three Dutch towns was about a lot more than traffic control: it secured their identity as trading centres. Article reports from a conference in Enschede aimed at persuading British authorities to have the confidence to follow suit.

1146 Morgan, B. P. *Some Aspects of Traffic Limitation in Large Urban Areas.* Salford: University of Salford (MSc Thesis), 1981.

1147 Nold, I. *Horizontal Traffic Calming Measures – Alternatives to Road Humps?* Northallerton: North Yorkshire County Council, 1994. 112 pp.

1148 Solomon, Keith T. Reduction of Vehicular Flow on Residential Streets. London: George Godwin, *International Forum Series*, Vol. 2, 1981, 209–220.

Various low-cost methods of discouraging vehicular flow through residential areas, including end, mid-block and diagonal closures, one-way flows, pavement narrowing and curving, and the provision of roundabouts, are explored in this paper. It is argued that such schemes should not be considered in isolation. They must take account of individual householders and sectional interests, be part of arterial road traffic management schemes and take cognisance of possible effects on public transport operations.

1149 Stonham, Peter. Traffic Calming: councils speed up efforts to turn the traffic tide. London: *Local Transport Today*, Feburuary 1991, 10–11.

More than sixty traffic calming schemes have been introduced in Britain over the past few years as a growing number of local authorities turn to a technique already widely adopted on the Continent. Article discusses the background to the current interest with two traffic calming specialists – Tim Pharoah and Carmen Hass-Klau.

1150 Tolley, Rodney. *Calming Traffic in Residential Areas.* Aberystwyth: Brefi Press, 1990. 142 pp.

Reviews traffic calming as a means of reducing the number and severity of accidents, ameliorating the adverse impacts of motorised travel on the environment and improving living conditions for residents.

1151 Topp, Hartmut H. Traffic Safety, Usability and Streetscape Effects of New Design Principle for Major Urban Roads. Amsterdam: *Transportation*, Vol. 16(4), 1990, 297–310.

Discusses experience in six German model cities of area-wide traffic calming, several research projects and the guidelines for major urban roads. Argues that traffic calming which is primarily based on the locational shift to main thoroughfares is socially unjust, because about one-quarter of the urban population live in those areas.

1152 Transport and Environment Studies. *Quality Streets: how traditional urban centres benefit from traffic-calming.* London: TEST, 1988. 252 pp.

Investigates area wide traffic restraint 'packages' and their effect first on the physical environment within the area, and second on the economic environment. Case studies are drawn from Britain and Europe.

Congestion

1153 Ampt, E. S. and **Jones, P. M.** *Attitudes and Responses to Traffic Congestion and Possible Future Counter-Measures: an exploratory study of household travel in Bristol.* Oxford: Oxford University, Transport Studies Unit, 1992. 76 pp.

1154 Arnott, R. J. Unpriced Transport Congestion. San Diego, CA: *Journal of Economic Theory*, Vol. 21(2), October 1979, 294–316.

Investigation into some features of an urban economy with unpriced transport congestion.

1155 Arnott, R., Lindsey, R. and **de Palma, A.** Route Choice with Heterogeneous Drivers and Group-Specific Congestion Costs. Amsterdam: *Regional Science & Urban Economics*, Vol. 22(1), March 1992, 71–102.

1156 Atash, Farhad. Mitigating Traffic Congestion in Suburbs: an evaluation of land-use strategies. Virginia: *Transportation Quarterly*, Vol. 47(4), October 1993, 507–524.

Focuses on land-use strategies to ease traffic congestion in suburban areas.

1157 Axhausen, Kay W., Emmerink, Richard H. M., Nijkamp, Peter and **Rietveld, Piet.** Effects of Information in Road Transportation Networks with Recurrent Congestion. Amsterdam: *Transportation*, Vol. 22(1), 1995, 21–53.

Aims to gain further insight into the implications of information provision to drivers on the performance of road transport networks with recurrent congestion. Three types of information provision mechanisms are considered: information based upon own-experience, after-trip information and real-time en route information.

1158 Banister, David. Urban Congestion and Gridlock in Britain. Oxford: *Built Environment*, Vol. 15(4), Numbers 3/4 1989, 166–175.

Argues that in order to solve traffic congestion, space on roads must be allocated according to priority of use and not by the market.

1159 Ben-Akiva, Moshe; Lefevre, Claude; Litinas, Nicolaos and **Palma,**

Andre de. Stochastic Equilibrium Model of Peak Period Traffic Congestion. Baltimore, MD: *Transportation Science*, Vol. 17(4), November 1983, 430–453.

Addresses the problem of peak period traffic congestion. Considers the queues and delays at a single point of insufficient capacity. A model is developed to predict the pattern of traffic volumes and travel times during a peak period.

1160 Bertrand, T. J. 'Second Best' Congestion Taxes in Transportation Systems. Washington, DC: *Econometrica*, Vol. 45(7), October 1977, 1703–1715.

Using assumptions on the effect of taxation on the level and structure of demand for transportation services, guidelines are provided for taxation (and subsidisation) in a multi-mode traffic system.

1161 Bertrand, Trent J. Congestion Costs in a Transport System, with an Application to Bangkok. London: *Journal of Transport Economics and Policy*, Vol. 12(3), September 1978, 244–279.

Presents a model to estimate the congestion costs created by various types of vehicles and the 'optimal' congestion taxes, and suggests how these taxes may be modified to allow for external constraints.

1162 Boardman, Anthony E. and **Lave, Lester B.** Highway Congestion and Congestion Tolls. London: *Journal of Urban Economics*, Vol. 4(3), July 1977, 340–359.

The speed-flow relationship is modelled, identifying private and social costs, and the implied congestion toll for a number of proposed formulations.

1163 Boyce, David E., Kim, Tschangho and **Kim, John.** The Role of Congestion of Transportation Networks in Urban Location and Travel Choices. Amsterdam: *Transportation*, Vol. 14, 1987, 53–62.

Issues arising in the use of network equilibrium models are described, and formulations of urban network prediction and design models are explored.

1164 Bradfield, Inai and **Owen, Wilfred.** *The Accessible City.* Washington, DC: Brookings Institution, 1972. 150 pp.

Addresses the problems of urban congestion and pollution caused by the automobile. Suggests that solutions depend on planning cities that are efficient, yet pleasant to live in.

1165 Buckley, D. J. and **Gooneratne, S. G.** Optimal Scheduling of Transport Improvements to Cater for Growing Traffic Congestion. London: *Journal of Transport Economics and Policy*, Vol. 8(2), May 1974, 122–135.

Argues that future changes in traffic flows must be considered in the timing of transport projects.

1166 Cervero, Robert. Land-Use Mixing and Suburban Mobility. Westport, CT: *Transportation Quarterly*, Vol. 42(3), July 1988, 429–446.

Looks at solutions to the traffic congestion encountered by suburban areas. Examines the potential mobility benefits of developing mixed-use suburban workplaces, where offices, shops, banks, restaurants and other activities are built side by side. The effects of current land-use mixes on the commuting choices of suburban workers are studied based on an empirical analysis of some of the largest suburban employment centres in the United States.

1167 Cervero, Robert and **Hall, Peter.** Containing Traffic Congestion in America. Oxford: *Built Environment*, Vol. 15(4), Numbers 3/4 1989, 176–184.

Examines the reasons and solutions for traffic congestion in America.

1168 Davis, Adrian and **Pharoah, Tim.** Setting Their Sights on Traffic Reduction. London: *Local Transport Today*, July 1992, 12–13.

Recent report for Friends of the Earth claims that traffic calming and restraint are not enough to tackle current congestion and environmental problems, and that local authorities should be planning to reduce overall traffic levels by 30 per cent. Article looks briefly at the wide array of measures being advocated to achieve such a reduction.

1169 Dewees, D. N. Estimating the Time Costs of Highway Congestion. Washington, DC: *Econometrica*, Vol. 47(6), November 1979, 1499–1512.

Uses a traffic simulation model to estimate the external cost imposed on motorists by increasing the number of vehicles on a traffic network. Model replicates the queuing of vehicles at traffic lights, the dispersion of platoons of vehicles as they move from one intersection to another, and the interaction of intersecting traffic flows on urban street networks.

1170 Dickins, I. *Traffic Congestion: the cost to the West Midlands.* Birmingham: Birmingham Polytechnic, School of Planning, 1991. 75 pp.

1171 Emmitt, Rosalind. Finding the Solution to Urban Traffic Congestion. London: *Transport*, Vol. 14, July/August 1993, 12–13.

1172 Eno Transportation Foundation. Report on the 23rd Annual Joint Conference of Eno Foundation Board of Directors and Board of Consultants. Westport, CT: *Transportation Quarterly*, Vol. 45(1), January 1991, 3–18.

Reports on the Foundation's Annual Joint Conference of its Board of Directors and Board of Consultants. The theme of the conference was 'The Growing Crisis in Urban Traffic Congestion' and both government and private roles were discussed.

1173 Evans, A. W. Road Congestion: the diagramatic analysis: comment. Chicago, IL: *Journal of Political Economy*, Vol. 100(1), February 1992, 211–217.

1174 Evans, Ruth and **Marlow, M.** *Urban Congestion Survey 1976: traffic flows and speeds in eight towns and five conurbations.* TRRL Supplementary Report 438. Crowthorne: Transport and Road Research Laboratory, 1978. 21 pp.

Outlines the survey techniques employed which include summaries of measurements made during weekday, daytime, off-peak and peak periods of urban traffic flow.

1175 Gurney, A. and **Smith, J.** *Community Effects of Traffic Congestion: a review of the London assessment study data.* Crowthorne: Transport and Road Research Laboratory, 1992. 54 pp.

1176 Henderson, J. V. Road Congestion: a reconsideration of pricing theory. London: *Journal of Urban Economics*, Vol. 1(3), July 1974, 346–365.

Examines the effect of congestion tolls upon the pattern of traffic flows.

1177 Howitt, Arnold M. Downtown Auto Restraint Policies: adopting and implementing urban transport innovations. London: *Journal of Transport Economics and Policy*, Vol. 14(2), May 1980, 155–168.

1178 Hughes, Graham and **Ison, Stephen.** The Cambridge Congestion Metering Scheme. London: *Transport*, Vol. 13, May/June 1992, 7–9.

Examines a pioneering traffic management scheme being implemented in Cambridge.

1179 Institution of Civil Engineers. *Congestion.* London: Thomas Telford, 1989. 100 pp.

Looks at the problem of traffic congestion and proposes that the problem can only be contained not solved. The nature and definition of congestion are identified and the costs, both direct and indirect, are examined.

1180 Jones, P. *Public Reactions to Possible Options for Dealing with Future Traffic and Parking Demands in Congested Urban Areas: summary.* Oxford: Oxford University, Transport Studies Unit, 1992. 22 pp.

1181 Kashima, Shigeru. Advanced Traffic Information Systems in Tokyo. Oxford: *Built Environment*, Vol. 15(4), Numbers 3/4 1989, 244–250.

Examines the various techniques used in Tokyo to reduce traffic congestion and squeeze more capacity out of the transport network.

1182 Khattak, Asad J., Koppelman, Frank S. and **Schofer, Joseph L.** Stated Preferences for Investigating Commuters' Diversion Propensity. Amsterdam: *Transportation*, Vol. 20, 1993, 107–127.

Evaluates the effects of real-time traffic information along with driver attributes, roadway characteristics and situational factors on drivers' willingness to divert from their regular route in response to information about traffic congestion.

1183 Larson, Thomas D. Metropolitan Congestion: towards a tolerable accommodation. Westport, CT: *Transportation Quarterly*, Vol. 42(4), October 1988, 489–498.

Suggests solutions to the problems of traffic congestion in the United States.

1184 Majid, M. S. M. *Traffic Congestion in Baghdad, with Special Reference to the Implementation of Traffic Projects.* Glasgow: University of Strathclyde (PhD Thesis), 1980.

1185 McConnell-Fay, Natalie. Tackling Traffic Congestion in the San Francisco Bay Area. Westport, CT: *Transportation Quarterly*, Vol. 40 (2), April 1986, 159–170.

Claims that traffic mitigation, land use and infrastructure planning are the key factors in tackling transportation problems.

1186 McDonald, John. Urban Highway Congestion. Dordrecht: *Transportation*, Vol. 22(4), 1995, 353–369.

Examines urban highway congestion pricing in situations where (for technical or political reasons) it is not possible to levy a congestion toll on a major portion of the urban road system.

1187 Meyer, Michael D. Dealing with Congestion from a Regional Perspective: the case of Massachusetts. Amsterdam: *Transportation*, Vol. 16(3), 1990, 197–219.

Argues that traffic congestion in many cases is an area wide phenomenon requiring consideration from a regional and programmatic viewpoint. Describes a ten-point congestion-relief programme developed for eastern Massachusetts.

1188 Orski, C. Kenneth. Can We Manage Our Way Out of Traffic Congestion? Westport, CT: *Transportation Quarterly*, Vol. 41(4), October 1987, 457–476.

Examines the strategy of 'congestion management'.

1189 Patankar, P. G. Bombay's Traffic Problems. London: *Transport Reviews*, Vol. 6(3), July–September 1986, 287–302.

Proposes solutions to Bombay's traffic problems through the implementation of an integrated transport plan.

1190 Pease, Jack. Edinburgh Traffic Plans Seek to Preserve the Past for the Future. London: *Local Transport Today*, September 1991, 10–11.

Examines Edinburgh's traffic plan which attempts to strike a balance between transport and the environment.

1191 Pring, K. *An Examination of the Problems Characteristic of the Inner Urban Ring of London and Some Possible Ways of Solving Them, in Particular Reference to Barnsbury.* Salford: University of Salford (MSc Thesis), 1971.

1192 Rathi, Ajay K. Traffic Metering: an effectiveness study. Westport, CT: *Transportation Quarterly*, Vol. 45(3), July 1991, 421–440.

Evaluates the external metering based control concept.

1193 Road Transport Research. *Congestion Control and Demand Management.* Paris: Organisation for Economic Co-operation and Development, 1994. 156 pp.

Presents a detailed catalogue of congestion management measures.

1194 Robinson, David. Peter Leeds: battling with congestion in Hong Kong. London: *Transport*, Vol. 3, January/February, 1983, 40–41.

An interview with Hong Kong's Traffic Commissioner, Peter Leeds.

1195 Rosenbloom, Sandra. Peak-Period Traffic Congestion: a state-of-the-art analysis and evaluation of effective solutions. Amsterdam: *Transportation*, Vol. 7, 1978, 167–191.

Reports on an analysis of a range of largely non-construction congestion reduction techniques.

1196 Shahia, Mrad D. Com. *A Transport Economic Investigation into Staggered Working Hours.* Pretoria: University of South Africa (PhD Thesis), 1986.

Focuses on the need for low cost solutions to urban peak-hour congestion. Argues that a system of staggered working hours could be introduced in Pretoria on the basis of a theoretical feasibility formulation.

1197 Sherman, R. Congestion Interdependence and Urban Transit Fares. Washington, DC: *Econometrica*, Vol. 39(3), May 1971, 565–576.

A general equilibrium model in which no price is available to ration urban road use, (in which both automobiles and buses affect the congestion experienced by either mode), is solved for combinations of first best and second best peak and off-peak urban transit fares.

1198 Solow, R. Congestion, Density and the Use of Land in Transportation. Oxford: *Swedish Journal of Economics*, Vol. 74(1), March 1972, 161–173.

A sketch of a model of equilibrium residential density and rent gradient in a monocentric city in which transportation cost depends only on distance from the central business district and income is equally distributed.

1199 Stonham, Peter. Congestion, Investment and the Art of the Possible. London: *Local Transport Today*, April 1989, 8–9.

Attempts to examine the background to what is increasingly being acknowledged to be a major crisis in matching supply and demand of urban transport.

1200 The Open University. *Economics of Traffic Congestion.* Bletchley: Open University Press, 1972. 36 pp.

Provides an account of the essential ideas of the economics of traffic congestion. Ancillary material is included in the form of graphs, statistics and short quotations.

1201 Thompson, Gerald L. and **Zawack, Daniel J.** A Dynamic Space-Time Network Flow Model for City Traffic Congestion. Baltimore, MD: *Transportation Science*, Vol. 21(3), 1987, 153–162.

A space-time network is developed that represents traffic flows over time for a capacitated road transportation system having one-way and two-way streets.

1202 Tzedakis, A. Different Vehicle Speeds and Congestion Costs. London: *Journal of Transport Economics and Policy*, Vol. 14(1), January 1980, 81–104.

A model is presented for the calculation of congestion costs imposed by a traffic of slow vehicles on a traffic of fast vehicles, where overtaking is not possible.

1203 Whitelegg, John (ed.). *Traffic Congestion: is there a way out?* Hawes: Leading Edge Press & Publishing Ltd., 1992. 192 pp.

Collection of papers on the subject of traffic congestion. Includes an article on ecological tax reform.

Freight

1204 Arnold-Baker, Charles. Moral Preventative Maintenance. Chichester: *Road Law*, Vol. 10(6), 1994, 375–383.

Recent cases involving road haulage operators whose contracts cannot be completed without exceeding the legal speed limits, cutting rest periods or failing to adequately maintain vehicles.

1205 Battilana, J. A. *The Cost of Using Light Vehicles for Town-Centre Deliveries and Collections.* TRRL Laboratory Report 710. Crowthorne: Transport and Road Research Laboratory, 1976. 20 pp.

Assesses some of the effects of a total ban on deliveries and collections with goods vehicles over three tons unladen weight in town centres. Data used was obtained from 48 companies whose vehicles stopped in Swindon, on a typical day in 1973.

1206 Bayliss, B. T. and **Edwards, S. L.** *Operating Costs in Road Freight Transport: a study of the costs of operating road goods vehicle fleets and of the performance and costs of running vehicles of different types and sizes.* London: HMSO, 1971. 181 pp.

1207 Bayliss, Brian T. The Structure of Road Haulage Industry in the United Kingdom, and Optimum Scale. London: *Journal of Transport Economics and Policy*, Vol. 20(2), May 1986, 153–172.

Road haulage firms grew larger after denationalisation in 1953. Argues that larger firms have scale economies in vehicle mix.

1208 Bayliss, Brian T. *The Road Haulage Industry Since 1968.* London: HMSO, 1973. 37 pp.

Examines the impact of the Transport Act 1968 on the road haulage industry and also up-dates some of the information collected in the Department of the Environment's 1965 survey 'Operating Costs in Road Freight Transport.'

1209 Bayliss, Brian T. *The Small Firm in the Road Haulage Industry: Research report No. 1. Committee of Inquiry on Small Firms.* London: HMSO, 1971. 50 pp.

Examines the reasons for the predominance of small operators in the British road haulage industry.

1210 Brown, Largent. *A Manager's Guide to International Road Freighting.* London: Kogan Page, 1986. 239 pp.

Examines the major aspects involved in international freighting.

1211 Buchan, K. and **Plowden, S.** *A New Framework for Freight Transport.* London: Civic Trust, 1995. 121 pp.

Investigates the increases in heavy traffic over the last two-and-a-half decades; specifically journey lengths, times and loads carried. The external costs of freight transport are measured, and reforms are recommended which include proposed changes to the regulatory and fiscal framework.

1212 Buckley, A. *Road Freight Surveys.* Bletchley: Open University Press, 1970. 80 pp.

1213 Buckley, P. and **Westbrook, M. D.** Market Definition and Assessing the Competitive Relationship between Rail and Truck Transportation. Peace Dale, RI: *Journal of Regional Science*, Vol. 31(3), August 1991, 329–346.

1214 Business Ratio Report. *Road Hauliers: an industry sector analysis.* 4th ed. London: Intercompany Comparisons, 1982.

Compares the financial performance of 100 road haulage companies over the 3 year period ending April 1981.

1215 Button, K. J. and **Pearman, A. D.** *The Economics of Urban Freight Transport.* London: Macmillan, 1981. 218 pp.

Provides a comprehensive study of the economics of urban freight transport. Includes details of the existing situation in Britain and many other countries.

1216 Cooper, J. C. and **Jessop, A. T.** *Planning Multi-Drop Deliveries.* Transport Studies Group Discussion Paper No.12. London: Polytechnic of Central London, 1983. 79 pp.

1217 Cooper, James. Lessons for Europe from Freight Deregulation in Australia, the United Kingdom and the United States of America. London: *Transport Reviews*, Vol. 11(1), January–March 1991, 85–104.

Compares the experiences of three countries which have undertaken economic deregulation of their freight sectors. Examines how freight sectors in Europe may be affected by current moves towards deregulation.

1218 Corcoran, P. J. and **Margason, G.** *Operational Evaluation of the*

Effects of Heavy Freight Vehicles. TRRL Supplementary Report 417. Crowthorne: Transport and Road Research Laboratory, 1978. 22 pp.

1219 Corcoran, P. J., Glover, M. H. and **Shane, B. A.** *Higher Gross Weight Goods Vehicles: operating costs and road damage factors.* Crowthorne: Transport and Road Research Laboratory, 1980. 65 pp.

Operational effects of permitting approved types of lorry to operate at more than 32 tons gross weight, the UK maximum. Looks at total operating costs, average vehicle length, axle weights, and road damage.

1220 Cundill, M. A. *A Comparative Analysis of Goods Vehicle Survey Data.* TRRL Supplementary Report 465. Crowthorne: Transport and Road Research Laboratory, 1979. 11 pp.

Contains analyses of data on goods vehicles and their activities in urban areas collected in recent surveys. Includes national goods vehicle statistics and an assessment of three urban areas: Swindon, Hull and London.

1221 Cundill, M. A. and **Shane, B. A.** *Trends in Road Goods Transport 1962–1977.* TRRL Supplementary Report 572. Crowthorne: Transport and Road Research Laboratory, 1980. 27 pp.

Considers vehicle stock, new registrations, goods movement, length of haul, vehicle utilisation and vehicle operation costs.

1222 Department of the Environment: Department of Transport: Transport and Road Research Laboratory. *The Management of Urban Freight Movements: the proceedings of a Seminar held at the Transport and Road Research Laboratory, Crowthorne, 20 and 21 May 1976.* TRRL Supplementary Report 309. Crowthorne: Transport and Road Research Laboratory, 1977. 141 pp.

Purpose of seminar to bring together wide cross section of those concerned with movement of goods vehicles in urban areas. The three main sessions were concerned with small town studies, whole town studies, and conurbation studies.

1223 Department of Transport. *Road Haulage Operators' Licensing: Report of the Independent Committee of Inquiry.* London: HMSO, 1979. 161 pp.

Examines the effectiveness of the Operators' Licensing system of road freight transport introduced by the Transport Act 1968.

1224 Economic Research Centre: European Conference of Ministers of Transport. *Report of the Twenty-Third Round Table on Transport Economics: Optimum Structure and Size of Road Haulage Firms:*

Positive and Negative Effects of Specialization. London: HMSO, 1974. 45 pp.

Round Table on Transport Economics held on 8/9 November, 1973, in Paris.

1225 *No Entry.*

1226 Greater London Council: SCPR: Transmark. *Goods Vehicle Survey Technical Manual: GLTS Vol. VI.* London: Greater London Council, 1976. 139 pp.

Survey of goods vehicles in London conducted with the aim of ascertaining why certain journeys were made, what types of goods were transported in what kind of vehicles and to which destinations.

1227 Greater London Council. *Heavy Lorries in London: report of the independent panel of inquiry into the effects of bans on heavy lorries in London: Volume 1.* London: Greater London Council, 1983. 125 pp.

Gives the conclusions of the inquiry into the effects of banning heavy lorries within the Greater London area. The possibility of a transfer from road to rail or water as means of freight transport is considered. The environmental impact of heavy lorries is examined.

1228 Greater London Council. *Heavy Lorries in London: report of the independent panel of inquiry into the effects of bans on heavy lorries in London: Volume 2.* London: Greater London Council, 1983. 80 pp.

Contains the annexes to the main report. Maps are included of the areas affected. Examples are provided from other European cities.

1229 Hart, Andrew. 1993 Community Transit: good or bad? *VAT Plan.* Vol. 19(7), 1993.

Documents the customs requirements for non-EC goods in transit.

1230 Highsted, Janice. *A Survey of Britain's Freight Forwarding Industry, with Special Reference to Leicestershire and Nottinghamshire: Public Sector Economic Research Centre (PSERC) Working Paper No. N2/80.* Leicester: Public Sector Economics Research Centre, 1980. 119 pp.

1231 Hughes, George A. *Company Freight Management: introduction to cost-effective transport.* Aldershot: Gower, 1969. 196 pp.

Deals with the requirements and pitfalls of accurate costing; financial investment in transport; meeting the actual transport needs of companies and the effect of the Transport Act 1968.

1232 Johnson, Johnny. *A Transport Manager's Guide to International Freighting.* London: Kogan Page, 1980. 118 pp.

Guide to the international movement of goods by road. Information on traffic for overseas destinations, regulations, documentation, port facilities, plus other countries' operating requirements.

1233 Koshal, Rajindar K. Economies of Scale: The Cost of Trucking: Econometric Analysis. London: *Journal of Transport Economics and Policy*, Vol. 6(2), May 1972, 147–151.

Claims that the Indian trucking industry enjoys economies of scale for distances below 1,000 kilometres.

1234 Lowe, D. The Problems of Over-Capacity in Delivery Vehicle Fleets. London: *Transport*, Vol. 1, March/April 1980, 23–25.

Claims that many firms involved in urban distribution continue to operate their own fleets despite the obvious disadvantages of high capital investment; the burden of legal responsibility; excessive cost through under utilisation; and the resultant increased traffic congestion in city centres.

1235 Lowe, David. *Quality Management in Road Transport.* Surrey: Fairplay Publications, 1992. 54 pp.

Guide for road hauliers and fleet operators who need to achieve certified quality assurance for their operations under the British Standard BS 5750, equivalent European (EN 2900) or International (ISO 9000) standards or accreditation by other standards bodies.

1236 Maejima, Tadafumi. An Application of Continuous Spatial Models to Freight Movements in Greater London. Amsterdam: *Transportation*, Vol. 8, 1979, 51–63.

Describes an application of continuous spatial models to freight movements in Greater London. Continuous spatial models are fitted to data on the densities of generation and attraction of the freight assuming that the density is dependent on the distance from the centre of the area.

1237 Ogden, K. W. *Urban Goods Movement: a guide to policy and planning.* Aldershot: Avebury, 1992.

1238 Polytechnic of Central London Transport Studies Group. *Carrying for Others: the role of the Own-Account Operator.* Transport Studies Group Discussion Paper No. 7. London: Polytechnic of Central London, 1978. 63 pp.

Report into the extent and circumstances in which own account operators carry other people's goods for hire-and-reward.

1239 Price Commission. *The Road Haulage Industry.* London: HMSO, 1978. 121 pp.

Looks at market size and structure, competition, pricing, management and efficiency, industrial relations and financial performance.

1240 Roudier, J. *Freight Collection and Delivery in Urban Areas: Report of the Thirty-first Round Table on Transport Economics: held in Paris on 20th and 21st November 1975.* Paris: Organisation for Economic Co-operation and Development, 1976. 87 pp.

Looks at volume and cost of freight traffic in towns, and at the possible ways of improving the urban freight transport system.

1241 Rushton, A. S. *Increased Goods Consolidation.* Bedford: The National Materials Handling Centre, 1978. 115 pp.

Investigates the extent of the consolidation of goods deliveries to the high street so as to indicate the trends that affect consolidation.

1242 Sharp, Clifford. The Optimum Allocation of Freight Traffic. London: *Journal of Transport Economics and Policy*, Vol. 5(3), September 1971, 344–356.

Methods are suggested for comparing cost and quality of service between outside hauliers (road or rail) and own transport.

1243 Sharp, Clifford. *Living with the Lorry: a study of the goods vehicle in the environment.* Leicester: University of Leicester, 1974. 194 pp.

Study sponsored by the Freight Transport Association and the Road Haulage Association. Looks at the unpleasant by-products of vehicle activities, i.e. noise, pollution, damage, the economic necessity of their existence, and the area of compromise.

1244 Slavin, H. L. *The Transport of Goods and Urban Spatial Structure.* Cambridge: University of Cambridge (PhD Thesis), 1979.

1245 Watson, Peter L. *Urban Goods Movement: a disaggregate approach.* Lexington, MA: Lexington Books, 1975. 110 pp.

Examination of the goods movement generation characteristics of manufacturing establishments, including the development of a proto-typical, second-generation model which estimates freight-orientated flows resulting from the activities of such establishments.

1246 Wilson, George. *Economic Analysis of Intercity Freight Transportation.* Bloomington, IN: Indiana University Press, 1980.

Analysis of the structure and problems of inter-city freight transportation including a look at the nature of demand and costs, pricing and regulation, and cost-benefit analysis.

1247 Worsford, F. J. *HGV's and Operator's Licences: the Surrey experience of controlling the impact of HGV's on the environment.* London: Transport Studies Group, University of Westminster, 1993, 43 pp.

Results of a study to investigate the effectiveness of legislation aimed at controlling the impact of HGVs on the local environment. Road traffic law requires all users of commercial heavy goods vehicles to hold an Operators licence ('O' licence). Since 1984 local authorities and residents have the right to object on environmental grounds to the granting of such licences. Surrey's experience shows that the legislation can be used effectively for the benefit of residents.

1248 Worsford, Frank. Road Transport and the Environment. *Environmental Information Bulletin*, No. 20, 1993, 12–16.

Details the response of the road freight industry to pressures to reduce environmental impact of HGVs.

1249 Worsford, Frank. Heavier Trucks: the 40–44 tonne truck debate. Chichester: *Road Law*, Vol. 11(4), 1995, 216–221.

Investment, infrastructure and subsidy

1250 Ahmed, Yusuf; O'Sullivan, Patrick and **Wilson, Derek.** *Road Investment Programming for Developing Countries: an Indonesian example.* Evanston, IL: Northwestern University, 1976.

Attempts to develop a practical model for investment planning which may be applied to transport problems in developing countries at the regional level. Approach based on region-wide optimisation of road transport by means of mathematical programming.

1251 Ashworth, Stephen. Developer's Contributions. *Parliamentary Reports*, Vol. 4(7), 1994, 239–240.

1252 Brademayer, B. F., El-Hawary, M., Markow, M. J., Moavenzadeh, F. and **Owais, M.** *Road Network Analysis for Transportation Investment in Egypt.* Washington DC: National Academy of Sciences, 1979.

An application of the Massachusetts Institute of Technology road investment analysis model for planning highway investments in Egypt.

1253 Butler, Eamonn (ed.). *Roads and the Private Sector.* London: Adam Smith Institute, 1982. 101 pp.

Arguments from various contributors to introduce private capital investment, as opposed to taxpayers investment, into road construction.

1254 Docwra, G. E. and **Kolsen, H. M.** Road Expenditure Policy in Australia. London: *Journal of Transport Economics and Policy*, Vol. 5(3), September 1971, 267–294.

1255 Hughes, Peter. Repossessing the High Street: Whitchurch builds on bypass opportunities. London: *Local Transport Today*, April 1992, 12–13.

Whitchurch is one of the six towns selected to take part in the Government's bypass demonstration project which will utilise town centre traffic calming to complement new bypasses. The aim is to find ways of sustaining the initial benefit brought to areas relieved of through traffic. Examines the measures planned for Whitchurch which provide an insight into the lessons which might be applied to other towns.

1256 Huntley, Peter. Which Route for Glasgow? public transport schemes fight roads for budget share. London: *Local Transport Today*, May, 1990, 10–11.

1257 Jones, David W. and **Altshuler, Alan** (ed.). *Urban Highway Investment and the Political Economy of Fiscal Entrenchment.* Lexington, MA: Lexington Books, 1980.

Builds a historical argument for the proposition that retrenchment is more likely to be a secular than a cyclic phenomenon.

1258 Michael, H. L. Impact of Intersection Controls in Urban Areas. London: George Godwin, *International Forum Series*, Vol. 2, 1981, 155–164.

Argues that greater emphasis needs to be given to the development and maintenance of optimal traffic flow at all urban intersections and not just those with the highest traffic volumes. Concludes that the potential represented by major investment made in road systems cannot be effectively realised without making use of the best traffic management available.

1259 Miyao, Takahiro. The Golden Rule of Urban Transportation Investment. London: *Journal of Urban Economics*, Vol. 4(4), October 1977, 448–458.

Aims to find an optimal taxation rule for transportion investment in an ever growing urban economy.

1260 Mullen, J. K. and **Williams, M.** The Contribution of Highway

Infrastructure to States' Economies. Rome: *International Journal of Transport Economics*, Vol. 19(2), June 1992, 149–163.

1261 Nilsson, Jan-Eric. Private Funding of Public Investments: a case of a voluntarily funded public road. London: *Journal of Transport Economics and Policy*, Vol. 24(2), May 1990, 157–170.

A projected road interchange at Bredden did not show a rate of return high enough for inclusion in the programme of the Swedish National Road Administration. After negotiations it was jointly funded by the Administration and local firms. Examines the conditions under which voluntary funding may be accepted and the various policies available to facilitate it.

1262 Sherman, Roger. Subsidies to Relieve Urban Traffic Congestion. London: *Journal of Transport Economics and Policy*, Vol. 6(1), January 1972, 22–31.

Subsidies to public transport may to some extent offset the failure to levy congestion charges on cars. Sets out the relevant criteria and concludes that bus subsidies would be appropriate in London, and probably in large US cities too.

1263 Sherrard, M. S. *The Long Term Economic Returns from Road Improvement Schemes.* Newcastle Upon Tyne: University of Newcastle Upon Tyne (MSc Thesis), 1972.

1264 Street, Andrew. *Local Authority Roads and Their Financing: a new approach.* London: British Road Federation, 1983. 15 pp.

1265 Transport 2000. *What are Roads Worth? Fair assessment for transport expenditure.* London: Transport 2000, 1991. 32 pp.

Proceedings of a conference held in April 1991.

Law

1266 Arnold-Baker, Charles. Some Environmental Provisions in the Transport Legislation: a critique. Chichester: *Road Law*, Vol. 10(7), 1994, 438–444.

1267 Butterworth's. *Road Traffic Service.* 2 vols. London: Butterworth, 1991.

Handbook of road traffic law.

1268 Butterworth's. *Mahaffy and Dodson on Road Traffic.* 3rd ed. London: Butterworth, 1989. 290 pp.

Contains the Road Traffic Act 1988, the Road Traffic Offenders Act 1988 and the Road Traffic (Consequential Provisions) Act 1988.

1269 Cooper, Simon. *Blackstone's Guide to the Road Traffic Act 1991.* London: Blackstone Press, 1991. 182 pp.

1270 Dix, M. C. and **Layzell, A. D.** *Road Users and the Police.* London: Croom Helm, 1983. 152 pp.

Explores why many drivers break the law, and how and when individual officers decide to intervene. Provides an examination of actual confrontations between motorists and the police.

1271 Halnan, Patrick and **Spencer, John.** *Wilkinson's Road Traffic Offences.* 10th ed. London: Oyez Publishing, 1980. 1093 pp.

1272 Jewell, Michael G. The 4 1/2 Hour Driving Rule in the European Court. Chichester: *Road Law*, Vol. 10(2), 1994, 72–77.

1273 Jones, Trevor and **Newburn, Tim.** The Future of Traffic Policing. London: *Policing*, Vol. 11(2), 1995, 131–142.

Examines the impact on traffic policing of extension of the government's privatisation programme.

1274 Kirk, Philip. Traffic Law for the Nineties: is the Government in time with the pace of change? London: *Local Transport Today*, May, 1989, 10–11.

The Government will be tabling plans to revise road traffic law in response to the North Committee report. Article examines what 'The Road User and the Law' will mean for those responsible for the management and policing of the highway.

1275 Marsh, Malcolm (ed.). *Butterworth's Road Traffic Handbook.* 2nd ed. London: Butterworth, 1993. 2029 pp.

1276 McMahon, Richard. *A Practical Approach to Road Traffic Law.* London: Blackstone Press, 1994. 313 pp.

1277 O'Hara, Robert A. *Guide to Highway Law for Architects, Engineers, Surveyors and Contractors.* London: E. & F.N. Spon, 1991. 141 pp.

1278 Singleton, E. Susan. The Citizen's Charter and Road Transport. Chichester: *Road Law*, Vol. 10(3), 1994, 152–154.

Pricing

1279 Abbie, Les and **Nevin, Michael.** What Price Roads? Oxford: *Transport Policy*, Vol. 1(1), October 1993, 68–73.

Summarises the results of a survey of eleven historic British cities undertaken by Touche Ross in 1992 to identify the central issues in the introduction of road pricing to complement traditional traffic management methods.

1280 Abbott, James. Key Role for Public Transport Funding Boost in Stockholm's Road Pricing Plans. London: *Urban Transport International*, November/December, 1990, 32–34.

Examines the introduction of road pricing in Sweden. Details how it has been planned and how the new system will operate.

1281 Abe, M. A. The Peak Load Pricing Problem in Urban Transportation. *Economic Studies Quarterly*, Vol. 24(3), December 1973, 54–62.

Claims that in no major area are pricing practices so irrational, so out of date, and so conducive to waste as in urban transportation, relative to others. The solution proposed is to accomplish Pareto-optimality by setting up proper price levels and redistributing income. Article extends three papers by Mohring, Marchand and Sherman.

1282 Armstrong-Wright, A. T. Road Pricing and User Restraint: opportunities and constraints in developing countries. Oxford: *Transportation Research*, Vol. 20A(2), March 1986, 123–127.

Examines the specific problems of developing countries in relation to urban traffic congestion. Looks at the attempts to introduce road pricing policies. Concludes that, although road pricing is technically feasible, its use is limited by political factors. Consequently second best policies that gradually introduce restraint are most favoured for many countries.

1283 Beesley, Michael E. and **Hensher, David A.** Private Toll Roads in Urban Areas. Amsterdam: *Transportation*, Vol. 16(4), 1990, 329–341.

Considers some economic and financial problems in the private sector provision of major road infrastructure within urban areas.

1284 Berglas, Eitan; Fresko, David and **Pines, David.** Right of Way and Congestion Toll. London: *Journal of Transport Economics and Policy*, Vol. 18(2), May 1984, 165–188.

Argues that under certain conditions buses, instead of being subsidised, should pay congestion tolls even when cars do not.

1285 Blair, B. *Road Charging in the '90s: an overview and guide to the literature.* London: British Library Board, September 1994. 88 pp.

1286 Catling, I. and **Dawson, J. A. L.** Electronic Road Pricing in Hong Kong. Oxford: *Transportation Research*, Vol. 20A(2), March 1987, 129–134.

Describes the pilot stage of the electronic road pricing project undertaken in Hong Kong between 1983 and 1985. Background and the technology of the project are discussed.

1287 Deakin, Elizabeth. Toll Roads: a new direction for US highways? Oxford: *Built Environment*, Vol. 15(4), Numbers 3/4 1989, 185–194.

Examines the emergence of privately funded toll roads in fast-developing suburban areas in the US. Poses the question of whether toll roads will only be built in locations of high demand and not in areas of the greatest need.

1288 Decorla-Souza, Patrick and **Kane, Anthony R.** Peak Period Tolls: precepts and prospects. Dordrecht: *Transportation*, Vol. 19(4), 1992, 293–311.

Presents the economic rationale for road pricing. Discusses the impacts of such tolls on congestion, air quality and economic development. Offers a long term strategy towards areawide implementation of peak period pricing.

1289 Department of Transport. *London Congestion Charging: charging technology.* London: Department of Transport, March 1993. 6 pp.

1290 Dorling, Nigel; Heyes, Martin; Jarvis, Richard and **Walpole, Brian.** Transport Management for London. London: *Journal of Transport Economics and Policy*, Vol. 8(2), May 1974, 152–160.

Claims that the price mechanism has been neglected in transport planning and that user costs should be adjusted by road pricing to arrest the decline in public transport.

1291 Elliot, Ward. Fumbling Toward the Edge of History: California's quest for a road-pricing experiment. Oxford: *Transportation Research*, Vol. 20(2), 1986, 151–156.

Examines the various efforts which have been made in California to introduce measures of fiscal restraint on car use since the early 1970s.

1292 Elliott, Ward. Peak-Hour Road Charges for Southern California: has their hour come around? Westport, CT: *Transportation Quarterly*, Vol. 46(4), 1992, 517–528.

Argues that the primary objections to congestion pricing may be evaporating in Southern California, and that experimental programmes should be implemented.

1293 Else, P. K. A Reformulation of the Theory of Optimum Congestion Taxes. London: *Journal of Transport Economics and Policy*, Vol. 15(3), September 1981, 217–232.

Suggests that the conventional approach to the theory of optimal congestion taxes might be reformulated.

1294 Else, Peter K. No Entry for Congestion Taxes. Oxford: *Transportation Research*, Vol. 20(2), 1986, 99–107.

Reviews some of the recent thinking on the theory of congestion taxes and considers some of the reasons why little practical interest has been shown in them despite the existence of an extensive academic literature.

1295 European Conference of Ministers of Transport. *Systems of Road Infrastructure Cost Average.* Report of the eightieth round table on transport economics. Paris: Organisation for Economic Co-operation and Development, 1989. 185 pp.

Proceedings of a seminar held in Paris in 1989 which focused on road pricing and similar methods in the form of tolls. Compares approaches adopted in a number of countries. Includes reports from Belgium, Denmark, France and Switzerland. Also includes a summary of the round table debate.

1296 European Conference of Ministers of Transport. *Charging for the Use of Urban Roads.* Report of the ninety-seventh round table on transport economics. Paris: Organisation for Economic Co-operation and Development, 1994. 174 pp.

Proceedings of a seminar held in Paris in 1993 which focused on the issues surrounding road pricing. Includes reports from Norway, the Netherlands and the United Kingdom. Also includes a summary of the round table debate.

1297 Evans, Andrew W. Road Congestion Pricing: when is it a good policy? London: *Journal of Transport Economics and Policy*, Vol. 26(3), September 1992, 213–244.

Makes use of an economic model of a congested road network in a stationary state to investigate two objections to road congestion pricing: it may be inequitable for the road users affected, and it generates perverse incentives for governments.

1298 Flowerdew, A. *Urban Traffic Congestion in Europe: road pricing and public transport finance.* London: Economist Intelligence Unit, May 1993. 81 pp.

1299 Giulliano, Genevieve. An Assessment of the Political Acceptability of Congestion Pricing. Dordrecht: *Transportation*, Vol. 9(4), 1992, 335–358.

Reviews changes in the transportation policy environment that have led to a renewed interest in implementing congestion pricing in metropolitan areas throughout the United States.

1300 Gomez-Ibanez, Jose A. The Political Economy of Highway Tolls and Congestion Pricing. Westport, CT: *Transportation Quarterly*, Vol. 46(3), 1992, 343–360.

Discusses the conflict between transport economists and environmentalists who view tolls as a means to manage demand, and the public which sees them simply as a means to finance capacity.

1301 Goodwin, P. *Road Pricing or Transport Planning?* Oxford: Oxford University, Transport Studies Unit, 1993. 13 pp.

1302 Goodwin, P. *The Case For and Against Urban Road Pricing: evidence to the House of Commons Transport Committee.* Oxford: Oxford University, Transport Studies Unit, 1994. 19 pp.

1303 Harrop, P. J. Charging for Road Use: future legal and policing aspects. Chichester: *Road Law*, Vol. 10(2), 1994, 85–97.

Discusses methods of charging for roads and the problems of enforcement bearing in mind the implications for civil liberties.

1304 Harrop, Peter. *Charging for Road Use Worldwide: an appraisal of road pricing, tolls and parking.* London: Financial Times Business Enterprises, 1993. 182 pp.

1305 Hau, Timothy D. Road Pricing in Hong Kong: a viable proposal. Oxford: *Built Environment*, Vol. 15(4), Numbers 3/4, 1989, 195–214.

Examines the political opposition to the implementation of suggested draconian measures to reduce the use of cars and lorries in Hong Kong. These measures include increased ownership taxes, increased fuel taxes, goods vehicle controls and electronic road pricing.

1306 Hensher, David A. Urban Tolled Roads and the Value of Travel Time Savings. Sydney: *Economic Record*, Vol. 66(193), June 1990, 146–156.

1307 Higgins, Thomas J. Road-Pricing Attempts in the United States. Oxford: *Transportation Research*, Vol. 20A(2), March 1987, 145–150.

Considers the attempts that have been made to introduce road pricing in the United States. Examines the reasons why such attempts have failed to progress beyond the discussion stage, and looks in particular at the political and institutional problems of implementation.

1308 Johansen, Frida. Toll Road Characteristics and Toll Road Experience in Selected South East Asia Countries. Oxford: *Transportation Research*, Vol. 23(6), 1989, 463–466.

Reviews toll road experiences in Indonesia, Malaysia, and Thailand.

1309 Kirkpatrick, C. H. *The Economics of Road User Charges in Less Developed Countries, with Special Reference to Kenya.* Loughborough: University of Loughborough (MSc Thesis), 1977.

1310 Lewis, Nigel C. *Road Pricing: theory and practice.* London: Thomas Telford, 1993. 122 pp.

Describes the theory of congestion charging using advanced electronic systems. The general principles and potential benefits are examined and a framework for good practice established.

1311 May, A. D. Traffic Restraint: a review of the alternatives. Oxford: *Transportation Research*, Vol. 20A(2), March 1986, 109–121.

Uses international examples to assess the role that road pricing plays as a means of urban traffic restraint. Identifies the major problems in the implementation of restraint policies.

1312 May, A. D. Road Pricing: an international perspective. Dordrecht: *Transportation*, Vol. 19(4), 1992, 313–333.

Reviews experience with road pricing in Europe and Asia. Considers the objectives of road pricing, and demonstrates that differences in objectives lead to differences in scheme design and performance.

1313 Mogridge, M. J. H. Road Pricing: the right solution for the right problem? Oxford: *Transportation Research*, Vol. 20A(2), March 1987, 157–167.

Aims to disprove that the theory of road pricing which asserts that the optimal speed of a road network is that where vehicles pay the marginal social cost of their journey.

1314 Morrison, Steven A. A Survey of Road Pricing. Oxford: *Transportation Research*, Vol. 20(2), 1986, 89–97.

Focuses on the wide-ranging literature on road pricing, drawing on not only the standard economic sources but also material from the engineering and planning literature. Theoretical issues are considered in the context of both empirical evidence of the practical viability of road pricing and the political-legal environment in which it must gain acceptance.

1315 MVA Consultancy. *The London Congestion Charging Research Programme: principal findings.* London: Government Office for London, 1995. 61 pp.

1316 Orins, Sandford F. Electronic Road Pricing: an idea whose time may never come. Oxford: *Transportation Research*, Vol. 22A(1), January 1988, 37–44.

Looks at Hong Kong's experiment with electronic road pricing. The government was unable to implement the scheme due to strong opposition from a public that perceived it as an invasion of privacy and a tax increase.

1317 Orski, C. Kenneth. Congestion Pricing: promise and limitations. Westport, CT: *Transportation Quarterly*, Vol. 46(2), April 1992, 157–167.

Introduction of area-wide congestion pricing schemes face political barriers to implementation. Considers pilot projects, such as the gradual introduction of peak period pricing in the context of new toll roads. Argues that once the idea of differential pricing has been tested and accepted, the way may be opened for wider schemes, involving the pricing of existing infrastructure use.

1318 Pease, Jack. Can Oldridge Take Cambridge to a 'First' in Restraint? London: *Local Transport Today*, October, 1990, 10–11.

While other cities have toyed with the idea of road pricing, firm plans are being laid in Cambridge for the implementation of a sophisticated 'congestion metering' scheme. The concept is the brainchild of surveyor Brian Oldridge who is interviewed for this report.

1319 Poole, Robert W. Introducing Congestion Pricing on a New Toll Road. Dordrecht: *Transportation*, Vol. 19(4), 1992, 383–396.

Proposes a demonstration project to test the effectiveness of 'congestion pricing' in an urban area. Reviews the general theoretical case for such pricing and summarises recent international interest in congestion pricing.

1320 Pretty, Robert L. Road Pricing: a solution for Hong Kong? Oxford: *Transportation Research*, Vol. 22A(5), September 1988, 319–327.

Examines the 1983 Government of the Territory of Hong Kong's decision to propose a system of charging mortorists directly for the use of congested roads. Despite the scheme's technical proficiency and ability to earn revenue well in excess of operating costs, there was doubt about equity and efficiency.

1321 PTRC. *Practical Possibilities for a Comprehensive Transport*

Policy With and Without Road Pricing. London: PTRC Education and Research Services, 1991. 52 pp.

Proceedings of a conference held in December 1990.

1322 Richardson, Harry W. A Note on the Distributional Effects of Road Pricing. London: *Journal of Transport Economics and Policy*, Vol. 8(1), January 1974, 82–85.

Road pricing is found to be regressive or ambiguous in its effects: the large group of lower-income motorists suffers, while gains or smaller losses accrue to wealthy motorists as well as to non-motorists.

1323 Royal Automobile Club. *Paying for Roads: a radical review.* London: Royal Automobile Club, May 1993. 23 pp.

1324 Seymer, Nigel. Demand Management: can the carrot beat the stick? London: *Local Transport Today*, December, 1989, 8–9.

Despite major problems of coping with the growth of car traffic in US big city areas, there is little thought of using road pricing as the solution. Article considers a three-pronged approach to encourage the use of public transport, promote ride-sharing and get the best out of available highway capacity.

1325 Small, Kenneth A. Using the Revenues from Congestion Pricing. Dordrecht: *Transportation*, Vol. 19(4), 1992, 359–381.

Examines the economic theory which states that the revenues from congestion pricing will be used to compensate highway users. Asks whether practical methods of using revenues come close to achieving this compensation, while still having appeal to important political groups.

1326 Sugimoto, Yuzo and **Poole, Robert W.** Congestion Relief Toll Tunnels. Dordrecht: *Transportation*, Vol. 22(4), 1995, 327–351.

Examines the development of a new type of transportation facility: that of congestion-relief toll tunnels in downtown areas.

1327 Takeuchi, K. *Urban Transport Pricing and the Internalization of External Cost.* Oxford: Oxford University (M.Litt Thesis), 1989.

The effect of road pricing is discussed in the context of whether subsidies should be given to public transport.

1328 Tite, Christopher. Road Charging. *Transport Law and Practice*, Vol. 1(7), 1994, 61–62.

Examines government proposals for the introduction of motorway tolls by electronic direct charging.

1329 Williams, Alan W. Should the User Pay? Dordrecht: *Transportation*, Vol. 22(2), 1995, 115–134.

Argues the case that historical analysis helps to understand current discussions on user-pays principles and practice. Demonstrates that the nature of funding systems is dominated by political considerations, and that user-pays systems lead to inadequate funding of infrastructure when politically controlled, but provide funds for expansion when 'market-driven'. Refers to the experience of interregional transport infrastructure in 19th-century England and 20th-century Australia.

Safety

1330 Adams, John. *Risk*. London: UCL Press, 1995. 228 pp.

Discusses the subject of risk and presents a synthesis of the concepts 'risk compensation' and 'cultural theory'. Within this context two chapters are included on road safety; one of which confines itself to seat belts and one of which considers other issues, such as safer vehicles and roads, bicycle and motorcycle helmets, and the abuse of alcohol.

1331 Andreassend, David C. Traffic Accidents in Melbourne, Taipei and Kuala Lumpur. London: George Godwin, *International Forum Series*, Vol. 2, 1981, 175–186.

To make adequate provision in planning for new towns or redeveloping old towns requires an understanding of the failings of the present street patterns in the town or country concerned. Analysis of traffic accidents by simple techniques can lead to a clearer understanding of system failure. A comparison is made of three cities in different countries, (Melbourne, Taipei and Kuala Lumpur). Paper illustrates the use of techniques in providing clear definitions of the problems in particular areas.

1332 Antwerp, Frederick van and **Miller, James H.** Control of Traffic in Residential Neighborhoods: some considerations for implementation. Amsterdam: *Transportation*, Vol. 10, 1981, 35–49.

The effect of motor vehicles upon older neighborhoods has received attention as residents of these areas seek to preserve the established quality of life. In order to reduce traffic flow in such neighborhoods, numerous techniques have been developed ranging from turn-prohibitions to physical barriers. Article reviews the major areas of conflict as revealed through court challenges.

1333 Armsby, P. *Road Accident Risk: an investigation into various assessment methodologies*. London: Middlesex Polytechnic (M.Phil Thesis), 1986.

Several techniques for assessing drivers' perceptions of hazards are investigated.

1334 Bolade, 'Tunji and Ogunsanya, A. Ade (eds). *Accident Control and Safety Measures in Mass Transit Operations in Nigeria*. Ibadan: Ibadan University Press, 1991. 291 pp.

Collection of papers which address the disturbing rate of road accidents in Nigeria. Divided into three parts it looks at general and conceptual issues, empirical issues, and policy and planning issues. Emphasises the need for corrective safety measures with specific reference to the Urban Mass Transportation System.

1335 Brindle, R. E. Local Street Management: observations on implementation problems. London: George Godwin, *International Forum Series*, Vol. 2, 1981, 187–196.

In Australia, as in many other parts of the world, concerns are expressed about the effects of inappropriate traffic within residential areas. However, there are widely divergent attitudes within the community to proposed measures. Article outlines three cases in Melbourne to demonstrate the difference that existing context, the motivation for change, and the nature of prior planning can make to the outcome.

1336 Bruhning, Ekkehard. Traffic Safety in Eastern and Western Europe at the beginning of the nineties. London: *Transport Reviews*, Vol. 13(3), July–September 1993, 265–276.

Evaluates the considerable differences which exist between European OECD countries in the area of traffic safety.

1337 Crilly, M. A. *Traffic Accident Fatalities in Liverpool*. Liverpool: University of Liverpool (MA Thesis), 1993.

Reports that traffic accident fatalities in Liverpool are predominantly male pedestrians. Most are killed close to their homes on major roads with a speed limit of 30 mph. Elderly people have the highest death rate from traffic accidents. Drivers involved with pedestrian fatalities are almost exclusively male and are significantly younger that the people they hit. Notes that alcohol had been consumed by a large proportion of those killed.

1338 Davis, Robert. *Death on the Streets: Cars and the mythology of road safety*. Hawes: Leading Edge Press, 1992. 302 pp.

Puts forward a strong argument against the car as a dangerous and destructive device. Divided into four parts, the first questions the official source of statistics claiming road safety trends as favourable. The second deals with education and training, enforcement and doctors. Part three looks at case studies on pedestrians, drink driving and traffic segregation. Part four looks at the costs of car use and suggests some proposals for improvement.

1339 Evans, Leonard. *Traffic Safety and the Driver*. New York: Van Nostrand Reinhold, 1991. 405 pp.

Concerned with the deaths, injuries and property damage from traffic crashes – their origin and nature, and ways to prevent their occurrence and reduce their severity.

1340 Ferry, Ted S. *Modern Accident Investigation and Analysis.* 2nd ed. New York: John Wiley and Sons, 1988. 306 pp.

General textbook covering the techniques needed to investigate accidents or review the work of those who do.

1341 Garbacz, Christopher. Traffic Fatalities in Taiwan. London: *Journal of Transport Economics and Policy*, Vol. 23(3), September 1989, 317–328.

Claims that fatalities increase with higher income and with the use of trucks and, especially, motorcycles. They are reduced by higher prices of petrol, higher costs of accidents and a more agricultural economy. Discusses the pros and cons of compelling motorcyclists to wear helmets.

1342 Garber, Nicholas J. and **Woo, Tzong-Shiou Hugh.** Effectiveness of Traffic Control Devices in Reducing Accident Rates in Urban Work Zones. Westport, CT: *Transportation Quarterly*, Vol. 45(2), 1991, 259–270.

1343 Gilad, Benjamin and **Loeb, Peter D.** The Efficacy and Cost-Effectiveness of Motor Vehicle Inspection: a state specific analysis using Time Series Data. London: *Journal of Transport Economics and Policy*, Vol. 18(2), May 1984, 145–164.

Reports that motor vehicle inspection in the State of New Jersey has significantly reduced the numbers of road accidents and deaths.

1344 Godwin, Stephen R. and **Kulash, Damian J.** The 55 mph Speed Limit on US Roads: issues involved. London: *Transport Reviews*, Vol. 8(3), July–September 1988, 219–235.

Reports that state and Federal experience with the national 55 mph (88 km/h) speed limit in the United States has shown it to be a major life-saving policy. Even though the effectiveness of this policy has diminished in recent years as highway speeds have decreased and other safety policies have made driving safer, 2000–4000 lives are nevertheless saved each year due to slower and more uniform highway speeds.

1345 Goldberg, Jeffrey and **Paz, Luis.** Locating Emergency Vehicle Bases When Service Time Depends on Call Location. Baltimore, MD: *Transportation Science*, Vol. 25(4), November 1991, 264–280.

Examines the problem of locating emergency vehicles in an urban area.

1346 Greater London Road Safety Unit. *Road Safety Studies.* London: Greater London Council, 1980. 39 pp.

Comprises a collection of papers on various aspects of road safety. Includes a section on pelican crossings and traffic signals. Also looks at junction safety experiments, a Greater London 'Ride Bright' campaign and its effect on the motorcyclist, the effects of mandatory school entrance markings, street lighting improvements; and the use of statistical tests in the analysis of accident and other associated data.

1347 Hakamies-Blomqvist, Lisa. *Older Drivers in Finland: traffic safety and behaviour.* Helsinki: Liikenneturva, 1994. 112 pp.

Presents a description of the accidents of older drivers (aged 65+) in Finland from the years 1984–1990.

1348 Hanna, Judith. Road Safety: getting speed, attitude and engineering changes to work together. London: *Local Transport Today,* November 1992, 12–13.

Seeks to ascertain whether public attitudes towards road safety, and the accessibility of exceeding speed limits, are beginning to change.

1349 Hillman, Mayer and **Plowden, Stephen.** *Danger on the Road: the needless scourge.* London: Policy Studies Institute, 1984. 239 pp.

Study of obstacles to the progress in the improvement of road safety.

1350 Hodgkinson, M. D. *The Relationship Between Road Accidents and Urban Structure.* Salford: University of Salford (PhD Thesis), 1973.

1351 Hughes, Peter. Traffic Cameras: early successes point the way to new applications. London: *Local Transport Today,* October 1993, 12–13.

New figures demonstrate that traffic cameras have brought about impressive reductions in speeding and red light running. It appears that the value of roadside cameras in curbing dangerous driving is now established beyond doubt. Article asks whether the police have the necessary resources to harness the full range of potential applications for camera technology.

1352 Irwin, G. A. *Risk and the Control of Technology: a comparative policy analysis of road traffic safety.* Manchester: University of Manchester (PhD Thesis), 1980.

1353 Jackson, R. Some Aspects of Transport-Related Accidents to Children in the UK. London: *Transport Reviews,* Vol. 9(3), July–September 1989, 267–278.

Considers transport-related accidents to children within the context of child development and within the overall framework of the interaction between the child, the agent causing the injury, and the environment.

1354 Jacobs, G. D. *Road Accidents in Developing Countries.* Guildford: Surrey University (PhD Thesis), 1976.

1355 Jadaan, Khair S. Traffic Safety in Gulf Countries with special reference to Kuwait. London: *Transport Reviews*, Vol. 8(3), July–September 1988, 249–265.
Review of the problem of road accidents in Gulf countries with special reference to Kuwait.

1356 Jamieson, A. S. *A Study of Road Accidents on Major Routes in Glasgow.* Glasgow: University of Strathclyde (MSc Thesis), 1979.

1357 Leisch, Jack E. Dynamics of Highway Design for Safety. Amsterdam: *Transportation*, Vol. 6, 1977, 71–83.
Examines proposals for improving highway safety including designing the geometric features of roadways in response to the characteristics and behaviour of drivers.

1358 Lewis, G. D. *A Study of Some Factors Influencing the Road Accident Rate for School Children for the Journeys to School During the Dark Hours.* Salford: University of Salford (MSc Thesis), 1971.

1359 Lightburn, A. D. C. *The Development of the Traffic Conflicts Technique: an approach to the study of road accidents.* Nottingham: University of Nottingham (PhD Thesis), 1984.

1360 Lockwood, C. R. and **Maycock, G.** The Accident Liability of British Car Drivers. London: *Transport Reviews*, Vol. 13(3), July–September 1993, 231–245.

1361 Lorenzen, Konrad. The Berlin U-Bahn Safety Plan. Brussels: *Public Transport International*, Vol. 42(2), July 1993, 59–60.
Examines the policies implemented in Berlin to find a solution to 'objective' safety problems, i.e. the actual position in terms of measured safety, and 'subjective' safety problems, i.e. how safe people feel.

1362 Machala, F. Reduced Speeds in Residential Areas. Brussels: *Public Transport International*, Vol. 43(2), March 1994, 47–48.

Examines the advantages and disadvantages of reduced speeds in urban areas from the operator's point of view.

1363 Mackay, Murray. Strategies for Safety. London: *Local Transport Today*, March 1990, 12–13.

As with the effects of transport on the environment, the human cost of injuries arising from road traffic accidents has been moving up the political agenda. Article discusses the main issues which need to be addressed in order to reduce the magnitude of the problem.

1364 Mackie, A. M. *Studies of the Influence of Propaganda and Advertising on Road Safety.* Salford: University of Salford (MSc Thesis), 1973.

1365 Mackie, A. and **Toothill, W.** *Transport Supplementary Grant for Safety Schemes: local authorities' schemes from 1992/93 allocations.* Crowthorne: Transport and Road Research Laboratory, 1995. 12 pp.

1366 Maclean, S., Rawcliffe, P. and **Roberts, J.** *Traffic Calmed Towns: an alternative to the East Grinstead by-pass proposals.* London: TEST, 1991. 18 pp.

1367 Marks, Harold. Traffic Protection for Residential Neighbourhoods. London: George Godwin, *International Forum Series*, Vol. 2, 1981, 233–242.

Study aims to determine the effectiveness of various traffic control devices and techniques in protecting residential neighbourhoods from extraneous through traffic. Summarises the experiences of numerous American cities in dealing with this problem.

1368 McGuigan, D. R. D. *The Relationship Between Accidents and Traffic at Road Junctions.* Glasgow: University of Strathclyde (MSc Thesis), 1980.

1369 McGuigan, D. R. D. *An Examination of Relationships Between Road Accidents and Traffic Flow.* Newcastle Upon Tyne: University of Newcastle Upon Tyne (PhD Thesis), 1988.

Suggests that the cost-effectiveness of road safety expenditure on low cost engineering remedial works could be improved through better identification of sites which offer the greatest potential for accident reduction.

1370 Miller, D. H. *The Collection and Use of Road and Traffic Information for Road Accident Investigation and Prevention.* Birmingham: Aston University (M.Phil Thesis), 1980.

1371 Omole, Wale. *Accidents on our Roads: causes and prevention.* Mokola: Akinola Books, 1985. 87 pp.

Examines the high numbers of road traffic accidents resulting in fatalities in Nigeria and suggests ways to prevent them.

1372 Organisation for Economic Co-operation and Development. *Traffic Safety in Residential Areas.* Paris: Organisation for Economic Co-operation and Development, 1979. 109 pp.

Report of the outcome of an OECD Road Research Group study in which experts from 14 countried collaborated to review the present situation regarding traffic safety in residential areas.

1373 Pease, Jack. Pressure Grows for New Moves to Curb Toll from Speeding. London: *Local Transport Today*, October 1991, 10–11.

1374 Peters, Melvyn J. Safely Trailing Behind: road safety and drawbar combinations. London: *Transport Reviews*, Vol. 11(4), October–December 1991, 325–346.

Changes in UK vehicle legislation have increased and will continue to increase the use of drawbar combinations, i.e. truck and trailer. Article reports serious misgivings about the overall effect of such a change on road safety.

1375 Polanis, Stanley F. Reducing Traffic Accidents Through Traffic Engineering. Westport, CT: *Transportation Quarterly*, Vol. 46(2), 1992, 235–242.

Examines results of a municipal safety improvement programme that makes the identification, treatment and evaluation of traffic accidents a regular part of the daily traffic engineering routine.

1376 Raffle, P. A. B. The Drinking Driver: a medical view. London: *Transport Reviews*, Vol. 9(4), October–December 1989, 315–345.

Accidents are the third main cause of death in Europe with 40 per cent of them due to road traffic accidents. Victims are mainly young male drivers/riders and elderly pedestrians. One-quarter of the deaths and 10 per cent of the injuries are associated with alcohol and the consumption of alcohol is generally increasing. Article considers the consequences of this.

1377 Retting, Richard A. Urban Traffic Crashes: New York City responds to the challenge. Westport, CT: *Transportation Quarterly*, Vol. 45(4), October 1991, 571–580.

Examines New York's innovative traffic safety programme that integrates activities in engineering, infrastructure maintenance, enforcement, education and research. Argues that the New York programme demonstrates the potential impact of local traffic safety efforts, and supports the view that motor vehicle collisions and injuries are preventable, not inevitable.

1378 Reynolds, R. E. *The Implications of the Economic Maximisation Paradigm for Road Safety Policies.* Cranfield: Cranfield Institute of Technology (PhD Thesis), 1985.

1379 Road Transport Research. *Marketing of Traffic Safety.* Paris: Organisation for Economic Co-operation and Development, 1993. 112 pp.

Highlights the substantial scope for innovative safety approaches through sociological analyses of road user groups; systematic communication processes; and back up marketing strategies.

1380 Road Transport Research. *Integrated Traffic Safety Management in Urban Areas.* Paris: Organisation for Economic Co-operation and Development, 1990. 120 pp.

Integrated traffic safety programmes are increasingly considered by urban authorities as an important element of public management. Report provides an up-to-date summary of current experience, highlighting the requirement for successful implementation.

1381 Ross, H. Laurence. *Confronting Drunk Driving: social policy for saving lives.* New Haven, CT: Yale University Press, 1992. 220 pp.

Examines the phenomenon of drink driving and the measures in law and policy for reducing its incidence.

1382 Rutherford, W. H. Compulsory Wearing of Seat Belts in the United Kingdom: the effect on patients and on fatalities. London: *Transport Reviews*, Vol. 7(3), July–September 1987, 245–257.

Study conducted in the years immediately before and after the introduction of seat belts. Confirms that a large number of improvements had occurred including a reduction in total number of patients; number of bed days; multiplicity of injuries; injuries to the brain and chest; and many facial injuries.

1383 Sani, B. M. *Gap Acceptance at Road Junctions in an Urban Area.* Dundee: University of Dundee (M. Sc. Thesis), 1977.

1384 Satterthwaite, S. P. *Sources of Variation in Road Accident Frequency.* London: University College London (PhD Thesis), 1978.

1385 Saunders, R. A. *Road Traffic Accidents and their Implications for Management.* Poole: Dorset Institute of Higher Education (PhD Thesis), 1987.

1386 Shoarian-Sattari, K. *Use of Vehicle Flow Parameters as Predictors of Road Traffic Accident Risk.* London: Queen Mary College (PhD Thesis), 1985.

Investigates the correlation between a number of traffic flow parameters and recorded accident density.

1387 Shoup, Donald C. Cost Effectiveness of Urban Traffic Law Enforcement. London: *Journal of Transport Economics and Policy*, Vol. 7(1), January 1973, 32–57.

1388 Shuhaibar, N. K. *Road Accidents in a Developing Country: characteristics and causes of accident rates in Kuwait.* London: Imperial College of Science and Technology (PhD Thesis), 1987.

Attempts to establish the nature, type and probable causes which lie behind the high rate of traffic accidents and casualties resulting in injuries and fatalities in a developing country such as Kuwait. Offers a systematic analysis and in-depth investigation of the statistical data available on traffic accidents.

1389 Stringer, Barney. Road Casualty Reduction: could new targets set a fairer assessment of risks for the vulnerable? London: *Local Transport Today*, April 1994, 12–13.

1390 Tight, Miles Richard. *Accident Involvement and Exposure to Risk for Children as Pedestrians on Urban Roads.* London: University College London (PhD Thesis), 1987. 542 pp.

Detailed literature review reveals the need for further study of several aspects of road accidents to child pedestrians in urban areas. Some of these aspects are explored using data for selected residential parts of five urban areas in Britain.

1391 Transport and Road Research Laboratory. *Children Should Be Seen and Not Hurt: children and road traffic accidents.* Crowthorne: Transport and Road Research Laboratory. 22 pp.

1392 World Health Organisation. *Road Traffic Accidents in Developing Countries.* WHO Technical Report Series 703. Geneva: World Health Organisation, 1984.

Report of a World Health Organisation meeting summarising a wide range of recommendations for reducing traffic accidents in developing countries.

1393 Worsey, G. M. *An Investigation of Statistical Relationships between Accident Rates and Road and Traffic on Two Urban Routes.* Newcastle Upon Tyne: University of Newcastle Upon Tyne (MSc Thesis), 1982.

Traffic

1394 Al-Anazi, F. K. *Vehicle Journey Time and Delay on Major Urban Highways.* Bradford: Bradford University (PhD Thesis), 1989.

Provides a model of traffic flow used for assessing the effect of a variety of managerial techniques on journey time and delay of vehicles along an urban signalised highway. In particular, the effect of providing a pedestrian facility (i.e. a pelican or zebra crossing) is tested.

1395 Alan M. Voorhees and Associates. *Traffic in the Conurbations.* London: British Road Federation, 1973. 47 pp.

Assessment of conurbations and the level of traffic saturation they are planning for. Comparisons are made between conurbations on the basis of present and future trip generation rates.

1396 Alastair Dick and Associates. *Gatwick Airport-London: traffic impact assessment of the BAA's future development proposals.* Tables and Figures. Surrey: Alastair Dick and Associates, 1979.

1397 Ananthararamiah, K. M. *Traffic Assignments and Network Efficiencies.* Birmingham: University of Birmingham (PhD Thesis), 1971.

1398 Anson, Geoff and **Willis, Kerry.** Planning with Vision: the development of traffic strategies for Melbourne. Dordrecht: *Transportation*, Vol. 20(1), 1993, 59–75.

Describes an approach to the development of metropolitan transport strategies based on community needs and values.

1399 Ardekani, Siamak and **Herman, Robert.** Urban Network-Wide Traffic Variables and Their Relations. Baltimore, MD: *Transportation Science*, Vol. 21(1), 1987, 1–16.

Reports on aerial photographic studies as a means of measuring network-wide traffic variables such as speed and flow.

1400 Bennett, David Winston and **Ogden, Kenneth Wade.** *Traffic Engineering Practice.* Monash, Victoria: Department of Civil Engineering, 1979.

Proceedings of a Workshop in Traffic Engineering Practice, held at Monash University in 1979. Provides coverage of practice in traffic theory, traffic planning and traffic management and design.

1401 Bourdrez, J. A. An Evaluation of the Traffic Management Plan for Groningen. London: George Godwin, *International Forum Series*, Vol. 2, 1981, 49–61.

Groningen, a town of about 160,000 inhabitants, is the main educational and cultural centre of the Netherlands. Several studies have been undertaken to determine the effects of various traffic measures. The main goals of the traffic management plan, i.e. to make the inner city more attractive for visitors and to reduce motorised traffic in the area, have been accomplished, although the plan, at least initially, had some adverse effect on economic activity.

1402 Buckley, D. J. (ed.). *Transportation and Traffic Theory.* New York: Elsevier, 1974. 816 pp.

Proceedings of the sixth international symposium on transportation and traffic theory, University of New South Wales, Sydney, Australia, 26–28 August 1974.

1403 Bunker, A. *A New Method of Assigning Traffic to Networks.* Canterbury: University of Kent at Canterbury (PhD Thesis), 1988.

Describes and compares various existing assignment models and discusses some of their drawbacks. A new stochastic assignment method is presented.

1404 Casement, Richard. *Urban Traffic: policies in congestion.* London: Economist Newspaper, 1972. 24 pp.

Brief examination of urban transport and the implications for growing cities with particular reference to the safety aspect and costs. Concentrates on Britain, although contrasts are made with America and Japan.

1405 Cervero, Robert. *Suburban Gridlock.* New Brunswick, NJ: Rutgers, 1986. 248 pp.

Looks at means to solve the problems associated with the growth of suburban traffic in the United States.

1406 Civic Trust. *Traffic Measures in Historic Towns: an introduction to good practice.* London: Civic Trust, 1993. 24 pp.

1407 Cornwell, P. R. *A Study of Lighting and Road Traffic.* Birmingham: University of Birmingham (PhD Thesis), 1971.

1408 Department of Transport. *Traffic in Towns: a study of the long term problems of traffic in urban areas.* London: HMSO, 1963. 223 pp.

Contains the reports of the Steering and Working Groups established in 1961 by the Minister of Transport to look at the problems posed by the rapid growth of motor traffic and the congested condition of towns.

1409 Doukas, Y. T. *Traffic Assignment at the Micro Level.* Uxbridge: Brunel University (PhD Thesis), 1981.

1410 European Conference of Ministers of Transport. *Influence of Measures Designed to Restrict the Use of Certain Transport Modes.* ECMT Round Table 42. Paris: Organisation for Economic Co-operation and Development, 1979. 59 pp.

Concentrates on non-fiscal measures (such as restricting parking spaces; providing bus only lanes; impeding vehicle access; and altering work times), as the means to reduce traffic.

1411 Ewell, Wallace E. Structuring Traffic Management Systems to Facilitate Integration with IVHS Innovations. Westport, CT: *Transportation Quarterly*, Vol. 46(4), 1992, 491–501.

Discusses some of the challenges of integrating future IVHS innovations with existing and planned traffic management systems.

1412 Fernando, Evelyn; Hedges, Barry and **Morton-Williams, Jean.** *Road Traffic and the Environment.* London: Social and Community Planning Research, 1978. 113 pp.

Findings of a survey, covering the whole of England, on the disturbance caused by road traffic.

1413 Goodwin, P. *Traffic Growth and the Dynamics of Sustainable Transport Policies.* Oxford: Oxford University, Transport Studies Unit, 1994. 16 pp.

1414 Greater London Council. *South East London Traffic and Environmental Problems: report of steering group.* London: Greater London Council, 1974. 31 pp.

1415 Greater London Council. *A Study of Supplementary Licensing.* London: Greater London Council, 1974. 100 pp.

Report on a study set up to investigate supplementary licensing and its practicability as a means of regulating the flow of traffic in London. Supplementary licensing would require drivers of certain vehicles to obtain a special licence to use their vehicles at specified times in designated areas.

1416 Hamerslag, R. and **Volmuller, J.** *Proceedings of the Ninth International Symposium on Transportation and Traffic Theory.* Utrecht: VNU Science Press, 1984. 597 pp.

Collection of technical papers concerned with transport and traffic theory.

1417 Hassan, M. U. *Traffic Generation and Prediction at Hospitals.* Leeds: University of Leeds (PhD Thesis), 1976.

1418 Herman, R. Traffic Dynamics through Human Interaction: reflections on some complex problems. Amsterdam: *Journal of Economic Behavior & Organization*, Vol. 15(2), March 1991, 303–311.

Examines the development of traffic flow theory over the last thirty-five years.

1419 Hughes, Peter. Road Traffic on a Plateau – but what happens next? London: *Local Transport Today*, September, 1993, 12–13.

Popular wisdom is that traffic, particularly in urban areas, is continuing to grow relentlessly, bringing ever higher levels of congestion and pollution. However, Department of Transport figures suggest that traffic growth has actually levelled out over the last four years. Article investigates the issue and asks whether the newly published National Travel Survey is already out of date, or whether the last few years were simply a short-term blip.

1420 Institute of Civil Engineers. *Traffic Data Collection.* London: Institute of Civil Engineers, 1978. 174 pp.

Proceedings of a conference held at the Institution of Civil Engineers in 1978 on the theme of the quality of traffic data and the means of collection.

1421 Institution of Highway Engineers: Highway and Traffic Technicians Association: County Surveyors' Society. *Report of the Conference on Traffic Engineering and Road Safety, Brighton, October 1973.* London: Printerhall Limited, 1974.

Proceedings of the Conference on Traffic Engineering and Road Safety. Includes an American and British viewpoint of traffic engineering practice; the status of the highway and traffic technician; transport policies and programmes in relation to local authorities; transportation methodology and techniques and public participation in policy formulation and decision making.

1422 Johansson, M. and Petterson, H. A. KomFram: a way to attractive and efficient public transport. Brussels: *Public Transport International*, Vol. 44(3), 1995, 27–30.

The KomFram traffic control and traffic information system is being implimented in the city of Göteborg. The overall objective is to improve the traffic situation within the city by using modern information and communication technologies. Article focuses on how the system might be used to reach strategic traffic goals.

1423 Jourdain, Susan. Red Routes or Red Faces: can parking blitz really cut congestion? London: *Local Transport Today*, June, 1990, 10–11.

Discussion on the pilot project for the Department of Transport's planned three hundred miles of 'Red-Route' urban clearways in London. Article examines the prospects for their success in improving traffic flow.

1424 Kershaw, R. C. *A Statistical Analysis of Traffic Flows on the Bristol Road Network, Based on the Annual Cordon Survey 1963–1969.* Bristol: University of Bristol (MSc Thesis), 1971.

1425 Lapierre, Rudolf. Comprehensive Traffic Control in Urban Areas. London: George Godwin, *International Forum Series*, Vol. 2, 1981, 15–23.
Reports developments in influencing the traffic process, traffic route, and manner of driving by using light signals, changeable direction signs and guide-signs in road networks.

1426 Lewis, David. Estimating the Influence of Public Transport on Road Traffic Levels in Greater London. London: *Journal of Transport Economics and Policy*, Vol. 11(2), May 1977, 155–168.

1427 London Research Centre. *Traffic Growth and Planning Policy.* London: Royal Town Planning Institute, 1991. 66 pp.

1428 Mogridge, M. J. H. *Travel in Towns: jam yesterday, jam today and jam tomorrow?* Basingstoke: Macmillan, 1990. 308 pp.
Attempts to show the stability of road speeds in the centres of large towns are very stable over long periods of time; and to show how they can be improved. Various sets of data on travel speeds available in London are examined as far back as 1863.

1429 Neill, J. *Paying the Price of Progress: an examination of contemporary police traffic management.* Glasgow: University of Strathclyde (M.Phil Thesis), 1993.
Focuses on traffic and the police and the amalgam of the two in traffic management. Plots the early development of vehicles and the response of local government to this development.

1430 Ngare, L. M. *Improved Traffic Network Control Using Transit.* Glasgow: University of Strathclyde (MSc Thesis), 1983.

1431 Nohr, M. (ed.). *Traffic and Transport: a consumers' guide to influencing the transport system.* London: Centre for Independent Transport Research in London, 1994. 87 pp.

1432 Ogunsanya, A. Ade. Improving Urban Traffic Flow by Restraint of Traffic: the case of Lagos, Nigeria. Amsterdam: *Transportation*, Vol. 12, 1983, 183–194.

Traffic restraint techniques, widely used to combat traffic congestion in the developed countries, have been tried in Lagos, Nigeria. Article examines the impact of the use of odd and even numbered vehicles on alternate days in reducing congestion on the urban roads.

1433 Organisation for Economic Co-operation and Development. *Better Towns with Less Traffic.* Paris: Organisation for Economic Co-operation and Development, 1976.

Proceedings of an OECD Conference held in Paris in April 1975. Contains seven case studies of cities pursuing comprehensive urban transport planning strategies involving novel elements. Describes Bologna's experiments in free public transport, daily licensing in Singapore and mass transit in the free standing nucleated town of Munich. Also contains summaries of sessions on specific problems such as parking, pedestrians and para-transit.

1434 Pharoah, Tim. *Less Traffic, Better Towns: Friends of the Earth's illustrated guide to traffic reduction.* London: Friends of the Earth, 1992. 70 pp.

Provides a guide to practical means to reduce traffic in city centres using examples of existing schemes in Britain and Europe. Argues the reasons why traffic should be reduced; the benefits of traffic restraint and reduction; and, finally, the strategies for putting restraint into action.

1435 Richards, Brian. *Transport in Cities.* London: Architecture Design and Technology Press, 1990. 145 pp.

Explores methods for restraining traffic, and the range of transport alternatives available.

1436 Salter, R. J. *Traffic Engineering Worked Examples.* 2nd ed. Basingstoke: Macmillan, 1989. 157 pp.

Provides a set of worked examples of a wide range of highway traffic engineering problems designed to illustrate the principles of highway traffic flow and the practical design of highway elements.

1437 Scott Wilson Kirkpatrick: Shankland Cox: Steer Davies Gleave. *Hasquad Report.* Hampshire: Scott Wilson Kirkpatrick, 1993. 60 pp.

HASQUAD is a study of orbital travel in south-west London within the M25. The study's origins lie in identified problems of access to Heathrow Airport from south-west London.

1438 Shepherd, Simon. Traffic Control in Over-Saturated Conditions. London: *Transport Reviews*, Vol. 14(1), January–March 1994, 13–14.

Provides an introduction to traffic control in general and goes on to describe types of congestion, objectives and approaches for congestion control. Mainly concerned with traffic signal control although other measures such as road pricing are described.

1439 Short, A. *Traffic Generation from Industrial Areas.* Glasgow: University of Strathclyde (MSc Thesis), 1983.

1440 Steele, J. R. *Traffic Flow Characteristics and an Assessment of Revised Capacity Standards.* Glasgow: University of Strathclyde (MSc Thesis), 1977.

1441 Stokes, G. *Traffic Growth and the Urban Environment.* Oxford: Oxford University, Transport Studies Unit, 1992. 10 pp.

Paper presented to the Institution of Civil Engineers Association of Municipal Engineers Annual Conference, in November 1992.

1442 Struthers, L. M. *Peak Hour Traffic in Central London.* London: University College London (M.Phil Thesis), 1971.

1443 Todd, Kenneth. Traffic Regulation and Public Policy. Westport, CT: *Transportation Quarterly*, Vol. 41(4), October 1987, 477–502.

Looks at methods used by the traffic engineer to control traffic, such as more pedestrian islands, better intersection designs and wider use of the yield sign.

1444 Topp, Hartmut H. A Critical Review of Current Illusions in Traffic Management and Control. Oxford: *Transport Policy*, Vol. 2(1), January 1995, 33–42.

Guidance and information systems, computer aided driving, parking control, park and ride terminals and freight transport management all raise the hope of solving traffic problems without major changes to transport policies and life styles. Critical review, however, shows that there is no all-saving intelligent technology which would allow basic decisions in transport policies to be avoided.

1445 Uren, J. *Traffic Studies Using Aerial Photography.* Leeds: University of Leeds (PhD Thesis), 1976.

1446 Voigt, Werner. Town Traffic in the German Democratic Republic. London: *Transport Reviews*, Vol. 8(3), July–September 1988, 183–195.

Starting with a description of the demographic and constructional development of towns in the German Democratic Republic, typical aspects of town traffic are considered, the traffic consequences of changes in town structure are discussed; and an account is given of the need for mobility of people in towns and how it is provided.

1447 Wooton Jeffreys Consultants: Department of Transport: Transport and Road Research Laboratory. *A study to show patterns of vehicle use in the London area.* Contractor Report 131. Crowthorne: Transport and Road Research Laboratory, 1989. 45 pp.

Report summarises the work carried out to evaluate the pattern of traffic flows, in particular journeys made in private and commercial vehicles, on the road network in the London area, for the production of route guidance systems such as Autoguide.

1448 Yuen, H. M. *Traffic Restraint in Singapore, with Special Reference to the Area Licensing Scheme.* Liverpool: University of Liverpool, 1980.

8 Buses

General

1449 Aldridge, John. Singapore Copes with Massive Crowds. Surrey: *City Transport*, December 1986/February 1987, 26–27.

Describes the way Singapore Bus Service handled heavy and increasing traffic as work progressed on the Mass Rapid Transit System.

1450 Armstrong-Wright, Alan and **Thiriez, Sebastian.** *Bus Services: reducing costs, raising standards.* Washington, DC: The World Bank, 1987. 97 pp.

Various developing countries are considered in terms of their bus services. Topics covered include ownership, variety of vehicles and services, co-operation between operators, the role of government, performance evaluation and standards of service. It argues that the most effective system would be a competitive industry composed of privately owned small firms which are free to choose their own combination of fares, routes, frequencies and vehicle types.

1451 Astrop, A., Balcombe, R. and **Fairhead, R.** *Bus Competition in Great Britain since 1986: a national review.* Crowthorne: Transport and Road Research Laboratory, 1992. 24 pp.

1452 Badejo, B. A. *Private Operation of Public Bus Services: the case of metropolitan Lagos, Nigeria.* London: London School of Economics and Political Science (PhD Thesis), 1990.

1453 Bhatt, Kiran U. and **Kirby, Ronald F.** *Guidelines on the Operation of Subscription Bus Services.* Washington, DC: Urban Institute, 1975. 76 pp.

Report based on ten case studies of urban bus services which were analysed in relation to their organisation and administrative operational systems. Subscription bus services are compared on criteria such as pollution, congestion and fuel consumption.

1454 Bocker, Geert; Bradburn, Peter; Goodwin, Phil; Hallett, Sharon; Jones, Peter; Kenny, Francesca and **Stokes, Gordon.** *Buses in Towns.* Preston: Transport Advisory Service, 1991. 64 pp.

Addresses the transport problems of cities of the 1990s, including congestion, pollution and noise. The bus as a form of public transport is examined in detail and ideas put forward for improving operation.

1455 Boucher, M. The Quebec Intercity Bus Industry: regulation, practices and performance. Quebec: *L'Actual Economics*, Vol. 69(4), December 1993, 271–312.

1456 Buchanan, Malcolm. How to Manage Post Deregulation. London: *Transport*, Vol. 9, January 1988, 17–19.

At the time of drafting the Buses White paper, there was much speculation over what its long-term effects on the structure and management of the bus industry were likely to be. Article reviews what actually happened.

1457 Bus and Coach Council. *The Bus: the key to urban mobility.* London: Bus and Coach Council, 1983. 20 pp.

Examines the role and prospects of the bus. Looks at the operating environment, legislation and financial support and makes recommendations for improvements.

1458 Bus and Coach Council. *The Future of the Bus: a special report from the Bus and Coach Council.* London: Bus and Coach Council, 1982. 59 pp.

Examines the role of the bus; the history of public involvement; the problems encountered in the 1980s; and recommendations for solutions.

1459 Bus and Coach Council. *Buses Mean Business: the solution to urban congestion.* London: Bus and Coach Council, 1990. 39 pp.

Puts forward the argument that buses provide a solution to traffic congestion.

1460 Butler, R. *Bus Operation in Hong Kong: a study of public and private enterprise.* London: University College London (PhD Thesis), 1971.

1461 Coles, O. B. and **Wabe, J. S.** *The Economics of Urban Bus Operations.* Warwick: University of Warwick, 1973. 126 pp.

Econometric analysis of the cost of, and demand for, bus services in urban areas.

1462 Dodgson, J. S. and **Topham, N.** (eds). *Bus Deregulation and Priva-*

tisation: an international perspective. Aldershot: Avebury, 1988. 223 pp.

Collection of papers which analyses developments in Australia, the UK, the USA and selected cities in South-East Asia.

1463 Faulks, Rex W. *Bus and Coach Operation.* 5th ed. London: Butterworth, 1987. 259 pp.

Covers the operation of buses and coaches, including reference to the Transport Act, 1985.

1464 Fetter, F. L. *Some Aspects of Urban Bus Operations in Rio de Janeiro.* Salford: University of Salford (MSc Thesis), 1981.

1465 Fevre, John Le. Urban Buses: wind of change blows at home and abroad. London: *Transport,* Vol. 2, March/April 1981, 15–18.

Discusses public transport problems in developing countries and looks at their relevance to urban transport in the United Kingdom.

1466 Giannopoulos, G. A. *Bus Planning and Operation in Urban Areas: a practical guide.* Aldershot: Avebury, 1989. 370 pp.

Covers the practical aspects of bus operation and planning, including the selection of appropriate vehicles; the configuration of a network; and the provision of bus stops. Problems and experiences of developing countries are considered.

1467 Hamer, Mike. The Bus Industry: a special report. London: *Transport,* Vol. 2, January/February 1981, 44–45.

Reviews a critical decade for the bus industry. Argues that the survival of the bus industry depends on coming to terms with the Transport Act, 1980.

1468 Hibbs, John. *Bus and Coach Management.* London: Chapman and Hall, 1985. 239 pp.

Focuses on the opportunities for private enterprise. Covers market strategy; pricing policies; traffic management; manpower management; and legal requirements and implications.

1469 Hibbs, John. *The Bus and Coach Industry: economics and organization.* London: J. M. Dent, 1975. 224 pp.

Radical analysis of the problems of bus and coach operation and management; using the criterion of satisfaction of the needs of potential and actual passengers.

1470 Hibbs, John. *How to Run the Buses.* London: John Baker, 1972. 72 pp.

1471 Hibbs, John. *The Bus and Coach Operator's Handbook.* London: Kogan Page, 1987. 198 pp.

Covers all aspects of the operation of the industry: routes and services; pay and staff relations; public relations; external controls; and competition and co-ordination.

1472 Higginson, Martin and **White, Peter.** Efficiency of Urban Buses. London: *Transport*, Vol. 3, March 1983, 18–20.

Examines the efficiency of British urban bus operators. Almost all operators in the local authority sector (including district and regional councils and London Transport) were examined, in an attempt to provide a picture both of aggregate trends during the 1970s, and cross-sectional comparisons.

1473 Huntley, Peter G. *Tendering and Local Bus Operation: the practical handbook.* Kingston-upon-Thames: Croner Publications, 1989. 173 pp.

Provides information on the deregulated world of bus operation and tendering. Includes sections on contracts; strategies for tendering; authorities and operators; marketing and publicity; concessionary fares; and finance.

1474 Lambden, William. *Bus and Coach Operation: principles and practice for the transport student.* 4th ed. London: Iliffe Books, 1969. 265 pp.

1475 Lim, Y. S. *A General Review of Bus Priority Systems.* Glasgow: University of Strathclyde (MSc Thesis), 1981.

1476 Marsh, Linda (ed.). *Bus Operations Research: Proceedings of the Fifth Annual Seminar, 18–20 July, 1973.* Leeds: University of Leeds, 1973.

Collection of seminar papers on such topics as bus and crew scheduling; urban transport problems; radio control; assessing bus priorities in London; and the redevelopment of rural services.

1477 Martin, P. H. *Bus Services in Small Towns.* TRRL Laboratory Report 848. Crowthorne: Transport and Road Research Laboratory, 1978. 15 pp.

Study of fixed route bus services operating in towns with populations of 5,000 to 30,000. Analysis of eight such services carried out to identify and quantify those factors which favour their operation. Demonstrates and assesses the potential for and advisability of extending this type of operation to other small towns.

1478 Meakin, R. T. *A Study of Driver-Blameworthy Bus Accidents in Bristol.* Birmingham: University of Birmingham (MSc Thesis), 1971.

1479 Oldfield, R. H. *The Effect of Income on Bus Travel.* TRRL Supplementary Report 644. Crowthorne: Transport and Road Research Laboratory, 1981. 15 pp.

Looks at cross-sectional data on bus travel as a function of household income in order to ascertain whether a demand elasticity can be estimated.

1480 Public Transport International. Adelaide's Northeast Busway. Brussels: *Public Transport International*, Vol. 42(1), March–April 1993, 86–88.

Reviews seven years of operating experience.

1481 Read, M. *Assessment of Bus Feeder Services to Rapid Transit Stations.* Leeds: University of Leeds (PhD Thesis), 1977.

1482 Roth, Gabriel and **Shephard, Anthony.** *Wheels Within Cities: private alternatives to public transport.* London: Adam Smith Institute, 1984. 89 pp.

Challenges the belief that only large-scale, publicly-owned transport systems are capable of providing cities with an efficient and integrated public transport network. Argues that centralised systems, relying on large buses, are inefficient.

1483 Sengupta, K. S. *Urban Public Transport in India, with Special Reference to Small Vehicle Modes and to Calcutta.* Warwick: University of Warwick (MSc Thesis), 1977.

1484 Souter, Brian. Business Growth for British Bus Companies. London: *Proceedings of the Chartered Institute of Transport*, Vol. 4(1), 1995, 25–33.

Frederick Speight Lecture, May 1994.

1485 White, Peter R. Bus Deregulation: a welfare balance sheet. London: *Journal of Transport Economics and Policy*, Vol. 24(3), September 1990.

Assesses the impact of deregulation over the period 1985/6 to 1988/9. Claims that after taking account of lower earnings and fuel costs, a substantial reduction in operating cost per bus-kilometre through improved productivity is shown. However, ridership losses were greater than expected and substantial losses to users through higher fares and service instability occurred. Overall, a small net benefit is shown in the metropolitan areas, but a net loss elsewhere.

1486 White, Peter. Bus and Coach Deregulation. London: *Global Transport*, Vol. 1, Spring 1995, 31–35.

Attempts to provide a broader view of the longer-run effects of bus and coach deregulation. Examines developments in Britain, Chile, New Zealand and Zimbabwe.

History

1487 Aldridge, John. *British Buses Before 1945.* London: Ian Allan, 1995. 128 pp.

Provides an account of the development of buses in Britain.

1488 Anderson, R. C. *A History of the Midland Red.* Newton Abbot: David and Charles, 1984. 192 pp.

Traces the history of the Midland Motor Omnibus Company (Midland Red) from its origins at the turn of the century through the inter-war years to the 1980s when it was a nationalised company.

1489 Baker, Michael. *Farewell to London's Trolleybuses.* London: Ian Allan, 1995. 112 pp.

Examines the rise and decline of London's trolleybus fleet.

1490 Barker, Theo. *Moving Millions: a pictorial history of London Transport.* London: Book Production Consultants, 1990. 132 pp.

1491 Barman, Christian. *The Man Who Built London Transport.* Newton Abbot: David and Charles, 1979. 287 pp.

Biography of Frank Pick.

1492 Blacker, Ken. *Trolleybus.* Middlesex: Capital Transport Publishing, 1975. 123 pp.

An illustrated examination of the thirty-one years of trolleybus operation in London.

1493 Blacker, Ken; Lunn, Ron and **Westgate, Reg.** *London's Buses: the independent era – 1922–1934.* Vol. 1. Hertfordshire: H. J. Publications, 1977. 491 pp.

Deals with independent operators who ran within the area now covered by London Transport.

1494 Blacker, Ken; Lunn, Ron and **Westgate, Reg.** *London's Buses, 1920–1939.* Vol. 2. London: H. J. Publications, 1983. 286 pp.

Continuation of the theme of the previous volume. Examines the independent operators in London from 1920 up to the outbreak of war in 1939.

1495 Cowley, S. *London Buses Then and Now.* London: Ian Allan, 1995. 128 pp.

Examines the changing nature of London's buses.

1496 Crawley, R. J., MacGregor, D. R. and **Simpson, F. D.** *The Years Between 1909 and 1969: Volume 2 The Eastern National Story from 1930.* Poole: Oxford Publishing, 1984. 207 pp.

History of the Eastern National Omnibus Company Ltd., from 1930 to 1969.

1497 Curtis, Colin H. *Forty Years With London Transport.* Derbyshire: Transport Publishing, 1990. 152 pp.

Autobiographical account of a forty year association with the bus industry in London.

1498 Day, John. R. *The Story of the London Bus: London and its buses from the horse bus to the present day.* London: London Transport, 1973. 148 pp.

Illustrated history of the bus in London. Covers how and why the bus first developed; the problems and successes of the horse buses; and the contribution made to the development of transport by the motor bus.

1499 Fairhurst, M., Mack, T. and **Rendle, G.** *Bus and Underground Travel in London: an analysis of the years 1966–1976.* Economic Research Report R235. London: London Transport Executive, March 1978. 17 pp.

Describes a research study intended to refine estimates of the sensitivity of London Transport's passenger demand to such factors as the level of fares; service; personal incomes; and car ownership.

1500 Gavin, Martin. *London Buses 1929–1939.* Shepperton: Ian Allen, 1990. 144 pp.

Account of the development of London's buses during the inter-war years.

1501 Glover, John. *Buses and Trains Since 1933.* Addlestone: Ian Allan, 1988. 64 pp.

1502 Goodwin, A. N. *Bus Services as an Integral Part of the British Railways Network.* Salford: University of Salford (MSc Thesis), 1989.

Traces the origins of the railway companies' involvement in road transport passenger operation; examines their role in the provision of road services incidental to their railway business; and sets out the legal and administrative structures which followed.

1503 Graves, Charles. *London Transport at War: 1939–1945.* Harpenden: Oldcastle Books, 1989. 95 pp.

Keeping the traffic of daily life moving during the worst days of the Blitz required extraordinary determination and ingenuity. This book tells how it was achieved by London Transport and its personnel.

1504 Green, Oliver and **Reed, John.** *The London Transport Golden Jubilee Book 1933–1983.* London: The Daily Telegraph, 1983. 192 pp.

Commemorates the 50th anniversary of the establishment of the London Passenger Transport Board.

1505 Hibbs, John. *The History of British Bus Services.* Newton Abbot: David and Charles, 1968. 280 pp.

Standard account of the origins and development of the British bus industry.

1506 Hibbs, John (ed.). *The Omnibus: readings in the history of road passenger transport.* Newton Abbot: David and Charles, 1971. 215 pp.

Selection of papers based on research conducted by The Omnibus Society including experimental vehicles in Edinburgh; London bus history; one hundred years of railway associated omnibus services; and passenger transport in Bristol during the Victorian era.

1507 Joyce, J. *Trolleybus Trails: a survey of British trolleybus systems.* London: Ian Allan, 1968. 118 pp.

Illustrated survey of Britain's trolleybus systems, including their development; routes; regions; and services.

1508 Klapper, Charles F. *Golden Age of Buses.* London: Routledge and Kegan Paul, 1978. 248 pp.

Charts the development of the bus from its origins in the 1800s to its period of maximum prosperity in the 1950s.

1509 London Omnibus Traction Society. *London Route Review 1934–1939.* London: London Omnibus Traction Society, 1991. 127 pp.

Comprehensive list of all central bus, tram and trolleybus routes as they were operating during October 1934; together with vehicle types and garages/depots from which they operated. Also includes a chronological list of all known route and vehicle type changes until the end of 1939 and summary of routes.

1510 London Omnibus Traction Society. *London Route Review*

1939–1945. London: London Omnibus Traction Society, 1993. 144 pp.

Account of London Transport's Central Area services during the Second World War.

1511 London Regional Transport. *Serving Greater London.* England: S. W. Sharman, 1986. 20 pp.

Introduces London Regional Transport and its principal subsidiary companies – London Buses and London Underground.

1512 Lumb, Geoff. *British Trolleybuses 1911–1972.* London: Ian Allan, 1995. 128 pp.

1513 MacDonald, Neil. *Midland Red North.* Venture Publications, 1995. 128 pp.

An illustrated history of the Midland Red North bus company which was formed from the old Midland Red Company when it was split into separate regional operations.

1514 Millar, Alan. *British Buses of the 1930s.* Cambridge: Patrick Stephens, 1982. 113 pp.

Details the development of bus design and operation during the 1930s.

1515 Millar, G. I. *Fifty Years of Public Service.* Belfast: Ulsterbus, 1987. 64 pp.

Traces the history of the publicly owned bus services within Northern Ireland from 1935 when the Northern Ireland Road Transport Board was formed.

1516 Morris, Stephen. *British Buses Since 1945.* London: Ian Allan, 1995. 128 pp.

Examines the fortunes of British bus manufacture during a period of increasing foreign competition.

1517 Mulley, C. A. *Public Control of the British Bus Industry: the origins and effects of legislation in the 1930's and 1940's.* London: London School of Economics and Political Science (PhD Thesis), 1990.

Focuses on the public control of motorised passenger carrying vehicles and the effect of control on the development of this sector of the transport industry.

1518 Mulley, Corinne. The Background to Bus Regulation in the 1930 Road Traffic Act: economic, political and personal influences in the

1920s. Manchester: *Journal of Transport History*, Vol. 4(2), September 1983, 1–19.

Describes the introduction of the Road Traffic Act of 1930 which marked the beginning of comprehensive State intervention in the control of omnibuses.

1519 Reed, John. *London Buses: past and present.* 2nd ed. Middlesex: Capital Transport Publishing, 1994. 80 pp.

Traces the progress of the bus through all its principal phases from horse power to diesel power and from the vision of one humble coachbuilder a century and a half ago to the massive operation administered by London Regional Transport in the 1990s.

1520 Sommerfield, Vernon. *London's Buses: the story of a hundred years.* London: St Catherine's, 1933. 118 pp.

Describes the development of both the omnibus and London since the 1830s.

1521 Taylor, Sheila. *A Journey Through Time: London Transport photographs 1880–1965.* London: Lawrence King, 1992. 159 pp.

1522 Townsin, Alan. Road Transport: then and now. London: *Transport*, Vol. 7, December 1986, 19–23.

Traces the similarities and differences between the road passenger transport scene of 1926 and that of the 1980s.

1523 Turns, Keith. *The Independent Bus: a historical survey of some independent bus operators.* Newton Abbot: David and Charles, 1974. 208 pp.

Seeks to destroy the myth of independent operators as either romantic rebels or vicious anti-passenger pirates.

1524 Waller, Wally. *The Busman's Story.* Sussex: New Horizon, 1982. 354 pp.

A London bus conductor and driver who finally became an inspector tells how he watched the busman's 'image' deteriorate in the eyes of the public during one of the worst periods in the history of London Transport.

1525 Warn, C. R. *The Development of Motor Bus Services in Northumberland, 1904–1975.* Newcastle Upon Tyne: University of Newcastle Upon Tyne (MA Thesis), 1977.

1526 Watts, Eric. *Fares Please: the history of passenger transport in Portsmouth.* Portsmouth: Milestone Publications, 1987. 128 pp.

Traces the history of public transport in Portsmouth from the 1840s to the 1980s.

1527 Woodworth, Frank. *Victoria Coach Station: the first fifty years: 1932–82.* Chatham: Rochester Press, 1982. 96 pp.

Theory and research

1528 Ailing, Luo. Chinese Problems and Swedish Solutions. Washington, DC: *Mass Transit*, July/August 1991, 46–50.

Buses are boarded 15 million times a day in Shanghai. Article attempts to discover the best way to maximise the efficiency of such an enormous system.

1529 Beesley, M. E. Collusion, Predation and Merger in the UK Bus Industry. London: *Journal of Transport Economics and Policy*, Vol. 24(3), September 1990, 295–310.

Claims that collusion, predation and merger should each be viewed as attempts by firms to restore and improve profits following deregulation in 1985.

1530 Berechman, Joseph and **Giuliano, Genevieve.** Economies of Scale in Bus Transit: a review of concepts and evidence. Amsterdam: *Transportation*, Vol. 12(4), 313–332.

1531 Bly, P. H. and **Oldfield, R. H.** Future Use of Stage Bus Services. Amsterdam: *Transportation*, Vol. 12, 1983, 45–59.

Considers the UK bus services. Breaks the demand into four user groups in an attempt to predict stage-bus service requirements in large cities. Looks at the probable effects of paying subsidies to reduce fares or enhance service levels.

1532 Bly, P. H. and **Oldfield, R. H.** An Analytic Assessment of Subsidies to Bus Services. Baltimore, MD: *Transportation Science*, Vol. 20(3), 1986, 200–212.

Presents a simple mathematical model of a bus service, in a way which allows the requirements for maximum benefit, and the rate of return on subsidy, to be solved analytically.

1533 Bly, P. H., Oldfield, R. H. and **Webster, F. V.** *Predicting the Use of Stage Service Buses in Great Britain.* TRRL Laboratory Report 1000. Crowthorne: Transport and Road Research Laboratory, 1981. 30 pp.

Bus patronage prediction model, constructed in two versions: the first categorises trips by purpose and type of traveller; the second divides trips by regions of the country.

1534 Bristow, A., Nash C. and **Mackie, P.** *Evaluation Criteria in the*

Allocation of Subsidies to Bus Operations. Swindon: Economic and Social Research Council. 19 pp.

1535 Buchanan, C. M. and **Urquhart, G. B.** *The Elasticities of Passenger Demand for Bus Services: a case study in Telford.* TRRL Supplementary Report 641. Crowthorne: Transport and Road Research Laboratory, 1981. 15 pp.

Substantial changes in bus fares/service levels which were introduced in Telford, Shropshire in 1978 provided a context to estimate elasticities of bus passenger demand using data collected in surveys before and after the implementation of changes.

1536 Button, K. J. and **O'Donnell, K. J.** *An Examination of the Cost Structures Associated with Providing Urban Bus Services in Britain: occasional research paper No.83.* Loughborough: University of Loughborough, 1984. 25 pp.

Examines the underlying cost structure associated with supplying urban bus services in Britain. A transpondental logarithmic cost model is employed and parameters estimated using data for 1980.

1537 Ceder, Avishai and **Marguier, Philippe H. J.** Passenger Waiting Strategies for Overlapping Bus Routes. Baltimore, MD: *Transportation Science*, Vol. 18(3), August 1984, 207–230.

Attempts to clarify the route-choice problem of transit passengers in many urban areas who have to deal with overlapping bus routes with some routes sharing common stops.

1538 Cervero, Robert. Profiling Profitable Bus Routes. Westport, CT: *Transportation Quarterly*, Vol. 44(2), April 1990, 183–202.

Analyses the service and ridership characteristics of bus routes that operate at a profit.

1539 Chua, Tiong An. The Planning of Urban Bus Routes and Frequencies: a survey. Amsterdam: *Transportation*, Vol. 12, 1983, 147–172.

Since the 1950s, bus patronage has declined and operational costs have increased. Most urban bus networks have developed over many years and despite changing conditions, few networks have undergone major reorganisation. Survey examines the reasons for this situation.

1540 City Transport. Deregulation: all right for some. Surrey: *City Transport*, Vol. 2(4), December 1987/February 1988, 25–28.

Presents an overview of the costs and benefits of bus deregulation one year after implementation.

1541 Coles, Oliver B. and **Wade, Stuart.** The Short and Long-Run Cost of Bus Transport in Urban Areas. London: *Journal of Transport Economics and Policy*, Vol. 9(2), May 1975, 127–140.

Reports evidence of diseconomies of scale in municipal bus operation. Examines costs between 1961 and 1971 and claims that the cost of a peak mile is increasing in proportion to total cost.

1542 Cornwell, Philip and **Cracknell, John.** Busway Transit: the neglected option? London: *Urban Transport International*, November/December 1990, 28–31.

Cheaper than light rail, more effective than buses on their own. Article addresses these claims for the latest busway systems and investigates why they remain out of favour.

1543 Cresswell, R. W. *Public Transport and Urban Structure: an examination of the Busway concept in areas of new urban development.* Cardiff: University of Wales Institute of Science and Technology (PhD Thesis), 1976. 172 pp.

1544 Danas, A. *Bus Passengers' Walking Distances, Arrivals at the Bus Stop and Waiting Times.* London: University College London (PhD Thesis), 1983.

1545 Department of the Environment: Department of Transport: Transport and Road Research Laboratory. *Factors Affecting Public Transport Patronage: the proceedings of a Symposium held by the Transport and Road Research Laboratory, Livingston, 14 June 1977.* TRRL Supplementary Report 413. Crowthorne: Transport and Road Research Laboratory, 1978. 65 pp.

Decline of bus patronage has had a major effect on the finances of most public transport operators. Examines demand factors; methodology of studies; patronage and main determinants of travel.

1546 Department of the Environment. *Bus Demonstration Project: bus feeder service to the local railway station.* London: Department of the Environment, 1975. 15 pp.

A bus feeder service was introduced in Formby in November 1970 to provide commuters with transport to the local railway station. Report examines the willingness of the public to accept a bus-rail transfer during their journey and also looks at the attractiveness of an integrated bus-rail mode to car commuters.

1547 Dodgson, J. S. and **Katsoulacos, Y.** Quality Competition in Bus

Services: some welfare implications of bus deregulation. London: *Journal of Transport Economics and Policy*, Vol. 22(3), September 1988, 263–282.

Uses a model of competition in vertically differentiated bus markets to identify the factors which determine whether consumer welfare increases or decreases when deregulation leads to quality competition.

1548 Duncan, J. B. *Interaction Between Vehicle Classes in Urban Streets, with Special Reference to Bus Operation.* Newcastle Upon Tyne: University of Newcastle Upon Tyne (MSc Thesis), 1975.

1549 El-Azm, A. A. *The Minimum Fleet Size Problem and Its Applications to Bus Scheduling.* Newcastle Upon Tyne: University of Newcastle Upon Tyne (PhD Thesis), 1982.

Addresses the problem of minimising the fleet size in the context of bus scheduling through the use of a Transportation-Assignment problem model.

1550 El-Reedy, T. Y. *Linking Traffic Signals to Favour Bus Movements.* Sheffield: University of Sheffield (PhD Thesis), 1977.

1551 El-Telbani, J. *The Contribution of Travel Times and Waiting Times to the Total Time Costs of Passengers by Bus: case studies in Sheffield.* Sheffield: University of Sheffield (M.Phil Thesis), 1992.

Attempts to determine the elements of travel time (made up of delay time and movement time) and to measure the determinants of passenger waiting time.

1552 Evans, Andrew W. Are Urban Bus Services Natural Monopolies? Amsterdam: *Transportation*, Vol. 18, 1991, 131–150.

Although Britain's urban bus services have been opened up to competition, most are still monopolies operated by the original incumbents. Article uses findings from case-studies to consider whether monopolistic practices have inherent advantages over competitive operation.

1553 Evans, Andrew. Theoretical Comparison of Competition with other Economic Regimes for Bus Services. London: *Journal of Transport Economics and Policy*, Vol. 21(1), January 1987, 7–36.

Uses a theoretical model to compare the economics of bus services operated under various regimes.

1554 Fernandez, Enrique and **Marcotte, Patrice.** Operators-Users Equilibrium Model in a Partially Regulated Transit System. Baltimore, MD: *Transportation Science*, Vol. 26(2), May 1992, 93–105.

Presents two formulations of a model for finding equilibrium passenger and operator flows in a partially regulated transit system where bus operators are free to choose the routes on which they offer public transport services.

1555 Frankena, Mark W. The Demand for Urban Bus Transit in Canada. London: *Journal of Transport Economics and Policy*, Vol. 12(3), September 1978, 280–303.

1556 Furth, Peter G. Alternating Deadheading in Bus Route Operations. Baltimore, MD: *Transportation Science*, Vol. 19(1), February 1985, 13–37.

Examines the process of alternating dead-heading as an operating strategy for urban bus routes that have a directional imbalance in passenger demand.

1557 Glaister, Stephen. Competition on an Urban Bus Route. London: *Journal of Transport Economics and Policy*, Vol. 19(1), January 1985, 65–82.

Claims that deregulation of the bus industry and reduction of costs and subsidy would probably lead to the introduction of smaller buses, giving faster and more frequent service but at higher fares. Observes that this could result in fewer big buses with resultant cost disadvantages to the less well off members of the travelling public.

1558 Golshani, F. *The Effects of Overtaking Rules upon Bus Service Regularity.* Warwick: University of Warwick (MSc Thesis), 1979.

1559 Green, A. J. *The Impact of Deregulation on the Perceptions of Urban Public Transport Users.* Plymouth: Polytechnic South West (PhD Thesis), 1990.

Four geographical areas within Plymouth are surveyed to provide an in-depth analysis and comparative study between different types of users and different levels of bus service provision.

1560 Hensher, David A. Productive Efficiency and Ownership of Urban Bus Services. Amsterdam: *Transportation*, Vol. 14, 1987, 209–225.

Established ownership of urban bus operations in Australia provides a unique opportunity to investigate the productivity differences between public and private bus service supply. Using duality theory which links economic indices of factor productivity to the cost structure of a firm, an empirical measure is developed of total and partial productivity of inputs.

1561 Heydecker, B. G. *Mathematical Analysis of Responsive Priority for Buses at Traffic Signals.* London: University College London (PhD Thesis), 1983.

1562 Higgins, Thomas J. Shuttle Buses: experience and planning implications. Westport, CT: *Transportation Quarterly*, Vol. 46(3), July 1992, 397–409.

Looks at the decisions to be faced when implementing a shuttle service. Reports on why some shuttle services are successful and other not and makes recommendations on planning, operations and costs.

1563 Higginson, Martin P. *The Efficiency of British Urban Bus Operation and Financing.* London: Council for National Academic Awards (PhD Thesis), 1987. 471 pp.

Study of the performance of the publicly owned bus undertakings in the local authority and nationalised sectors over the sixteen year period from 1970 to 1986.

1564 Higginson, Martin. *On the Buses: municipal bus operation under contrasting policies.* London: Polytechnic of Central London, 1980. 129 pp.

Sets out to monitor progress of a sample of British urban bus operators through the 1970s. Compares performance with that predicted by standardised elasticity model. Looks at Southampton, Northampton, Reading, Nottingham and Newport.

1565 Hopkin, Jean M. and **Oxley, P. R.** *The Effects of Bus Service Reductions in Urban Areas: case studies in Oxford and Manchester.* TRRL Research Report 186. Crowthorne: Transport and Road Research Laboratory, 1989. 21 pp.

Surveys of bus passengers using two bus routes in Oxford and Manchester were carried out before and after the services were reduced, and again a year later. Report summarises the results of a detailed analysis of the travel patterns of bus users on the routes, and their assessments of the effects of the changes.

1566 Hopkin, Jean M., Jones, P. M. and **Stokes, G.** *Bus Service Levels in Urban Areas: effects on bus use and travel behaviour.* TRRL Research Report 151. Crowthorne: Transport and Road Research Laboratory, 1988. 29 pp.

Report of an investigation into the effects of differences in bus service levels on patterns of travel by bus and other modes. Aims to measure elasticities of bus service levels for sub-groups of the population for different types of journey.

1567 Horowitz, Alan J. Subjective Value of Time in Bus Transit Travel. Amsterdam: *Transportation*, Vol. 10, 1981, 149–164.

A psychological scaling technique, magnitude estimation, is used to rate time spent on various elements of bus transit trips.

1568 Houshangi, H. *A Systematic Method for Planning Bus Route Network.* Glasgow: University of Strathclyde (MSc Thesis), 1980.

1569 Hussain, Khalifa Afzal. *Bus Logistics for Developing Countries: a comprehensive guide for bus route planning, bus scheduling and bus operations.* Dar es Salaam: Khalifa Afzal Hussain, 1980. 227 pp.

Guide to the operation of bus transport in developing countries. Covers the infrastructure needed; route planning; timetabling and bus schedules; marketing; fares and fare collection; inspectors and inspection system; and accidents, breakdowns and delays.

1570 Jackson, R. L. and **Johnston, I.** *Financially Viable Works Bus Services.* TRRL Supplementary Report 511. Crowthorne: Transport and Road Research Laboratory, 1979. 12 pp.

Study of a number of works bus and coach services operating with little or no financial support from employers. Speculates as to the advantages and disadvantages and also the potential of works bus operations.

1571 Jansson, Jan Owen. Marginal Cost Pricing of Scheduled Transport Services. London: *Journal of Transport Economics and Policy*, Vol. 13(3), September 1979, 268–294.

A development and generalisation of Truvey and Mohring's theory of optimal bus fares.

1572 Jansson, Jan Owen. A Simple Bus Line Model for Optimisation of Service Frequency. London: *Journal of Transport Economics and Policy*, Vol. 14(1), January 1990, 53–80.

Claims that if total social costs are to be minimised, bus frequencies should be higher than at present, especially in off-peak, and buses should be smaller.

1573 Kim, Moshe. Total Factor Productivity in Bus Transport. London: *Journal of Transport Economics and Policy*, Vol. 19(2), May 1985, 173–182.

Introduces a non-parametric technique for measuring total factor productivity.

1574 Koshal, Rajindar K. Economies of Scale in Bus Transport: some United States experience. London: *Journal of Transport Economics and Policy*, Vol. 6(2), May 1972, 151–153.

Claims that in the USA, the UK and India, there is no evidence of economies of scale in the bus industry.

1575 Krishnan, K. S. and **Nicolaidis, Gregory C.** A Methodology for

Planning Bus Service. Amsterdam: *Transportation*, Vol. 6, 1977, 249–263.

Provides a methodology to assist urban transportation planners to design bus services. Assesses the sensitivity of bus service characteristics upon intended bus usage using survey data collected in Orange County California. The methodology is based on a nonparametric statistical test.

1576 Lee, N. and **Steedman, I.** Economies of Scale in Bus Transport: some British municipal results. London: *Journal of Transport Economics and Policy*, Vol. 4(1), January 1970, 15–28.

Study prompted by the proposal to merge a number of municipal transport undertakings into Passenger Transport Authorities. Analyses figures showing various working expenses per bus-mile, and finds no evidence of scale economies. Claims that extension of one person operation appears to offer greater scope for economies than amalgamation.

1577 Lindau, L. A. *High-Flow Bus Operation on Urban Arterial Roads.* Southampton: University of Southampton (PhD Thesis), 1983.

1578 Lindsay, J. F. *Minibus Service W9: bus/minibus modal choice analysis and social cost-benefit assessment.* London Transport Operational Research Report 211. London: London Regional Transport, 1975. 64 pp.

Examines the factors influencing individuals' choice between the W9 minibus route and conventional bus services. Factors are then used to estimate the social costs and benefits resulting from the introduction of the W9.

1579 Lupton, D. R. *The Economic Implications of the Design of Bus Routes on Accessibility Criteria.* Leeds: University of Leeds (PhD Thesis), 1982.

1580 Madani, D. *Some Aspects of the Provision and Operation of Bus Services in Algiers.* Salford: University of Salford (MSc Thesis), 1984.

1581 Martin, P. H. *The Costs of Operating a Dial-A-Bus, Minibus and Conventional Bus Services.* TRRL Supplementary Report 409. Crowthorne: Transport and Road Research Laboratory, 1978. 16 pp.

Comparison of the costs of operating dial-a-bus, minibus and conventional bus services. Addresses the question of whether to operate minibuses or conventional buses.

1582 Matsoukis, E. C. *Transport Operations Research: bus priorities in* *contingency planning and a capacity restraint micro-assignment model*. Glasgow: University of Strathclyde (PhD Thesis), 1978.

1583 Mbara, T. C., Turner, R. P. and **White, P. R.** Cost Benefit Analysis of Urban Minibus Operations. Dordrecht: *Transportation*, Vol. 19(1), 1992, 59–74.

Extends on previous financial analyses of intensive urban minibus operations and applies a cost benefit analysis.

1584 Merewitz, Leonard. On Measuring the Efficiency of Public Enterprises: bus operating companies in the San Francisco Bay Area. Amsterdam: *Transportation*, Vol. 6, 1977, 45–55.

1585 Mitchell, I. W. Softly Softly Approach Pays Off for European Public Transport. London: *Transport*, Vol. 3, March/April, 1982, 18.

Article poses the question of why it is that in Western European cities the reliability of bus services can be taken for granted, while in the United Kingdom they often cannot.

1586 Nelson, J. D. *Innovative Bus Control for Congested Urban Corridors: the integration of convoying systems and passenger information*. Newcastle Upon Tyne: University of Newcastle Upon Tyne (PhD Thesis), 1991.

Focuses on the feasibility of linking bus convoy systems with on-line passenger information with the aim of improving conditions for bus operation and passengers in central urban corridors such as Oxford Street, London.

1587 Niiro, Katsuhiro. Demand for Buses in Japanese Medium Sized Cities. Amsterdam: *Transportation*, Vol. 16(4), 1990, 279–295.

Describes the cirumstances of Japanese bus services given that the increase in car ownership and the development in urban rapid rail networks have deprived the bus industry of passengers.

1588 Obeng, Kofi. Bus Transit Cost, Productivity and Factor Substitution. London: *Journal of Transport Economics and Policy*, Vol. 19(2), May 1985, 183–203.

Develops a neoclassical cost function from cross-sectional data pertaining to sixty-two bus transit systems. Cost function is used to study the effects of total factor productivity and input substitution on cost.

1589 Organisation for Economic Co-operation and Development. *Optimisation of Bus Operation in Urban Areas*. Paris: Organisation for Economic Co-operation and Development, 1972. 89 pp.

1590 Perrett, K. E. *Bus Registration Index: a national database of deregulated bus services: TRRL Research Report 229.* Crowthorne: Transport and Road Research Laboratory, 1989. 22 pp.

Provides an overview of the British Registration Index, describes its origins, and some of the key analyses for which it has been used.

1591 Pretty, R. L. Planning of Bus Transport for Developing Urban Form. Victoria: *Australian Road Research*, Vol. 18(2), June 1988, 82–88.

Explores bus networks in the context of urban form development. Proposes that a bus network with a ring route around the centre and radial routes to the centre is required for public transport users.

1592 Pretty, R. L. and **Ranaweera, D. J. K.** Ring Route Bus Scheduling: Brisbane's Great Circle Line. Victoria: *Australian Road Research*, Vol. 21(4), December 1991, 1–13.

Examines aspects of ring bus scheduling by establishing an equilibrium between ring and radial users.

1593 Pullen, W. T. *Measurement of the Quality of Local Bus Services with Respect to the Effects of Bus Deregulation in Scotland.* Newcastle Upon Tyne: University of Newcastle Upon Tyne (PhD Thesis), 1991.

Examines methods of definition and measurement of the quality of local bus services.

1594 Rajah, R. K. *Bus Priority and Service Performance.* Cardiff: University of Wales Institute of Science and Technology (PhD Thesis), 1988.

1595 Rana, P. S. *Reliability of Urban Bus Services as an Indicator of their Operational Effectiveness.* Newcastle Upon Tyne: University of Newcastle Upon Tyne (PhD Thesis), 1983.

1596 Rus, G. de *The Economics of Urban Bus Transport in Spain: an analysis of costs, demand and pricing.* Leeds: University of Leeds (PhD Thesis), 1989.

1597 Savage, I. P. *Economic Evaluation of Competition on Stage Carriage Bus Routes.* Leeds: University of Leeds (PhD Thesis), 1984.

Attempts to determine the economically optimal market structure for the local (stage) omnibus industry in the United Kingdom both by the development of appropriate models of bus markets, and by empirical observation of how bus markets operate.

1598 Savage, Ian. Analysis of Bus Costs and Revenues by Time Period. London: *Transport Reviews*, Vol. 9(1), January–March 1989, 1–17.

Describes the development of allocated and incremental cost and revenue techniques.

1599 Sawicki, D. S. Express Transit Systems Analysed. London: *Journal of Transport Economics and Policy*, Vol. 8(3), September 1974, 274–293.

Reports on research aimed at determining the benefits and costs of building a bus rapid-transit system in the Milwaukee region.

1600 Schmenner, Roger W. The Demand for Urban Bus Transit: a route by route analysis. London: *Journal of Transport Economics and Policy*, Vol. 10(1), January 1976, 68–86.

Considers the methods needed to identify urban bus transit demand in the context of declining demand due to decentralising urban areas.

1601 Sheffi, Yosef and **Powell, Warren B.** A Probabilistic Model of Bus Route Performance. Baltimore, MD: *Transportation Science*, Vol. 17(4), November 1993, 376–404.

Considers the problem of describing bus route performance as a first step toward developing strategies for improving service reliability.

1602 Trench, Sylvia. Bus Services in the Nottingham Area: some effects of the boundary system. London: *Journal of Transport Economics and Policy*, Vol. 5(2), May 1971, 163–172.

Reports on a project which suggests that substantial economies might be effected by route adjustments and allowing city passengers to use long-distance buses.

1603 Tyson, W. J. An Analysis of Trends in Bus Passenger Miles. London: *Journal of Transport Economics and Policy*, Vol. 8(1), January 1974, 40–47.

Reports that the number of trips has declined, but that average trip length has increased.

1604 Viton, Philip A. The Possibility of Profitable Bus Service. London: *Journal of Transport Economics and Policy*, Vol. 14(3), September 1980, 295–314.

Considers under what conditions express buses for commuters can be profitable.

1605 Viton, Philip A. The Question of Efficiency in Urban Bus Transportation. Ohio: *Journal of Regional Science*, Vol. 26(3), August 1986, 499–513.

Estimates a flexible frontier specification for the production of urban bus transit services in the United States.

1606 Webster, F.V. *Priority to Buses as Part of Traffic Management.* TRRL Laboratory Report 448. Crowthorne: Transport and Road Research Laboratory, 1972. 14 pp.

A paper which demonstrates how the saturation flow of cars and the time savings to buses are affected by the position of the end of the bus lane relative to the stop-line.

1607 Whelan, J. *A Framework for Evaluating the Validity of Retaining Bus Services in Pedestrian Areas.* Leeds: University of Leeds (PhD Thesis), 1988.

Develops a framework based on multicriteria evaluation techniques for assessing the desirability of retaining or excluding bus services from pedestrian areas.

1608 Wilson, Hoyt G. The Cost of Operating Buses in US Cities. London: *Journal of Transport Economics and Policy*, Vol. 11(1), January 1977, 68–91.

Presents a forecasting tool for estimating the costs of proposed new or extended bus systems.

1609 Young, A. P. *An Analysis of Urban Bus Priority Schemes.* Salford: University of Salford (MSc Thesis), 1972.

Policy

1610 Arnold, Barry and **Harris, Mike.** *Reshaping London's Buses.* Middlesex: Capital Transport Publishing, 1982. 127 pp.

Considers London Transport's Bus Reshaping Plan which envisaged large-scale reorganisation of routes coupled with new types of bus and automatic fare collecting equipment to enable the extension of one-person operation.

1611 Association of Metropolitan Authorities. *Ticket to Ride: policies for better buses.* London: Association of Metropolitan Authorities, 1994. 26 pp.

1612 Banister, David. Deregulating the Bus Industry in Britain: the proposals. London: *Transport Reviews*, Vol. 5(2), April–June 1985.

Outlines the arguments for and against the 'Buses' white paper and summarises the proposals.

1613 Battelino, Helen and **Smith, Nariida.** Developments in the Urban Bus Industry in New South Wales. Brussels: *Public Transport International*, Vol. 42(1), March–April 1993, 22–28.

1614 Bradburn, P. D. and **Hurdle, D. I.** *Planning for Buses in Greater London.* London: Greater London Council, 1981. 118 pp.

Three articles concerning respectively, town centres; highway schemes; and residential areas.

1615 Buchanan, C. M. Bus Policy: conclusions from a case study. Amsterdam: *Transportation*, Vol. 6, 1977, 333–343.

Policy conclusions from a bus study in Telford are summarised and discussed. Choice of bus routes and their combination into networks is examined. Alternative fares systems are compared and the implications for the fare levels necessary to cover costs are discussed.

1616 Button, K. J. The Effects of Regulatory Reform on the US Inter-city Bus Industry. London: *Transport Reviews*, Vol. 7(2), April–June 1987, 145–166.

Looks specifically at the comparatively neglected topic of the Bus Regulatory Reform Act 1982 which liberalised the regulations governing US inter-city bus transport. Details the changes, examines their rationale and assesses the impact they have exerted on the US inter-urban bus industry.

1617 Cheng, G. *Public Minibus Operation in Hong Kong: a case for evaluating the deregulation of public transport services.* London: University College London (M.Phil Thesis), 1985.

Attempts to assess the impact of the Hong Kong Government's policy of public transport deregulation in general, and the introduction of the public light bus system in particular.

1618 Chujoh, Ushio. Learning from Medium and Small Sized Bus Services in Developing Countries: is regulation necessary? Oxford: *Transportation Research*, Vol. 23A(1), January 1989, 19–28.

Examines competitive urban public transport modes under loose entry control in developing countries. Suggests that they may offer solutions to the urban transport problems of advanced countries.

1619 Department of Planning and Communications, London Borough of Camden. *Buses in Camden: a study of bus segregation in the central area of London.* London: London Borough of Camden, 1971. 49 pp.

1620 Department of the Environment: Transport and Road Research Laboratory. *Bus Priority: proceedings of a symposium held at TRRL.* TRRL Laboratory Report 570. Crowthorne: Transport and Road Research Laboratory, 1972. 156 pp.

Outlines the background, development, and prospects for bus priority schemes in the UK.

1621 Department of Transport: Scottish Office: Welsh Office. *Buses.* London: HMSO, 1985. 79 pp.

Covers a wide spectrum including safety and social need; the structure of bus operation; taxis and hire cars; regulation; subsidy and cross-subsidy; and the effects of the Transport Act 1980 on local bus services.

1622 Department of Transport. *Problems with Franchising.* London: HMSO, 1985. 10 pp.

1623 Department of Transport. *Buses: The Government's Response to the Second Report from the House of Commons' Transport Committee, Session – 1984–85.* London: HMSO, 1985. 23 pp.

1624 Downs, Charles. Private and Public Local Bus Services Compared: the case of New York City. Westport, CT: *Transportation Quarterly*, Vol. 42(4), October 1988, 553–570.

Seeks to determine whether private bus services provide lower cost provision of services in comparison to public bus services because they are private or because of some other characteristic. Based on a study of New York City's bus services.

1625 Dudley, G. F. *Implementation and Policy Change: aspects of Bus Passenger Transport in the U.K.* Keele: Keele University (PhD Thesis), 1982.

1626 Evans, Andrew W. Bus Accidents, Bus Deregulation and London. Dordrecht: *Transportation*, Vol. 21, 1994, 327–354.

Local bus services were deregulated in October 1986 in all areas of Britain except London. Government policy is to extend deregulation to London. Article analyses statistics on bus accidents from the national road accident database from 1981 to 1991 in order to compare results from London against those for the rest of Britain, and to consider whether deregulation has affected safety.

1627 Evans, Andrew. A Case Study of Bus Deregulation. London: *Journal of Transport Economics and Policy*, Vol. 22(3), September 1988, 283–306.

Hereford was a trial area in which buses were deregulated before national deregulation. Competitive tendering, introduced by the county council, was a success and was adopted nationally in the Transport Act 1985. Article examines the effects of competition and draws some conclusions for deregulation generally.

1628 Fairhurst, M. The Paradox of Urban Bus Deregulation. Brussels: *Public Transport International*, Vol. 41(3), 1992, 72–73.

1629 Ferguson, D., Hopkin, J. and **Perrett, K.** *Some Early Effects of the 1985 Transport Act in Strathclyde.* Crowthorne: Transport and Road Research Laboratory, 1989. 43 pp.

Report summarising the initial impact of the Transport Act 1985 on the Strathclyde region of Scotland.

1630 Foster, Christopher D. The Economics of Bus Deregulation in Britain. London: *Transport Reviews*, Vol. 5(3), September 1985, 207–214.

Reviews some of the arguments which have been put forward on the economics of bus deregulation. Argues that the experience of road haulage licensing is where the evidence suggests that liberalisation did not have the adverse effects that many predicted. Provides a relevant example for the bus industry.

1631 Glaister, Stephen and **Mulley, Corinne.** *Public Control of the British Bus Industry.* Aldershot: Gower, 1983. 139 pp.

Examines the origins, economic rationale and workings of the system of bus licensing in Britain from 1930 to 1980.

1632 Goldsack, Paul. Israel's Cooperative Approach to Bus Service. Washington, DC: *Mass Transit*, September 1987, 24–44.

Reviews Israel's bus services.

1633 Goodwin, Phil; Kenny, Francesca; Meadowcroft, Shirley; Pickup, Laurie; Stokes, Gordon and **Tyson, Bill.** *Bus Deregulation in the Metropolitan Areas.* Aldershot: Avebury, 1991. 264 pp.

Examines the development of competition and the competitive strategies of bus operators.Also examines the changes in the quality of bus services and fare levels and the subsequent changes in patronage levels.

1634 Gwilliam, K. M. and **Velde, D. M. van de.** The Potential for Regulatory Change in European Bus Markets. London: *Journal of Transport Economics and Policy*, Vol. 24(3), September 1990, 333–350.

Reviews the regimes of regulation of the bus industries of ten Western European countries. In each case the legal and institutional basis of regulation; the structure and performance of the industry under regulation; recent regulatory reform; and the potential for future reform, are discussed. An almost universal reluctance to accept British-style open entry to the industry is observed.

1635 Hendy, Peter. London Buses in the Private Sector. London: *Global Transport*, Vol. 2, Summer 1995, 17–19.

Details one London firm's moves towards privatisation.

1636 Heseltine, P. and **Mulley, C.** *Effects of Bus Deregulation and the Privatisation of the Scottish Bus Group.* Research report no. 84. Reading: University of Reading, 1980. 103 pp.

1637 Hibbs, John. International Comparisons of Bus Licensing. London: *Transport Reviews*, Vol. 6(3), July–September 1986, 259–272.

Seeks to provide a a taxonomy of licensing. Identifies the familiar principles of quality, quantity and price control, and examines them against the British licensing system introduced in 1930. Concludes that quantity control forms a more or less permeable barrier to contestability in the market for public road passenger transport.

1638 Hibbs, John. *Regulation: an international study of bus and coach licensing.* London: Transport Publishing Projects, 1985. 194 pp.

1639 Higginson, Martin; Gretton, John; Harrison, Anthony and **O'Leary, Laura** (eds). Competition and London's Bus Services, in Transport UK: an economic, social and policy audit. Berkshire: *Policy Journals*, 1987, 52–57.

Looks at bus operators outside London who are facing the challenge of deregulation in contrast to London Regional Transport with its system of competitive tendering.

1640 Huntley, Peter. Bus Priorities: Freeman asked to let Docklands show the way. London: *Local Transport Today*, August 1991, 12–13.

Public Transport Minister Roger Freeman has been presented with an innovative programme of bus priorities to help solve transport problems in London's Docklands. Article examines the proposals and asks whether they could be the catalyst for a new wave of bus priority schemes.

1641 Isaac, James K. Privatisation and Deregulation in the United Kingdom. Brussels: *International Union of Public Transport Revue*, Vol. 37(4), January 1989, 297–306.

Looks at the effects on local public transport two years on from the implementation of the Transport Act 1985 which introduced deregulation and competition into the bus industry. Considers whether it has achieved the intended result of reversing the trend of falling passenger numbers and rising subsidies. Comparison is made with other European countries. Article in English, with French and German translations.

1642 Kennedy, David. London Bus Tendering: an overview. London: *Transport Reviews*, Vol. 15(3), July–August 1995, 253–264.

Competitive tendering for bus services was introduced to London in 1984. Article focuses on the impact of tendering on costs, service quality and revenues.

1643 Khezwana, Maria; Maunder, David and **Mbara, Tatenda.** Assessing the Impact of Government Control on Harare's Bus Services. London: *Transport*, Vol. 14, May/June 1993, 3–4.

Summarises the findings of a two and a half year study funded by the Transport Research Laboratory's Overseas Centre on urban stage bus operations in Harare, Zimbabwe.

1644 Knowles, Richard (ed.). *Implications of the 1985 Transport Bill.* Salford: University of Salford, Transport Geography Study Group, 1985. 108 pp.

Focuses on aspects of the Government's policy towards bus transport: deregulation; abolition of fare controls; subsidy limitation; and privatisation.

1645 Leicester City Transport. *Park 'N' Ride: five years' experience: (1966–1971).* Leicester: Leicester City Transport, 1972. 24 pp.

1646 Mackie, Peter J., Gretton, John., Harrison, Anthony and **O'Leary, Laura.** (eds). Local Transport Under the Conservatives. Berkshire: *Policy Journals*, 1987, 36–45.

Investigates to what extent central government has taken over responsibility for transport from local authorities. Covers the institutional and financial framework.

1647 Mackie, Peter J., Nash, Chris and **Preston, John.** Bus Deregulation: ten years on. London: *Transport Reviews*, Vol. 15(3), July–August 1995, 229–251.

Identifies the principal areas of disagreement in the bus policy debate of 1984–85, and reviews the outcome of bus deregulation against that background.

1648 Monopolies and Mergers Commission. *A Report on Stage*

Carriage Services Supplied by Undertakings: Bristol Omnibus Co.: Cheltenham District Traction Company: City of Cardiff D.C.: Trent Motor Traction Co. London: HMSO, 1982. 449 pp.

1649 Moore, Barry J. C. The Municipal Bus Company: an appropriate ownership. London: *Proceedings of the Chartered Institute of Transport*, Vol. 2(4), November 1993.

Looks at the Government's drive to compel local authorities who own bus operations to sell them.

1650 National Bus Company. *The Role of the National Bus Company: organisation, planning, staff, training, maintenance, administration, and all associated requirements.* London: National Bus Company, 1973. 12 pp.

1651 Oram, R. L., Diamond, D. and **McLoughlin, J. B.** (eds). Peak Period Supplements: The contemporary economics of urban bus transport in the UK and USA. *Progress in Planning*, Vol. 12, Part 2. Oxford: Pergamon Press, 1979, 83–153.

Examines the worsening economic position of bus public transport in Britain and the USA. Details the constraints on management and the regulatory frameworks that have kept the industry from adjusting to the changing market.

1652 Pogun, Gulgun and **Satir, Ahmet.** Alternative Bus Scheduling Policies for an Exclusive Bus Lane. Oxford: *Transportation Research*, Vol. 20A(6), November 1986, 437–446.

Presents alternative operating policies for the exclusive bus lane. Based on the experience of the first exclusive bus lane built in Ankara in 1978.

1653 Public Transport Information Unit. *Buses for People – or buses for profit? social provision and commercial services.* Manchester: Public Transport Information Unit, 1995. 108 pp.

Examines the effects of the Transport Act 1985.

1654 Raciazek, Andre. Phoebus – A Project for Harmonising Operations of the 'European Bus'. Brussels: *Public Transport International*, Vol. 42(3), October 1993, 34–37.

Part of the advanced transport telematics programme of the European Community (DRI-VE-V2023), PHOEBUS is concerned with the implementation and evaluation of a range of public transport systems.

1655 Rigby, John. *London Regional Transport's Approach to Bus Serv-*

ice Tendering: Group Planning Report R261. London: London Transport, 1985. 16 pp.

Describes the initiative launched by LRT in the autumn of 1984 to achieve unit cost reductions and to test the market interest in supplying bus services. Provides an outline of the tendering process and a discussion of the reasons of this particular approach.

1656 Savage, Ian. *The Deregulation of Bus Services.* Aldershot: Gower, 1985. 267 pp.

Examines the strictly regulated route monopolies within the bus industry. Attempts to determine the economically optimal market structure for the local (stage) omnibus industry in the UK, by development of appropriate models of bus markets, and also by empirical observation.

1657 Siong, Tay Puan. Keeping People on the Move. London: *Transport*, Vol. 6, August, 1985, 11–15.

Examines the work of Singapore's bus service.

1658 Teer, Alan and **Young, Peter.** The Bordhill Bus Scheme. Chartered Institute of Transport Case Report. London: *Transport*, Vol. 6, December, 1985, 8–9.

Hampshire County Council in conjunction with Alder Valley District Council have introduced a mini-bus service to meet local demand. Article suggests pointers to local authorities on the potential of such services.

1659 Tyson, W. Urban Bus Deregulation: an update. London: *Local Transport Today*, October, 1989, 10–11.

Reports on the effects of deregulation in the conurbations.

1660 Tyson, W. J. Effects of Deregulation on Service Co-ordination in the Metropolitan Areas. London: *Journal of Transport Economics and Policy*, Vol. 24(3), September 1990, 283–294.

Examines the impact of deregulation on service co-ordination in the British conurbations outside London, and the different forms of co-ordination developed in the decade preceding 1985.

1661 Tyson, W. J. *Bus Deregulation Five Years On.* London: Association of Metropolitan Authorities, 1992. 40 pp.

Addresses questions relating to deregulation: has it created competition; can competition be sustained; has competition reduced costs and increased efficiency; has competition reduced fares and increased services; has all this increased patronage; and has financial support been reduced?

1662 Tyson, W. J. Five Years of Bus Deregulation in the United

Kingdom. Brussels: *Public Transport International*, Vol. 41(2), May 1992, 75.

Looks at the six Metropolitan Counties of England and the Strathclyde region of Scotland. Considers whether the Transport Act 1985 fulfilled its objectives to create competition and thereby reduce fares and raise the level of patronage. Article in English, with French and German translations.

1663 Tyson, W. J. Bus Deregulation in the UK: A review of the first year of full deregulation: Report addressed to the Association of Metropolitan Authorities and Passenger Transport Executive Group. Brussels: *International Union of Public Transport Revue*, Vol. 37(4), January 1989, 353–368.

Review of the first full year of bus deregulation in the Metropolitan Counties of England and the Strathclyde region of Scotland. It identifies the potential strengths and weaknesses of the framework introduced by the Transport Act 1985. Article in English, with French and German translations.

1664 Welsh Consumer Council. *Buses for People: the traveller and the local bus in Wales.* Cardiff: Welsh Consumer Council, 1991. 88 pp.

Study of the local bus industry in Wales, set against the background of the problems of traffic congestion and the need to balance private car users' needs with those of public transport users.

1665 White, Peter. Deregulation of Local Bus Services in Great Britain: an introductory review. London: *Transport Reviews*, Vol. 15(2), April–June 1995, 185–209.

Reviews the impact of the deregulation of local bus services in Britain under the Transport Act 1985.

1666 Wilson, T. *Effects of the De-Regulation of Express Coach Travel on Inter-City Public Transport in the U.K.* Glasgow: University of Strathclyde (MSc Thesis), 1983.

1667 Won, Jaimu. Bus Co-operative Systems in Korean Cities. Westport, CT: *Transportation Quarterly*, Vol. 40(2), April 1986, 277–287.

Looks at the bus cooperative systems that four Korean cities have implemented to overcome problems encountered with the operation and management of their bus service.

Fares

1668 City Transport. Getting the Best Out of Prepayment Fares. Surrey: *City Transport*, December 1986/February 1987, 19–21.

Examines the promotion, distribution, product design and pricing of prepaid ticket systems.

1669 City Transport. Brazil's Buses in Fares-Wages Trap. Surrey: *City Transport*, Vol. 2(4), December 1987/February 1988, 14–15.

Examines the position of private bus operators in Brazil.

1670 Diandas, John. Bus Profits Look Like Losses in India. London: *Proceedings of the Chartered Institute of Transport*, Vol. 4(1), 1995, 11–23.

Investigates the reasons why bus profits in India appear as losses for a range of reasons including arbitrary taxation and interest, and poor presentation of accounts.

1671 Heels, P. and **White, P. R.** *Fare Elasticities on Inter-Urban and Rural Bus Services.* London: Polytechnic of Central London, 1977. 77 pp.

Aims to establish a series of values for fare elasticity for different types of bus service outside major urban areas.

1672 Kerin, Paul D. Efficient Bus Fares. London: *Transport Reviews*, Vol. 12(1), January–March 1992, 33–47.

Focuses on two issues in the literature on efficient bus fares: efficient levels of fares and efficient fare-distance relations. The factors involved in determining efficient sets of bus fares are explored, and an attempt made to identify the reasons for the divergence of opinions on these issues found in the literature.

1673 Mellor, Andrew D. *Electronic Ticketing Systems: the use of microprocessor controlled ticket systems to produce management information in the bus industry.* Transport Studies Group: Research Report No. 11. London: Polytechnic of Central London, 1985. 90 pp.

Microprocessor controlled ticket systems retain much data that was previously lost. Discusses the possibility of using this data for performance monitoring and service planning.

1674 Mohring, Herbert and **Turvey, Ralph.** Optimal Bus Fares. London: *Journal of Transport Economics and Policy*, Vol. 9(3), September 1975, 280–286.

Considers how fares can be equated with marginal social costs, including the cost of passengers' time. Argues that fares should be higher on crowded buses to allow for the extra waiting time of would-be passengers.

1675 Naysmith, A. and **Watts, P. F.** *Urban Bus Revenue Collection:*

current methods and directions of development. TRRL Supplementary Report 629. Crowthorne: Transport and Road Research Laboratory, 1980. 24 pp.

Review of existing and future urban bus revenue collection methods in UK and other parts of the Western world.

1676 Pretty, R. L. and **Russell, D. J.** Bus Boarding Rates. Victoria: *Australian Road Research*, Vol. 18(3), September 1988, 145–152.

Study aiming to establish average boarding times of buses for four different types of passengers: a) those purchasing a ticket from the driver; b) those presenting a ticket requiring cancellation; c) those presenting a pass; and d) those boarding through a split entrance operated by a street ticket seller. Concludes that boarding rates can be improved by encouraging more passengers to have tickets requiring only to be shown or cancelled rather than bought for cash.

Investment, infrastructure and subsidy

1677 Arthur Anderson and Company: Department of the Environment: Department of Transport: Transport and Road Research Laboratory. *Bus Route Costing for Planning Purposes.* TRRL Supplementary Report 108UC. Crowthorne: Transport and Road Research Laboratory, 1974. 152 pp.

Aims to establish methods for structuring the total costs of bus companies in order that costs of individual services may be determined and costs related to route for budgeting and planning purposes.

1678 Browne, J. Quality of Bus Corridors in Dublin. Brussels: *Public Transport International*, Vol. 43(3), May 1994, 14–16.

Describes how a concerted improvement in the quality of the bus services of Dublin on a given route has resulted in a significant increase in traffic.

1679 Department of Transport. *Financing of Public Transport Services: The 'Buses' White Paper.* Volume I, minutes of the proceedings. London: HMSO, 1985. 123 pp.

1680 Finnamore, A. J. and **Jackson, R. L.** *Bus control systems: their application and justification.* TRRL Laboratory Report 851. Crowthorne: Transport and Road Research Laboratory, 1978. 20 pp.

Reviews present knowledge of bus control. Discusses the nature of problems to be overcome; types of control system available; and methods which can be applied to overcome problems. Presents results of experiments using surveys and simulation studies.

1681 Institute for Transport Studies, University of Leeds. *Cross-Subsidy in Urban Bus Operations: executive summary.* London: National Bus Company, 1984, 29 pp.

Study commissioned by the National Bus Company to consider the issue of cross-subsidy in the provision of networks of bus services.

1682 Kerridge, M. S. P. The Effect of the Bus Grant on Urban Transport. London: *Journal of Transport Economics and Policy*, Vol. 8(3), September 1974, 237–243.

Argues that the British government's grant scheme discriminates in favour of rear-engined rather than front-engined double-deck buses. Concludes that this creates an artificial impetus to one-person operation thereby generating serious disadvantages in congested areas.

1683 Peterson, B. E. Trunk Network for Buses in Central Stockholm. Brussels: *Public Transport International*, Vol. 43(2), March 1994, 33–35.

1684 Rhys, D. G. Economic Change in the Road Passenger Transport Study. London: *Journal of Transport Economics and Policy*, Vol. 6(3), September 1971, 240–253.

Considers the interaction between the payment of capital grants to operators of bus services by the Ministry of Transport, the restructuring of the bus operating sector and changes in vehicle design.

1685 Richardson, A. J. The Evaluation of Active Bus-Priority Signal Routes. Amsterdam: *Transportation*, Vol. 9, 1980, 173–189.

In an attempt to provide priority facilities for high occupancy vehicles, many cities have investigated or installed active bus priority signals at selected intersections. Article describes one such installation at the intersection of Bell Street and Oriel Road in Heidelberg, Victoria, Australia.

1686 Road Research Group. *Bus Lanes and Busway Systems.* Paris: Organisation for Economic Co-operation and Development, 1977. 125 pp.

Report prepared as result of OECD Groups meetings in Washington, Rome and Paris. Includes discussion, evaluation and inventory of local bus lanes in the member countries.

1687 Transport 2000. *Subsidising Bus Services: memorandum from Transport 2000 to the Select Committee on Transport.* London: Transport 2000, 1983. 23 pp.

Forms part of the evidence for the Select Committee's investigation into bus subsidies. Sets out the case for not only maintaining bus subsidies but for increasing them.

1688 Transport Committee of the House of Commons. *Financing of Public Transport Services: the 'Buses' White Paper 1985.* Volume III, *appendices.* London: HMSO, 1985. 355 pp.

1689 Transport Committee of the House of Commons. *Financing of Public Transport Services: the 'Buses' White Paper 1985*: Volume II, minutes of evidence. London: HMSO, 1985. 380 pp.

Labour, management and organisations

1690 Andrews, R. D. *A Survey of Bus Crew Scheduling Practices.* TRRL Report LR 576. Crowthorne: Transport and Road Research Laboratory, 1973. 38 pp.

1691 Babitsky, Timlynn; Gregerson, Hal and **Perry, James L.** Organizational Form and Performance in Urban Mass Transit. London: *Transport Reviews*, Vol. 8(2), April–June 1988, 125–143.
Analyses 20 studies from three countries (predominantly the USA) on the relationships between organisational form and fixed-route bus transit performance.

1692 Blumstein, Alfred and **Miller, Harold D.** Making Do: the effects of a mass transit strike on travel behaviour. Amsterdam: *Transportation*, Vol. 11(4), 1983, 361–382.
A brief bus strike in December 1976 in the City of Pittsburgh provided an opportunity for testing a variety of approaches to increase ride-sharing and reduce traffic congestion, and also for examining the effect of the strike on traffic congestion and on individual travel behaviour.

1693 Boyd, C. W. *One-Man Operation of Urban Bus Routes: system dynamics, costs and benefits.* Cranfield: Cranfield Institute of Technology (PhD Thesis), 1978.

1694 Boyd, Colin W. The Impact of Reduced Service Quality on Demand for Bus Travel. The case of One-Man Operation. London: *Journal of Transport Economics and Policy*, Vol. 15(2), May 1981, 167–178.
Introduction of one-person operations to urban bus routes in Great Britain was

generally expected to result in reduced passenger service quality. Results of a study confirm substantial adverse demand response to one-person operation from 1968 to 1974.

1695 Boyd, Colin W. Cost Savings from One-Man Operation of Buses: a re-evaluation. London: *Journal of Transport Economics and Policy*, Vol. 15(1), January 1981, 59–67.

Suggests that conversion of buses to one-person operation reduces costs by 15.6 per cent.

1696 Bramley, Philip and **Goodwin, P. B.** *One Person Operation of Buses in London.* Oxford: Oxford University, Transport Studies Unit, 1985. 87 pp.

1697 Brown, R. H. and **Nash, C. A.** Cost Savings from One-Man Operation of Buses. London: *Journal of Transport Economics and Policy*, Vol. 6(3), September 1972, 281–284.

Investigation of municipal bus undertakings from 1964 to 1969 suggests that an average cost saving of 13.7 per cent can be achieved on buses converted to one-person operation.

1698 Bryman, Alan; Gillingwater, David and **McGuinness, Iain.** Organizational Responses to the Deregulation of the Bus Industry in Britain. London: *Transport Reviews*, Vol. 14(4), October–December 1994, 341–361.

The bus industry, outside London, was deregulated in October 1986. Article documents the key trends within the industry which have emerged since 1986. Considers the implications of deregulation and privatisation from an organisational perspective at the level of the individual bus company.

1699 Chomitz, Kenneth M. and **Lave, Charles A.** Part-time Labour, Work Rules, and Urban Transit Costs. London: *Journal of Transport Economics and Policy*, Vol. 18(1), January 1984, 63–74.

Computer simulations are used in a study of the financial effects of possible changes in union work rules governing split shifts and the use of part-time drivers.

1700 Desrochers, Martin and **Soumis, Francois.** A Column Generation Approach to the Urban Transit Crew Scheduling Problem. Baltimore, MD: *Transportation Science*, Vol. 23(1), February 1989, 1–13.

1701 Fairhurst, M. H. The Impact on Receipts of Conversion to One-Man Bus Operation: some explanations and predictions. London:

Journal of Transport Economics and Policy, Vol. 8(3), September 1974, 223–236.

Sets out the findings of an analysis by London Transport of thirty services converted to one-person operation in 1970–71.

1702 Foster, Christopher and **Golay, Jeanne.** Some Curious Old Practices and their Relevance to Equilibrium in Bus Competition. London: *Journal of Transport Economics and Policy*, Vol. 20(2), May 1986, 191–216.

Claims that many of the bad practices of bus drivers will be prevented under the Transport Act 1985, or will be unprofitable. Others which may be revived are not necessarily harmful and may be conducive to competitive equilibrium.

1703 Gilks, J. S. *The Operation and Management of Stage Carriage Bus Services in England and Wales outside the areas of Passenger Transport Authorities and the Greater London Council.* Salford: University of Salford (MSc Thesis), 1973.

1704 Heseltine, P. M. and **Silcock, D. T.** The Effects of Bus Deregulation on Costs. London: *Journal of Transport Economics and Policy*, Vol. 24(3), September 1990, 239–254.

Reviews the way in which costs have changed since deregulation. Using information collected by interviews with management and union representatives in 46 companies operating within the metropolitan areas, it attempts to explain how cost savings have been achieved and particularly the impact of changes in wages and working practices.

1705 Heseltine, P. M. and **Silcock, D. T.** *Changes in Rates of Pay and Working Practices in the Bus Industry in Metropolitan areas since deregulation.* TRRL Contractor Report 162. Crowthorne: Transport and Road Research Laboratory, 1989. 58 pp.

1706 Malvaux, Francois. Modern, Efficient Bus Fleet Management. Brussels: *Public Transport International*, Vol. 43(1), January 1994, 37–38.

Reports on fleet management using a computerised system.

1707 Monopolies and Mergers Commission. *London Transport Executive: a report on the arrangements made by the Executive for the maintenance of buses and coaches.* London: HMSO, 1984. 200 pp.

1708 Morton, Norman. *One-Man Bus Operation.* University of Newcastle upon Tyne Department of Civil Engineering: Bulletin 41. New-castle upon Tyne: Oriel Press, 1969. 54 pp.

Report on the impact in urban areas of one-person bus operation. Examines the development of the one-person bus operation in Sunderland.

1709 Nash, C. A. Management Objectives, Fares and Service Levels in Bus Transport. London: *Journal of Transport Economics and Policy*, Vol. 12(1), January 1978, 70–85.

1710 Pelly, Roland. HGVs and Coaches: drivers' hours – EC court decision on breaks. Transport Law and Practice, Vol. 1(7), 1994, 62–63.

Council Regulation 3820/85 on the harmonisation of certain social legislation relating to road transport Art. 7. Provides an interpretation of EC rules on continuous driving and rest periods.

1711 Relton, A. E. *Some Aspects of Rostering and Unsocial Hours in Bus Operation.* Newcastle upon Tyne: University of Newcastle upon Tyne (PhD Thesis), 1983.

1712 Smith, David N. Managerial Strategies, Working Conditions and the Origins of Unionism: the case of the tramway and omnibus industry, 1870–91. Manchester: *Journal of Transport History*, Vol. 8(1), March 1987, 30–51.

Investigates the relationship between managerial strategies, working conditions and the development of worker resistance, using the British tramway and omnibus industry as an illustrative case study.

1713 Storey, Richard. Sources for the National Busworkers' Association. Manchester: *Journal of Transport History*, Vol. 4(1) March 1983, 81–83.

Attempts to draw attention to a significant group of source material for the study of the National Busworkers' Association.

1714 Watts, P. F. *Passenger Handling Performance of One-man Buses.* TRRL Supplementary Report 114 UC. Crowthorne: Transport and Road Research Laboratory, 1974. 12 pp.

Examines the development of one-person operation of buses in the UK.

1715 Webster, F. V. *The Importance of Cost Minimisation in Public Transport Operations.* TRRL Supplementary Report 766. Crow-thorne: Transport and Road Research Laboratory, 1983. 22 pp.

Examines the consequences of rising costs on the scope for setting fares and service levels; on car ownership and modal split; and on the location of activities.

Markets and marketing

1716 Al-Smadi, S. *The Marketing of Urban Bus Services in a Developing Country: the case of Greater Amman.* Edinburgh: Heriot-Watt University (PhD Thesis), 1992. 368 pp.

Examines the demand for bus services in Greater Amman and how these services might be more effectively marketed.

1717 Bly, P. H. and **Oldfield, R. H.** Competition between Minibuses and Regular Bus Services. London: *Journal of Transport Economics and Policy*, Vol. 20(1), January 1986, 47–68.

Argues that services run entirely by minibuses are unlikely to cover their costs. Suggests that minibuses running on the same routes as existing big bus services in London may do well, and may produce some net social benefit.

1718 Bradshaw, Bill. The Limitations of Competition in Developing the Market for Bus Services. London: *Proceedings of the Chartered Institute of Transport*, Vol. 2(4), November 1993, 24–39.

Considers the limitations of competition as a means of securing efficient outcomes, with particular reference to the bus industry.

1719 Cahm, Caroline and **Guiver, Jo.** *A Passengers' View of Bus Deregulation.* London: Buswatch, 1988. 121 pp.

Presents evidence from bus users about standards of services available to the public and ways in which standards and availability could be maintained and improved.

1720 Cohen, N. London's Buses: get on board. Brussels: *Public Transport International*, Vol. 43(5), September 1995, 28–31.

1721 Elmberg, Curt M. Dial-A-Ride with Customer Operated Dispatching. Amsterdam: *Transportation*, Vol. 7, 1978, 35–43.

Reports on a Dial-a-Ride scheme in the northeastern part of Göteborg, the second largest city in Sweden.

1722 Evans, Andrew. Competition and the Structure of Local Bus Markets. London: *Journal of Transport Economics and Policy*, Vol. 24(3), September 1990, 255–282.

After three years of deregulation, local bus routes in Britain are still mostly operated as monopolies, but enough have been operated competitively to have provided a lot of experience. This paper presents empirical evidence from case studies of competition, which is then used to explain the structure of the market.

1723 Goodwin, P. *Passenger Attitudes and Responses to Bus Deregulation Outside London: a summary of the evidence.* Oxford: Oxford University, Transport Studies Unit, 1993. 25 pp.

1724 Gwilliam, Ken M. Setting the Market Free: deregulation of the bus industry. London: *Journal of Transport Economics and Policy*, Vol. 23(1), January 1989, 29–44.

Consequences of the UK deregulation of the bus industry in the Transport Act 1985 are examined, with a focus on whether the market is contestable, and if so, whether this is a sufficient condition for welfare maximisation.

1725 Ireland, Norman J. A Product Differentiation Model of Bus Deregulation. London: *Journal of Transport Economics and Policy*, Vol. 25(2), May 1991, 153–162.

1726 Jones, T. S. Mervyn. Regular, Flexible and Friendly: how the bus can win custom. London: *Transport*, Vol. 9, July/August, 1988, 338–9.

1727 Mackie, Peter J. and **Preston, J. M.** *The Local Bus Market: a case for regulatory change.* Aldershot: Avebury, 1993.

1728 Morgan, Ian. Customer Satisfaction Through Quality Management. London: *Proceedings of the Chartered Institute of Transport*, Vol. 2(3), August 1993, 20–29.

1729 Seago, Philip. Anatomy of a Bus War: a small operator's perspective. London: *Proceedings of the Chartered Institute of Transport*, Vol. 1(3), Summer 1992, 29–36.

Describes the fortunes of Holosworth Transit Ltd, a small bus company who set up operations in competition with an established profitable bus operator.

1730 Transport and Road Research Laboratory. *Symposium on Unconventional Bus Services: summaries of papers and discussions.* TRRL Supplementary Report 336. Crowthorne: Transport and Road Research Laboratory, 1977. 43 pp.

Examines unconventional urban transport services such as Dial-a-Ride.

1731 Tunbridge, R. J. *A Comparison of Optimal Minibus, Dial-a-bus and Conventional Bus Services.* TRRL Laboratory Report 928. Crowthorne: Transport and Road Research Laboratory, 1980. 13 pp.

An assessment is made of the comparative performance of minibus, dial-a-bus and conventional bus services when operated at their optimal fare and frequency and in the absence of competing stage carriage services.

1732 West Yorkshire County Council: West Yorkshire Passenger Transport Executive. *Bradford Bus Study: final report.* London: R. Travers Morgan and Partners, 1976. 169 pp.

1733 West Yorkshire County Council: West Yorkshire Passenger Transport Executive. *Buses in Bradford: an interim report of the Bradford Bus Study.* London: Travers Morgan and Partners, 1974. 121 pp.

Examines public transport services in Bradford. Considers how bus services might be improved to provide reliable and attractive services more directly related to travel needs with particular regard to the distribution of passengers in and adjacent to the Central Area.

Vehicles

1734 Aldridge, John. City Bus Choice in a Changing Market. Surrey: *City Transport*, March/May 1987, 23–28.

Reports that long distance and the need for high spares stocks, as well as urban sprawl and an open attitude to manufacturer loyalty, are features underlying Australian operators' choice of new buses.

1735 Banister, D. J. and **Mackett, R. L.** The Minibus: theory and experience, and their implications. London: *Transport Reviews*, Vol. 10(3), July–September 1990, 189–214.

A major change brought about by the deregulation of buses in the UK has been the increase in the number of minibuses. Article attempts to identify the role of minibuses in urban areas. Compares theoretical expectations with empirical information on what has happened in practice.

1736 Blacker, Ken. *RT: the story of a London bus.* Middlesex: Capital Transport Publishing, 1979. 280 pp.

Details the history of the RT bus and its variants from its introduction in 1939 to its demise in 1979.

1737 Blacker, Ken. *The STLs.* Middlesex: Capital Transport Publishing, 1984. 200 pp.

Account of the STL's history from its introduction in 1932 to its demise almost a quarter of a century later.

1738 Booth, Gavin. *Leyland Atlantean.* London: Ian Allan, 1984. 96 pp.

Monograph on the Leyland Atlantean.

1739 Curtis, Colin H. *The Routemaster Bus.* Kent: Midas Books, 1981. 94 pp.

Details the history of the Routemaster bus from sketch plan to the 1980s.

1740 Darlot, D. The Accessibility of Lowered Buses in the City of the Future. Brussels: *Public Transport International*, Vol. 44(3), 1995, 33–35.

1741 Glaister, Stephen. Bus Deregulation, Competition and Vehicle Size. London: *Journal of Transport Economics and Policy*, Vol. 20(2), May 1986, 217–244.

Study of buses in Aberdeen suggests that, following deregulation, big buses are likely to face growing competition from minibuses.

1742 Godwin, Bill. Low Floors and Improved Layouts: trends in European bus design. London: *Urban Transport International*, January/February, 1991, 14–15.

1743 Godwin, Bill. Playing Safe. London: *Urban Transport International*, May/June 1988, 12–13.

Investigates how German bus builders are raising safety standards to meet new rules.

1744 Green, Oliver and **Rewse-Davies, Jeremy.** *Red Buses: designed for London – 150 years of transport design.* London: Lawrence King, 1995. 160 pp.

1745 Hamer, Mike. London's Minibus Poser. London: *Transport*, Vol. 3, May/June, 1983, 9–11.

Reports that attempts to introduce minibuses onto the streets of London have got off to a faltering start, despite Government enthusiasm for the idea.

1746 Huntley, Peter. Guided Bus: rapid transit on a tight budget? London: *Local Transport Today*, September 1992, 12–13.

Examines the costs and benefits of guided bus systems.

1747 Jack, Doug. *The Leyland Bus Mk 2.* Derbyshire: Transport Publishing, 1984. 524 pp.

Provides an account of 85 years of Leyland bus manufacture.

1748 Jenkinson, Keith A. *London's Cast-off Buses: 1945–1989.* Bradford: Autobus Review Publications, 1989. 96 pp.

Provides an insight into the disposal of more than 21,000 vehicles over a period of 45 years, illustrating the sales patterns that have emerged. Brief reference is also made to trams and trolleybuses.

1749 Keith, B. Guided Bus: some applications. London: *Proceedings of the Chartered Institute of Transport,* Vol. 2(2), May 1993, 26–35.

Considers the case for the guided bus as a possible alternative transport system for urban areas.

1750 Led, Jens Chr. The Duobus Project in Copenhagen. Brussels: *Public Transport International,* Vol. 43(1), January 1994, 22–24.

1751 Public Transport International. Buses Serve Cities World-Wide. Brussels: *Public Transport International,* Vol. 41, February 1993, 68–77.

Reviews the variety of vehicles in service throughout the world.

1752 South Yorkshire Passenger Transport Executive. *Articulated Buses: an evaluation of their potential use in Britain.* South Yorkshire: South Yorkshire Passenger Transport Executive, 1977. 39 pp.

Report prepared by the South Yorkshire Passenger Transport Executive to assist the Department of Transport, the South Yorkshire County Council, British Leyland and other UK operators in establishing the future prospects of articulated buses.

1753 Turner, Roy and **White, Peter.** Can Minibuses Really Attract Passengers Out of Cars? London: *Urban Transport International,* January/February, 1991, 23–25.

Reports that experience in Britain has demonstrated that converting a conventional urban bus service to minibuses operating at a higher frequency can actually attract passengers out of cars with consequent beneficial effects for the urban environment.

1754 Turner, Roy and **White, Peter.** Minibuses: the way ahead? London: *Transport,* Vol. 9, January, 1988, 23–25.

Considers the impact of minibuses on bus services in the UK and examines their future prospects.

1755 Turner, Roy; White, Peter; Gretton, John; Harrison, Anthony and **O'Leary, Laura** (eds). Does the Minibus Revolution Mean the End of the Big Bus? Berkshire: *Policy Journals*, 1987, 20–26.

Examines the circumstances in which minibuses are more profitable to operate than conventional buses.

1756 Urban Transport International. European Bus Industry: who's in good shape for the single market? London: *Urban Transport International*, August/September, 1990, 14–19.

Considers the implications for bus supply in Europe which will follow the withdrawal of barriers and the establishment of the single market in 1992.

1757 Walters, A. A. The Benefits of Minibuses: the case of Kuala Lumpur. London: *Journal of Transport Economics and Policy*, Vol. 13(3), September 1979, 320–335.

Reports that the introduction of 400 minibuses in Kuala Lumpur to compete with buses and taxis brought substantial benefits to operators and users.

1758 Wilkins, Van. Trolley Buses: return of the electric trolley bus. Washington, DC: *Mass Transit*, March/April 1992, 81–82.

Reviews the future of trolley buses in North America.

1759 Yearsley, Ian. Low Floors at Low Cost. London: *Urban Transport International*, October/November 1989, 8–9.

Low floor tramcars are being developed in several countries by a number of manufacturers and operators. Some systems, like that in Grenoble in France, have been designed entirely around the low floor concept. This article surveys the prospects of low floors, and the ways in which other operators are finding ways to integrate low floors with their conventional tramcars.

9   Cars and Automobiles

General

1760 Altshuler, Alan; Anderson, Martin; Jones, Daniel; Roos, Daniel and **Womack, James.** *The Future of the Automobile: the report of the MIT's International Automobile Program.* London: George Allen and Unwin, 1984. 321 pp.

1761 Barker, Theo (ed.). *The Economic and Social Effects of the Spread of Motor Vehicles.* Basingstoke: Macmillan, 1987. 324 pp.

Collection of essays designed to show the global economic and social effects of the ever escalating volume of motor vehicles. Specialists drawn from Europe, Asia, Africa and North America discuss the ways in which motor buses and trucks as well as cars and motor cycles increasingly affect most people's lives in the developing and developed parts of the world.

1762 Carpenter, S. M., Clarke, M. I., Dix, M. C., Pollard, H. R. T. and **Spencer, M. B.** *Car Use: a social and economic study.* Aldershot: Gower, 1983. 267 pp.

Survey of household travel patterns, with the car as the focus of the study.

1763 European Conference of Ministers of Transport. *The Future Use of the Car.* Paris: Organisation for Economic Co-operation and Development, 1982. 233 pp.

A volume of three reports. The first discusses studies which have been undertaken to ascertain and quantify forecasts of the ownership and use of a car. The second concentrates on fiscal policy and the associated costs of car use. Finally, the third investigates interrelationships between car use and changing space-time patterns in order to ascertain reasons for the development of urban policy aimed at controlling urban development.

1764 Foley, Donald Leslie. *Differentials in Personal Access to Household Motor Vehicles: five county San Francisco Bay area, 1971.* California: University of California, 1972. 61 pp.

In the United States, the past few decades have witnessed a significant progression from the household car to the personal car. Report aims to clarify the relationship between automobile availability at the household level and personal access to an automobile in order to measure the degree to which the shift from household car to personal car has been achieved.

1765 Hertz Leasing and Fleet Management. *The 'Executive's Car' Survey (1989).* Isleworth: Hertz Leasing and Fleet Management, 1989. 106 pp.

Examination of user and non-user attitudes towards the company car. The survey was initiated to provide the corporate decision-maker with unique data on the company car's effectiveness across a number of key areas ranging from recruitment to sales efficiency. Looks at whether fringe benefits such as the company car provide an effective incentive or motivational tool.

1766 Hutchings, Ken. *Urban transport: public or private? Fabian Research series 261.* London: Fabian Society, 1973. 24 pp.

Investigates an unanswered question in the Buchanan Report, that is, the limitation of car usage in our towns, and how that limitation is to be effected. Discussed in the context of London's traffic problems.

1767 Kenworthy, Jeffrey and **Newman, Peter W. G.** *Cities and Automobile Dependence: an international sourcebook.* Aldershot: Gower, 1989. 388 pp.

A study of urban form, transport and energy use in thirty-two cities from North America, Europe, Asia and Australia.

1768 Matthias, Howard. Understanding American Drivers. Westport, CT: *Transportation Quarterly*, Vol. 44(4), October 1990, 607–614.

Suggests that the reason for Americans' loyalty to their car, despite the high running costs, is that they have become psychologically brainwashed as to the importance of the automobile and driving.

1769 Mitchell, C. G. B. *The Influence of the Car on Personal Travel.* TRRL Supplementary Report 681. Crowthorne: Transport and Road Research Laboratory, 1981. 15 pp.

Report on the growth of the number of cars and of traffic. Examines the changes which occur in people's patterns of travel when they have a car available to them. Demonstrates that the popularity of the car as a means of transport creates problems for those without cars. Examples are given to illustrate ways in which these problems can be ameliorated.

1770 Mogridge, M. J. H. *The Car Market.* London: Pion, 1983. 197 pp.

Examines the UK car market in order to demonstrate how market processes work, particularly the statics and dynamics of supply–demand interaction.

1771 Nash, C. A. The Replacement of Road Transport Vehicles. London: *Journal of Transport Economics and Policy*, Vol. 10(1), January 1976, 150–166.

1772 Parkhurst, G. *A Case-Study of the Transport Debate in a Historic City Since Motorisation: ancient meadows, modern modes*. Oxford: Oxford University, Transport Studies Unit, 1992. 30 pp.

1773 Rhys, D. G. *The Motor Industry: an economic survey*. London: Butterworths, 1972. 486 pp.

Review of the motor industry from its origin through to its current structure and organisation both in Britain and abroad.

1774 Townroe, P. M. *Social and Political Consequences of the Motor Car*. Cheshire: St. Ann's Press, 1974. 189 pp.

Considers the motor car in its wider context; its development in partnership or in competition with other forms of transport and its impact on the life of the community.

Theory and technology

1775 Baker, Karen; Hirschman, Ira and **Pucher, John.** Factors Affecting Motor Vehicle Travel into New York City's Central Business District. Virginia: *Transportation Quarterly*, Vol. 47(4), October 1993, 61–77.

Documents trends in travel and modal splits for trips into the Manhattan central business district since World War II. Identifies factors that may have affected overall travel demand as well as the choice between automobile and mass transit.

1776 Banister, D. J. and **Gwilliam, K. M.** Patterns of Car Usage and Restraint Modelling. Amsterdam: *Transportation*, Vol. 6, 1977, 345–363.

Transport demand forecasting procedures have traditionally employed household based modal split models implicitly assuming a selection of modes for each trip based on relative generalised cost. However, detailed examination of the trip patterns of a sample of households in West Yorkshire shows that in fact there is little discretionary choice of public transport; public transport trips in car owning households generally being explained in terms of the specific unavailablity of the car for such trips.

1777 Berechman, Joseph and **Paaswell, Robert, E.** The Impact of Car Availability on Urban Transportation Behaviour. Amsterdam: *Transportation*, Vol. 6, 1977, 121–134.

Proposes that car availability is a variable which ought to be employed in planning studies to provide a more accurate picture of an individual's access to a car.

1778 Bos, G. G. J. *A Logistic Approach to the Demand for Private Cars.* Tilburg: Tilburg University Press, 1970. 165 pp.

1779 Button, Kenneth; Hine, John and **Ngoe, Ndoh.** Modelling Vehicle Ownership and Use in Low Income Countries. London: *Journal of Transport Economics and Policy*, Vol. 27(1), January 1993, 51–68.

Attempts to develop a forecasting framework to provide medium term projections for development and transport planning.

1780 Chen, Kan. Driver Information Systems: a North American perspective. Amsterdam: *Transportation*, Vol. 17(3), 1990, 251–262.

Driver information systems are considered as a major category of intelligent vehicle-highway systems which offer to improve the efficiency and safety of driving by means of an amalgamation of information technology with vehicle and highway technologies. Discusses the tradional North American strength in information technologies that are relevant to driver information systems.

1781 Costantino, James. The IVHS Strategic Plan for the United States. Westport, CT: *Transportation Quarterly*, Vol. 46(4), 1992, 481–490.

Describes the essential elements of an intelligent vehicle-highway system strategy, drawn up by IVHS America, an educational and scientific society established to plan, promote and coordinate the development and deployment of such systems in the USA.

1782 Davis, Christian F. and **Ridgeway, Hallas H.** Use of Video as an Aid in Driving. Westport, CT: *Transportation Quarterly*, Vol. 45(3), July 1991, 441–454.

Describes a study of the use of video to assist in motor vehicle navigation. Argues that efficient navigation is important in reducing traffic congestion, excess travel, fuel consumption, and air pollution.

1783 Hackworth, John. *How Many Cars in the 21st Century?* Bedford: Cranfield Press, 1988. 170 pp.

Examines and extends the existing ideas which underlie the mathematical prediction of changes in demand for consumer durables, including cars.

1784 Hazel, G. M. *The Spatial, Socio-Economic and Energy Influences on the Future of the Private Car.* Edinburgh: Heriot-Watt University (MSc Thesis), 1978.

1785 Hensher, David A. and **Smith, Nariida C.** A Structural Model of the Use of Automobiles by Households: a case study of urban Australia. London: *Transport Reviews*, Vol. 6(1), January–March 1986, 87–111.

Central to the development of transport energy plans are predictions of automobile use. Together with a knowledge of the fuel efficiency of the vehicle fleet, usage acts interdependently to determine the amount of fuel consumed. An econometric model system is developed, at the household level, which treats vehicle use, fuel cost, and vehicle fuel efficiency as functionally interdependent. Data is drawn from Wave 1 of a 4–wave panel of Sydney households.

1786 Hesher, D. A., Milthorpe, F. W. and **Smith, N. C.** The Demand for Vehicle Use in the Urban Household Sector: theory and empirical evidence. London: *Journal of Transport Economics and Policy*, Vol. 24(2), May 1990, 119–137.

Outlines a model of vehicle use and its theoretical integration with vehicle choice, based on an economic theory of individual choice behaviour.

1787 Jansson, Jan Owen. Car Demand Modelling and Forecasting: a new approach. London: *Journal of Transport Economics and Policy*, Vol. 23(2), May 1989, 125–140.

Longitudinal cohort analysis, where the cohorts are constituted by different generations (birth-years), proved necessary for explaining the post-war development of car ownership in Sweden.

1788 Jorgenstein, Finn and **Wentzel-Larsen, Tore.** Forecasting Car Holding, Scrappage and New Car Purchase in Norway. London: *Journal of Transport Economics and Policy*, Vol. 24(2), May 1990, 139–156.

1789 Kawashima, Horonao. Japanese Perspective of Driver Information Systems. Amsterdam: *Transportation*, Vol. 17(3), 1990, 263–284.

1790 Lewis, P. A. *Towards a Bio-cybernetic Model of a Car Driver's Behaviour.* Birmingham: University of Birmingham (PhD Thesis), 1973.

1791 Michon, John A. *Generic Intelligent Driver Support: a comprehensive report on GIDS.* London: Taylor and Francis, 1993. 252 pp.

Seeks to determine the requirements and design standards for an intelligent electronic co-driver system. The generic intelligent driver support concept is introduced, the system is described, its performance is evaluated and recommendations are made for successful implementation.

1792 Neumann, Edward S., Plummer, Ralph W. and **Romansky, Michael L.** Passenger Car Comfort and Travel Decisions: a physiological study. London: *Journal of Transport Economics and Policy*, Vol. 12(3), September 1978, 231–243.

Suggests that different degrees of heat and noise may affect the frequency and duration of trips.

1793 Reza, Ali M. and **Spiro, Michael H.** The Demand for Passenger Car Transport Service and for Gasoline. London: *Journal of Transport Economics and Policy*, Vol. 13(3), September 1979, 304–319.

Authors study the effects of changes in the price of gasoline on the demand for gasoline, for new cars and for quality in cars.

1794 Ritichie, Stephen G. A Knowledge-based Decision Support Architecture for Advanced Traffic Management. Oxford: *Transportation Research*, Vol. 24A(1), January 1990, 27–37.

Examines the operation of Intelligent Vehicle-Roadway Systems which provide for surveillance, control and management of integrated freeway and arterial networks.

1795 Robb, Margaret C. Route Information Systems for Motorists. London: *Transport Reviews*, Vol. 7(3), July–September 1987, 259–275.

Examines the conventional systems used by motorists for route-planning and navigation, and also a number of the experimental systems which have been developed in a number of countries throughout the world.

1796 Roberts, John. Sowing the Caraway Seed. Oxford: *Built Environment*, Vol. 15(4), Numbers 3/4, 1989, 215–230.

Examines the attempts to reduce the need to use a car and encourage less travel. These measures are seen as an alternative to developing a 'Green' car.

1797 Robertson, P. *A Study of the Importance of Travel Time Variability to Private Car Users.* Leeds: University of Leeds (MSc Thesis), 1987.

Investigates the reduction of variability of travel times which transport users experience as a result of a transport improvement.

1798 Seiffert, Ulrich and **Walzer, Peter.** *The Future for Automotive Technology.* London: Frances Pinter, 1984. 197 pp.

Reviews the trends in automobile technology.

1799 Shaoul, J. E. *An Analysis of the Effects of Driver Education.* Salford: University of Salford (PhD Thesis), 1972.

1800 Stamtiadis, Nikiforos. IVHS and the Older Driver. Virginia: *Transportation Quarterly*, Vol. 47(4), October 1993, 15–22.

Discusses the needs of older drivers within the context of the implementation of Intelligent Vehicle Highway Systems.

1801 Train, K. A Structured Logit Model of Auto Ownership and Mode Choice. Oxford: *Review of Economic Studies*, Vol. 47(2), January 1980, 357–370.

1802 Transport and Environment Studies. *Have Car Will Travel: a study of travel patterns in Manchester.* London: Transport and Environment Studies, 1992. 104 pp.

TEST believes that the congestion caused by cars can be solved by identifying why people need cars and then removing that need. Report forms one of the Trip Degeneration Series which attempt to identify ways in which the demand for travel can be reduced and modal shift effected from cars to 'greener' modes of transport. Two different travel patterns for two residential areas of Manchester were studied and an explanation offered for the differences found between them.

1803 Wright, Derek S. Current On Board Vehicle Systems. Amsterdam: *Transportation*, Vol. 17(3), 1990, 239–250.

Describes the aspects of vehicle technology and performance that are the focus for on board computing equipment, from engine management systems through to fully integrated driver decision support.

Policy

1804 Babunovic, Mark; Falvey, Rodney E., Frank, Jeff and **Fried, Harold O.** Fuel Economy Standards and Automobile Prices. London: *Journal of Transport Economics and Policy*, Vol. 20(1), January 1986, 31–46.

US law requires cars produced by each manufacturer to comply with average standards of fuel economy. Article claims that relative prices of large and small cars were adjusted during 1978 and 1979. In 1980 the standard was met through alterations in model characteristics and through changes in demand towards smaller cars.

1805 Bonnel, Patrick. Urban Car Policy in Europe. Oxford: *Transport Policy*, Vol. 2(2), April 1995, 83–95.

1806 Brown, R., Flavin, Christopher and **Norman, Colin.** *Running on Empty: the future of the automobile in an oil short world.* New York: W. W. Norton, 1979. 116 pp.

Written against the background of the oil crisis of the 1970s, the authors speculate on the demise of the automobile.

1807 Clorer, Steffen and **Pucher, John.** Taming the Automobile in Germany. Westport, CT: *Transportation Quarterly*, Vol. 46(3), July 1992, 383–395.

Examines some specific strategies for restricting automobile use that have been implemented in German cities. The city of Freiburg, Germany, is used as a case study as it has been an innovator in such efforts.

1808 Fauth, G. R. and **Gomez-Ibanez, J. A.** Downtown Auto Restraint Policies: the costs and benefits for Boston. London: *Journal of Transport Economics and Policy*, Vol. 14(2), May 1980, 133–153.

The Boston Metropolitan area was used as a case study in an analysis of the benefits and costs of several measures designed to restrain auto use and reduce congestion in the central area. The policies examined all produced positive net benefits, particularly during the peak period. Specifically, parking surcharges and area licence schemes were found to generate the highest amount of annual net benefit.

1809 Gakenheimer, Ralph (ed.). *The Automobile and the Environment: an international perspective.* Cambridge, MA: MIT Press, 1978. 494 pp.

Collection of papers which provides an international perspective to the consideration of alternatives to the unrestrained growth and density of private cars.

1810 Giannopoulos, G. A. National Policy Towards Cars: Greece. London: *Transport Reviews*, Vol. 5(1), January–March 1985, 1–18.

1811 Hoorn, Toon van der; Kroes, Eric and **Meijer, Hans.** National Policy Towards Cars: the Netherlands. London: *Transport Reviews*, Vol. 6(1), January–March 1986, 31–47.

Describes the historical development of Dutch motorisation after the Second World War and the policy of the Dutch Government towards the car. Developments are presented in a context of population growth and changes in population structure, in the economic situation, and in land use. Trends in the use of public transport and the bicycle are also highlighted.

1812 Kunert, Uwe. National Policy Towards Cars: the Federal Republic of Germany. London: *Transport Reviews*, Vol. 8(1), January–March 1988, 59–74.

Examines the main instruments that have been applied in West Germany to achieve car-related transport policy objectives, including the latest modifications in the tax system intended to foster the use of low emission vehicles.

1813 Mace, Shirley. National Policy Towards Cars: Hong Kong. London: *Transport Reviews*, Vol. 6(2), April–June 1986, 173–191.

1814 Madhavan, Shobhana and **Spencer, Andrew H.** The Car in South East Asia. Oxford: *Transportation Research*, Vol. 23(6), 1989, 425–437.

Discusses the dilemma of Southeast Asian national governments' anxiety to promote their car industries for the benefit of the economy and the complexities of dealing with urban congestion.

1815 Nieuwenhuis, Paul and **Wells, Peter** (eds). *Motor Vehicles in the Environment: principles and practice.* Chichester: John Wiley and Sons, 1994. 196 pp.

Highlights a number of issues which may form the basis of future legislation affecting the motor industry. Includes essays on the bicycle as part of a green integrated traffic system; the light rail option; the politics and paradoxes of greening the motor car in the UK; the greener truck; and the long-life car.

1816 Parkhurst, G. *A Comparison of Policies at Controlling Car Use in the Historic Cities of Oxford and York.* Oxford: Oxford University, Transport Studies Unit, 1993. 20 pp.

1817 Pharoah, Tim and **Topp, Hartmut.** Car-Free City Centres. Dordrecht: *Transportation*, Vol. 21(3), 1994, 231–247.

Examines the strategy of car-free city centres where car traffic is limited by area-wide bans. Looks at case studies from Bologna, Lübeck, Aachen, York and Nuremberg.

1818 Plowden, William. *The Motor Car and Politics in Britain.* Harmondsworth: Penguin Books, 1973. 496 pp.

Examines public policy towards the motor car from the early days of motoring to contemporary controversy about the environment and the needs to restrict motoring.

1819 Pucher, John. Modal Shift in Eastern Germany. Dordrecht: *Transportation*, Vol. 21(1), 1994, 1–22.

Examines the effects of the massive shift from public transport to the private automobile in Eastern Germany. Argues that urban transport policy within the East should adopt some of the strategies used for years in Western Germany to tame the automobile while at the same time allowing high levels of car ownership. Strategies include car-free zones; traffic calming; bicycle lanes; vehicle emission standards; and parking restrictions.

Car parking

1820 Arnott, R., de Palma, A and **Lindsey, R.** A Temporal and Spatial Equilibrium Analysis of Commuter Parking. Lausanne: *Journal of Public Economics*, Vol. 45(3), August 1991, 301–335.

1821 Axhausen, Kay W. and **Polak, John W.** Choice of Parking: stated preference approach. Amsterdam: *Transportation*, Vol. 18, 1991, 59–81.

Reports on two studies of parking carried out in the UK and Germany. Both studies used a stated preference approach in order to collect disaggregate data on travellers' responses to changes in parking attributes and used this data to build simple logit models of parking type choice.

1822 Banister, David. Congestion: market pricing for parking. Oxford: *Built Environment*, Vol. 15(4), Numbers 3/4 1989, 251–256.

Examines the mechanism of relating the costs of parking space to local office rate and rental levels in order to raise awareness of the full social costs of using the car in congested urban areas.

1823 Bixby, Bob. *A Study of Park and Ride Use and the Influence of Parking Availability on Patronage: Oxford.* Oxford Polytechnic working paper No. 35. Oxford: Oxford Polytechnic, 1978. 23 pp.

1824 British Parking Association Limited. *Off-Street Parking.* A report of the British Parking Association Seminar, London, 1970. London: British Parking Association, 1970. 47 pp.

1825 Brown, Mark. *Car Parking, the economics of policy enforcement.* Bedford: Cranfield Press, 1991. 171 pp.

Study in which the objectives of parking enforcement are expressed in quantitative economic terms. Describes surveys of the relationship between enforcement effort and compliance in Manchester, London and Brighton, and goes on to show how an economic model can be adapted as a framework for managing parking enforcement so as to minimise social costs.

1826 Cheshire County Planning Department. *Parking: planning standards.* Chester: Cheshire County Council, 1974. 29 pp.

1827 Cullinane, Kevin and **Polak, John.** Illegal Parking and the Enforcement of Parking Regulations: causes, effects and interactions. London: *Transport Reviews*, Vol. 12(1), January–March 1992, 49–75.

1828 Dickins, Ian S. J. Park and Ride Facilities on Light Rail Transit Systems. Amsterdam: *Transportation*, Vol. 18, 1991, 23–36.

Investigates the potential for park and ride facilities on light rail transit systems resulting from a postal survey of 51 European and North American cities.

1829 English Historic Towns Forum. *Bus-Based Park and Ride: a good practice guide.* English Historic Towns Forum, 1993. 64 pp.

1830 Eno Transportation Foundation. *Parking Garage Planning and Operation.* New York: Columbia University Press, 1978. 169 pp.

Study based on research from 118 cities in North America on 274 parking garages. The role of parking in the total urban transportation system is discussed as it relates to growing concern over social and environmental consequences and energy conservation implications in urban motor travel.

1831 Everett, Carol T. and **Miller, Gerald K.** Raising Commuter Parking Prices: an empirical study. Amsterdam: *Transportation*, Vol. 11, 1982, 105–129.

Parking price strategies have the potential for significantly altering travel behaviour in favour of high occupancy of vehicles, as well as reducing congestion, energy consumption and pollution. Reports that attempts aimed at eliminating employee parking subsidies provided an opportunity to examine the impact of commuter parking price changes.

1832 Gillen, David W. Estimation and Specification of the Effects of Parking Costs on Urban Transport Mode Choice. London: *Journal of Urban Economics*, Vol. 4(2), April 1977, 186–199.

The effect of changes in parking fees on urban transport mode choice are investigated in order to evaluate the claim that parking taxes are an effective substitute for road pricing in reducing congestion.

1833 Gillen, David W. Parking Policy, Parking Location Decisions and the Distribution of Congestion. Amsterdam: *Transportation*, Vol. 7, 1978, 69–85.

Develops and tests a model which characterises the parking location decisions of individual tripmakers. Designed to offer information concerning the effects of alternative parking policies on parking location decisions and the effects on the distribution of congestion in an urban area.

1834 Glazer, A. and **Niskanen, E.** Parking Fees and Congestion. *Regional Science of Urban Economics*, Vol. 22(1), March 1992, 123–132.

1835 Haworth, S. *Parking and Urban Land Use.* Manchester: University of Manchester Institute of Science and Technology (PhD Thesis), 1984. 542 pp.

1836 Higgins, Thomas J. Flexible Parking Requirements for Office Developments: new support for public parking and ridesharing. Amsterdam: *Transportation*, Vol. 12(4), 1985, 343–359.

Examines new flexible parking requirements in several North American cities.

1837 Hughes, Peter. Parking Controls and Traffic Restraint: can the matrix make the link? London: *Local Transport Today*, November, 1993, 12–13.

Constraints on parking capacity are increasingly being recognised as the most readily available tool in managing traffic demand, particularly in congested towns and cities. Hower, despite the fact that the principle of parking restraint is widely accepted, translating this into actual numerical standards is far more difficult. Article reviews the issue and looks at the solution offered by the London Advisory Committee.

1838 Hunt, J. D. *Modelling Commuter Parking Location Choice and its Influence on Mode Choice.* Cambridge: University of Cambridge (PhD Thesis), 1988.

Attempts to develop a hierarchical multinomial logit model of 1) parking location choice and 2) parking location and mode choice using disaggregate revealed preference observations.

1839 Huntley, Peter. Park and Ride: strategic modal shift or cheap overflow parking? London: *Local Transport Today*, July, 1993, 12–13.

Park and Ride is being backed by many towns as a solution to congestion and as an opportunity to boost public transport. Article looks at the current trends.

1840 Jain, Rajendra and **Mancini, Alan N.** Commuter Parking Lots – Vandalism and Deterrence: a Connecticut study. Westport, CT: *Transportation Quarterly*, Vol. 41(4), October 1987, 539–554.

Examines the problems of vandalism and theft taking place in Connecticut's car parks and the surveillance methods instituted to deter such acts.

1841 Jeong, B. *Identification of Parking Problems and Policy in the Metropolitan City: the case of Seoul, Korea.* Sheffield: University of Sheffield (PhD Thesis), 1992.

Argues that parking can no longer be viewed as an isolated issue, and parking policy should be considered as part of urban planning and the transport system. Explores the parking problem and policy in Seoul's central business district. It is orientated to the parking problem and characteristics, effects and implementation of parking policy.

1842 Khattak, Asad and **Polak, John.** Effect of Parking Information on Travelers' Knowledge and Behaviour. Dordrecht: *Transportation,* Vol. 20, 1993, 373–393.

The city of Nottingham in England tested a real-time parking information system designed to alleviate congestion on the City Centre parking facilities. Real-time information was disseminated through the radio, while historical information regarding parking locations was disseminated through newspaper advertisements and leaflets. The objective of this study is to assess impacts of the parking information system on travellers' knowledge and decisions.

1843 Kimber, R. M. *The Effects of Wheel Clamping in Central London.* TRRL Laboratory Report 1136. Crowthorne: Transport and Road Research Laboratory, 1984. 54 pp.

1844 Kirkus, Larry D. and **Segelhorst, Elbert W.** Parking Bias in Transit Choice. London: *Journal of Transport Economics and Policy,* Vol. 7(1), January 1973, 58–70.

Claims that the practice of subsidising the parking of employees' cars produces an undesirable bias against public transport.

1845 Laughlin, Colin A. *Introducing Car Park Charges.* Series 3. No. 27. London: Chartered Institute of Public Finance and Accountancy, 1985. 52 pp.

1846 Lester, Nick. On The Road to Success. London: *Local Government Chronicle,* 14 July 1995, 12–13.

Examines the implications for London Councils following shift in responsibility for enforcement of parking controls from the police to local authorities.

1847 Lusiba, J. G. *Drivers' Choice of Car Park.* Leeds: University of Leeds (MSc Thesis), 1987.

Examines the effects which a number of factors have on motorists' searching for a parking space and the walk from parking places to destinations.

1848 MacRae, John. Parking by Numbers. London: *Estates Gazette,* No. 9445, 1994, 133–134.

Considers the possible effects of PPG6 and PPG13 on planning for town centre and out of town development.

1849 MacRae, John. Driving Through the Solution. London: *Estates Gazette,* No. 9331, 1993, 56–57.

Analyses traffic and parking policies in historic towns.

1850 Matsoukis, Evangelos C. Privatization of Parking Management in Greece. Oxford: *Transport Policy,* Vol. 2(1), January 1995, 25–31.

In the city of Patras, which is the third most populated city in Greece, a new comprehensive parking management system was introduced in 1993. The main characteristics of the system include the introduction of paid parking for all legal places available in the city centre; the installation of appropriate equipment for ticket issuing; and the designation of street parking in three different zones, each with a different pricing policy. Article assesses the scheme on the basis of a 'before-and-after' study.

1851 McShane, Mary and **Meyer, Michael.** Parking Policy and Urban Goals: linking strategy to needs. Amsterdam: *Transportation,* Vol. 11, 1982, 131–152.

Parking management strategies have traditionally been used as a means of accommodating traffic demand, with little or no effort made to identify how such strategies might relate to other urban objectives. In this article, parking management strategies in the United States are classified according to the control they exert over the amount of aggregate parking supply; access to parking; spatial distribution of parking supply; or dollar price of parking.

1852 Nelson, R. B. A Tale of Four Cities and Their Car Parks. London: *Transport,* Vol. 9, March, 1988, 139–141.

In any major city or town, the subject of parking provision and pricing policy is often an emotive one. Looking at the United Kingdom and European cities, this article argues that they have much in common.

1853 Oppewal, Harmen; Timmermans, Harry and **Waerden, Peter van der.** Adaptive Choice Behaviour of Motorists in Congested Shopping Centre Parking Lots. Dordrecht: *Transportation,* Vol. 20(4) 1993, 395–408.

Currently existing models of parking choice behaviour typically focus on the choice of types of parking spaces. Aim of this article is to contribute to the growing literature on parking choice modelling by developing and testing a stated choice model of adaptive behaviour of motorists who are faced with fully occupied parking lots.

1854 Organisation for Economic Co-operation and Development. *Evaluation of Urban Parking Systems.* Paris: Organisation for Economic Co-operation and Development, 1980. 97 pp.

1855 Parkhurst, G. *Park and Ride: determining policy aims, evaluating their success.* Oxford: Oxford University, Transport Studies Unit, 1994. 12 pp.

1856 Parkhurst, G. and **Stokes, G.** *Park and Ride in Oxford and York.* Oxford: Oxford University, Transport Studies Unit, 1994. 71 pp.

1857 Parkhurst, Graham. Park and Ride: could it lead to an increase in car traffic? Oxford: *Transport Policy*, Vol. 2(1), January 1995, 15–23.

Examines the results of studies of park and ride carried out in Oxford and York during 1994.

1858 Pickett, M. (ed.). *Parking Control: from principle to practice.* Crowthorne: Transport and Road Research Laboratory, 1995. 159 pp.

1859 Regional Planning Research. *Parking: who pays?* London: Automobile Association, 1970. 160 pp.

Survey commissioned by the AA from Regional Planning Research which aimed to present a background of reliable information on the parking needs of motorists coupled with an indication as to how such needs might be adequately met.

1860 Segelhorst, Elbert W. Transit Validation for City Centres. London: *Journal of Transport Economics and Policy*, Vol. 5(1), January 1971, 28–39.

To counteract attractions of suburban shopping centres, retailers in central business districts often offer free parking to customers. Article proposes instead a scheme of transit validation to encourage the use of public transport.

1861 Shackleton, Jean. A Fighting Chance. Chichester: *Road Law*, Vol. 11(3), 1995, 161–164.

Looks at whether stipulations exist concerning the size and dimensions of parking spaces.

1862 Sheppard, Caroline. Parking in London. *Litigator*, July 1995, 309–311.

Examines the transfer of accountability for enforcing parking regulations to local authorities under the Road Traffic Act, 1991.

1863 Shoup, Donald C. and **Willson, Richard W.** Employer-Paid Parking: the problem and proposed solutions. Westport, CT: *Transportation Quarterly*, Vol. 46(2), April 1992, 169–192.

Examines the question of employer-paid parking providing the incentive for commuters to drive to work. Claims that this benefit for employees is at cross purposes with policies designed to reduce traffic congestion, energy consumption and air pollution.

1864 Shoup, Donald C. and **Willson, Richard W.** Parking Subsidies and Travel Choices: assessing the evidence. Amsterdam: *Transportation,* Vol. 17(2), 1990, 141–157.

Reviews empirical studies of how employer-paid parking affects employees' travel choices.

1865 Smith, L. H. *Park 'n' Ride: further developments.* Leicester: H. Cave, 1974. 24 pp.

Examination of Park and Ride in Leicester during the 1970s.

1866 Taylor, Michael A. P., Thompson, Russell G. and **Young, William.** A Review of Urban Car Parking Models. London: *Transport Reviews,* Vol. 11(1), January–March 1991, 63–84.

Car Parking is an issue of significance both at the local level and at the strategic level of planning. Parking policy and supply play a major role in the management of transportation systems in dense urban areas. Article examines parking as an integral component of urban transport systems.

1867 Thomson, J. M. *Some Characteristics of Motorists in Central London.* Greater London Papers: No. 13. London: Greater London Group, 1968. 63 pp.

Reports on 1966 survey of car parking in central London. Main purpose is to establish the number of parked cars; when they arrived and departed; duration of stay; and how full the parking sites were at different times of the day.

1868 Topp, Hartmut H. Parking Policies to Reduce Car Traffic in German Cities. London: *Transport Reviews,* Vol. 13(1), January–March 1993, 83–95.

Discusses parking policy is as part of a comprehensive approach of 'push and pull' strategies to reduce car traffic.

1869 Topp, Hartmut H. Parking Policies in Large Cities in Germany. Amsterdam: *Transportation,* Vol. 18, 1991, 3–21.

1870 Whitlock, Edward M. *Parking for Institutions and Special Events.* Connecticut: Eno Foundation for Transportation, 1982. 59 pp.

Examines the problems faced by hospitals, medical centres, universities and similar institutions in urban areas of providing adequate, controlled parking.

1871 Wilson, R. W. Estimating the Travel and Parking Demand Effects of Employer-Paid Parking. Amsterdam: *Regional Science & Urban Economics*, Vol. 22(1), March 1992, 133–145.

1872 Young, W. A Review of Parking Lot Design Models. London: *Transport Reviews*, 8(2), April–June 1988, 161–181.

The efficient design of parking lots is an important element in the development of the transport infrastructure. The design process often adopted is based on broad measures of parking demand, design manuals outlining the minimum size of the components and the experience of the designer. Recent improvements in these models have been aided by rapid developments in computer and graphics technology. Article reviews developments in models of parking lots.

1873 Young, W. Application of Some Recent Technological Developments that Assist in the Design of Car Parks. Victoria: *Australian Road Research*, Vol. 21(3), September 1991, 60–71.

Discusses the application of alternative technologies and methods for collecting and analysing parking data.

Car sharing

1874 Akiva, Moshe Ben and **Atherton, Terry J.** Methodology for Short-Range Travel Demand Prediction: analysis of carpooling incentives. London: *Journal of Transport Economics and Policy*, Vol. 11(3), September 1977, 224–261.

Carpooling can be encouraged by direct incentives and by disincentives to solo drivers. Combination can be effective in reducing congestion and fuel consumption. Article examines ways in which the process might be extended and improved.

1875 Atherton, T. J. and **Ben-Akiva, M. E.** Methodology for Short-Range Travel Demand Predictions: analysis of carpooling incentives. London: *Journal of Transport Economics and Policy*, Vol. 11(3), September 1977, 224–261.

Presents a methodology for short-range travel demand predictions based on disaggregate choice models and its application for predicting carpool demand. The models consider residential locations and work places as being fixed and predict automobile ownership, choice of mode for the work trip, and the frequency, destination and mode for non-work travel. The predicted effects of several significant carpooling incentives are presented.

1876 Automobile Association. *Travelling to Work: a study of employees' journey patterns and the AA carshare campaign.* Basingstoke: Automobile Association, 1992. 46 pp.

1877 Bain, R. and **Pettitt, T.** *Social Car Schemes: a comprehensive guide to organised car-sharing.* 2nd ed. Hyde: Community Transport Association, 1993. 76 pp.

1878 Beroldo, Steve. Casual Carpooling in the San Francisco Bay Area. Westport, CT: *Transportation Quarterly*, Vol. 44(1), January 1990, 133–150.

Report of a study into casual carpooling, which is an informal arrangement of single occupancy cars picking up passengers to take advantage of high occupancy vehicle bypass lanes.

1879 Bonsall, Peter. Car Sharing in the United Kingdom: a policy appraisal. London: *Journal of Transport Economics and Policy*, Vol. 15(1), January 1981, 35–44.

Car sharing schemes can be beneficial, but in Britain their main effect is normally to abstract patronage from public transport. Article provides guidance on the shaping and presentation of schemes.

1880 Brownstone, D. and **Golob, T. F.** The Effectiveness of Ridesharing Incentives: discrete-choice models of commuting in Southern California. Amsterdam: *Regional Science & Urban Economics*, Vol. 22(1), March 1992, 5–24.

1881 Ferguson, Erik. The Influence of Employer Ridesharing Programs on Employee Mode Choice. Amsterdam: *Transportation*, Vol. 17(2), 1990, 179–207.

Article examines a study where employer ridesharing programmes and employee mode choice were analysed using Southern California data. Problems in estimating the costs and benefits of employer ridesharing programmes were identified.

1882 Gordon, Steve and **Meyer, Michael D.** Public/Private-Sector Cooperation in Urban Transportation: lessons from ridesharing experiences in Connecticut. Amsterdam: *Transportation*, Vol. 11, 1982, 235–250.

Examples of public/private-sector interaction in two Connecticut cities, Hartford and Stamford, are used to illustrate the characteristics of successful transportation programme implementation.

1883 Green, G. R. *Car-sharing and Car-pooling – a review.* TRRL

Supplementary Report 358. Crowthorne: Transport and Road Research Laboratory,1978. 26 pp.

Literature review to assess the possible benefits and disbenefits of car-pooling and car-sharing in Britain. An Appendix gives an annotated list of the publications covered, which are mostly from the USA.

1884 Greening, P. A. K. and **Jackson, R. L.** Pooling for the Journey to Work: the outlook in Great Britain. Amsterdam: *Transportation*, Vol. 12, 1983, 97–116.

Considers the potential for bus, minibus and car pooling in Britain drawing from both relevant theoretical and economic studies and practical operational experience. Concludes that under reasonable assumptions about the transport situation in the next decade, pooling could become increasingly useful in solving travel problems of individual local groups, but that it is unlikely to become a major mode in terms of the numbers of trips carried. Relevant comparisons are made with like elements in the USA.

1885 Levin, Irwin P. Measuring Tradeoffs in Carpool Driving Arrangement Preferences. Amsterdam: *Transportation*, Vol. 11(1), 1982, 71–85.

Describes two experiments where evaluations were obtained of alternative carpooling situations varying in driving arrangement, size of carpool, distance travelled, and amount of time to pick up and deliver passengers.

1886 McCarthy, Patrick S. The Shared Vehicle Fleet: a study of its impact upon accessibility and vehicle ownership. London: *Journal of Transport Economics and Policy*, Vol. 18(1), January 1984, 75–94.

Reports on a study in which shared fleets provided each participating household with a small vehicle and the opportunity to call on larger vehicles when required. Gains in accessibility accrued chiefly to small, lower-income households. There was a decrease of 25 per cent in total vehicle ownership.

1887 Stevens, William F. Improving the Effectiveness of Ridesharing Programs. Westport, CT: *Transportation Quarterly*, Vol. 44(4), October 1990, 563–578.

Reports on a study structured to replicate recent findings regarding ridesharing influences and participants' behaviour. Set in the context of the declining influence of energy costs motivating ridesharing and the increase in non-energy factors.

1888 Teal, Roger F. Carpooling: who, how and why. Oxford: *Transportation Research*, Vol. 21A(3), May 1987, 203–214.

Analyses the characteristics of carpoolers, distinguishes among different types of carpoolers, identifies the key differences between carpoolers and drive alone and transit commuters, describes how commuters carpool, and offers explanations of why commuters carpool. Also addresses the feasibility of a substantial increase in carpool mode share.

Ownership

1889 Allanson, E. W. *Car Ownership Forecasting.* London: Gordon and Breach Science Publishers, 1982. 156 pp.

Comments on the development and performance of car ownership prediction procedures including a wide-ranging survey of the modelling techniques associated with such forecasting.

1890 Bates, John. *A Disaggregate Model of Household Car Ownership.* Research Report 20. London: Department of Transport, 1978. 79 pp.

Presents a car ownership model based on two equations and fitted by maximum likelihood methods to data from successive Family Expenditure Surveys using household income as the independent variable. Claims that, taking the model back to 1961, the growth in car ownership can be related entirely to the growth in real income and the relative fall in car prices.

1891 Bates, John; Lowe, Steve; Richards, Paul and **Roberts, Mike.** *The Factors Affecting Household Car Ownership.* Aldershot: Gower, 1981. 168 pp.

Identifies the factors which influence a household's choice of whether or not to own a car and decisions about multi-car ownership. Study based on a binomial logit model is applied to a large amount of unpublished household survey data.

1892 Button, K. J., Pearman, A. D. and **Fowkes, A. S.** *Car Ownership Modelling and Forecasting.* Aldershot: Gower, 1982. 157 pp.

Looks at existing forecasting models for car ownership and at forecasting techniques, on a national and local level.

1893 Button, K. J. and **Pearman, A. D.** Some Problems in Forecasting Car Ownership for Urban Areas. London: George Godwin, *International Forum Series,* Vol. 1, 1981, 157–168.

Presents the findings of a research project on car ownership being undertaken under the auspices of the Social Science Research Council.

1894 Downes, J. D. *The Distribution of Household Car Ownership.* TRRL Supplementary Report 250. Crowthorne: Transport and Road Research Laboratory, 1976. 18 pp.

1895 Eldridge, Derek and **Mogridge, Martin.** *Car Ownership in London.* Research Report 10. London: Greater London Council, 1970. 67 pp.

Outlines the methods used to forecast car ownership for households in London from 1970–1990.

1896 Fairhurst, M. H. The Influence of Public Transport on Car Ownership in London. London: *Journal of Transport Economics and Policy,* Vol. 9(3), September 1975, 193–208.

Reports that variations in car ownership between districts may be accounted for by household income, household size and access to public transport. Claims that transport planning can influence not only modal split in the short term but future decisions by households on whether to own a car.

1897 Forbartha, An Foras. *Car Ownership Forecasts 1995–2005.* Dublin: National Institute for Physical Planning and Construction Research, 1984. 28 pp.

Report providing forecasts of car ownership for the years 1995 to 2005. Indicates that income levels as measured by Gross National Product are the most important determinant of car ownership.

1898 Gallez, Caroline. Identifying the Long-Term Dynamics of Car Ownership: a demographic approach. London: *Transport Reviews,* Vol. 14(1), January–March 1994, 83–102.

Presents a new approach for long term forecasting of vehicle ownership and the household total car fleet, based on a proven demographic method: longitudinal analysis.

1899 Geeson, A. J. *Geographical Aspects of Car Ownership and Availability in the Bristol Area.* Bristol: University of Bristol (PhD Thesis), 1981.

1900 Golob, Thomas F. The Causal Influences of Income and Car Ownership on Trip Generation by Mode. London: *Journal of Transport Economics and Policy,* Vol. 23(2), May 1989, 141–162.

Develops a simultaneous equations model to explain car ownership and trip generation by mode at the household level.

1901 Goodwin, P. B. Car Ownership and Public Transport Use: revisiting the interaction. Dordrecht: *Transportation,* Vol. 20, 1993, 21–33.

1902 Hopkin, Jean M. *The Role of an Understanding of Social Factors in Forecasting Car Ownership.* TRRL Supplementary Report 695. Crowthorne: Transport and Road Research Laboratory, 1981. 21 pp.

Examines established car ownership forecasting techniques and reviews the case for change.

1903 Kitamura, Ryuichi. A Causal Analysis of Car Ownership and Transit Use. Amsterdam: *Transportation*, Vol. 17(2), 1989, 155–173.

Suggests that increase in car use, which is a consequence of increasing car ownership, may not be suppressed by improving public transit.

1904 Lawrence, Peter (ed.). *Vehicle Leasing and Contract Hire.* London: Confederation of British Industry, 1984. 54 pp.

1905 Mogridge, M. J. H. *Improvements to the Department of Transport's Techniques of Car Ownership Forecasting.* London: Martin Mogridge Associates, 1985. 67 pp.

Examines short-term problems with a cross-sectional causal model for car ownership forecasting.

1906 Mogridge, M. J. H. Prediction of Car Ownership and Use Revisited: the beginning of the end? London: *Journal of Transport Economics and Policy*, Vol. 23(1), January 1989, 55–74.

The 1973 oil crisis and subsequent developments have re-emphasised the long-term cycles in the economy, and the Schumpeter changes in power sources and associated technology which drive them. Article reflects on what this may mean for car ownership and use, using new data on time and money budgets. Increasing car ownership but decreasing use are suggested.

1907 Niiro, K. *Impact of Public Transport Service on Regional Car Ownership and Passenger Demand.* Leeds: University of Leeds (M.Phil Thesis), 1988.

Considers the structure and dynamics of the regional passenger transport markets.

1908 Olszewski, Piotr and **Turner, David J.** New Methods of Controlling Vehicle Ownership and Usage in Singapore. Dordrecht: *Transportation*, Vol. 20, 1993, 355–371.

Over the years Singapore has introduced several fiscal measures aimed at restraining car ownership and usage and thus preventing traffic congestion. Two new methods have recently been added: the 'Vehicle Quota System' which limits the number of new vehicles registered each month, and the 'Weekend Car Scheme' which allows cars to be registered for use during off-peak hours only, with substantial financial savings offered to the owners. Article looks at the implementation of these schemes.

1909 Organisation for Economic Co-operation and Development. *Car*

Ownership and Use. Paris: Organisation for Economic Co-operation and Development, 1982. 107 pp.

Reviews the socio-economic factors affecting car ownership and use in OECD countries and assesses forecasting models.

1910 Said, Galal M. Modelling Household Car Ownership in the Gulf States: the case of Kuwait. London: *Journal of Transport Economics and Policy*, Vol. 26(2), May 1992, 121–138.

1911 Sien, Chia Lin and **Spencer, Andrew H.** National Policy Towards Cars: Singapore. London: *Transport Reviews*, Vol. 5(4), October–December 1985, 301–323.

1912 Silberston, Aubrey. Automobile Use and the Standard of Living in East and West. London: *Journal of Transport Economics and Policy*, Vol. 4(1), 1970, 3–14.

Analyses figures of automobiles (and all vehicles) per 1,000 population in various regions. Found that automobile use is related to gross domestic product (or net material product), but that the number of automobiles in socialist countries was far below expectations from the pattern in free-market countries.

1913 Smith, M. J. *Regional Variations in Car Ownership in the United Kingdom: a geographic and economic analysis of the factors affecting the level of passenger car ownership.* London: London School of Economics and Political Science (PhD Thesis), 1971.

1914 Tanner, J. C. *Saturation Levels in Car Ownership Models: some recent data.* TRRL Supplementary Report 669. Crowthorne: Transport and Road Research Laboratory, 1981. 27 pp.

Report on car ownership statistics; on holding driving licences; and on annual kilometres per car; largely obtained through the 1978–79 National Travel Survey and the similar 1977–78 Nationwide Personal Transportation Study of the United States.

1915 Tanner, J. C. *Car Ownership Trends and Forecasts.* TRRL Laboratory Report 799. Crowthorne: Transport and Road Research Laboratory, 1977. 117 pp.

Reports on a range of forecasts on numbers of cars on the basis of alternative assumptions about future levels of economic growth and fuel prices.

1916 Tanner, J. C. *Choice of Model Structure for Car Ownership Forecasting.* TRRL Supplementary Report 523. Crowthorne: Transport and Road Research Laboratory, 1979. 32 pp.

Explores issues raised by the car ownership element of the Regional Highway Traffic Model and the report of the Advisory Committee on Trunk Road Assessment.

1917 Tanner, J. C. *A Lagged Model for Car Ownership Forecasting.* TRRL Laboratory Report 1072. Crowthorne: Transport and Road Research Laboratory, 1983. 17 pp.

Taxis and hire cars

1918 Acton, Peter. Polegate Pioneers Pay Cars. London: *Transport*, Vol. 2, May/June, 1981, 33–34.

Reports on East Sussex County Council's shared taxi scheme at Polegate to supplement the declining bus service.

1919 Beesley, M. E. Competition and Supply in London Taxis. London: *Journal of Transport Economics and Policy*, Vol. 13(1), January 1979, 102–132.

1920 Berglund, Mary and **Teal, Roger F.** *The Impact of Taxicab Deregulation in the USA.* London: Journal of Transport Economics and Policy, Vol. 21(1), January 1987, 37–56.

Examines the results of taxi deregulation in various North American cities and offers explanations, based on industrial organisation concepts, of why this policy has largely failed to produce benefits for either consumers or providers.

1921 Bourgeois, Francoise and **Piozin, Francoise.** The 'Redheads' of Niamey: an original way of providing urban transport. London: *Transport Reviews*, Vol. 6(4), October–December 1986, 331–346.

Examines the operation of shared taxis in Niamey (Niger).

1922 Burby, Raymond J., Feibel, Charles E. and **Gilbert, Gorman.** Taxicab Operating Characteristics in the United States. Amsterdam: *Transportation*, Vol. 12, 1983, 173–182.

Reports on a 1982 national survey of US taxicab operators which sought to assess the economic, operational and organisational status of the industry and also to determine how these characteristics have been changing in response to rising costs and an economic recession.

1923 Coe, G. A. and **Jackson, R. L.** *Some New Evidence Relating to Quantity Control in the Taxi Industry.* TRRL Supplementary Report

797. Crowthorne: Transport and Road Research Laboratory, 1983. 21 pp.

Quantity control of the local taxi trade is the norm in England and Wales, outside London. Report attempts to shed light on the justification for quantity control.

1924 Coe, G. A. and **Jackson, R. L.** *Taxi and Private Hire Car Industries in England and Wales.* TRRL Laboratory Report 1011. Crowthorne: Transport and Road Research Laboratory, 1981. 20 pp.

1925 Departmental Committee. *Report of the Departmental Committee on the London Taxicab Trade.* London: HMSO, 1970. 216 pp.

Report of an inquiry into the operation, structure and economics of the taxicab and private hire car trades in London.

1926 Douglas, George W. Price Regulation and Optimal Service Standards: The Taxicab industry. London: *Journal of Transport Economics and Policy*, Vol. 6(2), May 1972, 116–127.

Examines the principles governing the setting of efficient prices to attain maximum use of the taxicab service.

1927 Economic Research Centre: European Conference of Ministers of Transport. *Organisation of Taxi Services in Towns: Report of the Fifty-fourth Round Table on Transport Economics: held in Paris on 12th – 13th March 1981.* Paris. Organisation for Economic Co-operation and Development, 1981. 131 pp.

1928 European Conference of Ministers of Transport. *Access to Taxis: transport for people with mobility handicaps.* Paris: Organisation for Economic Co-operation and Development, 1992. 177 pp.

Report of an ECMT seminar which examines the role of the taxi for people with mobility disabilities. Includes contributions from taxi operators and designers.

1929 *No Entry.*

1930 Farkas, Z. Andrew and **Rouville, Matthew de.** The Potential of the Jitney: a case study of the Baltimore Metropolitan Area. Westport, CT: *Transportation Quarterly*, Vol. 42(1), January 1988, 89–105.

Using the Baltimore Metropolitan Area as a case study, the potential for jitney or shared-ride taxi services as a viable means of public transportation within a metropolitan area is discussed.

1931 Finch, D. *The 1989 TRRL London Taxi Survey.* Crowthorne: Transport and Road Research Laboratory. 26 pp.

1932 Foerster, James F. and **Gilbert, Gorman.** Taxicab Deregulation: economic consequences and regulatory choices. Amsterdam: *Transportation*, Vol. 8, 1979, 371–387.

The regulation of taxicab services is receiving an increasing amount of attention by city governments. At issue is the question of whether local regulations should limit the supply of taxicabs and whether the regulations should control taxi fares. Article discusses the effects of deregulation within a framework of eight regulatory scenarios involving different price, entry and industrial concentration factors.

1933 Greening, P. A. K. and **Jackson, R. L.** *Shared Taxi Operation: cost considerations.* TRRL Supplementary Report 793. Crowthorne: Transport and Road Research Laboratory, 1983. 12 pp.

Considers when and where the use of shared taxi services might be justified in the light of cost considerations.

1934 Hackner, Jonas and **Nyberg, Sten.** Deregulating Taxi Services: a word of caution. London: *Journal of Transport Economics and Policy*, Vol. 29(2), May 1995, 195–208.

Examines pricing and capacity decisions in markets for phone-ordered taxicabs.

1935 Kirby, Ronald F. Innovations in the Regulation and Operation of Taxicabs. Amsterdam: *Transportation*, Vol. 10, 1981, 61–86.

Reviews a number of innovations in the regulation and operation of taxicabs in U.S. cities. Discusses the growing involvement of various levels of government in public transportation programmes which affect the taxicab industry, and identifies the opportunities and problems created for the industry by this increased governmental activity.

1936 Lister, A. *Shared Taxi Services: a case study of Greater Nottingham.* Nottingham: University of Nottingham (PhD Thesis), 1992. 240 pp.

Attempts to assess why there are so few shared taxi ride services in operation and examines the potential for such services.

1937 McKnight, Claire E. and **Pagano, Anthony M.** Economies of Scale in the Taxicab Industry: some empirical evidence from the United States. London: *Journal of Transport Economics and Policy*, Vol. 17(3), September 1983, 299–314.

Multiple regression analysis was used to estimate the relationship between taxicab company costs and size. Results of both the cost per passenger trip and cost per passenger mile models imply a U-shaped average cost curve for small to medium taxicab firms.

1938 Nemer, Terry and **Teal, Roger F.** Privatization of Urban Transit: the Los Angeles Jitney experience. Amsterdam: *Transportation*, Vol. 13(1), 1986, 5–22.

Reports on a recent attempt to provide private transit in the form of a jitney service in downtown Los Angeles. Describes the process undertaken to initiate jitney service and the resultant organisation's structure and operation.

1939 Papayanis, Nicholas. The Development of the Paris Cab Trade, 1855–1914. Manchester: *Journal of Transport History*, Vol. 8(1), March 1987, 52–65.

1940 Price Commission. *Prices, Costs and Margins in the Provision of Taxicab and Private Hire Car Services.* London: HMSO, 1978. 58 pp.

Examines both the licensed hackney carriage and the private hire car. Focuses on London, Glasgow, Liverpool, Manchester, Hastings, Rhymney Valley (South Wales), Worcester, Yeovil and York.

1941 Shreiber, Chanoch. The Economic Reasons for Price and Entry Regulation of Taxicabs. London: *Journal of Transport Economics and Policy*, Vol. 9(3), September 1975, 268–279.

Article claims that in a free market the charges for taxicabs tend to be high. Regulation in New York City has not been properly designed to achieve economic efficiency. Abolition of the present restriction on entry will increase congestion and pollution and also attract more passengers from public transport.

1942 Takyi, Isaac K. An Evaluation of Jitney Systems in Developing Countries. Westport, CT: *Transportation Quarterly*, Vol. 44(1), January 1990, 163–177.

The jitney or shared ride taxi services are favoured in developing countries' cities because they run faster, provide a source of income to many who would otherwise be unemployed and operate without subsidies. Article attempts to measure its strengths and weaknesses.

1943 Toner, J. P. *The Demand for Taxis and the Value of Time: a welfare analysis.* Leeds: University of Leeds, Institute for Transport Studies, August 1991. 31 pp.

1944 Toner, J. P. *The Economics of Regulation of the Taxi Trade in British Towns.* Leeds: University of Leeds (PhD Thesis), 1990.

Reviews the effects of the Transport Act 1985 on taxi licensing, and claims that regulation is not undertaken by Councils trying to achieve any notion of optimality, but rather with the focus on public order issues.

1945 White, Peter. Fighting Off a 'Mini Challenge.' London: *Transport*, Vol. 10, January, 1989, 13–15.

1946 Williams, David J. Changes in Real Income and the Demand for Taxicabs. Amsterdam: *Transportation*, Vol. 10, 1981, 51–59.

Examines the possible future of the taxicab industry within the context of a familiar economic-growth model. The future capability of the taxicab industry to check increases in real costs is shown to be an important determinant in the industry's long-term viability.

10 Pedestrians and Bicycles

General

1947 Abdulla, H. M. *A Study of the Pedestrian Delay and Behaviour in Glasgow City Centre.* Glasgow: University of Strathclyde (MSc Thesis), 1983.

1948 Balshone, Bruce L., Deering, Paul L., McCarl, Brian D. *Bicycle Transit: its planning and design.* New York: Praeger, 1975. 164 pp.
Argues for the bicycle as a primary means of transportation. Looks at the history of the bicyle, planning, design, legislation, and prospects for the future.

1949 Bell, M. and **Dolphin, R.** *Bicycles and Motorcycles: urban road usage.* Crowthorne: Transport and Road Research Laboratory, 1990. 61 pp.

1950 Bendixson, Terence. *Instead of Cars.* Harmondsworth: Pelican Books, 1977. 254 pp.
Considers the alternatives to cars including buses, trains, pedestrian walkways, taxis and bicycles.

1951 Black, Alan. Analysis of Census Data on Walking to Work and Working at Home. Westport, CT: *Transportation Quarterly*, Vol. 44(1), January 1990, 107–120.
Considers the mode of transport most neglected by urban transportation planners, that of walking. Describes an exploratory study to establish what urban characteristics are related to walking to work and working at home.

1952 Bunting, P. M. *Costs and User Benefits of Passenger Conveyors.* Loughborough: University of Loughborough (MSc Thesis), 1976.

1953 Carrington, Burr. Moving Downtown. Washington, DC: *Mass Transit*, September 1988, 76–83.

Article claims that although proposals for people-movers are now common-place, few manufacturers survive the harsh realities of the market.

1954 Elkington, John; McGlynn, Roger and **Roberts, John.** *The Pedestrian: planning and research.* London: Transport and Environment Studies, 1976. 235 pp.

1955 European Conference of Ministers of Transport. *Short-Distance Passenger Travel.* Report of the ninety-sixth round table on transport economics. Paris: Organisation for Economic Co-operation and Development, 1994. 130 pp.

Proceedings of a conference held in Paris in June 1993. Examines the concept of 'people movers' – or short-distance mechanised transport systems which could serve short distance travel needs.

1956 Forester, John. *Bicycle Transportation.* New York: Cambridge University Press, 1977. 394 pp.

Outlines the complete process of cycling transportation design and offers a recommended cycling transportation programme.

1957 Friends of the Earth. *Cycling and the Healthy City.* London: Friends of the Earth, 1991. 74 pp.

Proceedings of a one day conference held in London in 1990.

1958 Gercans, G. and **Harland, G.** *Cycle Routes.* Crowthorne: Transport and Road Research Laboratory, 1993. 30 pp.

1959 Greater London Council. *Pedestrianised Streets: GLC study tour of Europe and America.* London: Greater London Council, 1973. 245 pp.

1960 Harbidge, J., Henley, S. and **Jones, R.** *Kempston Urban Cycle Route Project After Study.* Crowthorne: Transport and Road Research Laboratory, 1993. 130 pp.

1961 Harrison, A. E. The Origins and Growth of the UK Cycle Industry to 1900. Manchester: *Journal of Transport History,* Vol. 6(1), March 1985, 41–70.

Examines the techniques of production and the economic and social forces which generated the bicycle industry during the last thirty years of the nine-teenth century.

1962 Hass-Klau, Carmen. Impact of Pedestrianisation and Traffic

Calming on Retailing: a review of the evidence from Germany and the United Kingdom. Oxford: *Transport Policy*, Vol. 1(1), October 1993, 21–31.

Claims that pedestrianisation and traffic calming have a positive effect on retailing, with shops inside pedestrian areas being more successful than those outside.

1963 Hillman, Mayer and **Whalley, Anne.** *Walking is Transport.* London: Policy Studies Institute, 1979. 119 pp.

An analysis of 'walk journeys' drawn from national surveys made in 1972/73 and 1975/76 by the Department of Environment and the Department of Transport respectively. Reviews the extent of walking as an element of total travel and in the lives of different people, and for different purposes.

1964 Holmes, G. and **Jackson, S.** *Nottingham Urban Cycle Route Project.* Crowthorne: Transport and Road Research Laboratory, 1993. 64 pp.

1965 Hopkinson, P. and **May, A.** *Perceptions of the Pedestrian Environment.* Crowthorne: Transport and Road Research Laboratory, 1992. 61 pp.

1966 Lowe, Marcia D. *The Bicycle: vehicle for a small planet.* Washington, DC: Worldwatch Institute, 1989. 62 pp.

Examination of the way in which bicycles are used throughout the world.

1967 McGurn, James. *On Your Bicycle: an illustrated history of cycling.* London: John Murray, 1987. 208 pp.

Examines the development of bicycle technology and the social implications and economic importance of the bicycle.

1968 Morgan, J. and **Trevelyan, P.** *Cycling in Pedestrian Areas.* Crowthorne: Transport and Road Research Laboratory, 1987. 59 pp.

1969 Morton, J. *Walking Conditions for Elderly People in the United Kingdom.* London: Pedestrians Association, 1993. 44 pp.

1970 Nwabughuogu, Anthony I. The Role of the Bicycle Transport in the Economic Development of Eastern Nigeria, 1930–45. Manchester: *Journal of Transport History*, Vol. 5(1), March 1984, 91–98.

1971 O'Flaherty, Coleman A. and **Tough, John M.** *Passenger Convey-*

ors: *an innovatory form of communal transport.* Shepperton: Ian Allen, 1971. 176 pp.

Examines the history and prospects of moving pavements as a suitable means to move large numbers of people in an urban environment.

1972 Rajgor, G. Norris Signals Support for Council Cycling Initiatives. Dartford: *Public Service & Local Government,* May/June 1995, 21–22.

Looks at the recent creation of a national bicycle network by the Minister for Local Transport and Road Safety.

1973 Richards, Brian. *Moving in Cities.* London: Studio Vista, 1976. 104 pp.

Examines aspects of urban mobility including pedestrian safety and improved walking conditions; the use of the bicyle; moving pavements; and automatic vehicles.

1974 Robertson, Kent A. Pedestrian Skywalk Systems: downtown's great hope or pathways to ruin. Westport, CT: *Transportation Quarterly,* Vol. 42(3), July 1988, 457–484.

Examines skywalk systems in five cities in the midwest United States: Cincinnati, Des Moines, Duluth, Minneapolis and St. Paul. Evaluates skywalks on the bases of usage; access and orientation; economic activities; design and aesthetics; and use as a downtown redevelopment tool.

1975 Tolley, Rodney (ed.). *The Greening of Urban Transport: planning for walking and cycling in Western cities.* London: Belhaven Press, 1990. 309 pp.

Collection of essays presenting the arguments for incorporating 'green modes' in modern city transport plans. Addresses the principles of green transport planning and outlines the environmental, social and economic issues. Provides examples of successful traffic restraint and exclusion schemes in a variety of urban settings and policy environments.

1976 Transport and Environment Studies. *Buses and Pedestrian Areas.* London: London Transport, 1981. 52 pp.

A study showing ten examples of cities that have conciously made access by bus to pedestrianised areas as good as by car. Concludes that much could be done to improve conditions for bus users wishing to reach and leave pedestrianised shopping areas.

1977 Trench, Sylvia and **Taner, Oc** (eds). *Current Issues in Planning.* Aldershot: Gower, 1990. 236 pp.

Examines various aspects of pedestrianisation including the pedestrian in public policy; walking in the city; women as pedestrians; making residential areas safer for children; the introduction of pedestrianisation in Copenhagen; and the evaluation of pedestrianisation schemes.

1978 Vamplew, C. *Bicycle Ownership and Use in Cleveland: findings from the 1993 Cleveland Social Survey.* Middlesborough: Cleveland County Council, 1994. 10 pp.

1979 Wright, Charles L. Urban Transport, Health and Synergy. Westport, CT: *Transportation Quarterly*, Vol. 45(3), July 1991.

Investigate the advantages of integrating frequent walks and bike rides into daily transportation activities.

1980 Zhihao, Wang. Bicycles in Large Cities in China. London: *Transport Reviews*, Vol. 9(2), April–June 1989, 171–182.

Examines the role of the bicycle as a means of transport in China. Considers such issues as the production of bicycles; bicycles in large cities; the problems of bicycle traffic; and road design and regulation.

Theory

1981 Ashford, N., Atha, J. and **Hawkins, N. M.** *Behavioural Observations of Passengers Boarding a Slow Speed Conveyor.* Loughborough: University of Loughborough, 1974. 57 pp.

1982 Auriat, Denise. *Walking as a Form of Transport: cutting congestion in Edmonton.* Toronto: Toronto Press, 1988. 125 pp.

Makes the case for reducing road congestion through the provision of pedestrian walkways and the raising of public awareness of alternatives to the automobile.

1983 Catchpole, Tim and **Parker, John.** *A Pedestrian Network for Central London.* London: Greater London Council, 1983. 35 pp.

Describes the development of pedestrianised areas in central London and how they might be consolidated into a designed network of pedestrian routes.

1984 Finch, Helen and **Morgan, J. M.** *Attitudes to Cycling.* TRRL Research Report 14. Crowthorne: Transport and Road Research Laboratory, 1985. 18 pp.

1985 Fruin, J. J. *Pedestrian Planning and Design.* New York: Naudep Press, 1971. 206 pp.

Attempts to establish the importance of walking in urban design and to identify the problems of pedestrians in modern cities. The human physiological and psychological factors that affect the planning and design of pedestrian spaces are examined.

1986 Garbrecht, Daniel. Frequency Distributions of Pedestrians in a Rectangular Grid. London: *Journal of Transport Economics and Policy*, Vol. 4(1), January 1970, 66–88.

1987 Lovemark, Olof. New Approaches to Pedestrian Problems. London: *Journal of Transport Economics and Policy*, Vol. 6(1), January 1972, 3–10.

Claims that mistaken ideas on pedestrian behaviour are responsible for many defects in planning and provides several examples.

1988 Miller, David; Papacostas, C. S. and **Willey, Mark.** A Longitudinal Comparison of Bicycle and Moped Use by University Students. Westport, CT: *Transportation Quarterly*, Vol. 45(3), July 1991, 391–408.

Reports on a 1988 survey which provided information on bicycle and moped usage by University of Hawaii students. A comparison is made with a similar study conducted a decade earlier. Includes comparisons of overall modal choices, shifts from other modes of travel to bicycles and mopeds; user characteristics; riding habits; and user-specified problem areas.

1989 Mori, Masmitsu and **Tsukaguchi, Hiroshi.** A New Method for Evaluation of Service in Pedestrian Facilities. Oxford: *Transportation Research*, Vol. 21A(3), May 1987.

Examines the pedestrian movement in urban areas of Japan with the object of finding a suitable method for evaluating sidewalks.

1990 Richards, Brian. *New Movement in Cities.* 2nd ed. London: Studio Vista, 1969. 95 pp.

Concerned primarily with the movement of people rather than cars, and with short distance rather than long distance movement.

1991 Robertson, Kent A. Downtown Pedestrian Malls in Sweden and the United States. Westport, CT: *Transportation Quarterly*, Vol. 46(1), 1992, 37–55.

Evaluates, compares and explains the key similarities and differences between pedestrian streets in the US and Sweden using six case studies from each country.

1992 Sandrock, Keith. Heuristic Estimation of Pedestrian Traffic Volumes. Oxford: *Transportation Research*, Vol. 22A(2), 1988, 89–95.

Describes the method of monitoring pedestrian volumes in the Johannesburg Central Business District.

1993 Xanthopoulos, N. *Pedestrian Movement in Liverpool: a study of design factors.* Edinburgh: University of Edinburgh (MSc Thesis), 1970.

1994 Ying, Li Jia. Management of Bicycling in Urban Areas. Westport, CT: *Transportation Quarterly*, Vol. 41(4), October 1987, 619–629.

Examines various means of managing bicycle traffic in relation to motor vehicles and pedestrians.

Policy

1995 Bannister, Chris and **Groome, David.** *Planning for Cycling in the 1980s: Occasional Paper Number 10.* Manchester: University of Manchester Department of Town and Country Planning, 1983. 89 pp.

Report of a conference held in 1982. Examines such issues as improved facilities for cyclists and the provision of cycle routes on disused railways.

1996 Cyclists' Touring Club. *Cycling as Transport: the way forward; policy statement.* Godalming : Cyclists' Touring Club, 1993. 8 pp.

1997 Davenport, Peter. Derailed. London: *Global Transport*, Vol. 2, Summer 1995, 73–75.

Outlines Seattle's attempt to solve city road congestion. Includes consideration of the role of the bicycle; provision of cycle paths and lanes; and the ability to transport cycles by bus.

1998 Davies, D. *Trust Pedal Power: a review of Transport Policies and Programmes for 1994/1995 with regard to cycling.* Cyclists' Public Affairs Group, June 1994. 32 pp.

1999 Efrat, Joseph. Planning a Favourable Environment for Bicycle Use in Towns. London: George Godwin, *International Forum Series*, Vol. 2, 1981, 123–136.

Examines the available methods to promote safe and pleasant cycling conditions.

2000 Fergusson, M. and **Rowell, A.** *Bikes Not Fumes: the emission and*

health benefits of a modal shift from motor vehicles to cycling.
Godalming: Cyclists' Touring Club, 1991. 27 pp.

2001 Gilmour, James. Designing the Best Way to Boost Bicycle Use.
London: *Local Transport Today*, May 1992, 12–13.

Examines the experiences of local authorities in their attempts to encourage
cycling by providing cycleways.

**2002 Grimshaw, John; Holder, Andrew; Kuiper, Jan; McRobie,
George; Ratcliffe, Terry** and **Trevelyan, Peter.** *Setting the Wheels in
Motion: towards a national cycling policy.* London: Intermediate
Technology Publications, 1982. 75 pp.

Collection of articles examining planning; the international experience; cycling
campaigning groups; cycleways; examples of cycle facilities in the UK and
solutions to the practical problems of designing cycleways.

2003 Hanna, Judith. International Evidence Shows Cycling Coming of
Age in Transport Policy. London: *Local Transport Today*, September
1993, 12–13.

Considers the ways in which cycling can help deliver sustainable transport
objectives, while improving public fitness and health.

2004 Hudson, Mike; Levy, Caren; Macrory, Richard; Nicholson, John
and **Snelson, Peter.** *Bicycle Planning: policy and practice.* London:
Architectural Press, 1982. 135 pp.

Compares and contrasts the different cycling policies of Holland, Germany,
France and the USA.

2005 Institution of Highways and Transportation. *Providing for the
Cyclist: guidelines.* London: Institution of Highways and Transportation, 1983. 60 pp.

Provides guidelines for those responsible for providing facilities for cyclists.
Claims that, relative to the distance travelled, cycling is nine times more
dangerous than travelling by car.

2006 Levinson, Herbert S. Streets for People and Transit. Westport, CT:
Transportation Quarterly, Vol. 40(4), October 1986, 503–520.

Traces the development of pedestrian and transit streets, discusses the principles that underlie planning and design, and gives illustrative examples of
projects that have been built.

2007 Levy, Caren. *On Our Bikes?: a survey of local authority cycle planning in Britain.* London: Friends of the Earth, 1982, 57 pp.

2008 Mathew, Don. *The Bike is Back: a bicycles policy for Britain.* London: Friends of the Earth, 1980. 24 pp.

Claims that increased cycle use can generate individual benefits and national gains in the field of energy conservation and job creation.

2009 McClintock, Hugh (ed.). *The Bicycle and City Traffic: principles and practice.* London: Belhaven Press, 1992. 211 pp.

Makes the case that cycling has many advantages but also increases certain risks. Examines developments in Western Europe and the USA.

2010 Noland, Robert B. and **Kunreuther, Howard.** Short-Run and Long-Run Policies for Increasing Bicycle Transportation for Daily Commuter Trips. Oxford: *Transport Policy,* Vol. 2(1), January 1995, 67–79.

Analyses data collected in the Philadelphia metropolitan area which suggests that two general approaches can be taken to improve bicycle transportation and make bicycling safer and more convenient.

2011 Ochia, Krys. Bicyle Programs and Provision of Bikeway Facilities in the U.S. Virginia: *Transportation Quarterly,* Vol. 47(4), October 1993, 445–456.

Reports on the progress managers have made in implementing policies and plans to promote bicyle use, especially as a commuter mode.

2012 Roberts, John. *Pedestrian Precincts in Britain.* London: Transport and Environment Studies , 1981. 166 pp.

Investigates the number, type and location of pedestrian precincts within the UK. Considers their dimensions and the kinds of face-lift that most have received. Looks at the way various types of transport convey people and goods to and from the precinct. Speculates on the future prospects for precincts.

2013 Schweig, Karl-Heinz. Pedestrian-Related Goals and Innovations, Step by Step. Westport, CT: *Transportation Quarterly,* Vol. 44(4), October 1990, 595–606.

Examines the former Federal Republic of Germany's policies for realising improvements for pedestrians and other weak road users and also achieving a traffic situation compatible with their cities.

Safety

2014 Abdul-Jabbar, J. A. A. A. *An Evaluation of Pelican Crossings on Roundabout Approaches in Urban Areas.* Cardiff: University of Cardiff (PhD Thesis), 1992.

Describes a study of pedestrian crossing facilities close to roundabout entries. The objective was to evaluate the benefits to pedestrians of providing a pelican crossing, and the effect of the crossing on the roundabout capacity.

2015 Abeysuriya, A. G. K. de S. *Analysis of Various Measures of Pedestrian Crossing Activity as an Aid to Determining the Environmental Traffic Capacity of Shopping Streets.* Leeds: University of Leeds (PhD Thesis), 1979.

2016 Al-Neami, A. H. K. *Design of Pedestrian Facilities at Signal Controlled Junctions.* Cardiff: University of Cardiff (PhD Thesis), 1992.

Describes a study of pedestrian behaviour and delay at signal controlled junctions. The objective was to develop tools, based on observed behaviour, to evaluate alternative techniques and strategies for assisting pedestrians.

2017 Bar-Ziv, J. and **Hakkert, A. S.** Accident Risk and Delays at Mid-Block Pedestrian Crossings. London: George Godwin, *International Forum Series*, Vol. 2, 1981, 165–174.

2018 Chapman, Antony J., Foot, Hugh C. and **Wade, Frances M.** (eds). *Pedestrian Accidents.* Chichester: John Wiley and Sons, 1982. 354 pp.

Divided into three sections, focusing in turn on the pedestrian; the driver and the vehicle; and the environment. Contains a comprehensive, annotated bibliography.

2019 Cleary, J. *Cycle Facilities and Cyclists' Safety in Greater Nottingham.* Nottingham: University of Nottingham (PhD Thesis), 1993.

Examines the provision of a network of cycle routes. Suggests that while such infrastructure had a place in improving the safety and attractiveness of cycling as a mode of transport, its value has been undermined by a deterioration in the general road environment where the majority of cycle journeys must still take place.

2020 Clennell, Simon. Coping with a Safety Crisis. London: *Urban Transport International*, December 1988/January 1989, 22–23.

Reflects on the accidents which have occurred at pedestrian crossings and have delayed the launch of Hong Kong's light rail transit system.

2021 Colborne, H. V. *Factors Affecting the Safety of Young Children as Pedestrians.* Salford: University of Salford (MSc Thesis), 1972.

2022 Creswell, C. *Pedestrian Crossing Facilities.* Cardiff: University of Wales Institute of Science and Technology (PhD Thesis), 1978.

2023 Dickins, Ian. Pedestrian Safety and Traffic Calming. London: *Proceedings of the Chartered Institute of Transport*, Vol. 1(2), Winter 1991, 32–42.

Examines the welfare of pedestrians, and the means to safeguard them through the application of traffic calming.

2024 Goodwin, P. B. and **Hutchinson, T. P.** The Risk of Walking. Amsterdam: *Transportation*, Vol. 6, 1977, 217–230.

Analysis of National Travel Survey data which relates accident risk to age; sex; time of day; day of week; and month of year.

2025 Hass-Klau, C. H. M. *The History of Protecting Pedestrians and Residents from the Effects of Wheeled and Motor Traffic with Special Reference to Britain, Germany and the United States.* Reading: University of Reading (PhD Thesis), 1989.

Examines British, German and American responses to the emergence of the automobile from the late 19th century until 1989. Specifically concerned with the protection of pedestrians, residents and worker road users.

2026 Hine, J. *Pedestrian Travel Experiences and Perceptions of Safety: analysis of results from an in-depth interview technique.* Edinburgh: Heriot-Watt University, School of Planning and Housing, 1995. 64 pp.

2027 Hudson, Mike. *The Bicycle Planning Book.* London: Friends of the Earth, 1978. 154 pp.

Examines how cycling can be made safe in large towns, easily and without great expense. Argues that the bicycle is energy-efficient and a form of transport which does not pollute the atmosphere. Suggests ways in which local authorities might plan the urban environment to accommodate cyclists. The author aims to demonstrate how provisions may be made to accommodate cyclists and thus provide a new perspective on planning the urban environment.

2028 Pease, Jack. Improving Pedestrian Safety: councils look for ways to quicken the pace. London: *Local Transport Today*, November 1993, 12–13.

Examines ways in which local authorities are trying new ways of tackling pedestrian safety problems.

2029 Pillai, K. S. *A Study of Traffic Behaviour at a Pedestrian Crossing.* Birmingham: University of Birmingham (PhD Thesis), 1972.

2030 Shipley, F. *The Southampton Western Approach Cycle Route: cyclist flows and accidents.* Project report no. 93. Crowthorne: Transport and Road Research Laboratory, 1994. 14 pp.

2031 Todd, Kenneth. Pedestrian Regulation in the United States: a critical review. Westport, CT: *Transportation Quarterly*, Vol. 46(4), 1992, 541–559.
Discusses the conflict between car drivers and pedestrians.

2032 Unwin, N. C. *Cycling: promoting the public health benefits and reducing the risks.* Manchester: University of Manchester (MSc Thesis), 1992.
Investigates why Manchester University students do or do not cycle and their views of how cycle safety could be improved. Attitudes to cycle helmets were investigated using the health belief model as a guide.

2033 Walsh, Bernadine. Cycling: Cambridge Bids to Bridge the Safety Gap. London: *Local Transport Today*, May 1990, 10–11.
Reports on the promotion of cycling undertaken by Cambridge City Council.

2034 Young, A. *A Study of Skid Resistance and Accidents at Pedestrian Crossings in London.* Salford: University of Salford (MSc Thesis), 1978.

11 Railways

General

2035 Carpenter, T. T. *The Environmental Impact of Railways.* Chichester: John Wiley and Sons, 1994. 385 pp.

Examines the main planning and management issues relating to the ways in which railways impact on the environment.

2036 Crampton, Graham and **Evans, Alan W.** Myth, Reality and Employment in London. London: *Journal of Transport Economics and Policy*, Vol. 23(1), January 1989, 89–108.

Discusses the importance of rail commuting and identifies the need for greater investment in railways.

2037 Glaister, Stephen. Some Characteristics of Rail Commuter Demand. London: *Journal of Transport Economics and Policy*, Vol. 17(2), May 1983, 115–132.

Suggests that annual season tickets are too cheap, and that cheap day tickets are too expensive.

2038 Hall, Peter and **Smith, Edward.** *Better Use of Rail Ways: geographical papers.* London: George Over Ltd., 1976. 132 pp.

Examines the main engineering and economic considerations affecting the conversion of a railway to a road and the replacement of trains with buses and lorries.

2039 Hellewell, D. Scott. New Developments in Light Rail. London: *Proceedings of the Chartered Institute of Transport*, Vol. 3(4), November 1994, 17–24.

Examines the increased interest in rail systems, both heavy and light, by local authorities since the advent of bus deregulation.

2040 Hope, Richard and **Yearsley, Ian** (eds). *Urban Railways and*

Rapid Transit: a railway gazette management study manual. London: IPC Transport Press, 1972. 95 pp.

Collection of articles covering the main facets of urban rail planning and operation.

2041 Howard, G. *Light, Heavy or Innovative? a review of current systems.* Paper from the proceedings of 'Light Transit Systems' organised by the Institution of Civil Engineers. London: Thomas Telford, 1990, 101–118.

Building new urban railways using existing heavy rail technology has become increasingly difficult in recent years because of their high costs and environmental implications. Alternative technologies have become available, particularly where peak demand ranges from 10,000 to 20,000 passengers an hour. Article describes some of them.

2042 Mackett, Roger L. Railways in London. London: *Transport Reviews*, Vol. 15(1), January–March 1995, 45–58.

Examines the role of railways in London and the problems arising from the development of two systems: the Underground and Network SouthEast.

2043 Nash, C. A. Policies Towards Suburban Rail Services in Britain and the Federal Republic of Germany: a comparison. London: *Transport Reviews*, Vol. 5(3), July–September 1985, 269–282.

Compares the major role played by suburban rail (S-Bahn) systems in West German Cities with the much more limited role of rail in the British conurbations.

2044 Smith, Edward. An Economic Comparison of Urban Railways and Express Bus Services. London: *Journal of Transport Economics and Policy*, Vol. 7(1), January 1973, 20–31.

Examines evidence from several countries which suggests that the construction of new urban railways is likely to be less economically viable than the provision of express bus services.

2045 White, Peter R. Catching up with Europe in the Urban Rail Sector. London: *Transport*, Vol. 3, January/February 1983, 17–18.

The results of the Glasgow Rail Impact Study published in November 1982, together with reports on rail developments in Tyne and Wear; Merseyside; and the West Midlands, were presented at a symposium in Glasgow at the end of 1982. Article contrasts the state of urban rail in Britain with that in Europe.

2046 Wilmshurst, J. *The Overseas Development Administration Approach to Rail Mass Transit.* London: Thomas Telford, 1990, 319–326.

Outlines the Overseas Development Administration's appraisal procedures and examines the possibilities for rail mass transit systems in low income countries.

Theory

2047 Baron, Paul. Momentum Towards Automated Systems Growing. London: *Transport*, Vol. 6, December 1985, 21–22.

In the past two decades, there has been a significant increase in the number of heavy and light-rail urban mass transit systems throughout the world. Article reviews these along with current and future technology.

2048 Catling, David T. Selecting a New Rail System. Brussels: *Public Transport International*, Vol. 43(4), July 1994, 13–26.

Examines how a transport authority can choose between a new and a modernised rail system.

2049 *No Entry.*

2050 Foster, Christopher; Posner, Michael and **Sherman, Michael.** *A Report on the Potential for the Conversion of Some Railway Routes in London into Roads.* The Steering Committee Report. London: Department of Public Affairs, British Railways Board, 1984. 59 pp.

Explores the notion that the conversion of all railway routes could offer better public service if they were converted into roads. Primarily concerned with the potential for conversion of some lightly used routes.

2051 Fowkes, T. and **Nash, C.** *Analysing Demand for Rail Travel.* Aldershot: Avebury, 1991. 191 pp.

2052 Hopkinson, C., Nash, C. and **Tweddle, G.** *The Future of Railways and Roads.* London: Institute for Public Policy Research, 1991. 20 pp.

2053 Howard, D. F. *Project Management.* Paper from the proceedings of 'Urban Railways and the Civil Engineer' organised by the Institution of Civil Engineers. London: Thomas Telford, 1987, 41–52.

Railways are increasingly being built as a solution to urban transport problems. Their construction is a complex process which begins when a project is first mooted and is only complete once the railway is running and final accounts have been settled. Article examines the various stages in order to outline the role of project management and the wide range of disciplines and expertise involved.

2054 Joy, Stewart. Railway Costs and Planning. London: *Journal of Transport Economics and Policy*, Vol. 23(1), January 1989, 45–54.

Examines the various costs involved in running a railway.

2055 Kiepper, Alan F. Rail Transport: the future is now. Brussels: *Public Transport International*, Vol. 42(2), July 1993, 55–58.

2056 Local Transport Today. Managing Mobility in the London Megalopolis: is more really better? London: *Local Transport Today*, April 1993, 12–13.

Considers whether the 'new build' approach for London's transport needs is appropriate or whether improvement of existing transport systems is a more pressing need.

2057 Wardman, M. Forecasting the Impact of Service Quality Changes for Inter-Urban Rail Travel. London: *Journal of Transport Economics and Policy*, Vol. 28(3), September 1994, 287–306.

Investment and infrastructure

2058 Allen, John G. Public-Private Joint Development at Rapid Transit Stations. Westport, CT: *Transportation Quarterly*, Vol. 40(3), July 1986, 317–333.

Examines the pre-requisites for a successful joint public-private development at rapid transit stations, and examines the experience of several North American cities.

2059 Ashburner, D. S. and **Richardson, R.** *Commercial Options and Implementations.* Paper from the proceedings of 'Light Transit Systems' organised by the Institution of Civil Engineers. London: Thomas Telford, 1990, 227–237.

Privately funded projects in urban transport infrastructure are experiencing a renaissance, but ideas on the forms of contract and associated risks are still developing. Article discusses aspects of the Trafalgar House approach and comments on current and recent projects.

2060 Banks, Sandra. On the Right Track or off the Rails? Building New Rail and Guided Transport Systems: Transport and Works Act

1992 in perspective. *Parliamentary Reports,* Vol. 2(4), 1993, 154–157.

Examines aspects of the development and planning procedures of the Transport and Works Act 1992.

2061 Campion, R. J. *The Redevelopment of Liverpool Street Station.* Paper from the proceedings of 'Urban Railways and the Civil Engineer' organised by the Institution of Civil Engineers. London: Thomas Telford, 1987, 97–112.

The remodelling of London's Liverpool Street station has been financed from the proceeds of associated property development. Article examines the main design and planning considerations involved.

2062 City Transport. France Sees a Rebirth of the Tramcar. Surrey: *City Transport,* March–May 1987, 29–31.

Revival of interest in light rail has already produced two new tramway systems and created manufacturing capability which will enable France to build for export.

2063 Clennell, Simon. Private Capital Boosts Hong Kong Metro. London: *Urban Transport International,* October/November 1989, 22–23.

2064 Hayashi, Yoshitsugu. Issues in Financing Urban Rail Transit Projects and Value Captures. Oxford: *Transportation Research,* Vol. 23(1), 1989, 35–44.

Examines the financing system of urban rail transit projects in Japan and analyses the possible menus for fund-raising from the viewpoint of imbalance between benefit receivers and cost burdeners on the bases of benefit principle.

2065 Hillman, Ellis and **Trench, Richard.** *London Under London: a subterranean guide.* 2nd ed. London: John Murray, 1993. 240 pp.

Covers the underground infrastructure of the metropolis, including the tubes.

2066 Huntley, Peter. New Lines for London. London: *Local Transport Today,* July 1989, 10–11.

Examines the London Rail Study of 1989 which proposed major new capacity transport routes to deal with mounting congestion in London. This article looks at the options examined so far.

2067 James, William K. Railways: government recognises the environmental benefits of rail. *Transport Law and Practice,* Vol. 1(6), 1994, 50–51.

Reports on the provisions of Section 8 of the Railways Act 1993 making available grants for certain environmental benefits of railways.

2068 Jenkin, P. *Urban Railways: system choice.* Paper from the proceedings of 'Urban Railways and the Civil Engineer' organised by the Institution of Civil Engineers. London: Thomas Telford, 1987, 9–25.

Argues that the evaluation of system options must take into consideration financial and economic targets; plus appropriate infrastructure and technology, together with other special factors.

2069 Kanemoto, Yoshitsugo. Pricing and Investment Policies in a System of Competitive Commuter Railways. Oxford: *Review of Economic Studies*, Vol. 51(4), October 1984, 665–81.

Develops a simple spatial equilibrium model of a city served by competing commuter railways and analyses the effects of different transportation policies on pricing and investment decisions.

2070 Leckey, J. J. *The Organisation and Capital Structure of the Irish North Western Railway.* Belfast: Queen's University (MSc Thesis), 1973.

2071 Martin and Voorhees Associates: Scottish Development Department: Transport and Road Research Laboratory. *The Glasgow Rail Impact Study: a study of the impact of investment in the Argyle Line and Glasgow Underground: final report.* Edinburgh: Central Research Unit, 1982. 111 pp.

2072 McIntosh, A. P. J. *Urban Land Investment in Relation to Rail Transport.* Reading: University of Reading (M.Phil Thesis), 1978.

2073 Nilsson, Jan-Eric. Second Best Problems in Railway Infrastructure Pricing and Investment. London: *Journal of Transport Economics and Policy*, Vol. 26(3), September 1992, 245–261.

In 1988 the Swedish nationalised railway company was separated into the State Railways (in charge of running rail transport), and the National Rail Administration (responsible for investment in and maintenance of rail infrastructure). Article analyses optimal pricing of rail infrastructure use and optimality conditions for rail and road investment.

2074 Schabas, M. *Light Rail Transit to Stimulate Development: the developer's perspective.* Paper from the proceedings of 'Light Transit

Systems' organised by the Institution of Civil Engineers. London: Thomas Telford, 1990, 47–60.

Examines Olympia and York's involvement in the financing of London's Docklands Light Railway and looks also at the potential for other private contributions to other urban railway projects in London and around the world.

2075 Stopher, Peter R. Financing Urban Rail Projects: the case of Los Angeles. Dordrecht: *Transportation*, Vol. 20(3), 1993, 229–250.

Examines the potential use of the financing strategy of value capture or benefit assessment for an urban mass transportation project. Describes the legal background to the use of benefit assessment, and the process of implementation for the first phase of the Los Angeles Metro Rail Project.

2076 Tarr, R. J. Private Finance and Light Rail. Brussels: *Public Transport International*, Vol. 43(4), July 1994, 27–30.

2077 Transport 2000. *Transport Policy Tomorrow*. London: Transport 2000, 1976. 58 pp.

Considers the impact of rail investment and rail subsidies in the context of transport policy generally.

2078 Tyson, W. J. *Evaluating Alternative Proposals*. Paper from the proceedings of 'Light Transit Systems' organised by the Institution of Civil Engineers. London: Thomas Telford, 1990, 61–67.

Argues that although light rapid transit is cheaper than conventional railways to construct and to operate, it is a substantial investment which needs to be systematically evaluated.

2079 Urban Transport International. A Battle of the Giants. London: *Urban Transport International*, November/December 1990, 14–19.

Claims that Europe's light railway industry is in the midst of massive structural change as the big groups fight it out to win a slice of the boom in orders. Article looks at the market for light rail.

Safety

2080 Follenfant, H. G. *Reconstructing London's Underground*. London: London Transport, 1974. 184 pp.

A former London Transport Chief Civil Engineer describes the refurbishment of London's Underground.

2081 Holden, C. B. *Safety Requirements for Light Rail*. Paper from the proceedings of 'Light Transit Systems' organised by the Institution of Civil Engineers. London: Thomas Telford, 1990, 201–225.

The Railway Inspectorate is responsible for advising the Secretary of State for Transport on whether or not a new LRT system is safe to be opened to the public for the carriage of passengers. Article examines safety procedures and describes the current situation, summarises the recently issued Provisional Guidance Note on street-running, and previews the contents of the Department of Transport's Requirements for LRT systems.

2082 Holloway, Sally. *Moorgate: anatomy of a railway disaster.* Newton Abbot: David and Charles, 1988. 208 pp.

An account of the Moorgate tube disaster of February 1975 which resulted in 42 deaths and 82 serious injuries.

2083 Jones-Lee, M. and **Loomes, G.** Towards a Willingness-to-Pay Based Value of Underground Safety. London: *Journal of Transport Economics and Policy*, Vol. 28(1), January 1994, 83–98.

2084 Jones-Lee, Michael. Transport Safety: getting value for money. Aurora, Ont.: *Canadian Patent Reporter*, Vol. 3(4), 1993, 196–203.

2085 Kozar, Christian. Three Years Spent Reclaiming Lost Ground. Brussels: *Public Transport International*, Vol. 41(1), February 1992.

The Director of the Environment and Security Department of the French metro system assesses the results of programmes launched in 1989 to improve the safety and sense of security of passengers. Article in English with French and German translations.

2086 Rose, C. F. *The Safety of Urban Railways with Particular Reference to Civil Engineering.* Paper from the proceedings of 'Urban Railways and the Civil Engineer' organised by the Institution of Civil Engineers. London: Thomas Telford, 1987, 113–121.

Describes the role of the UK Government in regulating safety on railways in general and urban railways in particular and the role and function of the Railway Inspectorate. Also discusses the safety elements of various aspects of the design and planning of an urban railway.

2087 Walmsley, D. *Light Rail Accidents in Europe and North America.* Crowthorne: Transport and Road Research Laboratory, 1992. 30 pp.

2088 Williams, P. *The Maintenance of Old Structures on the London Underground.* Paper from the proceedings of 'Urban Railways and the Civil Engineer' organised by the Institution of Civil Engineers. London: Thomas Telford, 1987, 203–215.

The London Underground railway system was formed by the amalgamation of a number of railway companies. The earliest structures date back to the 1860s. A large number of these original structures are still used. The early tunnels are brick and the tube tunnels are either cast iron or concrete lined. All structures are inspected at regular intervals and this article recounts some of the problems that arise and how they are treated.

12 Heavy Railways

History

2089 Barrie, D. S. M. *South Wales*. The Regional History of the Railways of Great Britain. Vol. 12. Newton Abbot: David and Charles, 1980. 296 pp.

2090 Benest, K. R. *Metropolitan Electric Locomotives*. Hertfordshire: London Underground Railway Society, 1983. 108 pp.
Illustrated history of the British Westinghouse Locomotives; the Thomson-Houston Locomotives; and the Metropolitan-Vickers Locomotives deployed on the Metropolitan railway.

2091 Biddle, Gordon. *Great Railway Stations of Britain*. Newton Abbot: David and Charles, 1986. 240 pp.

2092 Binney, Marcus; Foehl, Axel and Hamm, Manfred. *Great Railway Stations of Europe*. London: Thames and Hudson, 1984. 144 pp.

2093 Body, Geoffrey. *Railways of the Eastern Region. Vol. 1: southern operating area*. Wellingborough: Patrick Stephens, 1986. 216 pp.
Field guide to the southern operational area of British Rail's Eastern Region, broadly from the Thames to the Humber. Includes details of London and South Yorkshire suburban services past and present.

2094 Bonavia, M. R. Shaped by State Involvement. London: *Transport*, Vol. 7, December 1986, 25–26.
Examines the expanded role of government in the affairs of British railways in the aftermath of the First World War, in transport as in other fields.

2095 Brodribb, John. *The Eastern Region Before Beeching*. London: Ian Allan, 1994. 128 pp.
Examines the Eastern and North Eastern Regions of British Rail in the years between nationalisation and the Beeching cuts in the era before dieselisation.

2096 Butt, R. V. J. *The Directory of Railway Stations.* Yeovil: Patrick Stephens, 1995. 296 pp.

Details every public and private passenger station; halt; platform; and stopping place; past and present, within the British Isles.

2097 Christiansen, R. *The West Midlands.* The Regional History of the Railways of Great Britain. Vol. 7. 2nd rev. ed. Newton Abbot: David and Charles, 1983. 305 pp.

2098 Christiansen, Rex. *Regional Rail Centres: North West.* London: Ian Allan, 1995. 142 pp.

Provides a history of railway development in one of the most densely populated and heavily industrialised districts of Britain.

2099 Coleman, Terry. *The Railway Navvies.* Harmondsworth: Penguin Books, 1986. 256 pp.

A history of the men who made the railways.

2100 Coles, C. R. L. *Railways Through London.* London: Ian Allan, 1983. 128 pp.

A largely pictorial description of London's railways.

2101 Condit, Carl W. *The Port of New York.* Chicago: University of Chicago Press, 1981. 399 pp.

A history of the rail and terminal system from the Grand Central Electrification to the 1980s.

2102 Connor, J. E. and **Halford, B. L.** *The Forgotten Stations of Greater London.* Colchester: Connor and Butler, 1991. 139 pp.

Gazetteer of disused and renamed passenger stations within the area covered by the Greater London Boroughs.

2103 Course, Edwin. *London's Railways Then and Now.* London: Batsford, 1987. 119 pp.

Traces the history of forty-eight London railway 'undertakings' from their origins to their current state.

2104 Demoro, Kristen A. Preserving the Golden Age of Urban Rail. Washington, DC: *Mass Transit*, September 1987, 90–91.

A review of an urban railway museum in Sacramento.

2105 Edmonds, Alexander. *History of the Metropolitan District Rail-*

way Company to June 1908. London: London Transport, 1973. 243 pp.

A historical account of those Parliamentary powers which were secured by the Metropolitan District Railway Company and a detailed description of the civil engineering work involved in their implementation.

2106 Edwards, Dennis and **Pigram, Ron.** *The Golden Years of the Metropolitan Railway.* Kent: Midas Books, 1983. 128 pp.

History of the Metropolitan Railway. Offers glimpses of life during the steam days of the railway in the settings of Middlesex and Hertfordshire and also from its headquarters in London's Baker Street.

2107 Gadsen, E. J. S. *Metropolitan Steam.* Middlesex: Roundhouse, 1963. 43 pp.

Of the smaller railway companies operating in London, the Metropolitan possessed some of the most interesting locomotives. This book describes their development from the days of 'Fowler's Ghost' to the modern express tanks of the 1930s.

2108 Gammell, C. J. *LNER Branch Lines.* Sparkford: Oxford Publishing, 1993. 192 pp.

Traces the development of the London and North Eastern Railway's branch lines, including its numerous suburban services.

2109 Glover, John. *London's Railways Today.* Newton Abbot: David and Charles, 1981. 32 pp.

Illustrated account of the rail services covering a radius of 35 miles from the centre of London.

2110 Hall, Stanley. *Rail Centres: Manchester.* London: Ian Allan, 1995. 192 pp.

Provides a detailed historical survey of the railways of Manchester from the earliest days in the region to the latest developments.

2111 Heale, K. *North East England.* The Regional History of the Railways of Great Britain Series. Vol. 4. Newton Abbot: David and Charles.

2112 Hendry, Powell R. and **Hendry, Preston R.** *Paddington to the Mersey: the GWR's forgotten route from London to Birkenhead.* Sparkford: Oxford Publishing, 1992. 144 pp.

Examines the Great Western Railway's route from Paddington via Birmingham to Birkenhead, including its urban and suburban connections.

2113 Higgins, John F. Railways in Ireland. London: *Transport*, Vol. 1, March/April 1980, 27–29.

2114 Holt, G. O. *The North West.* The Regional History of the Railways of Great Britain. Vol. 10. 2nd ed. Newton Abbot: David and Charles, 1986. 279 pp.

2115 Jackson, Alan A. *London's Local Railways.* Newton Abbott: David and Charles, 1978. 384 pp.

Surveys 50 railway lines of varying types and importance within London, exploring their social and historical impact. Also includes an account of various unfulfilled schemes for new lines.

2116 Jackson, Alan A. *London's Termini.* 2nd ed. Newton Abbot: David and Charles, 1985. 397 pp.

2117 Jackson, Alan A. *London's Metropolitan Railway.* Newton Abbott: David and Charles, 1986. 416 pp.

A history of London's Metropolitan Railway.

2118 Jobling, D. G. *Development Over Urban Railways.* Paper from the proceedings of 'Urban Railways and the Civil Engineer' organised by the Institution of Civil Engineers. London: Thomas Telford, 1987, 149–163.

Examines some of the early buildings erected over the cut and cover of urban railways. Discusses the case for commercial development over urban railways.

2119 Joy, D. *South and West Yorkshire.* The Regional History of the Railways of Great Britain. Vol. 8. 2nd rev. ed. Newton Abbot: David and Charles, 1984. 317 pp.

2120 Leleux, R. *The East Midlands.* The Regional History of the Railways of Great Britain. Vol. 9. 2nd rev. ed. Newton Abbot: David and Charles, 1984. 268 pp.

2121 Morris, R. and **Rodger, R.** (eds). *The Victorian City: a reader in British urban history 1820–1914.* London: Longman.

Contains an important essay by J. Kellett on railways as an agent of internal change in Victorian cities.

2122 Mulligan, Fergus. *One Hundred and Fifty Years of Irish Railways.* Belfast: The Appletree Press, 1983. 192 pp.

Explores the history of Irish railways both in the Republic and in Ulster over the last 150 years.

2123 Nicholls, P. H. *British Rail in South Gloucestershire, 1971–81.* Bath: University of Bath (MSc Thesis), 1972.

2124 Simmons, Jack. Suburban Traffic at King's Cross 1852–1914. Manchester: *Journal of Transport History,* Vol. 6(1), March 1985, 71–78.
Describes the traffic management difficulties encountered by King's Cross railway terminus during the period 1852–1914.

2125 Thomas, J. *Scotland.* The Regional History of the Railways of Great Britain Series. Vol. 6. Newton Abbot: David and Charles, 1971. 288 pp.

2126 Turnock, David. *Railways in the British Isles: landscape, land use and society.* London: Adam and Charles Black, 1982. 259 pp.

2127 Waters, Lawrence. *Railways at Cardiff.* London: Ian Allan, 1995. 96 pp.
Traces the historical development of railways in Cardiff from the arrival of the Taff Vale Railway, through to nationalisation and the modern era.

2128 White, H. P. *Greater London.* The Regional History of the Railways of Great Britain Series. Vol. 3. Newton Abbot: David and Charles, 1984. 237 pp.
Describes the influence on London of the world's most complex railway system. Defining London in an introductory chapter, the author then deals with the different sectors which make up the whole network. Deals with the role played by the Underground. Also provides an extensive account of the Great Eastern's policies which helped the development of the working-class suburbs.

2129 White, H. P. *Forgotten Railways.* Newton Abbot: David and Charles, 1986. 240 pp.
Charts the history of closed railway lines. Includes a chapter on closed urban railways and a section on the forgotten railway in the landscape.

2130 Yuzawa, Takeshi. The Introduction of Electric Railways in Britain and Japan. Manchester: *Journal of Transport History,* Vol. 6(1), March 1985, 1–22.
Examines the differences of introduction of electric railways in Britain and

Japan and questions Britain's adherence to steam trains at the turn of the century.

Theory

2131 Bleyer, Bill. Double-Deckers Increase Ridership. Washington, DC: *Mass Transit*, March 1990, 18–21.

Examines the growing popularity of the bi-level railway coach.

2132 Buckman, J. C. *The Locational Effects of a Railway Closure: a case study of the withdrawal of passenger services from the Steyning line in March 1966.* Bristol: University of Bristol (MSc Thesis), 1972.

2133 Dodgson, J. S. Railway Costs and Closures. London: *Journal of Transport Economics and Policy*, Vol. 18(3), September 1984, 219–236.

Network Studies in the recent Serpell Report provide conclusive evidence that substantial savings would result from closure of lightly-used railway lines.

2134 Economic Research Centre: European Conference of Ministers of Transport. *Scope for Railway Transport in Urban Areas: Report of the Forty-seventh Round Table on Transport Economics, held in Hamburg on 25 and 26 June, 1979.* Paris: Organisation for Economic Co-operation and Development, 1980. 375 pp.

Looks specifically at case study reports from Liverpool and Newcastle.

2135 Ford, Roger. Widening Users' Options. London: *Transport*, Vol. 11, June 1990, 141–145.

Claims that prospects for railways have rarely been brighter as congestion clogs roads and environmental pressures grow.

2136 Galvez-Perez, T. E. *Assessment of Operating Policies in Public Transport: a comprehensive model applied to a rail service.* Leeds: University of Leeds (PhD Thesis), 1989.

2137 McDonough, Carol C. The Demand for Commuter Rail Transport. London: *Journal of Transport Economics and Policy*, Vol. 7(2), May 1973, 134–143.

Claims that the quickest and most expensive mode, preferred by those who can afford it, is rail with a car journey from home to station. Notes also that efficient public transport to and from suburban stations should increase rail demand.

2138 McFarland, Henry. Ramsey Pricing of Inputs with Downstream Monopoly Power and Regulation: implications for railroad rate setting. London: *Journal of Transport Economics and Policy*, Vol. 20(1), January 1986, 81–90.

2139 McGeehan, H. Forecasting the Demand for Inter-urban Railway Travel in the Republic of Ireland. London: *Journal of Transport Economics and Policy*, Vol. 18(3), September 1984, 275–292.

Aims to determine a short-run demand model capable of giving accurate forecasts of passenger miles.

2140 McGeehan, Harry. Railway Costs and Productivity Growth: the case of the Republic of Ireland: 1973–1983. London: *Journal of Transport Economics and Policy*, Vol. 27(1), January 1993, 19–32.

Measures productivity growth in Irish railways for the period 1973–83, using a translog cost approach.

2141 Owen, A. D. and **Phillips, G. D. A.** The Characteristics of Railway Passenger Demand: an econometric investigation. London: *Journal of Transport Economics and Policy*, Vol. 21(3), September 1987, 231–254.

Represents the main results of a study into the major determinants of passenger demand for rail travel in the UK based upon British Rail's monthly NPAAS data for the period 1973–84.

2142 Potter, Stephen. *On the Right Lines? the limits of technological innovation.* London: Frances Pinter, 1987. 160 pp.

Discusses the British Advanced Passenger Train (APT) from the research stage to the construction of prototypes. Includes a comparison of the development of high-speed rail services in Britain and abroad. Also discusses the technical difficulties encountered with the diesel high speed train.

2143 Richards, G. The Economics of the Cambrian Coast Line. London: *Journal of Transport Economics and Policy*, Vol. 6(3), September 1972, 308–320.

Critical analysis of the official Cambrian Coast Line Study leads to the conclusion that retention of the line for ten years would result, not in a loss as shown, but in a large net benefit to the community.

2144 Shipman, William D. Rail Passenger Subsidies and Benefit-Cost Considerations. London: *Journal of Transport Economics and Policy*, Vol. 5(1), January 1971, 3–27.

Argues that rail passenger subsidies are undesirable; people enjoy driving to work, and the true answer to congestion may be the break-up of cities by drastic decentralisation. Claims that except for development purposes in corridor transport, rail subsidies may only delay desirable long-run solutions.

2145 Trotter, S. D. The Price-Discriminating Public Enterprise, with Special Reference to British Rail. London: *Journal of Transport Economics and Policy*, Vol. 19(1), January 1985, 41–64.

Article combines consideration of the possible objectives of a public enterprise with a discussion on price discrimination. Claims that British Rail is well placed for discriminatory pricing, but there are limits to what is practicable and desirable.

2146 Urban Transport International. Rail Technology: intelligent trains for cross rail. London: *Urban Transport International*, Vol. 1, 1993, 24–25.

A report on the testing by British Rail of databus systems and data radio links for its new cross London trains.

Policy

2147 Brew, John. Rail Chief Moves to Commercialisation. Brussels: *Public Transport International*, Vol. 42(1), March–April 1993, 36–42.

Article argues that public transport must match private sector benchmarks to achieve peak performance and commerciality.

2148 Centre for Independent Transport Research. *British Rail and Underground Stations in Hackney.* London: Centre for Independent Transport Research in London, 1986. 139 pp.

2149 European Conference of Ministers of Transport. *Privatisation of Railways.* Report of the ninetieth round table on transport economics. Paris: Organisation for Economic Co-operation and Development, 1993. 162 pp.

Attempts to clarify the issues and analyse a number of examples of the privatisation of railways. Defines the obstacles to privatisation and shows the difficulties inherent in such projects and the scope for implementing them.

2150 Gibb, Richard A. Imposing Dependence: South Africa's manipulation of regional railways. London: *Transport Reviews*, Vol. 11(1), January–March 1991, 19–39.

Examines the evolution and the nature of varying levels of interdependence within the Southern African transport sector. Highlights the different regional policies adopted by Pretoria.

2151 Glaister, Stephen and **Travers, Tony.** *New Directions for British Railways?: the political economy of privatisation and regulation.* London: Institute of Economic Affairs, 1993. 66 pp.
Critically examines the Conservative Government's proposals for privatisation of British Rail.

2152 Gylee, Malcolm and **Hibbs, John.** *Off the Rails. International Freedom Foundation, 1993.* 32 pp.
Looks at the European Community's elimination of true private participation in rail operation. Recommends that the EC should confine itself to a strategic overview and that transport should be divorced from member states' policies.

2153 Hamer, Mick. Commuter Railways Fare Well Under the Microscope. London: *Transport,* Vol. 1, November/December 1980, 22–23.
Claims that British Rail's commuter services in London and the South East have emerged from their scrutiny by the Monopolies and Mergers Commission with a relatively clean bill of health.

2154 Huntley, Peter. BR Provincial: ready for a new local route. London: *Local Transport Today,* May 1989, 8–9.
Claims that local authorities could be set to take over control of local rail services, following suggestions by the Monopolies and Mergers Commission arising from its examination of the affairs of British Rail's Provincial sector.

2155 Jenkins, Hugh. Oh! Mister Porter, What Shall I Do? the comedy of misdirection, and the prospects for railways after privatisation: London: *Proceedings of the Chartered Institute of Transport,* Vol. 2(4), November 1993, 3–23.
Discusses the future of Britain's railways after privatisation.

2156 Leydon, K. A. *Irish Railway Policy in the Context of the Common Transport Policy of the EEC.* Dublin: University of Dublin (MA Thesis), 1972.

2157 Nash, C. A. Rail Policy and Performance in Australia. London: *Transport Reviews,* Vol. 5(4), October–December 1985, 289–300.
Review of rail policy and performance of the rail system in Australia which draws comparisons with the rail systems of Western Europe.

2158 Parkes, Michael; Mouawad, Daniel C. and **Scott, Michael J.**

King's Cross Railwaylands: towards a people's plan. London: King's Cross Railwaylands Group, 1991. 84 pp.

Presents a community view of how the King's Cross railway land site might be used to meet the needs of local people.

2159 Salveson, Paul. *British Rail: the radical alternative to privatisation.* Manchester: Centre for Local Economic Strategies, 1989. 158 pp.

2160 Urban Transport International. Designers Add Flair to Dutch SM90 Commuter Trains. London: *Urban Transport International*, January/February 1991, 19–20.

Reports that the Netherlands Railway company have given designers a new freedom in creating the specification for a new generation of local passenger trains.

2161 Williams, Charles. *Can Competition Come to the Railways?* London: Public Finance Foundation, 1992. 78 pp.

Discusses the viability of privatising British Rail.

2162 Yearsley, Ian. Investment Leads to Growth. Surrey: *City Transport*, Vol. 2(4), 1987, 7–10.

The director of British Rail's Network SouthEast, Chris Green, explains how a marketing approach is working on the predominantly commuter rail services centred on London.

13 Light Railways

History

2163 Baddeley, G. E. *The Tramways of Croydon.* London: Light Rail Transit Association, 1983. 208 pp.

2164 Bobrick, Benson. *Labyrinths of Iron: the history of the world's subways.* New York: Newsweek Books, 1981. 351 pp.

A story of the world's subways from Egyptian times to the 1970s.

2165 Buckley, R. J. *History of Tramways from Horse to Rapid Transit.* Newton Abbot: David and Charles, 1975. 184 pp.

Survey of the tramways from the introduction of railed horse drawn transport in the mid-1800s, through its heyday around World War I, its subsequent decline, and present-day revival in new form.

2166 Buckley, Richard J. Capital Cost as a Reason for the Abandonment of First-Generation Tramways in Britain. Manchester: *Journal of Transport History,* Vol. 10(2), September 1989, 99–112.

Within the context of renewed interest in tramways as a form of urban transport the reason for their decline from the 1930s is re-examined. Article questions whether it was competition from motor buses that caused their demise.

2167 Burrows, V. E. *Tramways in Metropolitan Essex: Vol. 1.* Essex: V. E. Burrows, 1967. 163 pp.

Traces the story of tramways in Essex from the origins to electrification.

2168 Burrows, V. E. *Tramways in Metropolitan Essex: Vol. 2.* Essex: V. E. Burrows, 1976. 220 pp.

Traces the histories of the East Ham, Ilford, Barking and West Ham systems from their inception until their acquisition by the London Passenger Transport Board.

2169 Collins, Paul. *The Tram Book.* London: Ian Allan, 1995. 112 pp.

Comprehensive survey which examines how Britain's tramway systems were operated and maintained.

2170 Cooper, Terence (ed.). *The Wheels Used to Talk to Us.* Sheffield: Tallis, 1978. 172 pp.

Autobiographical account of life on London County Council's trams.

2171 Cooper, Terry and **Gent, John.** *Around London by Tram.* Sheffield: Sheaf Publishing, 1981. 154 pp.

Collection of more than 200 postcards looking at the richly varied London street scene as it was in the years between 1900 and 1930.

2172 Economic and Operational Research Office, London Transport. *Variations in the Demand for Bus and Rail Travel in London up to 1974.* Economic Research Report R210. London: London Transport, 1975. 23 pp.

Statistical analysis of weekly bus and Underground receipts.

2173 Gill, Dennis. *Heritage Trams: an illustrated guide.* Stockport: Trambooks, 1991. 48 pp.

Illustrated directory and guide to sites and museums which exhibit trams.

2174 Gladwin, D. D. *Trams on the Road.* London: Batsford, 1990. 128 pp.

Pictorial history of trams, from horse-drawn to electric powered.

2175 Hesketh, Peter. *Trams of the North West.* London: Ian Allan, 1995. 128 pp.

Examines the development of tramways in the North West region of England, including the towns of Blackpool, Carlisle, Barrow and Morecambe.

2176 Higginson, Martin (ed.). *Tramway London: background to the abandonment of London's trams 1931–1952.* London: Light Rail Transit Association, 1993. 71 pp.

Collection of papers prompted by the revival of interest in light rail in London and consequently the search for reasons for the demise of trams.

2177 Jones, P. *The Spread of Urban Tramway Services in the British Isles: a scales approach.* Aberdeen: Aberdeen University (PhD Thesis), 1977.

2178 Joyce, J. *Trams in Colour Since 1945.* London: Blandford Press, 1970. 157 pp.

Depicts the twilight of the tramcar as part of the urban transport scene in Britain.

2179 Kidner, R. W. *The London Tramcar 1861–1952.* Locomotion Papers Number 7. Dorset: The Oakwood Press, 1992. 45 pp.

2180 Klapper, Charles F. *The Golden Age of Tramways.* Newton Abbot: David and Charles, 1974. 327 pp.
Standard account of the rise and decline of Britain's tramways.

2181 Marshall, Prince. *Wheels of London.* New Jersey: Haessner Publishing, 1974. 142 pp.
Review of trams and trolleybuses in London supported by over four hundred photographs and illustrations.

2182 McCarthy, James D. *Boston's Light Rail Transit Prepares for the Next Hundred Years.* Paper presented at the National Conference on 'Light Rail Transit: new system successes at affordable prices'. Washington, DC: Transportation Research Board, National Research Council, 1989, 286–308.
Reviews some of the accomplishments of light rail in Boston over the past century and takes a look at what the future may hold.

2183 McKay, John P. *Tramways and Trolleys: the rise of urban mass transport in Europe.* Princeton, NJ: Princeton University Press, 1976. 266 pp.
Examines the impact of tramways and trolleys on the urban environment and the lives of city dwellers.

2184 Muller, A. E. G. *The Buenos Aires Underground System (SUBTE): stagnation ... and revival?* Paper from the proceedings of 'Rail Mass Transit for Developing Countries' organised by the Institution of Civil Engineers. London: Thomas Telford, 1990, 189–204.
Examines the development, relative decline and prospects for revival of the Buenos Aires underground system.

2185 Nock, O. S. *Underground Railways of the World.* London: Adam and Charles Black, 1974. 208 pp.
Examines the underground railways of the world including those of London, Paris, New York, Madrid, Moscow and San Francisco.

2186 Oakley, E. R. *London County Council Tramways. Volume 1. South London.* London: London Tramways History Group, 1989, 1–488.

Details the origins, development and consolidation of the tramway systems south of the Thames which eventually became part of the London County Council's Tramways.

2187 Oakley, E. R. *The London County Council Tramways: Volume 2: North London.* London: London Tramways History Group, 1991, 489–986.

Details the origins, development and consolidation of the railway systems north of the Thames which eventually became part of the London County Council's Tramways.

2188 Oakley, E. R. and **Withey, C. L.** *Improving London's Trams (1932–7): Part 1: the LCC prototypes.* Hertfordshire: Light Rail Transit Association Publications, 1988. 28 pp.

Examines the move to improve the quality of trams in the face of competition from omnibuses.

2189 Oakley, E. R., Packer, A. D., Smeeton, C. S. and **Willoughby, D. W.** *London County Council Tramways Handbook.* 3rd ed. London: Tramway and Light Railway Society, 1977. 97 pp.

Provides an overview of the London County Council tramways. Also examines routes, services and rolling stock.

2190 Oakley, Edward R. *The British Horse Tram Era with Special Reference to the Metropolitan Areas Around London: a personal survey.* Kent: Nemo Productions, 1979. 44 pp.

2191 Ochojna, A. D. *Lines of Class Distinction: an economic and social history of the British tramcar, with special reference to Edinburgh and Glasgow.* Edinburgh: University of Edinburgh (PhD Thesis), 1977.

2192 Ryder, Andrew. What Went Wrong with Poland's Warsaw Metro? Virginia: *Transportation Quarterly*, Vol. 47(4), October 1993, 79–89.

Provides a history of the construction of the Warsaw metro, examines the possible alternatives that were available and discusses the problems encountered.

2193 Smeeton, C. S. *The London United Tramways: Volume 1–origins to 1912.* London: Light Rail Transit Association, 1994. 288 pp.

Charts the history of the London United Tramways, the first electric street tramway system in the Greater London area to be worked from a fixed power source.

2194 Snell, John and **Whitehouse, Patrick.** *Narrow Gauge Railways of the British Isles.* 2nd ed. Newton Abbot: David and Charles, 1984. 160 pp.

Traces the origins and development of narrow gauge railways,

2195 Trevisiol, Robert. Wagner's Metro is a Hundred Years Old. Brussels: *Public Transport International*, Vol. 43(2), March 1994, 46–47.

An illustrated history of the metro in Vienna.

2196 Wilson, Geoffrey. *London United Tramways: a history 1894–1933.* London: George Allen and Unwin, 1971. 240 pp.

2197 Wiseman, R. J. S. *Classic Tramcars.* London: Ian Allan, 1986. 216 pp.

Examines the evolution of the electric tramcar.

2198 Yearsley, Ian. Some Financial Causes of Tramway Decline in Great Britain. London: *Proceedings of the Chartered Institute of Transport*, Vol. 3(4), November 1994, 25–33.

Brief history of the electric tramway in Great Britain and its demise through financial causes.

Theory

2199 Allport, R. J. Appropriate Mass Transit for Developing Cities. London: *Transport Reviews*, Vol. 6(4), October–December 1986, 365–384.

Examines the development of the metro in Manila, capital of the Philippines, where an innovative system of metropolitan planning and administration provides an example of 'appropriate' investment for developing cities.

2200 Allport, R. J., Thomson, J. M. and **Fouracre, P. R.** *Rail Mass Transit in Developing Cities: the TRRL study.* Paper from the proceedings of 'Rail Mass Transit for Developing Countries' organised by the Institution of Civil Engineers. London: Thomas Telford, 1990, 21–39.

Many third world cities have recently built metros. Article examines the findings of the Overseas Development Association which looked into how such metros have fared and whether they were justified in either financial or economic terms.

2201 Anderson, J. E. *Personal Rapid Transit.* Minneapolis, MN: University of Minnesota, 1972. 520 pp.

Collection of twenty-eight papers which examine personal rapid transit from an economic and operational perspective.

2202 Bakker, J. J. Design Principles for Bus-Light Rail Transit Integration in Edmonton. London: George Godwin, *International Forum Series*, Vol. 2, 1981, 75–95.

Examines how well light rail transit has been integrated with Edmonton's urban bus system.

2203 Barry, Michael. *Through the Cities: the revolution in light rail.* Dublin: Frankfort Press, 1991. 255 pp.

2204 Bates, Michael and **Lee, Leo.** *At-Grade or Not At-Grade: the early traffic question in LRT route planning.* Paper presented at the National Conference on 'Light Rail Transit: new system successes at affordable prices'. Washington, DC: Transportation Research Board, National Research Council, 1989, 351–367.

Article examines analytical tools which provide effective methods for dealing with traffic issues in the feasibility and planning stages of LRT lines where early decisions have to be made between horizontal and vertical route alignment alternatives.

2205 Bonz, M. *Running Light Railways: experience in Europe.* Paper from the proceedings of 'Light Transit Systems' organised by the Institution of Civil Engineers. London: Thomas Telford, 1990, 259–264.

Article reports on experiences of light rail operation and outlines some requirements relevant to new operations. Includes a detailed presentation of the operational conditions of a German light rail transit system.

2206 Bownes, J. S. *Glasgow Underground: a study in urban transport planning.* Glasgow: University of Strathclyde (MSc Thesis), 1976.

2207 British Rail: London Regional Transport. *Light Rail for London ? – a report for the BR/LRT Liaison Group.* London: British Rail, London Regional Transport, 1986. 23 pp.

Reviews the potential for light rail in Greater London as an intermediate mode between the bus and conventional suburban and underground railways.

2208 Bugoz, G. N. *Rapid Transit Systems in Developing Countries.* Sheffield: University of Sheffield (PhD Thesis), 1980.

2209 Cassanova, Lilia; Hornilia, Linda and **Nierras, Jaime U.** Improving the Urban Planning and Management Process and Performance: Metro Manila. Nagoya, Japan: *Regional Development Dialogue*, 13(1), Spring 1992, 122–148.

Analyses Metro Manila in relation to land use control measures and regulation.

2210 Collins, B. T. *Light Transit to Stimulate Development: the London Docklands experience.* Paper from the proceedings of 'Light Transit Systems' organised by the Institution of Civil Engineers. London: Thomas Telford, 1990, 33–46.

Examines the inter-relationship between the Docklands Light Railway and the regeneration of the London Docklands and suggests some tentative conclusions that may be applicable elsewhere in British cities.

2211 Davidson, Peter. Estimating Ridership for Bristol's LRT. Transport planning Applications Stated Preference Special Report No.2. London: *Local Transport Today*, January 1990, 12–13.

2212 Davies, Gordon W. The Effect of a Subway on the Spatial Distribution of Population. London: *Journal of Transport Economics and Policy*, Vol. 10(2), May 1976, 126–136.

Examines how the Yonge Street subway line led to a marked increase in density of population in bordering areas.

2213 Davoudi, S., Gillard, A. and **Healey, P.** *The Longer Term Effects of the Tyne and Wear Metro.* Crowthorne: Transport and Road Research Laboratory, 1993. 83 pp.

2214 Dewees, D. N. A Comparison of Streetcar and Subway Service Quality. London: *Journal of Transport Economics and Policy*, Vol. 13(3), September 1979, 295–240.

Argues that replacement of a streetcar service by a subway brings benefits for longer trips; but for travellers starting between stations, with waiting and walking time weighted more heavily than travel time, the streetcar may be better for trips of up to five miles.

2215 Dickins, Ian. *An Introduction to Light Rail Transit in Europe: departmental working paper 32.* Birmingham: Birmingham Polytechnic, 1988. 61 pp.

Report produced as part of the preparatory work on the proposed Midland Metro LRT system. Examines current European practice in the planning and operation of LRT systems.

2216 Duran, F. M. *The Impact of the Decisions' Game on a Project.* Paper from the proceedings of 'Rail Mass Transit for Developing Countries' organised by the Institution of Civil Engineers. London: Thomas Telford, 1990, 269–279.

Examines the principal elements involved in the decision making process for a metro system being built in the city of Medellín, Colombia.

2217 European Conference of Ministers of Transport. *Scope for the Use of Certain Old-Established Urban Transport Techniques: trams and trolleybuses.* ECMT Round Table 38. Paris: Organisation for Economic Co-operation and Development, 1978. 73 pp.

2218 Ford, Roger. Equipment Market Goes Lightweight. London: *Transport*, Vol. 8, December 1987, 257–258.

Reports that, having concentrated on the series of new heavy rail metros promoted during the last decade, many project engineers and equipment manufacturers are now focusing their attention on developments in the lighter end of the market.

2219 Fox, Peter and **Taplin, Michael** (eds). *Light Rail Review.* London: Light Rail Transit Association, 1989. 64 pp.

Collection of articles written to coincide with an international conference on Light Rail held in 1989. Includes a world list of urban tramway and light rail systems.

2220 Gates, J. R. *Operating a Light Railway in Britain.* Paper from the proceedings of 'Light Transit Systems' organised by the Institution of Civil Engineers. London: Thomas Telford, 1990, 247–258.

2221 Goldsack, Paul. European Light Rail Review. Washington, DC: *Mass Transit*, June 1988, 17–24.

Reviews the situation in Europe (particularly cities such as Amsterdam, Birmingham, Geneva and Belgium's Liège and Rochefort) in order to reveal imaginative approaches to rail transit.

2222 Hall, Peter and **Hass-Klau, Carmen.** *Can Rail Save the City? – the impacts of rail rapid transit and pedestrianisation on British and German cities.* Aldershot: Gower, 1985. 241 pp.

2223 Hall, Peter; Hass-Klau, Carmen; Gretton, John; Harrison, Anthony and **O'Leary, Laura** (eds). Urban Transport: time for a fresh look. Berkshire: *Policy Journals*, 1987, 83–86.

Article examines the viability of investment in rapid transport systems.

2224 Hartley, Trevor. Keeping on the Light Side. London: *Transport*, Vol. 8, December 1987, 253–256.

Light Rail Transit systems have been installed or upgraded in a number of cities in the United States in recent years and there is a growing list of proposals for new systems, both in the United States and in the United Kingdom. Article reviews these developments.

2225 Hellewell, D. Scott. The Light Solution. London: *Urban Transport International*, July/August 1988, 8–10.

Reviews the advantages which give LRT the edge over other modes of public transport.

2226 Henry, Lyndon. *Ridership Forecasting Considerations in Comparisons of Light Rail and Motor Bus Modes.* Paper presented at the National Conference on 'Light Rail Transit: new system successes at affordable prices'. Washington, DC: Transportation Research Board, National Research Council, 1989, 163–189.

Claims that from the standpoint of ridership forecasting, light rail transit and motor bus modes vary in their attributes. Argues that specific modal attributes can be rated for LRT, busway and street bus systems and analysed, but that while LRT is rated highest in this comparison, the implications for mode choice behaviour require more intensive research.

2227 Higgins, Thomas J. Coordinating Buses and Rapid Rail in the San Francisco Bay Area: the case of Bay Area rapid transit. Amsterdam: *Transportation*, Vol. 10, 1981, 357–371.

Examines attempts by planners and policy makers to bring about the coordination of rail and bus transit in the San Francisco Bay Area.

2228 Hondius, Harry. How Can Tramways and Light Rail Be Made More Readily Affordable? Brussels: *Public Transport International*, Vol. 44(3), 1995, 71–77.

Considers the comparative economic efficiency of light rail and buses.

2229 Hope, Richard (ed.). *Developing Metros 88: metros, trams, light rail, commuter rail.* Sussex: Reed Business Publishing, 1988. 81 pp.

Annual collection of international features and reports.

2230 Hope, Richard (ed.). *Developing Metros 89: metros, trams, light rail, commuter rail.* Sussex: Reed Business Publishing, 1989. 40 pp.

Annual collection of features and reports.

2231 Hughes, Peter. Road Trains and People Movers: toy trains or serious transport? London: *Local Transport Today*, June 1994, 12–13.

Reviews the prospects of 'road-trains', mini-trams, and other people-movers.

2232 Huntley, Peter. Advanced Thinking in Avon? London: *Local Transport Today*, June 1989, 8–9.

Examines the progress of Britain's only privately-conceived urban rail project.

2233 Institute of Civil Engineers. *Rail Mass Transit for Developing Countries: proceedings of the conference organized by the Institute of Civil Engineers, and held in London on 9–10 October 1989.* London: Thomas Telford, 1990. 393 pp.

Study of the arguments for and against metros, based on analyses of the advantages and problems encountered in several cities of the world.

2234 Joos, E. *Light Transit to Combat Congestion.* Paper from the proceedings of 'Light Transit Systems' organised by the Institution of Civil Engineers. London: Thomas Telford, 1990, 19–32.

Examines the 'Zurich Model' which helps to ease congestion by redistributing road areas, giving more space for short range public passenger transport and pedestrians and less for private motoring.

2235 Joy, Stewart. Light Rail's Niches and Boundaries in Australian and Asian Cities. Westport, CT: *Transportation Quarterly*, Vol. 44(3), July 1990, 467–476.

Examines under which conditions light rail conversions would prove the solution for large flows of people in cities in Pacific Rim countries.

2236 Keys, S. *Moving People Within Urban Areas.* Paper from the proceedings of 'Light Transit Systems' organised by the Institution of Civil Engineers. London: Thomas Telford, 1990, 119–132.

Considers the potential role of light transit systems for moving people within urban centres.

2237 Knight, Robert L. and **Trygg, Lisa L.** Evidence of Land Use Impact of Rapid Transit Systems. Amsterdam: *Transportation*, Vol. 6, 1977, 231–247.

Article claims that rapid transit can have substantial growth-focusing impacts, but only if other supporting factors are present.

2238 Last, A. *Ridership Prediction and Revenue Estimation.* Paper from the proceedings of 'Light Transit Systems' organised by the Institution of Civil Engineers. London: Thomas Telford, 1990, 69–81.

Claims that appropriate, sensitive demand and revenue forecasts are essential for the successful planning of Light Transit Systems. Reviews forecasting methods, outlines some of the techniques that are available; and illustrates the application of the methods to specific schemes.

2239 Liberatore, M., McConnon, J. and **Legostaev, E. A.** *42nd International Congress: Montreal 1977.* Brussels: International Union of Public Transport, 1977. 36 pp.

Contains two papers presented at the 42nd international congress, the first by Liberatore and McConnon, 'The Place of Metropolitan Railways and Other Forms of Tracked Transport to Serve the Needs of Large Cities'. The second by Legostaev is 'Passenger Information and Orientation Systems in Metropolitan Railways'. The latter paper looks at ways of conveying information to railway passengers and also the visual systems of some underground railways.

2240 London Centre for Transport Planning. *Light Rail: the way forward for London?* London: London Centre for Transport Planning, 1987. 65 pp.

Contains three papers: 'The Concept of Light Rail' by Tim Morton, a senior transportation planner; 'Plans for Light Rail in London' by Jon Willis, the transport planner for Docklands Light Railway; and 'Light Rail Systems in German Cities: the social aspects' by Carmen Hass-Klau, a freelance writer on the environmental and social aspects of transport and planning.

2241 Martin, Joseph; Phraner, S. David and **Wilkins, John D.** *Hudson River Waterfront Transitway System.* Paper presented at the National Conference on 'Light Rail Transit: new system successes at affordable prices'. Washington, DC: Transportation Research Board, National Research Council, 1989, 225–250.

2242 McSpedon, Edward. *Building Light Rail Transit in Existing Rail Corridors – panacea or nightmare?* Paper presented at the National Conference on 'Light Rail Transit: new system successes at affordable prices'. Washington, DC: Transportation Research Board, National Research Council, 1989, 426–441.

The Los Angeles County Transportation Commission is constructing a 21 mile LRT line between the cities of Long Beach and Los Angeles. Sixteen miles of this line are being constructed on right-of-way acquired from and shared with the Southern Pacific. Examines some of the challenging aspects of this project such as the need to maintain railroad operations while relocating the freight line and constructing LRT.

2243 Meakin, R. T. *Hong Kong's Mass Transit Railway: vital and viable.* Paper from the proceedings of 'Rail Mass Transit for Developing Countries' organised by the Institution of Civil Engineers. London: Thomas Telford, 1990, 125–143.

Reports on the success of Hong Kong's mass transit railway in meeting the objectives of enhancing mobility while meeting financial targets.

2244 North, B. H. (ed.). *Light Transit Systems.* London: Thomas Telford, 1990. 282 pp.

Collection of papers presented at a symposium held to discuss the feasibility of running light transit systems. Issues addressed are: funding; engineering feasibility; public consultation; environmental impact; safety; and legal aspects of operation.

2245 Pastor, George J. *The Case for Automated Guideway Transit.* Paper presented at the National Conference on 'Light Rail Transit: new system successes at affordable prices'. Washington, DC: Transportation Research Board, National Research Council, 1989, 79–88.

Automated-guideway transit (AGT) is a class of transit system characterised by fleets of driverless transit vehicles operating under computer control on exclusive rights-of-way paths. This paper puts the case that, in certain applications, AGT is more than competitive with conventional transit, and that, under certain conditions, AGT systems can return sufficient revenues to match and even exceed their total operating and maintenance costs at acceptable fare levels.

2246 Potter, Stephen. *The Beckton Travel Survey.* London: Metropolitan Transport Research Unit, 1993. 33 pp.

Study of travel patterns in Beckton before the opening of the extension of the Docklands Light Railway.

2247 Profillidis, Vassilios A. Criteria for the Optimum Design of an LRT Depot. Brussels: *Public Transport International*, Vol. 41(2), May 1992, 50–59.

Examines the functions of a light rail transit depot. Article in English, with French and German translations.

2248 Quidort, Michel. Light Rail: a review of developments. Brussels: *Public Transport International*, Vol. 41, February 1993, 78–89.

2249 Rose, E. A. and Truelove, P. Social Impact and Transport Technology: some policy considerations. London: George Godwin, *International Forum Series*, Vol. 1, 1981, 47–58.

Examines the question of how far transportation investment decisions can and should be informed by social considerations.

2250 Scaillet, Michel. Guided Light Transit: the tramway on tyres. Brussels: *Public Transport International*, Vol. 44(3), 1995, 21–22.

2251 Schumann, John W. *What's New in North American Light Rail Transit Projects?* Paper presented at the National Conference on 'Light Rail Transit: new system successes at affordable prices'. Washington, DC: Transportation Research Board, National Research Council, 1989, 8–42.

Summary of the progress of North American light rail transit systems during recent years. Existing system rehabilitation and new project planning, design, construction, and start-up activities are also considered.

2252 Scudamore, D. M. *The Potential in Edinburgh for Rapid Transit.* Edinburgh: Heriot-Watt University (MSc Thesis), 1970.

2253 Sullivan, Brian E. Light Rail Transit in Canada. Amsterdam: *Transportation*, Vol. 9, 1980, 75–82.

Describes current light rail transit planning and operation in Canada's major cities and smaller communities.

2254 Taplin, M. R. *Light Transit Proposals in British Cities: a review.* Paper from the proceedings of 'Light Transit Systems' organised by the Institution of Civil Engineers. London: Thomas Telford, 1990, 5–17.

2255 Taplin, M. R. *Light Rail Transit Today.* Milton Keynes: Light Rail Transit Association, 1983. 64 pp.

Makes the case for the development of LRT systems in the UK. Argues that LRT systems fill the technology gap between the bus and the metro or urban railway.

2256 Taplin, Michael. Light Rail Takes Regional Rail to the City Centre. Brussels: *Public Transport International*, Vol. 41(3), 1992, 28–29.

Examines the possibilities of converting regional rail to light rail; sharing tracks between light and regional railways; and how main-line railways can be linked with tram systems. Article is also translated into French and German.

2257 Taylor, Stewart F. Light Rail Transit in the United States. Amsterdam: *Transportation*, Vol. 9, 1980, 67–74.

Reviews recent light rail transit developments in four American cities; two of which have undertaken to rehabilitate and upgrade their existing surface street railway systems; two of which have embarked on construction of entirely new light rail systems.

2258 Tinajero, Roberta. Rail Transit Makes a Comeback in Los Angeles County. Washington, DC: *Mass Transit*, September/October 1992, 54–60.

Examines the construction of an underground metro line which is to be part of a planned 400 mile metro system.

2259 Transportation Research Board. *Light Rail Transit: new system successes at affordable prices.* Washington, DC: National Research Council, 1989. 665 pp.

Proceedings of the National Conference on Light Rail Transit held in May 1988 in San Jose, California. Divided into five parts, part one provides an overview; part two looks at policy and planning considerations; part three looks at new light rail transit systems and lessons learned from new systems; part four looks at system design and vehicle performance; part five looks at operations and maintenance.

2260 Tyneside Passenger Transport Executive. *Tyneside Rapid Transit Analysis.* London: Alan M. Voorhees and Associates, 1972. 130 pp.

Considers various aspects of the public transport system in Tyneside and Wearside.

2261 Venturato, Tony and **Wolsfeld, Richard.** *Alternative Light Rail Transit Implementation Methods for Hennepin County, Minnesota.* Paper presented at the National Conference on 'Light Rail Transit: new system successes at affordable prices'. Washington, DC: Transportation Research Board, National Research Council, 1989, 251–268.

2262 Vuchic, Vukan R. *The Great Debate: potential roles of different transit modes.* Paper presented at the National Conference on 'Light Rail Transit: new system successes at affordable prices'. Washington, DC: Transportation Research Board, National Research Council, 1989, 62–65.

2263 Walker, Peter J. *The Case for Light Railway Rapid Transit.* Cardiff: Light Railway Transport League, 1969. 50 pp.

2264 Weinstein, Gary A., Williamson, Raymond C. and **Wintch, Thomas M.** *Preliminary Geometric Design Analysis for Light Rail Transit.* Paper presented at the National Conference on 'Light Rail Transit: new system successes at affordable prices'. Washington, DC: Transportation Research Board, National Research Council, 1989, 368–386.

Describes preliminary geometric design for LRT; the design sketch formats that were used, and the two-step procedure that was applied.

2265 Williams, Alan F. *Rapid Transit Systems in the UK: problems and prospects.* Aberystwyth: Institute of British Geographers, 1985. 200 pp.

2266 Winn, R. F. F. *A Costing Model for Light Rail Transit Operations.* Leeds: University of Leeds (MSc Thesis), 1987.

Investigates the building of an LRT financial cost model capable of being used to test changes in peaking, alignment length and alignment type. The model is applied to a hypothetical corridor to test the effects of the variables on financial costs and also to compare LRT, bus and conventional rail.

2267 Wood, Chris. *Street Trams for London.* London: Centre for Independent Transport Research in London, 1994. 182 pp.

Argues the case for locally orientated tramways as well as strategic, long distance systems. Case studies are included from Amsterdam, Göteborg, Oslo, Paris, Stockholm and Zurich.

Policy

2268 Abd El-Bary, F., El-Baradei, M., El-Fiky, F., Godard, X., Huzayyin, A. S. and **Nourel-Din, M.** *Cairo Regional Metro Line: an overview on the project.* Paper from the proceedings of 'Rail Mass Transit for Developing Countries' organised by the Institution of Civil Engineers. London: Thomas Telford, 1990, 241–254.

Cairo regional metro line has recently entered service extending for 42.5km with a 4.5km tunnel under the city centre. Article provides an overview of the project stages including history; institutions; construction; experience gained; and traffic circulation during construction.

2269 Acton, Peter. UK's First Public Monorail Gets off the Ground. London: *Transport*, Vol. 1, September/October 1980, 69–71.

Details the manufacture of a monorail in Rhyl, North Wales.

2270 Babendererde, S. *Lyons Metro: crossing the Rhône/Saône.* Paper from the proceedings of 'Urban Railways and the Civil Engineer' organised by the Institution of Civil Engineers. London: Thomas Telford, 1987, 181–191.

Examines the construction problems faced by the company building the Lyons metro and in particular the problems posed by the tunnel between the Guillotière and St Jean stations, and thus beneath the Rhône and Saône rivers.

2271 Barat, J. *Rio de Janeiro Mass Transportation System: the role* *played by metro lines*. Paper from the proceedings of 'Rail Mass Transit for Developing Countries' organised by the Institution of Civil Engineers. London: Thomas Telford, 1990, 205–221.

2272 Bayliss, David. *What's New in European and Other International Light Rail Transit Projects?* Paper presented at the National Conference on 'Light Rail Transit: new system successes at affordable prices'. Washington, DC: Transportation Research Board, National Research Council, 1989, 43–61.

Examines the pattern and nature of recent developments in light rail transit outside North America. Includes both conventional street tramways and unconventional automated systems. Details the distribution of light rail operations and the broad pattern of recent innovation in Western Europe with fuller accounts given of the developments of Hanover and Grenoble.

2273 Caba, Susan. Calcutta's Metro Instills Pride and Cuts Commutes. Washington, DC: *Mass Transit*, September 1987, 88–92.

2274 City Transport. How Light Rail Transit Can Cut the Costs. Surrey: *City Transport*, March/May 1987, 17–19.

Article reports how co-operation between public and private sector industries and authorities has provided a full scale light rail in Manchester.

2275 City Transport. Light Rail Revives in the Rust Belt. Surrey: *City Transport*, Vol. 2(4), December 1987/February 1988, 30.

Examines the emergence of light rail as a means of bringing new life to city centres in an area of the United States where heavy industry has departed.

2276 Claydon, C. *Light Transit Systems, Parliamentary Procedures and Options*. Paper from the proceedings of 'Light Transit Systems' organised by the Institution of Civil Engineers. London: Thomas Telford, 1990, 189–200.

2277 Dalvi, M. Q. *Calcutta Metro*. Paper from the proceedings of 'Rail Mass Transit for Developing Countries' organised by the Institution of Civil Engineers. London: Thomas Telford, 1990, 255–268.

Article describes the origin and economic justification of the Metro, the problems faced in its construction and funding; and finally its operation and impact.

2278 Dans, J. P. *The Metro Manila LRT System: its future*. Paper from the proceedings of 'Rail Mass Transit for Developing Countries' organised by the Institution of Civil Engineers. London: Thomas Telford, 1990, 159–173.

2279 Davis, D. E. Urban Transport, Dependent Development and Change: lessons from a case study of Mexico City's subway. Ottawa: *Canadian Journal of Development Studies*, Vol. 12(2), 1991, 329–355.

2280 Demoro, Harre W. The Sacramento LRT System: simple and successful. Washington, DC: *Mass Transit*, July/August 1988, 15–16.

Reviews the success of the Sacramento LRT system which was built on an economy model, using existing right-of-way where possible, and providing only one track for both directions along two-thirds of the route.

2281 Dutt, Ashok K. and **Mukhopadhyay, Anupa.** The Mass Rapid Transit System in Calcutta: a clean, efficient and well maintained metro. Brussels: *Public Transport International*, Vol. 41(1), February 1992, 70–81.

Describes the construction and service of the Calcutta Metro opened in stages from 1984. Article in English, with French and German translations.

2282 Figueroa, O. *Santiago Metro: integration and public transport.* Paper from the proceedings of 'Rail Mass Transit for Developing Countries' organised by the Institution of Civil Engineers. London: Thomas Telford, 1990, 307–317.

Reports on competition between Santiago's publicly owned metro and deregulated buses.

2283 Goldsack, Paul J. Lyons: world's first fully automatic heavy metro. Washington, DC: *Mass Transit*, June 1987, 10–12.

Reviews the impact which the new fully automated heavy metro system is likely to have on Lyons.

2284 Gonsalves, B. F. *Structures: Docklands light railway.* Paper from the proceedings of 'Urban Railways and the Civil Engineer' organised by the Institution of Civil Engineers. London: Thomas Telford, 1987, 135–148.

Article argues that an attractive feature of urban railways for designers and for constructors is that they are made to carry lightweight, relatively small scale rolling stock. Structures can be made simpler and less ponderous than those generally associated with railway construction work.

2285 Hamer, Andrew Marshall. *The Selling of Rail Rapid Transit.* Lexington, MA: D. C. Heath, 1976. 336 pp.

Critical study of the arguments given for the expansion of rail transit systems in the 1970s. Claims that powerful lobbyists for rapid rail transit systems were merely promoting their own interests with no real examination of the issues.

2286 Hamer, Mick. Lille Metro: on the right track. London: *Transport*, Vol. 3, July/August 1982, 7–9.

Reports that, as the United Kingdom endures the turmoil of a rail system locked in dispute over flexible rostering, and manning levels in general, the French city of Lille has been running passenger trials on its unmanned metro trains.

2287 Hellewell, D. Scott. Manchester's Light Rail Landmark. Brussels: *Public Transport International*, Vol. 41(3), 1992, 16–17.

Argues that the Manchester Metrolink provides an example of the type of high quality public transport needed to satisfy motorists displaced by measures to control traffic congestion.

2288 Mexia, Antonio and **Viegas, Jose Manuel.** Lisbon Metro Expands its Network. Brussels: *Public Transport International*, Vol. 42(4), November/December 1993, 32–38.

2289 Muller, Georges. Grenoble's Street Running Success Sets Light Rail Trend. London: *Urban Transport International*, November/ December 1990, 25–27.

Compares light railways and their operation in Grenoble and Strasbourg.

2290 Murin, William J. *Mass Transit Policy Planning: an incremental approach.* Lexington, MA: D. C. Heath, 1971. 123 pp.

Investigates some of the values and consequences of the construction of the Metro system in the Washington DC metropolitan area in the 1970s.

2291 Ng Cheuk Hon. *Hong Kong's Mass Transit Railway: a study of planning process.* London: University College London (M.Phil Thesis), 1980.

2292 Ogden, E. and **Senior, J.** *Metrolink.* Glossop: Transport Publishing Company, 1992. 152 pp.

Describes the development of Manchester's Metrolink; the first new street-running light rail system in Britain.

2293 Peschkes, Robert. *World Gazetteer of Tram, Trolleybus, and Rapid Transit Systems.* London: Rapid Transit Publications, 1993. 200 pp.

2294 Predl, Wolfgang. Modernising Light Rail Vehicles in Germany's New Federal States. Brussels: *Public Transport International*, Vol. 43(4), July 1994, 50.

Within the context of measures to develop public transport in the new federal states of Germany, this article puts the argument forward that the restoration of tramway systems will have an essential part to play.

2295 Reed, Fred A. Teheran: the Middle East's newest metro. Washington, DC: *Mass Transit*, April 1988, 32–33.

Construction of the Iranian capital's projected 45 kilometre subway network got underway in early 1987. Article reviews many aspects of the Middle East's newest metro.

2296 Schumann, John W. *RT Metro: from Sacramento's community dream to operating reality.* Paper presented at the National Conference on 'Light Rail Transit: new system successes at affordable prices'. Washington, DC: Transportation Research Board, National Research Council, 1989, 387–407.

Sacramento's RT Metro was built for the lowest capital cost per route mile to date of any new state funded rail system – US$9.6 million. Article describes the planning and design approach leading to this achievement.

2297 Shaw, Stephen. Quality Through Equality in Toronto's Mass Transit System. London: *Transport*, Vol. 14, March/April, 1993, 3–4.

2298 Strandberg, Keith. Hong Kong's Mass Transit Railway: leaving a legacy for Hong Kong's future. Washington, DC: *Mass Transit*, January/February 1989, 22–24.

2299 Taplin, Michael. Light Rail Renaissance in North America. Brussels: *International Union of Public Transport Revue*, Vol. 37(4), January 1989, 311–320.

Looks at the revival of the light rail and tramway in Canada and the United States from the early 1970s. Provides a brief summary of the types of system used in each city. Article in English with French and German translations.

2300 Urban Transport International. Shared Tracks Make Light Rail S-Bahn Simple for Karlsruhe. London: *Urban Transport International*, January/February 1991, 26–27.

Article reports on the success of trams running alongside DB trains in a German city's latest innovation.

2301 Urban Transport International. Confident Start: Hong Kong plans to extend its light rail system as phase one comes on stream. London: *Urban Transport International*, September/October 1988, 18–19.

Examines the latest addition to Hong Kong's extensive transport infrastructure, the Tuen Mun light rail system.

2302 Wade, Joe. Why Hong Kong Chose Light Rail. Surrey: *City Transport*, Vol. 2(4), December 1987/February 1988, 11–13.

Explains why light rapid transit was chosen for a busy corridor between new towns in Hong Kong.

2303 Yearsley, Ian. Why Docklands Chose Automation. Surrey: *City Transport*, Vol. 2(2), June–August 1987, 12–14.

Discusses the operating pattern and development of London's Docklands Light Railway.

2304 Young, A. P. *Development and Implementation of Greater Manchester's Light Rail Transit.* Paper presented at the National Conference on 'Light Rail Transit: new system successes at affordable prices'. Washington, DC: Transportation Research Board, National Research Council, 1989, 135–146.

The first new-generation light rail transit line to involve street operation in Britain includes 31km of track which utilises much of suburban railway infrastructure and provides new highway-based links across the city centre. Article describes the background to the project; the options considered; and the development of the chosen scheme through a period of major administrative and regulatory change.

14 London Underground

History

2305 Bennet, A. E. and **Borley, H. V.** *London Transport Railways: a list of opening, closing and renaming of lines and stations.* Newton Abbot: David and Charles, 1963. 32 pp.

Provides a reference work of the dates of opening and closing of lines and stations, and the renaming of stations, of all the former railways which merged into the London Transport system.

2306 Bruce, Graeme J. *Tube Trains Under London.* London: London Transport, 1977. 114 pp.

Short illustrated history of London Transport tube rolling stock.

2307 Croome, Desmond F. and **Jackson, Alan A.** *Rails Through the Clay: a history of London's tube railways.* London: George Allen and Unwin, 1962. 406 pp.

Standard account of the evolution, engineering and operation of the London Underground.

2308 Day, John R. *The Story of London's Underground.* London: London Transport, 1979. 160 pp.

Tells the story of London's Underground from the early days of the Metropolitan Railway tunnels between Paddington and Farringdon in 1863 to the late 1970s.

2309 Day, John and **Fenton, William.** *The Last Drop: the steam age on the underground from 1863 to 1971.* London: London Transport, 1971.

2310 Douglas, Hugh. *The Underground Story.* London: Robert Hale, 1963. 208 pp.

History of London's Underground from the early days to the building of the Victoria Line.

2311 Edwards, Dennis and **Pigram, Ron.** *London Underground's Suburbs.* London: Baton Transport, 1986. 137 pp.

Study of the development of the London Underground into the surrounding counties of Middlesex, Hertfordshire and Surrey.

2312 Garland, Ken. *Mr Beck's Underground Map: a history.* London: Capital Transport, 1994. 80 pp.

Describes the origins and development of the London Underground's famous map.

2313 Green, Oliver. *The London Underground: an illustrated history.* London: Ian Allan, 1987. 80 pp.

History of the development of London Underground from a Victorian steam railway just four miles long to the extensive electric railway covering some 250 route miles today.

2314 Green, Oliver. *Underground Art: London Transport Posters 1908 to the Present.* London: Studio Vista, 1990. 144 pp.

Extensively illustrated account of the development of London Underground's advertising campaign through the use of posters. Contains much information on the development of the tubes in the metropolis.

2315 Howson, H. F. *London's Underground.* London: Ian Allan, 1981. 159 pp.

Illustrated account of the development of London's Underground.

2316 Leboff, David. *London Underground Stations.* London : Ian Allan, 1994. 160 pp.

2317 Lee, Charles E. *The Piccadilly Line: a brief history.* London: London Transport, 1973. 26 pp.

2318 Lee, Charles E. *The Northern Line: a brief history.* London: London Transport, 1973. 31 pp.

2319 Lee, Charles E. *The East London Line and the Thames Tunnel: a brief history.* London: London Transport, 1976. 24 pp.

2320 Lee, Charles E. *100 Years of the District.* London: London Transport, 1968. 32 pp.

Historical review of London Underground's District Line during its first hundred years from the 1860s to the 1960s.

2321 Lee, Charles E. *The Bakerloo Line: a brief history.* London: London Transport, 1973. 23 pp.

2322 Lee, Charles E. *The Central Line: a brief history.* London: London Transport, 1973. 32 pp.

2323 Lee, Charles E. *The Metropolitan Line: a brief history.* London: London Transport, 1973. 32 pp.

2324 Levey, Michael F. *London Transport Posters.* Oxford: Phaidon Press, 1976. 80 pp.

2325 Morrison, Herbert. *Socialisation and Transport: the organisation of socialised industries with particular reference to the London Passenger Transport Bill.* London: Constable, 1933.

Seminal account of the growing trend towards the regulation, rationalisation and public ownership of London's road passenger and underground transport networks.

2326 Passingham, W. J. *The Romance of London's Underground.* New York: Benjamin Blom, 1972. 243 pp.

Illustrated historical account of the beginning of the London Underground and the men who created it. Describes the beginning of London's traffic problem and the growth of the Metropolitan railway; the first tube and electric railways; and the Post Office underground network.

2327 Thomas, J. P. *Handling London's Underground Traffic.* London: London Underground, 1928. 230 pp.

Account of the methods adopted in the handling of London's sub-surface systems of transport which pays particular regard to the many innovations of which the London Underground were the pioneers.

Theory

2328 Forsyth, E. *The Effects of Real-Time Information on the Perceptions of Time and Experienced Stress and Arousal of Passengers on the Northern Line of the London Underground.* Newcastle Upon Tyne: University of Newcastle Upon Tyne (M.Phil Thesis), 1988.

Attempts to evaluate London Underground's Northern Line dot-matrix indicators, with particular regard to its impact on passengers' perceptions of time and experienced stress and arousal.

2329 London Strategic Policy Unit. *Notes from the Underground.*

Popular Planning Transport Guide No. 3. London: London Strategic Policy Unit, 1986. 131 pp.

Survey of the London Underground system in the mid-1980s.

2330 Maxwell, W. W. *The Contribution of the Underground Railway to City Transport.* Transport and Road Research Laboratory Conference on moving people in cities, 5–6 April 1973. Crowthorne: Transport Road and Research Laboratory, 1973. 14 pp.

2331 McWilliams, Douglas. The Economic Benefits of Refurbishing the London Underground. Brussels: *Public Transport International*, Vol. 43(3), May 1994, 16–19.

Examines the effect on the United Kingdom's economy of differing levels of investment in the refurbishment of the London Underground.

2332 Rice, P. *Queuing and Stochastic Aspects of Urban Railway Capacity with Special Reference to London Transport Underground Railways.* London: University College London (PhD Thesis), 1976.

Policy

2333 Davies, Malory. Taking the Jubilee Line to Stratford. London: *Global Transport*, Vol. 3, Summer 1995, 18–23.

Considers whether the new Jubilee Line extension will meet the expectations of London Underground and its passengers.

2334 Godwin, Bill. Out of the Ashes. Washington, DC: *Mass Transit*, May 1990, 22–26.

Examines the rebuilding of London Underground with a new emphasis on safety following the tragic fire at the King's Cross Station in November, 1987.

2335 Parsons, John. Total Control. London: *Urban Transport International*, May/June 1988, 21–22.

Examines the efforts to ease overcrowding on the London Underground and a crackdown on fraud.

15 Environment

General

2336 Alexandre, Ariel. The Need to Reconcile Transport and the Environment. London: *Global Transport*, Vol. 1, Spring 1995, 15–20.

Argues that a balance needs to be struck between transport requirements and their social impact.

2337 Arnold-Baker, Charles. Yells, Smells and Jams. Chichester: *Road Law*, Vol. 9(1), 1993, 18–20.

Reports on the thermal energy conservation programme.

2338 Banister, David and **Button, Kenneth** (eds). *Transport, the Environment and Sustainable Development.* London: E. and F.N. Spon, 1993. 275 pp.

Examines the relationships between transport, urban structure and environmental degradation.

2339 Barde, Jean-Philippe and **Button, Kenneth** (eds). *Transport Policy and the Environment: six case studies.* London: Earthscan, 1990. 211 pp.

Case studies aim to identify and analyse the elements in transport policy which can induce adverse environmental effects. Reports from the United States, the Federal Republic of Germany, France, the Netherlands, Greece and Italy.

2340 Billings, R., Crowley, J. A. and **Moran, R.** *Research and Technology Strategy to Help Overcome the Environmental Problems in Relation to Transport.* SAST Project 3. Paris: Organisation for Economic Co-operation and Development, 1992.

2341 Colin Buchanan and Partners. *Greenwich and Deptford Management Study: a report to the Greater London Council.* London: Colin Buchanan and Partners, 1972. 49 pp.

Study of traffic movement and the environment within the Greenwich-Blackheath area together with proposals for a diversion scheme.

2342 Conway, Harry. Need to Change Old Attitudes. London: *Transport*, Vol. 11, October 1990, 243–244.

Reports on how the transport industry is coming to terms with the environment.

2343 Council for the Protection of Rural England. *Transport and the Environment.* London: Council for the Protection of Rural England, 1992. 47 pp.

The Council for the Protection of Rural England's submission to the Royal Commission on Environmental Pollution.

2344 Environment Directorate. *Environmental Implications of Options in Urban Mobility.* Paris: Organisation for Economic Co-operation and Development, 1973.

2345 European Conference of Ministers of Transport. *Urban Transport and the Environment: 10–12 July 1979.* IV. Conclusions. Paris: Organisation for Economic Co-operation and Development, 1980. 15 pp.

Considers pedestrians and cyclists; traffic in residential areas; transportation management; financing; land use; political and economic considerations; flexibility and reversibility.

2346 European Conference of Ministers of Transport. *Internalising The Social Costs of Transport.* Paris: Organisation for Economic Co-operation and Development, 1994. 191 pp.

Presents the results of a 1994 OECD/ECMT seminar on the external costs of transport services, such as the social costs of noise, air pollution, increased risk of accidents and traffic congestion. Examines how the economic burden of transport policies can be shared.

2347 Fiala, Ernst. Individual Transport in Cities. London: George Godwin, *International Forum Series*, Vol. 2, 1981, 113–122.

Examines the contribution of the automobile to individual mobility.

2348 FitzRoy, F. and **Smith, I.** *Improving Urban Transport and the Environment: taxes or buses?* St Andrews: St Andrews University, 1992. 20 pp.

2349 Fraker, Harrison; Lambert, Joseph E., Marckel, Daniel J. and

Tambornino, Mark. Streets, Parks and Houses. Oxford: *Transport Policy*, Vol. 1(3), June 1994, 160–173.

Describes the results of an urban design process which examined the remains of a neighbourhood's ecological structure; the existing infrastructure; transit improvements and needs; land-use and zoning; issues of crime and housing needs.

2350 **Frederick, Stephanie J.** and **Small, Kenneth A.** Cost-Effectiveness of Emissions Control Strategies for Transit Buses: the role of photochemical pollutants. Oxford: *Transportation Research*, Vol. 23(3), 1989, 217–227.

2351 **Gigg, M. F.** *The Visual Intrusion of Moving Traffic.* Sheffield: University of Sheffield (PhD Thesis), 1981.

2352 **Ham, Joop van; Kroon, Martin** and **Smit, Ruthger** (eds). *Freight Transport and the Environment.* London: Elsevier, 1991. 355 pp.

Examines goods transport and its environmental consequences. Addresses political and practical issues of utilising railways and waterways and how care of the environment can be considered alongside current logistical trends.

2353 **Hart, T.** and **Wayne, F.** *Greening Transport: providing acceptable alternatives to past trends.* Glasgow: Glasgow University, Scottish Transport Studies Group, October 1990. 40 pp.

2354 **Higman, R.** *Local Responses to 1989 Traffic Forecasts: a survey.* London: Friends of the Earth, 1991. 12 pp.

2355 **Hopkinson, P. G.** *Methods for Measuring Environmental Disturbances Affecting Residents and Pedestrians: a contribution to rail project appraisal.* Leeds: University of Leeds (PhD Thesis), 1988.

Examines some of the methods which are used to measure how individuals perceive and evaluate exposure to different levels of railway and road transport related environmental impact.

2356 **Jennings, Tony** and **Sharp, Clifford.** *Transport and the Environment.* Leicester: Leicester University Press, 1976. 229 pp.

Examines the impact of transport operations on the environment. Noise, air pollution, vibration, accidents, delays caused by slow-moving vehicles, road wear, visual intrusion and the severance of communities are all analysed in detail. The role of central and local government is considered, particular attention being given to methods of allowing for environmental benefits when planning new transport investment.

2357 Knight, Donald. Report of the 24th Annual Joint Conference of the Eno Transportation Foundation Board of Directors and Board of Advisors. Westport, CT: *Transportation Quarterly*, Vol. 46(2), 1992, 3–17.

Examines the conflict between sustaining mobility and simultaneously meeting environment and energy challenges.

2358 Lee, James A. *The Environment, Public Health, and Human Ecology: considerations for economic development.* Baltimore, MD: Johns Hopkins University Press, 1985.

2359 Lichfield, Nathaniel and **Proudlove, Alan.** *Conservation and Traffic: a case study of York.* York: Sessions Book Trust, 1976. 132 pp.

2360 Lyons, William M. Policy Innovations of the US Intermodal Surface Transportation Efficiency Act and Clean Air Act Amendments. Dordrecht: *Transportation*, Vol. 22(3), 1995, 217–240.

Examines the Intermodal Surface Transportation Efficiency Act 1991 and the Clean Air Act Amendments 1990 which in combination have the objective of moving US cities toward integrated transportation and air quality planning.

2361 Organisation for Economic Co-operation and Development. *Problems of Environmental Economics.* Paris: Organisation for Economic Co-operation and Development, 1971.

2362 Organisation for Economic Co-operation and Development. *Environmental Effects of Automotive Transport.* Paris: Organisation for Economic Co-operation and Development, 1986. 172 pp.

Forms part of the work of the OECD programme on the Comparative Assessment of the Environmental Implications of Various Energy Systems. Discusses the economic tradeoffs involved in seeking an environmentally acceptable transport package. Reviews methods for obtaining environmental improvements economically.

2363 Organisation for Economic Co-operation and Development. *Market and Government Failures in Environmental Management: the case of transport.* Paris: Organisation for Economic Co-operation and Development, 1992. 90 pp.

Analyses the kinds of government intervention in transport such as pricing, taxation and regulations, which often result in environmental degradation.

2364 Oron, Yitzhak; Pines, David and **Sheshinski, Eytan.** The Effect of

Nuisances Associated with Urban Traffic on Suburbanization and Land Values. London: *Journal of Urban Economics*, Vol. 1(4), October 1974, 382–394.

Considers the nuisance which urban motor vehicle traffic inflicts on the quality of the residential neighbourhood environment: pollution, noise and congestion. Analyses the impact of these nuisances by comparing competitive equilibrium and optimum allocations, employing a standard urban area model into which the the nuisances of motor vehicle traffic have been introduced.

2365 Pease, Jack. Tide of Environmentalism Carries the Standing Committee on Trunk Road Assessment Findings Forward. London: *Local Transport Today*, March 1992, 10–11.

2366 Plowden, Stephen. *Towns Against Traffic*. London: André Deutsch, 1972. 183 pp.

Examines the causes of decline in the quality of urban living and the ability of people to move around safely and conveniently within the urban environment.

2367 Preston, Barbara. *The Impact of the Motor Car*. Tregaron: Brefi Press, 1990. 205 pp.

Discusses the impact of the car on the environment within a British context.

2368 Road Research Group. *Roads and the Urban Environment: proceedings of the symposium on roads and the urban environment held at the Ministry for Public Works in Madrid on 14th, 15th and 16th October 1974*. Paris: Organisation for Economic Co-operation and Development, 1975. 191 pp.

Reports on research results in the fields of traffic noise and vibration; noise abatement; air pollution and economic and regulatory aspects. Also considers the development and application of comprehensive environmental approaches in planning new urban roads.

2369 Smith, Gavin. *Getting Around: transport today and tomorrow*. New South Wales: Pluto Press, 1984. 97 pp.

Describes a transport utopia providing a vision of what a people-orientated transport system could look like.

2370 Southampton Federation of Residents and Allied Associations. *The Portswood Link? the case against the Portswood link motorway*. Southampton: Southampton Federation of Residents and Allied Associations, 1973.

2371 Stokes, G. and **Taylor, B.** *Public Attitudes to Transport and the*

Environment: results from the 1993 British Social Attitudes Survey. Oxford: Oxford University, Transport Studies Unit, 1994. 20 pp.

2372 Transport and Environment Studies. *Environmental Effects of European Intercity Transport.* Paris: Organisation for Economic Co-operation and Development, 1973. 92 pp.

Examines the effects of transport on the environment. Reports on the incremental effects of increasing mobility and concludes that such increases could rapidly accelerate the worsening of Europe's environmental quality and subject many more people than now to the unpleasant side-effects of transport.

2373 Transport and Road Research Laboratory. *Roads and the Environment.* A collection of papers prepared at TRRL: TRRL Supplementary Report 536. Crowthorne: Department of the Environment, Department of Transport, 1980. 90 pp.

Analysis of topics including noise, low frequency sound, vibration, exhaust emissions and the visual impact of roads.

2374 Walbank, M. J. *Community Assessment of the Environmental Impacts of a Transport Service.* Manchester: University of Manchester (MSc Thesis), 1978.

2375 Watkins, L. H. *Environmental Impact of Roads and Traffic.* Essex: Applied Science Publishers, 1981. 263 pp.

Examines the problems of environmental intrusion including noise, vibration, exhaust emission and roadside pollution.

2376 Westerman, H. L. Roads and Environments. Victoria: *Australian Road Research*, Vol. 20(4), December 1990, 5–23.

Considers the conflict arising where roads carrying heavy traffic penetrate into areas intended to be precincts. Summarises research on friction and impact, and policies and guidelines.

2377 Whitelegg, J. The Future of Urban Transport. Victoria: *Australian Road Research*, Vol. 21(2), September 1991, 12–22.

Examines the evidence of economic, social and environmental damage caused by the automobile to cities. Argues that alternative development paths are available and that it is more a matter of political will than technical inadequacies that is proving to be the constraint.

2378 World Bank. *Making Development Sustainable: the World Bank Group and the environment.* Washington, DC: The World Bank, 1994. 270 pp.

Report on the World Bank's projects for 1994 and in particular its effort to incorporate environmental concerns into all aspects of its work.

Policy

2379 Automobile Association. *Transport and the Environment: a policy statement.* Basingstoke: Automobile Association, 1992. 18 pp.

2380 Batisse, Francois. European Transit and the Environment. Washington, DC: *Mass Transit*, September/October 1990, 43–48.
Article reviews the environmental issues of transport and the future prospects for reform.

2381 Button, Kenneth. *Transport, the Environment and Economic Policy.* Cheltenham: Edward Elgar Publishing, 1993. 153 pp.
Examines the environmental costs of transport. Discusses all modes of transport and their effects on major problems such as greenhouse gases, depletion of non-renewable resources, urban sprawl and acid rain.

2382 Convisser, Martin and **Altshuler, Alan** (eds). Transportation and the Environment, in *Current Issues in Transportation Policy*. Lexington, MA: Lexington Books, 1980. Chapter 3.
Examines the impact of transportation improvements on parks and sites of historic and cultural significance. Also – standards to control environmental pollution; community disruptions from transportation; considerations relating to bicyclists; pedestrians; physically handicapped; elderly; highway beautification and billboard control, land use and urban growth.

2383 Cullinane, S. *Attitudes Towards the Car in the UK: some implications for policies on congestion and the environment.* Oxford: Oxford University, Transport Studies Unit, 1992. 13 pp.

2384 Durrant, Lovell White. 'Green Shift' in Draft Transportation Guidance. *In-House Law*, May 1993, 66.
Consultation Document on draft planning policy guidance note on transport and the environment to replace PPG13.

2385 European Conference of Ministers of Transport. *Urban Travel and Sustainable Development.* Paris: Organisation for Economic Co-operation and Development, 1995. 238 pp.
Report of a three year enquiry into urban travel and sustainability. Examines the

role of economic incentives and disincentives; the role of land-use planning; the potential of traffic calming and other approaches to traffic management and the use of marketing, telematics and other innovations to improve public transport.

2386 Francis, Malcolm. York: un-sticking transport in a honeypot. London: *Local Transport Today*, September 1990, 10–11.

Report focuses on the city of York and its ability, or inability, to cope with the pressures of three million visitors a year.

2387 Goodwin, P. *Are Transport Policies Driven by Health Concerns?* Oxford: Oxford University, Transport Studies Unit, 1994. 25 pp.

2388 Heggie, Ian G. and **Rothenberg, J. G.** (eds). *Transport and the Urban Environment.* London: Macmillan, 1974. 273 pp.

Proceedings of a conference held by the International Economic Association at Lyngby, Denmark. The material included relates to the study of the character and determinants of urban development and structure, the relationship between these and environmental quality, and the public policy issues which arise because of this relationship.

2389 Hensher, David A. Socially and Environmentally Appropriate Urban Futures for the Motor Car. Dordrecht: *Transportation*, Vol. 20(1), 1993, 1–19.

2390 Hewitt, Patricia. *A Cleaner, Faster London: road pricing, transport policy and the environment.* Green Paper No. 1. London: Institute for Public Policy Research, 1989. 44 pp.

Considers how best to protect the environment against the environmental costs of traffic congestion and pollution, particularly in Central London. Looks at 'Road Pricing' as a means to encourage more discriminating car use.

2391 Hughes, Peter. Sustainable Transport: a new 'green' urgency in the air? London: *Local Transport Today*, March 1992, 10–11.

Following the launch of another green paper on 'sustainable mobility' by the European Community, this article aims to analyse the conflict between transport and environmental protection.

2392 Mathew, Don. *Getting There: a transport policy by Friends of the Earth.* London: Friends of the Earth, 1987. 48 pp.

2393 McKee, Graham and **Sillar, M.** State Transit Meets Increasing Environmental Responsibilities. Brussels: *Public Transport International*, Vol. 42(1), March–April 1993, 64–68.

Makes the case that the State Transit Authority of New South Wales clearly recognises environmental factors when operating bus and ferry services.

2394 Nishioka, Shuzo. Traffic Pollution: control policy and research trend. Oxford: *Transportation Research*, Vol. 23A(1), January 1989, 73–81.
Focuses on measures to control traffic pollution in Japan.

2395 Ono, Yuji. Japan's Sustainable Transport Policy Towards the 21st Century. Oxford: *Transport Policy*, Vol. 1(1), October 1993, 32–42.
Examines Japan's transport policy in the light of growing concern over environmental problems and energy issues.

2396 Organisation for Economic Co-operation and Development. *Urban Transport and the Environment.* OECD/ECMT Seminar 1979. Paris: Organisation for Economic Co-operation and Development, 1979. 283 pp.

2397 Organisation for Economic Co-operation and Development. *Management-Orientated Urban Transport Policies to Improve the Environment.* Paris: Organisation for Economic Co-operation and Development, 1978. 299 pp.
Study of twelve cities that have made successful efforts to enhance environmental conditions, improve public transport and assist movement by foot and by bicycle while maintaining access for travellers by car.

2398 Parkhurst, G. *UK Transport Policy Developments in 1991: environmental relevance.* Oxford: Oxford University, Transport Studies Unit, 1992. 32 pp.

2399 Postlethwaite, Robert. Sustainable Transport: Government Environment Policy: friend of the public transport industry? *Transport Law and Practice*, Vol. 1(6), 1994, 46–48.
Article examines contradictions in the British government's transport policy.

2400 Serageldin, Ismael. Environmentally Sustainable Urban Trans port: defining a global policy. Victoria: *Australian Transport and Freight Magazine*, Vol. 36(5), 1993, 13–16.
Article provides a definition of sustainable development in terms of urban transport.

2401 Serageldin, Ismael. Environmentally Sustainable Urban Transport: defining a global policy. Brussels: *Public Transport International*, Vol. 42(2), July 1993, 17–24.

Examines the strategies required to promote a global environmentally friendly urban transport policy.

2402 Sharp, Clifford. The Environmental Impact of Transport and the Public Interest. London: *Journal of Transport Economics and Policy*, Vol. 13(1), January 1979, 88.

Article argues that policies designed to reduce the damage to the environment caused by transport shoud be judged by the criterion of the public interest, i.e. a net increase in welfare.

2403 Transport 2000. *Travelling Cleaner: Dutch and British transport policy compared.* London: Transport 2000, February 1992. 58 pp.

2404 Transport and Environment Studies. *The Accessible City.* London: Campaign to Improve London's Transport Research Unit, 1985. 112 pp.

Examines the ability of people and goods to reach highly active areas of cities quickly, cheaply and pleasurably while maintaining environmental quality in areas passed through and at the destination.

2405 Virley, Simon. The Effect of Fuel Price Increases on Road Transport CO_2 Emissions. Oxford: *Transport Policy*, Vol. 1(1), October 1993, 43–48.

Examines the effect of higher fuel prices on UK road transport CO_2 emissions using an econometric model of road transport fuel consumption.

Planning

2406 Antoniou, Jim. *Environmental Management: planning for traffic.* London: McGraw-Hill, 1971. 171 pp.

Examines the organisation of traffic within towns and cities.

2407 Barat, Josef. Integrated Metropolitan Transport: reconciling efficiency, equity and environmental improvement. Liverpool: *Third World Planning Review*, Vol. 7, August 1985, 241–261.

Article investigates the structure of Brazilian transport with a view to defining a national urban transport policy.

2408 Barbe, Hans B. The Four Transitions from Traffic Engineering to

Environmental Planning. London: George Godwin, *International Forum Series*, Vol. 1, 1981, 23–28.

2409 Barnard, Louise. The Concept of Sustainable Development and its Impact on the Planning Process. Parliamentary Reports, Vol. 2(9), 1993, 394–397.

Investigates the incorporation of sustainable development policies into local plans and the important consequences for transport of draft PPG13.

2410 Campaign to Improve London Transport. *Changing to Green.* London: Transport and Environment Studies, 1986. 114 pp.

Study of the relationship between access, environmental quality and economic performance of central areas of cities, in this case the Central area of the London Borough of Camden, and Holborn. Argues that by removing inessential traffic and reallocating the movement space among pedestrians, cyclists and public transport the environment can be improved and economic prosperity increased.

2411 Cohn, Louis F. and **McVoy, Gary R.** *Environmental Analysis of Transportation Systems.* New York: Wiley-Interscience Publication, 1982. 374 pp.

Addresses the technical questions of noise, air quality and terrestrial and aquatic ecology using predictive modelling techniques.

2412 Colman, James. *Streets for Living.* Victoria: Australian Road Research Board, 1978. 92 pp.

Considers the design of residential streets from the perspective that their principal social function is to provide public space for social contact of various kinds.

2413 Day, M. and **Ringer, J.** *Environmental Impact: problems and opportunities.* Paper from the proceedings of 'Light Transit Systems' organised by the Institution of Civil Engineers. London: Thomas Telford, 1990, 167–187.

Examines the application of environmental assessment to the development of light transit systems.

2414 Doak, Edward J. and **Weiner, Paul.** *Environmental Factors in Transportation Planning.* Lexington, MA: Lexington Books, 1972. 283 pp.

Considers how environmental factors which are not reflected in the market can be integrated with the calculation of monetary impacts.

2415 Department of Transport: Department of the Environment.

Transport. Planning Policy Guidance Note PPG13 issued by the Department of the Environment and the Department of Transport, March 1994. *Journal of Planning Law*, May 1994, 423–424.

Revised guidance with the objectives of reducing journeys by road and reliance on private cars.

2416 Hill, Brian. Planning: balancing transport and environment. London: *Chartered Surveyor Weekly*, Vol. 43(7), 1993, 72–73.

Examines the Department of the Environment's consultation paper – Planning Policy Guidance on Transport.

2417 Krell, Karl. Using Urban Planning Concepts to Reduce Travel and Improve the Environment. London: George Godwin, *International Forum Series*, Vol. 1, 1981, 39–45.

Examines the possible readjustment of work and living space as a means of avoiding commuter traffic.

2418 Llewelyn–Davies Weeks Forestier. *Motorways in the Urban Environment*. London: British Road Federation, 1971. 102 pp.

Examines the local environmental implications of urban motorway development and the ways in which motorways could be satisfactorily integrated into existing urban areas.

2419 McKee, William A. and **Matingly, M. J.** Environmental Traffic Management: the end of the road? Amsterdam: *Transportation*, Vol. 6, 1977, 365–377.

Questions aspects of the technical soundness and public acceptability of environmental traffic management schemes of the kind advocated in the Buchanan Report, 'Traffic in Towns'.

2420 Pease, Jack. Leicester Plans its Transport for Model 'Environment City'. London: *Local Transport Today*, April 1991, 10–11.

Leicester is taking steps to be a model to show that sustainable development can actually work. Article seeks to analyse the extent of the progress which has been achieved in respect of urban transport.

2421 Russell, John R. E. Traffic Integration and Environmental Traffic Management in Denmark. London: *Transport Reviews*, Vol. 8(1), January–March 1988, 39–58.

Assesses Danish attempts to integrate traffic with the urban environment.

2422 Stone, Tabor R. *Beyond the Automobile: reshaping the trans-*

portation environment. Englewood Cliffs, NJ: Prentice Hall, 1971. 148 pp.

Argues the necessity of a large scale commitment to rail and bus transit systems in preference to the expansion of the road system.

Safety and crime

2423 Abbot, V., Hammerton, M. and **Jones-Lee, M. W.** The Consistency and Coherence of Attitudes to Physical Risk: some empirical evidence. London: *Journal of Transport Economics and Policy*, Vol. 16(2), May 1982, 181–200.

A questionnaire was found to be successful in establishing people's valuation of, and willingness to pay for, the prevention of transport accidents.

2424 Atkins, S. T. Personal Security as a Transport Issue: a state-of-the-art review. London: *Transport Reviews*, Vol. 10(2), April–June 1990, 111–125.

Reports that the possibility of experiencing assault, robbery, harassment or other anti-social behaviour has become an important influence on traveller decision-making. Reviews the extent and nature of the problem and looks at the range of possible responses from the authorities.

2425 Atkins, Stephen T. *Critical Paths: Designing for Secure Travel.* London: Design Council, 1989. 96 pp.

Sets out the general principles by which the design, operation and management of transport systems can significantly reduce both the opportunities for crime and the fear of crime.

2426 Brucati, Patricia S. Safety First. Washington, DC: *Mass Transit*, May/June, 1991, 18–19.

New York State's Public Transportation Safety Board is the only one of its kind in the USA. Article examines how it works.

2427 European Conference of Ministers of Transport. *Delinquency and Vandalism in Public Transport.* Report of the seventy-seventh Round Table on transport economics. Paris: Organisation for Economic Co-operation and Development, 1989. 165 pp.

Provides an analysis of the social and psychological causes of vandalism and the defacing of facilities on public transport systems.

2428 Evans, Andrew. The Evaluation of Public Transport Safety

Measures. Brussels: *Public Transport International*, Vol. 43(3), May 1994, 32–35.

2429 Hammerton, M., Jones-Lee, M. W. and **Philips, P. R.** The Value of Safety: results of a national sample survey. Oxford: *Economic Journal*, Vol. 95, 1985, 49–72.

Study, based on a questionnaire, of willingness to pay for reductions in the risk of death or injury on transport systems in the UK.

2430 Hensher, David A. and **Lowndes, J. F. L.** *Environmental Design for the Passenger.* Paper from the proceedings of 'Urban Railways and the Civil Engineer' organised by the Institution of Civil Engineers. London: Thomas Telford, 1987, 67–80.

Argues that the control of the environment, particularly in relation to the safety and comfort of passengers, is an important consideration in the design of transport systems.

2431 Issac, James. Cooperation Between Operators and Public Authorities in Birmingham. Brussels: *Public Transport International*, Vol. 42(2), July 1993, 43–46.

Report on a campaign against vandalism, graffiti and assaults.

2432 Jansson, Jan Owen. Accident Externality Charges. London: *Journal of Transport Economics and Policy*, Vol. 28(1), January 1994, 31–43.

2433 Levine, Ned and **Wachs, Martin.** Bus Crime in Los Angeles. 1: measuring the incidence. Oxford: *Transportation Research*, Vol. 20(4), July 1986, 273–284.

Discusses a method for estimating the number of transit crimes and examines sources of information loss within existing transit crime statistics.

2434 Levine, Ned and **Wachs, Martin.** Bus Crime in Los Angeles. 2: victims and public impact. Oxford: *Transportation Research*, Vol. 20A(4), July 1986, 285–293.

Examines the impact of bus crime in Los Angeles using data from a large victimisation survey which found that frequency of bus use was the most important correlate of being victimised. Looks at perceptions of bus safety, and the impact of crime on subsequent bus use.

2435 Logan, Laura. How Safe Is Your Passenger? London: *Proceedings of the Chartered Institute of Transport*, Vol. 2(3), August 1993, 10–19.

Gives a review of personal security issues on public transport systems in five European cities; Birmingham, Copenhagen, Paris, Stuttgart, and Turin.

2436 Main, Timothy. An Economic Evaluation of Child Restraints. London: *Journal of Transport Economics and Policy*, Vol. 19(1), January 1985, 23–40.

Sets out the economic costs and benefits of using restraints for children in cars from the point of view of parents.

2437 McLead, Marcia. A Tale of Two Cities. London: *Urban Transport International*, October/November 1989, 17–20.

Argues that New York City Transit Authority's problems of graffiti, vandalism and violence are due, in part at least, to the age and size of its bus and subway network, and to the criminal problems inherent within the city itself. Contrasts this situation with that prevailing in Washington.

2438 Mellor, Andrew. Wiping Out Vandalism. London: *Urban Transport International*, May/June 1988, 15–16.

Investigates ways in which fleet operators can stem the rising tide of crime.

2439 Moises, Jose-Alvaro and **Stolcke, Verena.** Urban Transport and Popular Violence: the case of Brazil. Oxford: *Past and Present*. 86, February 1980, 175–192.

Investigation, largely based on newspaper reports, into the riots on surburban railways which took place in Rio de Janeiro and São Paulo during the late 1970s.

2440 O'Connor, Michael. Solving the Graffiti Problem on the New York City Transit System. Brussels: *Public Transport International*, Vol. 41(1), February 1992, 91.

Describes how the problem graffiti was tackled on the New York City subway system. Claims that from being the subway system that suffered most from graffiti it is now one of the cleanest in the world. Article in English, with French and German translations.

2441 O'Reilly, D. The Value of Road Safety: UK research on the valuation of preventing non-fatal injuries. London: *Journal of Transport Economics and Policy*, Vol. 28(1), January 1994, 45–59.

2442 Whitford, M. J. *Getting Rid of Graffiti: a practical guide to graffiti removal and anti-graffiti protection.* London: E. and F.N. Spon, 1992. 160 pp.

Study based on London Underground's experience of removing and protecting surfaces from graffiti.

2443 Yearsley, Ian. UK Operators Combat Crime. Brussels: *Public Transport International*, Vol. 41(1), February 1992, 36–42.

Examines the various strategies and techniques used by public transport operators in Britain to deal with vandalism and violence. Closed circuit television; passenger alarm units; and security control rooms are discussed together with ways to deal with graffiti and aggressive passengers. Article in English, with French and German translations.

Air pollution

2444 Arnold-Baker, Charles. Transport and Air Pollution at Avignon. Chichester: *Road Law*, Vol. 10(5), 1994, 288–308.

European Commission's 3rd International Symposium on Transport and Air Pollution, Avignon; contains the list of submitted papers.

2445 Barrett, George M. Transport Emissions and Travel Behaviour: a critical review of recent European Union and UK policy initiatives. Dordrecht: *Transportation*, Vol. 22(3), 1995, 295–323.

Examines the shift of UK transport policy in response to concerns about the environmental impacts of road transport.

2446 Croke, Kevin and **Zerbe, Richard O.** *Urban Transportation for the Environment.* Massachusetts: Ballinger Publishing, 1975. 182 pp.

Presents an integrated engineering-economic investigation, including the development of an interdisciplinary methodology, for assessing the merits of different transportation measures.

2447 Department of the Environment and Department of Transport. *Reducing Transport Emissions Through Planning.* London: HMSO, 1993.

2448 European Conference of Ministers of Transport. *Transport Policy and Global Warming.* Paris: Organisation for Economic Co-operation and Development, 1993. 241 pp.

Report of an ECMT seminar on the subject of global warming and the contribution of the transport sector to this. Focuses on the transport policy options likely to stabilise and reduce greenhouse gas emissions.

2449 Glazer, Amihai; Klein, Daniel B. and **Lave, Charles.** Clean on Paper, Dirty on the Road: troubles with California's smog check. London: *Journal of Transport Economics and Policy*, Vol. 29(1), January 1995, 85–92.

Reports on the inadequacies of California's attempt to reduce air pollution caused by automobiles.

2450 Hall, Jane V. The Role of Transport Control Measures in Jointly Reducing Congestion and Air Pollution. London: *Journal of Transport Economics and Policy*, Vol. 29(1), January 1995, 93–104.

Examines transport control measures, such as reducing the demand for travel, or creating disincentives to car use, and improving alternatives to single-occupancy vehicles.

2451 Horowitz, Joel L. *Air Quality Analysis for Urban Transportation Planning.* Cambridge, MA: MIT Press, 1982. 386 pp.

Describes the key factors involved in evaluating the air quality impact of changes in the design and operation of urban transport systems.

2452 Hughes, Peter. *Personal Transport and the Greenhouse Effect.* London: Earthscan, 1993. 175 pp.

Explores the links between greenhouse gas emissions and personal transport and develops a number of scenarios based on projections of future economic and development trends combined with possible policy responses.

2453 Hughes, Peter. City Air Pollution: will new monitoring evidence make the case for action? London: *Local Transport Today*, April 1992, 10–11.

Article looks at whether enough will be done to prevent urban smog caused by road traffic.

2454 Kessler, Jon and **Schroeder, William.** Meeting Mobility and Air Quality Goals: strategies that work. Dordrecht: *Transportation*, Vol. 22(3), 1995, 241–272.

Examines the guidance necessary for urban areas responsible for meeting the goals of US federal legislation on air quality.

2455 McKinnon, Alan C. and **Woodburn, Allan.** The Consolidation of Retail Deliveries: its effect on CO2 emissions. Oxford: *Transport Policy*, Vol. 1(2), March 1994, 125–136.

Over the past twenty years, large British retailers have transformed the system of shop delivery by centralising inventory at distribution centres and delivering supplies in large consolidated loads. Article assesses the likely effects of the system on CO2 levels and suggests that any reductions upstream of the shop are likely to have been more than offset by the greater use of cars on shopping trips.

2456 Organisation for Economic Co-operation and Development.

Motor Vehicle Pollution: reduction strategies beyond 2010. Paris: Organisation for Economic Co-operation and Development, 1995. 133 pp.

Seeks to determine the impact that stricter, comprehensive control programmes could have on motor vehicle emissions over the next thirty to forty years.

2457 Poulton, M. L. *Alternative Engines for Road Vehicles*. Southampton: Computational Mechanics Publications, 1994. 164 pp.

Examines engine technologies within the context of attempting to minimise fuel consumption and exhaust emission.

2458 Shrouds, James M. Challenges and Opportunities for Transportation: implementation of the Clean Air Act Amendments of 1990 and the Intermodal Surface Transportation Efficiency Act of 1991. Dordrecht: *Transportation*, Vol. 22(3), 1995, 193–215.

Examines the Federal Clean Air Act Amendments of 1990 which are intended to significantly affect transportation decision-making not only to achieve air quality goals but also to affect broader environmental goals related to land use, travel mode choice, and reductions in vehicle miles travelled.

2459 Small, Kenneth A. Estimating the Air Pollution Costs of Transport Modes. London: *Journal of Transport Economics and Policy*, Vol. 11(2), May 1977, 109–132.

Claims that damage from air pollution appears not to justify large reductions in automobile travel in typical urban areas in the USA; but does justify significant expenditure on control of pollution.

2460 Urban Transport International. Cutting Down on Bus Engine Exhaust Emissions. London: *Urban Transport International*, Vol. 1, 1993, 11–15.

Reports that engine manufacturers are considering a range of options from turbo-charging to particulate traps, in order to render engine exhaust fumes more compatible with environmental demands.

2461 Wachs, Martin. Learning from Los Angeles: transport, urban form, and air quality. Dordrecht: *Transportation*, Vol. 20(4), 1993, 329–354.

Los Angeles is well known as an automobile-orientated low density community, yet recent transportation policies have emphasised greater capital investment in rail transportation than in highways, and recent policies have attempted to discourage automobile usage through demand management. Article reports that while these policies have accomplished small shifts towards public transport, and somewhat lower dependence upon singly occupied automobiles for commuting, the costs of change have been very high.

2462 Wang, Michael Q. Cost Savings of Using a Marketable Permit System for Regulating Light-Duty Vehicle Emissions. Oxford: *Transport Policy*, Vol. 1(4), October 1994, 221–232.

In the USA, each individual vehicle is required to meet uniform per-mile emission standards. Article argues that the uniform standard system does not allow vehicle manufacturers flexibility in achieving emission reduction goals for motor vehicles.

2463 Watkins, L. H. *Air Pollution from Road Vehicles.* London: HMSO, 1991. 152 pp.

Transport and Road Research Laboratory review of the facts about air pollution by vehicle exhausts.

Noise pollution

2464 Abott, P. and **Layfield, S.** *Vehicle and Traffic Noise Surveys Alongside Speed Control Cushions in York.* Project report no. 103. Crowthorne: Transport and Road Research Laboratory, 1995. 25 pp.

2465 Adams, Melville S. and **McManus, Francis.** *Noise and Noise Law.* London: Wiley Chancery Law, 1994. 204 pp.

Contains a chapter on 'environmental noise', including noise generated by road, air and rail transport.

2466 Alexandre, A., Barde, J. and **Pearce, D. W.** The Practical Determination of a Charge for Noise Pollution. London: *Journal of Transport Economics and Policy*, Vol. 14(2), May 1980, 205–220.

After reviewing various proposals for taxing traffic and aircraft noise, article offers a formula aimed at reducing noise at source and raising revenue to be used for mitigating noise in the environment.

2467 Birden, D. W. *The Development of Appropriate Noise Scales for the Prediction of Community Response to New Urban Light Rail Systems.* London: South Bank Polytechnic (PhD Thesis), 1990.

Discusses a series of subjective tests that were proposed to assess the ability of the dB(A), a weighted Sound Pressure Level, to assess the impact of noise dominated by low frequency energy. The background to these tests is the higher than predicted levels of noise annoyance reported by people living close to the Docklands Light Railway following its opening in 1987.

2468 Brachya, Valerie. Minimising Traffic Noise in Planning New Residential Areas. London: George Godwin, *International Forum Series*, Vol. 2, 1981, 221–232.

Examines five different ways in which noise levels can be reduced: removing noise at source; reducing noise at source; intercepting noise en route from source; to receptor; reducing noise at receptor; and reducing sensitivity of receptor.

2469 Cashell, R. H. M. *A Study of Traffic Noise in Urban Conditions.* Belfast: Queen's University (MSc Thesis), 1979.

2470 Department of the Environment: Department of Transport: Transport and Road Research Laboratory. *Roads and the Environment.* TRRL Supplementary Report 536. Crowthorne: Transport and Road Research Laboratory, 1980. 90 pp.

Discusses environmental research carried out at TRRL under two main headings; the first concerns factors such as noise and vibration, the second describes research concerned with an overall appraisal of schemes.

2471 Feitelson, Eran. Transportation Noise, Property Rights, and Institutional Structure: the Israeli experience in perspective. Oxford: *Transportation Research*, Vol. 23(5), 1989, 349–358.

Discusses the application of 'noise rights' to dealing with transportation noise.

2472 Hughes, Peter. Trying to Put a Price on Peace as Concern Grows at Noise Nuisance. London: *Local Transport Today*, January, 1993, 10–11.

Efforts are being made to apply proper weight to the environmental externalities of transport, with noise among the most tangible side-effects of road traffic and a growing concern for rail lines too. Article reviews the issue and observes that the adverse impact of noise is notoriously difficult to quantify.

2473 Jones, R. R. K. *An Investigation of Road Traffic Noise Characteristics in Restricted Flow Situations.* Bradford: University of Bradford (PhD Thesis), 1979.

2474 Jougla, J. P. *The Environmental Impact of Urban Railways Within the Community.* Paper from the proceedings of 'Urban Railways and the Civil Engineer' organised by the Institution of Civil Engineers. London: Thomas Telford, 1987, 81–95.

Noise and vibrations from heavy or light rail systems have become a major concern for the railway track engineer. Article reviews the main methods of reducing airborne and groundborne noise as well as considering various types of anti-vibration track.

2475 Nelson, Jon P. Highway Noise and Property Values. A survey of recent evidence. London: *Journal of Transport Economics and Policy*, Vol. 16(2), May 1982, 117–138.

Survey of nine studies of areas in Canada and U.S.A. suggests that traffic noise on a main highway decreased the price of a house by between 8 and 10 per cent.

2476 Nelson, P. M. (ed.). *Transportation Noise Reference Book*. London: Butterworths, 1987.

Provides a comprehensive account of transportation noise and vibration, and the methods of control that are available.

2477 Rosall, A. W. *The Measurement and Analysis of Road Traffic Noise*. Salford: University of Salford (MSc Thesis), 1978.

2478 Thancanamootoo, S. *Impact of Noise from Urban Railway Operations*. Newcastle Upon Tyne: University of Newcastle Upon Tyne (PhD Thesis), 1987.

Examines the noise nuisance that results from the operation of urban railways and reports on a case-study of the impact of the Tyneside Metro on residents living in close proximity to the railway tracks.

16 Theory and Research

General

2479 Anderson, Ake E. and **Batten, David F.** Creative Nodes, Logistical Networks, and the Future of the Metropolis. Amsterdam: *Transportation*, Vol. 14, 1987, 281–293.

A paradigmatic shift away from traditional quantitative methods towards qualitative dynamic analysis is proposed in order to fully comprehend the future of the metropolis.

2480 Andrikopoulos, A. A. and **Brox, J. A.** Canadian Inter-City Passenger Transportation: a simultaneous equation approach. Rome: *International Journal of Transport Economics*, Vol. 17(3), October 1990, 311–328.

2481 Axhausen, Kay and **Garling, Tommy.** Activity-Based Approaches to Travel Analysis: conceptual frameworks, models, and research problems. London: *Transport Reviews*, Vol. 12(4), October–December 1992, 323–341.

Review of conceptualisations and models of activity scheduling.

2482 Barnard, P. O. Use of an Activity Diary Survey to Examine Travel and Activity Reporting in a Home Interview Survey: an example using data from Adelaide, Amsterdam: *Transportation*, Vol. 13(4), 1986, 329–357.

Presents research which uses results from an activity diary survey to comment on the quality of data collected in a home interview travel survey. Discusses the possible implications of the deficiencies of using home interview surveys when investigating a range of urban transport issues.

2483 Bendixson, Terrence. *Without Wheels.* Bloomington, IN: Indiana University Press, 1975. 256 pp.

Examines the alternatives to the private automobile as a practical mode of transport within an urban environment.

2484 Bentley, G. A., Bruce, A. and **Jones, D. R.** *Intra-urban Journeys and Activity Linkages.* Watford: Building Research Establishment, 1977. 7 pp.

Examines the linkages between successive stages of multi-stage journeys.

2485 Bers, Eric L. The Functional Approach to Transit Balance. London: George Godwin, *International Forum Series*, Vol. 1, 1981, 105–115.

Presents a comprehensive approach to transit planning and operations based on corridor travel requirements and the three basic trip components: collection, line-haul and distribution.

2486 Black, Ian; Gillie, Richard; Henderson, Richard and **Thomas, Terry.** *Advanced Urban Transport.* Farnborough: Saxon House, 1975. 212 pp.

A report on the findings of the research which was commissioned in 1972 by the British Science Research Council. Assesses the possibility and desirability of introducing small, reserved-route public transport systems into towns.

2487 Blackburn, J. C. *Mental Maps and Intra-Urban Travel.* Reading: University of Reading (M.Phil Thesis), 1977.

2488 Bly, P. H., Dasgupta, M., Johnston, R. H., Pauley, N. and **Webster, F. V.** Changing Patterns of Urban Travel: Part 1. Urbanization, household travel and car ownership. London: *Transport Reviews*, Vol. 6(1), January–March 1986, 49–86.

First part of a report sponsored by the European Conference of Ministers of Transport aimed at explaining transport trends in cities, identifying likely future changes and assessing the implications for transport policy.

2489 Bly, P. H., Dasgupta, M., Johnston, R. H., Pauley, N. and **Webster, F. V.** Changing Patterns of Urban Travel: Part 2. Public transport and future patterns of travel. London: *Transport Reviews*, Vol. 6(2), April–June 1986, 129–172.

Second part of a report sponsored by the European Conference of Ministers of Transport which examines changes in public transport use; considers the interactions between the various underlying trends; speculates on future travel patterns by public and private means; and considers the likely impact of land use and transport policies.

2490 Bly, P., Hunt, P. and **Maycock, G.** *Future Scenarios for Inland Surface Transport: an examination of future research needs.* Crowthorne: Transport and Road Research Laboratory, 1995. 75 pp.

2491 Bos, Dieter. Distributional Effects of Maximisation of Passenger Miles. London: *Journal of Transport Economics and Policy*, Vol. 12(3), September 1978, 322–329.

2492 Bradley, Mark. Realism and Adaption in Designing Hypothetical Travel Choice Concepts. London: *Journal of Transport Economics and Policy*, Vol. 22(1), January 1988, 121–137.
Examines many of the aspects of stated preference applications which may affect the validity of the data, and then describes a number of recent developments addressing these issues.

2493 Braga, M. G. de C. Research Trends in Urban Transport Science: some empiricial evidence from academic research. Oxford: *Transportation Research*, Vol. 22A(1), January 1988, 57–70.
Changes in paradigm are detected and analysed through the use of data from academic research leading to higher degrees in both the UK and the USA over a period of twenty years.

2494 Busby, R. H. *Some Aspects of the Development of Transport Patterns in Hertfordshire, 1830–1980.* Salford: University of Salford (MSc Thesis), 1983.

2495 Catanese, Anthony J. (ed.). *New Perspectives in Urban Transportation Research.* Lexington, MA: D. C. Heath, 1972. 273 pp.
Provides an overview of systems analysis in the urban transportation planning process.

2496 Cervero, Robert. Futuristic Transit and Futuristic Cities. Westport, CT: *Transportation Quarterly*, Vol. 46(2), April 1992, 193–204.
Speculates on how emerging technology such as 'smart roads' and 'smart cars' will shape the city of the future.

2497 Chapman, Honor and **Lichfield, Nathaniel.** The Urban Transport Problem and Modal Choice. London: *Journal of Transport Economics and Policy*, Vol. 5(3), September 1971, 247–266.
Concentrates on one aspect of the general problem of urban transport, that of modal split, the distribution of travellers by mode.

2498 Clarke, M. I. *Understanding Travel Behaviour.* Aldershot: Gower, 1983. 281 pp.

Provides a new way of describing travel behaviour in terms of a model that has an explicit behavioural basis.

2499 Clarke, Mike and **Jones, Peter.** The Significance and Measurement of Variability in Travel Behaviour. Amsterdam: *Transportation*, Vol. 15(1), 1988, 65–87.

Examines the policy and analytical rationale for using multi-day data; illustrates different ways of measuring variability; and finally discusses issues relating to the collection of suitable data for such analyses.

2500 Collings, J. J. and **Glaister, S.** Maximisation of Passenger Miles in Theory and Practice. London: *Journal of Transport Economics and Policy*, Vol. 12(3), September 1978, 304–322.

2501 Council for Science and Society. *Access For All? technology and urban movement.* London: Council for Science and Society, 1986. 119 pp.

Examines the impact of technological developments on the demand for and means of transport within Britain.

2502 Curdes, G. and **Giannopoulos, G. A.** Innovations in Urban Transport and the Influence on Urban Form: an historical review. London: *Transport Reviews*, Vol. 12(1), January–March 1992, 15–32.

Draws on work of the international collaborative programme URBINNO on innovation and urban development.

2503 Dalvi, Quasim and **Hencher, David A.** (eds). *Determinants of Travel Choice.* Farnborough: Saxon House, 1978. 394 pp.

Comprehensive introduction to the literature on the determinants of travel choice.

2504 Durnell, K. G. *A Review of Inter-Urban Travel, with Particular Reference to a Special Study of Mode Choice.* Birmingham: University of Birmingham (MSc Thesis), 1971.

2505 Eagland, R. M. *Factors Affecting Modal Split in Urban Transportation.* Bradford: University of Bradford (MSc Thesis), 1970.

2506 Gottschalk, Bernd. Transport of the Future. London: *Global Transport*, Vol. 2, Summer 1995, 21–23.

Considers the many aspects of innovative technology; environmentally friendly logistical concepts; and intelligent management as a way forward for transport.

2507 Greater London Council: SCPR: Transmark. *External Cordon and Screen Line Survey Report.* GLTS Vol. II. London: Greater London Council, 1976. 89 pp.

Considers the use of external cordon and screen-line roadside interviews to supplement other methods of data collection.

2508 Greater London Transport. *Address Zone Coding Manual.* Greater London Transportation Survey: Volume VII. London: Greater London Transport, 1974. 46 pp.

Describes the operation which translates addresses written in free style into a five-digit numerical code used for computer processing.

2509 Harberger, Arnold C. *Project Evaluation.* Chicago, IL: Chicago University Press, 1972.

Collection of essays, including one which relates specifically to transport projects.

2510 Holst, O. *European Transport: crucial problems and research needs – a long-term analysis.* Paris: Organisation for Economic Co-operation and Development, 1982. 107 pp.

2511 Jehiel, Philippe. Equilibrium on a Traffic Corridor with Several Congested Modes. Baltimore, MD: *Transportation Science,* Vol. 27(1), February 1993, 16–38.

Examines the user equilibrium on a traffic corridor with several congested modes, a continuum of entry points and a single exit point.

2512 Jones, P. *Social Trends in Transport.* Oxford: Oxford University, Transport Studies Unit, 1992. 24 pp.

2513 Kanafani, Adib and **Knudsen, Tore.** *Definition and Measurement of Accessibility in Urban Areas.* Research Report No 54. Trondheim: Institute of Transportation and Traffic Engineering, 1974. 38 pp.

Investigates alternative conceptual and methodological frameworks for the characterisation of accessibility in urban areas.

2514 Kitamura, Ryuichi. An Evaluation of Activity-Based Travel Analysis. Amsterdam: *Transportation,* Vol. 15(1), 1988.

Review and assessment of the contributions made by 'activity-based approaches' to the understanding and forecasting of travel behaviour.

2515 Knappers, Peter and **Muller, Theo.** Optimized Transfer Opportunities in Public Transport. Baltimore, MD: *Transportation Science*, Vol. 29(1), February 1995, 101–105.

2516 Koenig, J. G. Indicators of Urban Accessibility: theory and application. Amsterdam: *Transportation*, Vol. 9, 1980, 145–172.

Reviews various existing theoretical bases with special emphasis on recent behavioural approaches.

2517 Koppelman, Frank S. and **Pas, Eric I.** An Examination of the Determinants of Day to Day Variability in Individuals' Urban Travel Behaviour. Amsterdam: *Transportation*, Vol. 14, 1987, 3–20.

Develops and examines hypotheses regarding the determinants of intrapersonal variability in urban travel behaviour.

2518 Lambert, G. *Resource Depletion and Passenger Transport Development.* Loughborough: University of Loughborough (MSc Thesis), 1978.

2519 Larkinson, J. and **Rickard, J. H.** (eds). *Longer Term Issues in Transport.* Aldershot: Avebury, 1991. 549 pp.

Proceedings of a research conference sponsored by the Department of Transport in July 1990 covering the developments likely to influence the pattern of transport over the next decade.

2520 Massot, M. H. Sensitivity of Public Transport Demand to the Level of Transport Service in French Cities Without Underground. London: *Transport Reviews*, Vol. 14(2), April–June 1994, 135–149.

Examines the sensitivity of the demand for public transport from different population clusters against the level of service.

2521 Maxwell, W. W. *42nd International Congress: Montreal 1977.* Brussels: International Union of Public Transport, 1977. 16 pp.

Contains a paper on 'Automation of the control of public transport operations' which looks at rail and bus systems.

2522 May, A. D. and **Patterson, N. S.** Transport Problems as Perceived by Inner City Firms. Amsterdam: *Transportation*, Vol. 12, 1983, 225–241.

Suggests that transport problems are a major irritant to inner city firms but are unlikely to cause them to leave an area.

2523 Mohring, Herbert. Land Rent and Transport Improvements: some urban parables. Amsterdam: *Transportation*, Vol. 20, 1993, 267–283.

Defines a transportation improvement's 'impact zone' as the area within which resident households and business firms regularly utilise the improvement.

2524 Morichi, Shigeru and **Nakamura, Hideo.** Transportation Research Activities in Japan. Oxford: *Transportation Research*, Vol. 23(1), 1989, 1–5.

Examines the state of transportation research activities in Japan.

2525 Nash, C. A. *Replacement Policies in the Road Transport Industry.* Leeds: University of Leeds (PhD Thesis), 1973.

2526 Newton, B. J. *A Study of Inter-Nodal Public Transport Networks in the South West.* Bath: University of Bath (MSc Thesis), 1978.

2527 Oliver, Robert M. and **Potts, Renfrey B.** *Flows in Transportation Networks.* New York: Academic Press, 1972. 192 pp.

2528 Organisation for Economic Co-operation and Development. *Challenge and Opportunities for Tomorrow.* Paris: Organisation for Economic Co-operation and Development, 1989. 179 pp.

Focuses on how research, new technologies and international co-operation can enhance social and economic interchange for future road transport and communication systems.

2529 Pas, Eric I. and **Sundar, Subramanian.** Intrapersonal Variability in Daily Urban Travel Behaviour: some additional evidence. Amsterdam: *Transportation*, Vol. 22, 1995, 135–150.

Examines day-to-day variability in urban travel using a three-day travel data set collected in Seattle, WA. Replicates and extends previous work dealing with day-to-day variability in trip-making behaviour that was conducted using data collected in Reading, England, in the early 1970s.

2530 Peng, S. K. City Type, City Size, Trade Patterns and Interurban Transport Costs in a Spatial Economy. *Journal of Environmental Planning*, Vol. 23(11), November 1991, 114–128.

2531 Prashker, Joseph N. Direct Analysis of the Perceived Importance of Attributes of Reliability of Travel Modes in Urban Travel. Amsterdam: *Transportation*, Vol. 8, 1979, 329–346.

Reports that reliability of travel modes was found to be the most important characteristic of transportation systems in several attitudinal investigations of individual travel behaviour.

2532 Quandt, Richard E. (ed.). *The Demand for Travel: theory and measurement.* Lexington, MA: D.C. Heath, 1970. 300 pp.

Collection of essays on the demand for passenger transport.

2533 Rozin, Vadim Markovich. Urban Culture: man and the environment. Moscow: *Voprosy Filosofii*, Vol. 34, January 1980, 43–54.

Discusses urban transport in relation to trade, the division of zones; stratifications within social groups; the amount of leisure time available; education; work; and the role of the individual in both the public and private sphere.

2534 Rumar, Kare. Driver Requirements and Road Traffic Informatics. Amsterdam: *Transportation*, Vol. 17(3), 1990, 215–229.

Provides a historical perspective of the driver's role as a link in the driver-vehicle-road-traffic control-chain.

2535 Salter, D. R. *Automatic Vehicle Classification in Urban Areas.* Nottingham: University of Nottingham (PhD Thesis), 1983.

2536 Silva Rosa, M. da. *Linear Programming and Problems of Flow in Networks.* Birmingham: University of Birmingham (PhD Thesis), 1973.

2537 Stein, Martin. Social Impact Assessment Techniques and their Application to Transportation Decisions. *Traffic Quarterly*, Vol. 31(2), 1977, 320–325.

Deals with social impact assessment methodologies primarily related to urban transport.

2538 Stuart, Darwin. Focusing the Transit Alternatives Analysis Process. Amsterdam: *Transportation*, Vol. 12(4), 1985, 277–292.

Explores the role of transit alternative analyses, or comparative assessments of alternative modes and service levels for improving urban transit at corridor or system-wide scales. Case studies involving the Southwest Corridor of Chicago and the Dallas Area Rapid Transit Authority are reviewed.

2539 Swiss Association of Traffic Engineers. *Modal Split in Function of Various Parameters: report on current methods.* Zurich: Swiss Association of Traffic Engineers, 1970. 22 pp.

Investigates which parameters affect modal split; what the effect of the parameters is on modal split; and in what way modal split can be influenced.

2540 Taylor, M. A. P. Urban Public Transport Research in Australia 1969–1989: a review. Victoria: *Australian Road Research*, Vol. 20(1), March 1990.

Presents a review of research on urban public transport in Australia over the preiod 1969 to 1989. Includes an annotated bibliography of Australian research on urban public transport during the same period.

2541 Tolley, K. H. *Investigation of Communications and Travel Expenditure Patterns Using Family Expenditure Survey Data.* Leeds: University of Leeds (M.Phil Thesis), 1988.

Investigates variations in patterns and types of interactions in household expenditures on travel and communications components.

2542 Transportation Research Board. *Research for Public Transit: new directions.* Washington, DC: Transportation Research Board, 1987. 146 pp.

Report of a study which reviewed a public transportation research programme within the United States. Covers the evolution of the public transportation industry and programmes and priorities within transit research since 1962.

2543 Transportation Research Board. *A Look Ahead: Year 2020.* Washington, DC: Transportation Research Board, 1988. 551 pp.

Proceedings of a conference on long-range trends and requirements for US highway and public transit systems. Considers economic growth and vitality; demographics and life-style; energy and environment; patterns of future development; personal mobility; new technology and communications; and finally resources and institutional arrangements.

2544 Viton, P. A. Consolidations of Scale and Scope in Urban Transit. Amsterdam: *Regional Science & Urban Economics*, Vol. 22(1), March 1992, 25–49.

2545 Wigan, M. R. Changes in the Relationships Between Transport, Communications and Urban Form. Amsterdam: *Transportation*, Vol. 14, 1988, 395–417.

Claims that transport, communication and urban form cover an overlapping area of rising academic and practical concern. Article traces several of the many themes brought together under different professional banners and demonstrates how a confluence of interest is emerging.

2546 Willis, David K. IVHS Technologies: promising palliatives or popular poppycock? Westport, CT: *Transportation Quarterly*, Vol. 44(1), January 1990, 73–84.

Examines the interest in intelligent vehicle/highway systems technologies. Attempts to assess whether the expectations that they will reduce urban traffic congestion, improve highway safety, and increase highway transportation productivity are realistic.

2547 Yagar, Sam. *Transport Risk Assessment.* Waterloo, Ont.: University of Waterloo Press, 1984. 266 pp.

Presents the proceedings of a Symposium on Risk in Transport held in 1983 at the University of Waterloo.

2548 Yearsley, Ian. Self-Sufficiency Taking Hold in Urban Transport. London: *Transport*, Vol. 9, June 1988, 273–275.

Examines the moves to self-sufficiency in manufacture for public transportation in the cities of the Pacific Rim.

Computers and telecommunications

2549 Ali, A. T. *Computer Vision-Aided Road Traffic Analysis.* Uxbridge: Brunel University (PhD Thesis), 1993.

Considers the application of real-time computer vision and parallel processing techniques to monitor and analyse road traffic automatically.

2550 Baggaley, D. A. Computing Passenger Miles in London Transport. London: *Journal of Transport Economics and Policy*, Vol. 10(1), January 1976, 87–89.

Describes methods used to compute passenger miles by London Transport, which has various systems of graduated and flat fares, period tickets, and tickets for free travel.

2551 Ball, Michael; Bodin, Lawrence and **Dial, Robert.** A Matching Based Heuristic for Scheduling Mass Transit Crews and Vehicles. Baltimore, MD: *Transportation Science*, Vol. 17(1), February 1983, 4–31.

Describes a computerised procedure for scheduling mass transit crews and vehicles.

2552 Bell, Michael and **Bonsall, Peter** (eds). *Information Technology Applications in Transport.* Utrecht: VNU Science Press, 1987. 384 pp.

2553 Bouree, Kasia; Van Der Peet, G.; Roach, Helen and **Staub, Lutz.** Transmodel, a Framework for Interoperability of Software Packages in Public Transport. Brussels: *Public Transport International*, Vol. 43(4), July 1994, 80–81.

2554 Callaghan, Martin J. Computer Assistance to Management Information Systems in the London Underground. London: *Transport Reviews*, Vol. 10(1), January–March 1990, 49–58.

Identifies the classes of information technology systems in transport with reference to London Underground and considers, in particular, management information systems.

2555 Chua, T. A. *A Computer-Assisted Method for Planning Urban Bus Services.* Newcastle Upon Tyne: University of Newcastle Upon Tyne (PhD Thesis), 1985.

2556 Coombe, R. D. Review of Computer Software for Traffic Engineers. London: *Transport Reviews*, Vol. 9(3), July–September 1989, 217–234.

Considers the range of programmes now available and in common usage for the design and appraisal of traffic management schemes in the UK.

2557 Deakin, Elizabeth and **Garrison, William L.** Travel, Work, and Telecommunications: a view of the electronics revolution and its potential impacts. Oxford: *Transportation Research*, Vol. 22A(4), 1988, 239–245.

Reviews the substitution of communications for travel.

2558 Ducatel, K. and **Hepworth, M.** *Transport in the Information Age: wheels and wires.* London: Belhaven Press, 1992. 217 pp.

Examines the impact of information technology on transport and its potential for modernising infrastructure and rethinking transport policy.

2559 Giannopoulos, G. A. The Influence of Telecommunications on Transport Operations. London: *Transport Reviews*, Vol. 9(1), January–March 1989, 19–43.

Examines the impact of telecommunications and information technology on the operation of transport systems in general.

2560 Giaoutzi, Maria and **Nijkamp, Peter.** New Information Technology and Spatial Transport Development. London: *Transport Reviews*, Vol 9(4), October–December 1989, 347–360.

Assesses the impact of technological dynamics as reflected in the new information technology.

2561 Gipps, P. G., Taylor, M. A. P. and **Young, W.** *Microcomputers in Traffic Engineering.* Taunton: Research Studies Press, 1989. 489 pp.

Describes the characteristics of available microcomputer hardware and software for traffic engineering use and shows how computer models can become interactive tools within the design process. Covers aspects of traffic flow theory, network and route choice modelling, discrete event simulation, queuing theory and statistics.

2562 Grol, Hendrikus Johannes Maria van. *Traffic Assignment Problems Solved by Special Purpose Hardware with Emphasis on Real Time Applications.* The Hague: Hendrikus Johannes Maria van Grol (PhD Thesis), 1992. 230 pp.

2563 Hengeveld, Willem; Sommerville, Fraser; Underwood, Geoffrey and **Underwood, Jean D. M.** *Information Technology on the Move: technical and behavioural evaluations of mobile telecommunications.* Chichester: John Wiley and Sons, 1994. 245 pp.

Introduces the fundamental concepts and terminology of road traffic informatics.

2564 Heres, Luc and **Winter, Niek de.** Towards a Standardized European Road Network Database. Amsterdam: *Transportation*, Vol. 17(3), 1990, 301–312.

Discusses two DRIVE (Dedicated Road Infrastructure Vehicle Safety in Europe) projects, PANDORA and Task Force EDRM which are investigating the surveying and digitising techniques necessary for Driver Information Systems.

2565 Keen, Len. Risk Management and Public Transport. Brussels: *Public Transport International*, Vol. 41(1), February 1992, 46–58.

Explains how a computer-based programme giving statistical analysis of accidents helps management cut costs. Article in English, with French and German translations.

2566 Keong, Chin Kian. The GLIDE system – Singapore's urban traffic control system. London: *Transport Reviews*, Vol. 13(4), October–December 1993, 295–305.

Examines Singapore's dynamic computerised traffic control system, known locally as the GLIDE system.

2567 Klamt, D. and **Lauber, R.** (eds). *Control on Transport Systems.* Oxford: Pergamon Press, 1984. 374 pp.

Proceedings of the 4th International Federation of Automatic Control; International Federation of Information Processing; and International Federation of Operational Research Societies. Conference held in Baden-Baden, Germany, 20–22 April 1983.

2568 Lassave, Pierre and **Meyere, Alain.** Overview of New Technology Information Systems for Public Transport Passengers in French Towns. London: *Transport Reviews*, Vol. 10(1), January–March 1988, 29–47.

Recent development of dynamic information systems for public transport passengers in numerous French towns and cities is based on two major technological innovations: videotex, which is in more widespread public use in France than anywhere else, and electronic control of bus fleets. Article provides a survey of developments.

2569 Leeds University. *An Intelligent Traffic System for Vulnerable Road Users: final report.* Leeds: University of Leeds, Institute for Transport Studies, 1992. 69 pp.

2570 Maltby, David. Financial Appraisals of a Microcomputer-Based Referencing system for a Local Bus Travel Enquiry Service. London: *Transport Reviews*, Vol. 10(4), October–December 1990, 353–360.

Compares the likely benefits and costs associated with investing in an IBM clone microcomputer-based referencing system for helping clerks to answer telephone enquiries about local bus services.

2571 McCartney, J. D. *Multi-Level Control of Urban Traffic Networks Using Microprocessors.* Glasgow: University of Strathclyde (PhD Thesis), 1980.

2572 Mokhtarian, Patricia Lyon. A Typology of Relationships Between Telecommunications and Transportation. Oxford: *Transportation Research*, Vol. 24A(3), May 1990, 231–242.

Defines the relationship between telecommunications and transportation, by expanding on linkages already identified in the literature; by identifying additional relationships; and by putting these relationships into a conceptual framework.

2573 Neville-Smith, M. J. *The Design, Commissioning and Preliminary Traffic Studies Using a Hardware Traffic Simulator.* Manchester: University of Manchester Institute of Science and Technology (PhD Thesis), 1977.

2574 Pagano, Anthony M. and **Verdin, Jo Ann.** Implementing Computer Technology in Transportation. Westport, CT: *Transportation Quarterly*, Vol. 41(3), July 1987, 381–396.

Analyses the strategies that transport managers can utilise to influence the introduction and implementation of computer technology.

2575 Public Transport International. Technology and Environment. Brussels: *Public Transport International*, Vol. 42(1), March–April 1993, 60–62.

2576 Reid, A. A. L. *The Impact of Telecommunications Innovation on the Demand for Passenger Transportation.* London: University College London (PhD Thesis), 1976.

2577 Rodwell, Peter (ed.). *The Road Transport Industry's Guide to Software: microcomputing for the professions.* London: Frances Pinter, 1985. 163 pp.

Reviews the main software packages and aims to provide practical help in assessing users' special requirements.

2578 Salomon, Ilan. Telecommunications and Travel Relationships: a review. Oxford: *Transportation Research*, Vol. 20A(3), May 1986, 223–238.

Reviews and assesses the interactions between telecommunications and transportation and proposes a research agenda.

2579 Taylor, Michael A. P. Knowledge-Based Systems for Transport Network Analysis: a fifth generation perspective on transport network problems. Oxford: *Transportation Research*, Vol. 24A(1), January 1990, 3–14.

Considers the formative steps in the development of an expert system for route selection in transport networks.

2580 Wren, Anthony. *Computers in Transport Planning and Operation.* London: Ian Allan, 1971. 152 pp.

An awareness guide to the wide range of transport projects in which computers could be of value.

Cost-benefit analysis

2581 Abelson, Peter. Cost Benefit Analysis of Proposed Major Rail Development in Lagos, Nigeria. London: *Transport Reviews*, Vol. 15(3), July–August 1995, 265–289.

2582 Beesley, M. E., Gist, P., Glaister, S., Diamond, D. and **McLoughlin, J. B.** (eds). *Cost Benefit Analysis and London's Transport Policies: Progress in Planning:* Vol. 19, Part 3. Oxford: Pergamon Press, 1983. 269 pp.

2583 Brod, Daniel and **Lewis, David L.** *Making Benefit-Cost Analysis Work.* Aldershot: Avebury, 1996. 279 pp.

Commissioned and prepared for Transport Canada – the Canadian Department of Transportation – this study develops a new strategy for economic decision making.

2584 Cole, W. S. *A Cost Benefit Approach to Environmental Evaluation of Transport Expenditure.* Salford: University of Salford (MSc Thesis), 1982.

2585 Dajani, J., Egan, M. M. and **McElroy, M. B.** The Redistributive Impact of the Atlanta Mass Transit System. Baltimore, MD: *Southern Economic Journal*, Vol. 42(1), July 1985, 49–60.

The 1983 annual costs and benefits of adopting Atlanta's newly approved rapid transit system as compared to retaining an all-highway system are projected and distributed across small neighborhoods in Atlanta.

2586 Department of Transport. *Getting the Best Roads for our Money: the COBA method of appraisal.* London: Department of Transport, 1983.

Comparison of the costs of road schemes using a cost benefit analysis with the benefits derived by users, and expresses results as monetary valuation. Environmental considerations are not included.

2587 Dodgson, J. S. and **Topham, N.** Benefit-Cost Rules for Urban Transit Subsidies: an integration of allocational, distributional, and public finance issues. London: *Journal of Transport Economics and Policy*, Vol. 21(1), January 1987, 57–72.

Derives comprehensive benefit-cost rules for urban transit subsidies which encompass the overall impact of increases in subsidies on social welfare.

2588 Evans, R. D. Fare Revenue and Cost-Benefit Analysis. London: *Journal of Transport Economics and Policy*, Vol. 6(3), September 1972, 321–323.

Suggests that the Cambrian Coast Line Study ought to have included as a benefit of the line the saving of goods bought with their fare money by people who no longer travel.

2589 Everett, Michael. Benefit-Cost Analysis for Labour Intensive Transportation Systems. Amsterdam: *Transportation*, Vol. 6, 1977, 57–70.

Claims that labour-intensive systems, such as bikeways and pedestrianways, suffer in transportation planning in part because traditonal benefit-cost analysis focuses on narrow, private transportation savings.

2590 Georgi, Hanspeter. *Cost-Benefit Analysis and Public Investment in Transport.* London: Butterworth, 1973. 214 pp.

Demonstrates the means of introducing economic criteria into public expenditure through cost-benefit analysis.

2591 Haney, D. G. Problems, Misconceptions and Errors in Benefit-Cost Analyses of Transit Systems. *Highway Research Record*, Vol. 314, 1970, 98–113.

2592 Henderson, J. V. Peak Shifting and Cost-Benefit Miscalculations. Amsterdam: *Regional Science & Urban Economics*, Vol. 22(1), March 1992, 103–121.

2593 Jennings, A. and **Sharp, C. H.** More Powerful Engines for Lorries? an exercise in cost-benefit analysis. London: *Journal of Transport Economics and Policy*, Vol. 6(2), May 1972, 154–166.

Suggests that a legal minimum power-to-weight ratio of 8 bhp per ton would produce approximately equal costs and benefits for vehicles under 30 tons gross weight; cost would exceed benefits for larger vehicles. Benefits would exceed costs for a minimum of 6 bhp per ton.

2594 Kanemoto, Yoshitsugo. Cost-Benefit Analysis and the Second Best Land Use for Transportation. London: *Journal of Urban Economics*, Vol. 4(4), October 1977, 483–503.

2595 Kuhn, Tillo E. *The Economics of Transportation Planning in Urban Areas.* New York: National Bureau of Economic Research, 1965.

Transport planning guide to the cost-benefit approach.

2596 Langdon, M. G. *A Comparative Cost/Benefit Assessment of Minitram and Other Urban Transport Systems.* TRRL Laboratory Report 747. Crowthorne: Transport and Road Research Laboratory, 1977. 25 pp.

Summary account of a cost/benefit analysis of several hypothetical fixed track automatic passenger transport systems in an urban scenario based on the West Midlands.

2597 Robson, Arthur J. Cost-Benefit Analysis and the Use of Urban

Land for Transportation. London: *Journal of Urban Economics*, Vol. 3(2), April 1976, 180–191.

Investigates the allocation of resources, particularly land, within a suburban city where transportation is subject to congestion.

2598 Sawicki, David S. Break-Even Benefit-Cost Analysis of Alternative Express Transit Systems. London: *Journal of Transport Economics and Policy*, Vol. 8(3), September 1974, 274–293.

Milwaukee commissioned research into the comparative merits of its existing Freeway Flier express bus; a controlled access system giving the Flier right of way and restricting access of automobiles on congested roads; and a busway with its own right of way.

2599 Squire, L. *The Social Cost-Benefit of Road Projects in Developing Countries.* Cambridge: University of Cambridge (PhD Thesis), 1976.

Economics

2600 Andrikopoulos, A. A., Loijidis, J. and **Prodomidis, K. P.** Technological Change and Scale Economies in Urban Transportation. Rome: *International Journal of Transport Economics*, Vol. 19(2), June 1992, 127–148.

2601 Bani-Kashani, Reza. Discrete Mode-Choice Analysis of Urban Travel Demand by the Analytic Hierarchy Process. Amsterdam: *Transportation*, Vol. 16(1), 1989, 81–96.

Develops a new procedure for the problem of multimodal urban corridor travel demand estimation by using the Analytic Hierarchy Process.

2602 Barrett, S. D. C. *The Economics of Surface Public Transport in Ireland.* Dublin: University of Dublin (PhD Thesis), 1972.

2603 Beesley, M. E. Transport Research and Economics. London: *Journal of Transport Economics and Policy*, Vol. 23(1), January 1989, 17–28.

2604 Bell, Michael E. and **Feitelson, Eran.** US Economic Restructuring and Demand for Transportation Services. Westport, CT: *Transportation Quarterly*, Vol. 45(4), October 1991, 517–538.

Questions whether the analytical tools used by transport economists are still adequate to analyse the link between transportation and economic development.

2605 Berechman, J. and **Pines, D.** Financing Road Capacity and Returns to Scale Under Marginal Cost Pricing: a note. London: *Journal of Transport Economics and Policy*, Vol. 25(2), May 1991, 177–182.

Examines the relationship between toll revenue and capacity cost under marginal cost pricing.

2606 Berechman, Joseph. Costs, Economies of Scale and Factor Demand in Road Transport. London: *Journal of Transport Economics and Policy*, Vol. 17(1), January 1983, 7–24.

Deploys a general translog cost function to show that there are economies of scale in bus transport in Israel.

2607 Berechman, Joseph; Hirschman, Ira; McKnight, Claire; Paaswell, Robert E. and **Pucher, John.** Bridge and Tunnel Toll Elasticities in New York. Dordrecht: *Transportation*, Vol. 22, 1995, 97–113.

Statistical analysis of Triborough Bridge and Tunnel Authority crossings in New York City to determine the impact of toll increases in traffic volumes and revenue.

2608 Blauwens, G. The Optimal Output of Transport in an Imperfect Economic Environment. London: *Journal of Transport Economics and Policy*, Vol. 6(3), September 1972, 285–293.

2609 Brandeneau, Margaret and **Chiu, Samuel S.** Location of Competing Facilities in a User-Optimizing Environment with Market Externalities. Baltimore, MD: *Transportation Science*, Vol. 28(12), May 1994, 125–140.

Considers a location problem in which customers select a facility based not only on the travel time or distance to the facility (as is commonly assumed in location models), but also on negative externalities associated with the market share of the facility.

2610 Brown, Richard J. A Rational Approach to Trip Generation. London: George Godwin, *International Forum Series*, Vol. 1, 1981, 117–126.

Claims that the trip generation phase of transportation planning is the first stage and thus the foundation of the travel demand estimation process.

2611 Brownlee, A. T. *The Application of an Economic Demand Model to the Transport Planning Process.* Newcastle Upon Tyne: University of Newcastle Upon Tyne (PhD Thesis), 1976.

2612 Burns, Lawrence D. Consumer Preferences Relative to the Price and Network Capability of Small Urban Vehicles. Amsterdam: *Transportation*, Vol. 8, 1979, 219–236.

Preferences of consumers for small urban vehicle concepts differing only with respect to their hypothetical purchase prices and network capabilities are analysed using statistical techniques based on psychological scaling theories.

2613 Button, Kenneth; Deadman, Derek and **Sharp, Clifford.** The Economics of Tolled Road Crossings. London: *Journal of Transport Economics and Policy*, Vol. 20(2), May 1986.

Examines the different practices adopted by the USA and UK in levying tolls on transport infrastructure.

2614 Cameron, Michael. A Consumer Surplus Analysis of Market-Based Demand Management Policies in Southern California. Oxford: *Transport Policy*, Vol. 1(4), October 1994, 213–220.

Makes a quantitative case for implementation of market-based demand management policies, such as congestion pricing, to reduce urban traffic congestion and mobile-source air pollution. Also demonstrates the usefulness of the consumer surplus model for performing transportation policy analysis.

2615 Carpenter, Susan and **Jones, Peter** (eds). *Recent Advances in Travel Demand Analysis.* Aldershot: Gower, 1983. 474 pp.

2616 Crane, L. M., Fuller, S. W. and **Pinnoi, N.** Estimating Demand for Public Roads in Texas. Clemson, SC: *Review of Regional Studies*, Vol. 24(2), Autumn 1994, 195–209.

2617 Cryer, Jonathan; Kyte, Michael and **Stoner, James.** A Time-Series Analysis of Public Transit Ridership in Portland, Oregon, 1971–1982. Oxford: *Transportation Research*, Vol. 22A(5), 1988, 345–359.

Examines the factors affecting changes in transit ridership in Portland, Oregon during the period 1971 through 1982. A time-series methodology is used to investigate the effects of service level, travel costs, and market size at the system, sector and route levels.

2618 Dafermos, Stella and **Sparrow, F. T.** Optimal Resource Allocation and Toll Patterns in User-Optimised Transport Networks. London: *Journal of Transport Economics and Policy*, Vol 5(2), May 1971, 184–200.

Claims that where travellers are free to choose their own routes, the way to ensure maximum benefit from investments is to levy congestion tolls based on the path taken from origin to destination, rather on use of a particular link.

2619 Daly, A. J. and **Gale, H. S.** *Elasticity of Demand for Public Trans-*

port. TRRL Supplementary Report 68 UC. Crowthorne: Transport and Road Research Laboratory, 1974. 36 pp.

Report describing the findings of a review of the literature on public transport demand models.

2620 Daor, Erella. The Effect of Income on Trip-Making Behaviour. London: George Godwin, *International Forum Series*, Vol. 1, 1981, 127–140.

2621 Dargay, J. and **Goodwin, P.** *Transport Evaluation in a Desequilibrium World: some problems of dynamics.* Oxford: Oxford University, Transport Studies Unit, 1994. 23 pp.

2622 Dodgson, J. S., Katsoulacos, Y. and **Newton, C. R.** Application of the Economic Modelling Approach to the Investigation of Predation. London: *Journal of Transport Economics and Policy*, Vol. 23(2), May 1993, 153–171.

Concerned with the identification of predatory behaviour in the bus industry. An economic model of competition is used to determine competitive equilibria in markets where predation is alleged.

2623 Domencich, Thomas A. and **McFadden, Daniel.** *Urban Travel Demand: a behavioral analysis.* Oxford: North-Holland Publishing, 1975. 215 pp.

Provides a comprehensive guide to modelling consumer behaviour in the face of discrete choices. The theory of choice in the face of discrete alternatives and application of the theory to the demand for travel is developed.

2624 Economic Research Centre: European Conference of Ministers of Transport. *Economic Criteria for the Maintenance, Modification or Creation of Public Urban and Suburban Transport Services.* Report of the Twenty-Fourth Round Table on Transport Economics. Paris: Organisation for Economic Co-operation and Development, 1975. 76 pp.

2625 Fowkes, Tony and **Wardman, Mark.** The Design of Stated Preference Travel Choice Experiments, with Special Reference to Inter-Personal Taste Variations. London: *Journal of Transport Economics and Policy*, Vol. 22(1), January 1988, 27–44.

Sets out guidelines for the satisfactory design of Stated Preference experiments. In particular, the importance of incorporating appropriate boundary values for the trade-offs between attributes is stressed.

2626 Giannacopoulos, A. *Optimisation Algorithm for Mass Transportation.* London: Imperial College of Science and Technology (PhD Thesis), 1982.

2627 Goodwin, P. B. A Review of New Demand Elasticities with Special Reference to Short and Long Run Effects of Price Changes. London: *Journal of Transport Economics and Policy,* Vol. 26(2), May 1992, 155–170.

Suggests that increases in real fuel prices would lead to a short run reduction in both traffic and consumption, due to more careful driving and differential responses for different journeys.

2628 Goodwin, P. B. *Some Causes and Effects of Variations in the Structure of Demand for Urban Passenger Transport.* London: University College London (PhD Thesis), 1976.

2629 Gwilliam, K. M. Economic Evaluation of Urban Transport Projects. London: *Transportation Planning and Technology,* Vol. 1(2), 1972, 123–141.

2630 Hensher, David A., Barnard, Peter O. and **Truong, Truong P.** The Role of Stated Preference Methods in Studies of Travel Choice. London: *Journal of Transport Economics and Policy,* Vol. 22(1), January 1988, 45–58.

Clarifies the relationship between theory and method used to justify the stated preference approach.

2631 Hibbs, John. *On the Move... A Market for Mobility on the Roads.* Hobart Paper 121. London: Institute of Economic Affairs, 1993. 95 pp.

Analysis of the suboptimal allocation of resources arising from incompatible financial, fiscal and regulatory regimes for the various modes of inland transport.

2632 Jackson, J. *Inter-Urban Travel Demand in Great Britain.* Manchester: University of Manchester (MA Thesis), 1973.

2633 Jones, Ian S. *Urban Transport Appraisal.* London: Macmillan, 1977. 144 pp.

An economic approach basically concerned with those impacts of projects to which a monetary value can be given.

2634 Kanafani, Adib and **Lan, Lawrence W.** Economics of Park and

Shop Discounts: a case of Bundled Pricing Strategy. London: *Journal of Transport Economics and Policy*, Vol. 27(3), September 1993, 291–304.

Economic implications of two 'park-and-shop' discount programmes are analysed.

2635 Keeler, T. E. (ed.). *Research in Transportation Economics.* Greenwich, CT: JAI Press, 1983. 235 pp.

Covers a range of topics including the impact on urban expressways of higher fuel prices; bus priorities and congestion pricing; and the determination of Pareto optimal urban transport equilibria. Also examines regulation and deregulation, with papers on the trucking industry, unregulated airline markets, and determination of price and investment for airport runways.

2636 Keeler, Theodore E. (ed.). *Research in Transportation Economics: a research annual.* Volume 2, 1985. Greenwich, CT: JAI Press, 1985. 259 pp.

2637 Kroes, Eric P. and **Sheldon, Robert J.** Stated Preference Methods. London: *Journal of Transport Economics and Policy*, Vol. 23(1), January 1988, 11–26.

Concerned with stated preference methods and their use in the transport sector, particularly within the areas of preference evaluation, demand analysis and forecasting.

2638 Kunert, Uwe. Past Trends and Future Scenarios for Passenger Travel Demand in Regions of West Germany. London: *Transport Reviews*, Vol. 10(3), July–September 1990, 245–267.

Passenger travel in West Germany is diverse as a result of personal and household characteristics of the travellers, the settlement structure, the topography, the quality of transport supply, etc. Article examines general trends in transport demand, then focuses on urban areas.

2639 Laffieriere, R. A Travel Demand Forecasting Dilemma: to pivot or not? Vancouver: *Logistics and Transportation Review*, Vol. 30(1), March 1994, 21–29.

2640 Lago, Armando M., Mayworm, Patrick and **McEnroe, J. Matthew.** Transit Service Elasticities: evidence from demonstrations and demand models. London: *Journal of Transport Economics and Policy*, Vol. 15(2), May 1981, 99–120.

Claims that transit service is inelastic, with off-peak-service elasticities 50 to 100 per cent higher than for peak periods. Service elasticities are higher in lower service areas, and ridership is more responsive to improvements in headways than to in-vehicle time.

2641 Meyburg, Arnim H. and **Stopher, Peter R.** *Transport Systems Evaluation.* Lexington, MA: Lexington Books, 1976. 179 pp.

Considers the alternative evaluation techniques for transportation-system strategies, in particular focusing on two principal procedures, namely economic evaluation and cost-effective evaluation.

2642 Mills, Gordon. Economic Appraisal and Reappraisal of an Inter-Urban Road in Great Britain. London: *Journal of Transport Economics and Policy*, Vol. 11(1), January 1977, 3–23.

A relief road for Wellington, Somerset, opened in 1971, was built to a modest standard as it was to be superseded by the extension of the M5 motorway. Article claims that reappraisal shows the low-cost road is successful: Wellington has been improved by traffic diversion.

2643 Ministry of Overseas Development. *A Guide to the Economic Appraisal of Projects in Developing Countries.* London: HMSO, 1977.

2644 Mitchell, D. J. *Some Aspects of Demand Actuated Public Transport Systems.* Birmingham: University of Birmingham (PhD Thesis), 1972.

2645 Oldfield, R. *Elasticities of Demand for Travel.* TRRL Supplementary Report 116 UC. Crowthorne: Transport and Road Research Laboratory, 1974. 17 pp.

Report into the degree to which travellers respond to changes in the cost of their journey as measured by the elasticity of demand.

2646 Ortuzar, Juan de Dios (ed.). *Simplified Transport Demand Modelling.* London: PTRC Education and Research Services, 1992. 153 pp.

2647 Oum, Tae Hoon; Waters, W. G. and **Yong, Jong-Say.** Concepts of Price Elasticities of Transport Demand and Recent Empirical Estimates. London: *Journal of Transport Economics and Policy*, Vol. 26(2), May 1992, 139–154.

An interpretative survey of recent estimates of price elasticities of demand for various modes of transport.

2648 Pas, Eric I. A Flexible and Integrated Methodology for Analytical Classification of Daily Travel-Activity Behaviour. Baltimore, MD: *Transportation Science*, Vol. 17(4), November 1983, 405–429.

Discusses the importance of incorporating the derived demand nature of urban person movement and the interdependence of the elemental travel episodes (trips) in analyses of urban travel behaviour.

2649 Plowden, Stephen. Indirect Taxation of Motorway and Alternative Consumption. London: *Journal of Transport Economics and Policy*, Vol. 7(3), September 1973, 250–258.

Article presents a statistical comparison of the amounts paid in indirect taxation on the cost of running motor vehicles and on the alternative expenditure which might be incurred by consumers if roads were not built.

2650 Rose, Geoffrey. Transit Passenger Response: short and long term elasticities using time series analysis. Amsterdam: *Transportation*, Vol. 13(2), 1986, 131–144.

Investigates the effects of price and service changes on transit ridership. The concept of elasticity is introduced and the traditional methods for estimating elasticities are discussed. In addition, short and long term elasticities are investigated.

2651 Rus, Gines de. Public Transport Demand Elasticities in Spain. London: *Journal of Transport Economics and Policy*, Vol. 24(2), May 1990, 189–202.

Argues that patronage of public transport in Spanish cities could be increased by adjustment of the proportionate charges for cash fares and multiple-ride tickets, and by increasing fares to provide higher frequencies.

2652 Steinberg, Richard and **Stone, Richard E.** The Prevalence of Paradoxes in Transportation Equilibrium Problems. Baltimore, MD: *Transportation Science*, Vol. 22(4), November 1988, 231–241.

Considers a congested transportation network, where the cost along each arc is affine, i.e. consists of a fixed cost plus a variable cost proportional to the flow.

2653 Train, Kenneth. Optimal Transit Prices under Increasing Returns to Scale and a Loss Constraint. London: *Journal of Transport Economics and Policy*, Vol. 11(2), May 1977, 185–194.

Argues that welfare loss might be reduced by requiring total revenues from all units in an urban transport system to meet a proportion of total costs, instead of applying the constraint to each unit separately. Prices are calculated for East Bay Area, San Francisco.

2654 Tyson, W. J. *The Economics of the Work-Peak in Road Passenger Transport.* Manchester: University of Manchester (MA Thesis), 1970.

2655 Vitton, Philip A. Quasi-Optimal Pricing and the Structure of Urban Transportation. Oxford: *Transportation Research*, Vol. 20A(4), July 1986, 295–305.

Investigates a set of causes for the divergence of the acutal (poor) position of urban transit from its optimal (pervasive) structure.

2656 Wardman, M. *An Evaluation of the Use of Stated Preference and Transfer Price Data in Forecasting the Demand for Travel.* Leeds: University of Leeds (PhD Thesis), 1987.

Evaluates the use of stated preference and transfer price data for travel demand forecasting.

2657 Williams, R. L. *The Matching of Transport Systems and Urban Travel Demands.* Salford: University of Salford (MSc Thesis), 1973.

2658 Winston, Clifford. Conceptual Developments in the Economics of Transportation: an interpretive survey. Nashville, TN: *Journal of Economic Literature*, Vol. 23(1), 1985, 57–94.

Survey of the literature on transport economics in the United States with emphasis on regulation.

2659 Xu, K. Re-Evaluating Returns to Scale in Transport. London: *Journal of Transport Economics and Policy*, Vol. 28(3), September 1994, 275–286.

Econometrics

2660 Betz, M. J. and **Brady, C. R.** An Evaluation of Regression Analysis and the Gravity Model in the Phoenix Urban Area. London: *Journal of Transport Economics and Policy*, Vol. 5(1), January 1971, 76–90.

Regression equations for generation were developed and gravity models calibrated on 1957 data. The 1964 zone-to-zone traffic demand was then 'forecast' for a larger area, actual data being used for the independent variables.

2661 Burns, M. R. and **Faurot, D. J.** An Econometric Forecasting Model of Revenues from Urban Parking Facilities. New York: *Journal of Economics and Business*, Vol. 44(2), May 1992, 143–150.

2662 Donnea, F. X. de. *The Determinants of Transport Mode Choice in Dutch Cities: some disaggregate stochastic models.* Groningen: Rotterdam University Press, 1971. 229 pp.

Provides an econometric analysis of consumer behaviour with respect to transport mode choice in Dutch cities.

2663 Douglas, A. A. *The Application of Least-Square Multiple Regression Analysis to Trip Generation Estimation.* Glasgow: University of Strathclyde (MSc Thesis), 1970.

2664 Harker, Patrick T. Multiple Equilibrium Behaviors on Networks. Baltimore, MD: *Transportation Science*, Vol. 22(1), February 1988, 39–46.

2665 Hensher, David A. Discrete/Continuous Econometric Models and their Application to Transport Analysis. London: *Transport Reviews*, Vol. 7(3), July–September 1987, 227–244.
Provides a general overview of the basic elements of discrete/continuous econometric modelling with an emphasis on transport applications.

2666 Nijkamp, Peter and **Reggiani, Aura.** Chaos Theory and Spatial Dynamics. London: *Journal of Transport Economics and Policy*, Vol. 25(1), January 1991, 81–96.
Seeks to link chaos theory to spatial interaction analysis by focusing attention on the conditions under which a general utility function related to a dynamic logit model for spatial interaction analysis will exhibit chaotic behaviour.

2667 Petretto, Alessandro and **Viviani, Alessandro.** An Econometric Model for Cross Sectional Analysis of the Production of Urban Transport Service. *Economic Notes*, Vol. 1, 1984, 35–65.
Attempts to analyse the technological structure of urban transport service production by means of 'direct' estimation of the production function. Results demonstrate the role of environmental variables and their significant relationship with traditional productive factors in determining the production level of urban transport service.

2668 Sharma, Subramanian. *An Analysis of Transportation and Central City Economic Activity in Small and Medium Urban Areas.* Cambridge, MA: Massachusetts Institute of Technology (PhD Thesis), 1987. 183 pp.
Claims that changes in demographic and economic activity can be related to transportation improvements if consistent patterns of changes can be observed in demographic and economic activities among a large number of cities.

2669 Sheffi, Yosef. *Urban Transportation Networks: equilibrium analysis with mathematical programming methods.* Englewood Cliffs, NJ: Prentice Hall, 1985. 399 pp.

2670 Small, Kenneth A. The Scheduling of Consumer Activities: work trips. Princeton, NJ: *American Economic Review*, Vol. 72(3), June 1982, 467–479.

Generalises allocation of time models to encompass scheduling decisions, then derives an econometric model for work trips. Results demonstrate that many commuters respond to a trade off, dependent on worker and employer characteristics, between travelling under uncongested conditions and travelling at a more preferred time of day. Model appears capable of explaining the 'shifting peak' phenomenon by which the duration of a peak period changes more than the peak level of activity.

Fuels

2671 Al-Naif, K. *The Relationship Between Fuel Consumption and the Distance from the Centre of Glasgow.* Glasgow: University of Strathclyde (MSc Thesis), 1981.

2672 Andoh, C. O. *Strategies for Reducing Urban Passenger Transport Fuel Consumption in a Developing Country.* London: University College London (PhD Thesis), 1989.

2673 Ardekani, Siamak and **Herman, Robert.** The Influence of Stops on Vehicle Fuel Consumption in Urban Traffic. Baltimore, MD: *Transportation Science*, Vol. 19(1), February 1985, 1–12.

Establishes a simple linear relation between fuel consumption per unit distance and trip timer per unit distance for fuel data collected in Austin and Dallas, Texas, and Matamoros, Mexico.

2674 Arnold-Baker, Charles. More About 'Thermie'. Chichester: *Road Law*, Vol. 10(2), 1994, 97–99.

CEC project for giving financial encouragement to practical experiments in conservation of energy and examples of transport projects.

2675 Butler, C. and **Culshaw, F.** *A Review of the Potential of Biodiesel as a Transport Fuel.* London: HMSO, 1993.

2676 Cheeseman, I. C. The Energy Needs of Transport. London: *Transport*, Vol. 1, March/April 1980, 9–13.

2677 Collins, P. H. and **Flower, S. P.** *The Possible Effects of Petrol Rationing on Travel in London.* Economic Research Report R 214. London: London Transport Executive, 1975. 15 pp.

Describes the results of a survey of 1000 car owning households in the Greater London area which was undertaken in 1973 for London Transport. At that time the threat of petrol rationing was imminent and the survey was undertaken to elicit car users' likely response. Results provide a useful indication of car drivers' perception of public transport as an alternative mode.

2678 Difiglio, Carmen. Timing of Methanol Supply and Demand: implications for alternative transportation fuel policies. Oxford: *Transportation Research*, Vol. 23(3), 1989, 229–241.

Examines potential expansion rates of the world methanol industry.

2679 Dolan, Kari; Figueroa, Maria Josefina; Schipper, Lee and **Steiner, Ruth.** Fuel Prices and Economy: factors affecting land travel. Oxford: *Transport Policy*, Vol. 1(1), October 1993, 6–20.

Examines some preliminary findings on how fuel prices and other factors are linked with automobile fuel use, travel and fuel economy. It is shown that there is a clear cross-sectional relationship between fuel prices and both on-road (actual) fleet fuel intensity and new-car test fuel intensity.

2680 Ferreira, L. J. A. *Energy Conservation in Road Passenger Transport: the role of urban transport managment.* Leeds: University of Leeds (PhD Thesis), 1984.

Focuses on two objectives: 1) to develop urban fuel consumption estimation procedures for the U.K. to be used in conjunction with conventional traffic assignment models and more detailed simulation assignment models; and 2) to assess the likely fuel consumption impacts of urban transport management measures.

2681 Gore, B. M. Alternative Fuels for Passenger Carrying Vehicles. Brussels: *Public Transport International*, Vol. 43(1), January 1994, 15–19.

Examination of the alternative fuels which could be used for passenger transport, and in particular, their application to the bus.

2682 Greene, David I. Motor Fuel Choice: an econometric analysis. Oxford: *Transportation Research*, Vol. 23(3), 1989, 243–253.

Investigates the sensitivity of fuel choice to fuel prices using data on purchases of regular, premium, leaded, and unleaded grades of gasoline.

2683 Hardenberg, Horst O. *Samuel Morey and his Atmospheric Engine.* Warrendale: Society of Automotive Engineers, Inc., 1992. 114 pp.

Describes Samuel Morey's development of an atmospheric engine in the early

1800s which burned a blend of alcohol and turpentine, mixed with air in a heated surface carburettor.

2684 Hillman, Mayer and **Whalley, Anne.** *Energy and Personal Travel: obstacles to conservation.* London: Policy Studies Institute, 1983. 304 pp.

Identifies the institutional aids and obstacles to the implementation of measures of saving energy used for transport. Examines the grounds for reducing the use of oil; switching to alternative fuels; and the factors which discourage transfer to less energy intensive travel methods.

2685 Hussain, A. M. *Some Aspects of Fuel Consumption by Road Traffic.* Glasgow: University of Strathclyde (MSc Thesis), 1977.

2686 International Energy Agency. *Fuel Efficiency of Passenger Cars.* Paris: Organisation for Economic Co-operation and Development 1991. 91 pp.

Provides an overview of the evolution of car fuel efficiency. Examines factors affecting fuel demand – such as the development and structure of the fleet – and reviews pricing and taxation policies.

2687 International Energy Agency. *Substitute Fuels for Road Transport: a technology assessment.* Paris: Organisation for Economic Co-operation and Development, 1990. 114 pp.

Assesses the prospects for fuels which might substitute for gasoline in cars and trucks over the next twenty years. Those considered are natural gas, alcohol fuels, and fuels derived from heavy oils. Analyses the availability and economics of these fuels, the technical problems of using them in road vehicles; and the effects of their use on the environment. Recommends research and development strategies to help realise each fuel's potential.

2688 International Energy Agency. *Cars and Climate Change.* Paris: Organisation for Economic Co-operation and Development, 1993. 236 pp.

Examines the potential for emission reductions, through car fuel economy and alternative fuels.

2689 International Energy Agency. *Biofuels.* Paris: Organisation for Economic Co-operation and Development, 1994. 115 pp.

Presents an analysis of the costs, energy use and greenhouse gas emissions involved in producing and using ethanol from maize, wheat and sugarbeet, 'biodiesel' from rapeseed oil, and methanol from wood. Comparisons are made with gasoline and diesel.

2690 Jackson, M. D., Moyer, C. B. and **Unnasch, S.** Air Quality Programs as Driving Forces for a Transition to Methanol Use. Oxford: *Transportation Research*, Vol. 23(3), 1989, 209–216.

Studies the effectiveness of substituting methanol for gasoline and diesel fuel.

2691 Kenworthy, Jeffrey and **Newman, Peter W. G.** The Transport Energy Trade-Off: fuel-efficient traffic versus fuel-efficient cities. Oxford: *Transportation Research*, Vol. 22A(3), 1988, 163–174.

Discusses the implications for traffic engineering programmes and road funding of the trade-off between fuel-efficient traffic and fuel-efficient cities.

2692 Lones, Trevor. The Age of the Alcohol Car Dawns in Brazil. London: *Transport*, Vol. 1, September/October 1980, 31–32.

2693 MacKenzie, J. and **Nadis, Steve.** *Car Trouble.* Boston, MA: Beacon Press, 1993. 229 pp.

Examines new technology and clean fuels and assesses their potential for solving the problems of pollution and traffic congestion and also for reviving the automobile industry.

2694 MacKenzie, James J. *The Keys to the Car: electric and hydrogen vehicles for the 21st Century.* World Resources Institute, 1994. 128 pp.

Examines the problems posed by oil-powered vehicles. Looks at emerging vehicle technologies; electric vehicles; the impacts of zero-emission vehicles; and, finally, provides a summary and policy recommendations.

2695 Maria, Sam de. Natural Gas Vehicle Development in Australia. Brussels: *Public Transport International*, Vol. 42(1), March/April 1993, 52–54.

Describes tests undertaken on various natural gas powered engines in an attempt to provide a better environment.

2696 Martin, D. J. and **Shock, R. A. W.** *Energy Use and Energy Efficiency in UK Transport up to the Year 2010.* London: HMSO, 1989. 409 pp.

Examines the pattern of use and current demand for energy in UK transport; the factors most likely to affect future demand; and the potential impact of measures for improving energy efficiency.

2697 Mass Transit. Fueling the Future of Mass Transit. Washington, DC: *Mass Transit*, March/April 1993, 70–77.

Reports on the use of alternative fuel by US local authorities.

2698 Mellow, Andrew. Power Struggle. London: *Urban Transport International*, December 1988/January 1989, 17–18.

Review on the testing of alternative fuels and how they may prove a spur to more cost-effective diesel bus design.

2699 Metro Magazine. Buses Bear Brunt of Cleaning Nation's Air. *Metro Magazine*, March/April 1992, 24–32.

Reports on alternative fuels; particulate traps; and the growth of new technology in the bus industry.

2700 Money, Lloyd J. *Transportation Energy and the Future.* Englewood Cliffs, NJ: Prentice Hall, 1984. 142 pp.

Considers the intersection of transportation and energy and argues that transportation is almost completely dependent upon petroleum and that petroleum is in limited supply. Examines the limits of present petroleum based transportation and the development of technological alternatives.

2701 Organisation for Economic Co-operation and Development. *Choosing an Alternative Transportation Fuel: air pollution and greenhouse gas impacts.* Paris: Organisation for Economic Co-operation and Development, 1993. 149 pp.

Synthesises the available literature on alternative fuels with particular attention to the air pollution impacts of each possible solution.

2702 Poulton, M. L. *Alternative Fuels for Road Vehicles.* Southampton: Computational Mechanics Publications, 1994. 212 pp.

Review of alternative fuels for motor vehicles and a discussion of their potential development in the future. Prospects for conventional petrol and diesel fuels are discussed, including their reformulation, as well as synthetic fuels; vegetable oils; and other biofuels; alcohols; gases; and electricity.

2703 Public Transport International. Diesohol ... Future Fuel. Brussels: *Public Transport International*, Vol. 42(1), March/April 1993, 56–58.

Discusses diesohol, a new fuel mixture which promises to be better for the environment.

2704 Ross, Christopher. Alternative Fuels: solar solutions. Washington, DC: *Mass Transit*, May/June 1992, 36–37.

Examines the potential for solar bus installations.

2705 Santini, Danilo J. Interactions Among Transportation Fuel Substitution, Vehicle Quantity Growth, and National Economic Growth. Oxford: *Transportation Research*, Vol. 23(3), 1989, 183–207.

Hypotheses concerning the micro- and macroeconomic effects of historically important fuel switches in the vehicles operating on the dominant US transportation modes are statistically tested using nineteenth and twentieth century data.

2706 Schipper, Lee and **Tax, Wienke.** New Car Test and Actual Fuel Economy: yet another gap? Oxford: *Transport Policy*, Vol. 1(4), October 1994, 257–265.

Reports that automobile fuel economy derived from tests varies greatly from that obtained from actual daily use and suggests some mitigation techniques to close the test/actual fuel economy gap.

2707 Simpson, Richard. Green Special: compressed natural gas the future – but not for everyone. Peterborough: *Coach and Bus Week*, Issue 172, June 1995, 28–29.

Examines the environmental advantages of using natural gas (methane) as a fuel.

2708 *No Entry.*

2709 Urban Transport International. Stockholm Experiments with Ethanol Buses. London: *Urban Transport International*, August/ September 1990, 20–21.

Considers why bus manufacturers and operators are joining in the quest for environment-friendly powerplants.

Models

2710 Ableson, P. W. and **Flowerdew, A. D. J.** Models for the Economic Evaluation of Road Maintenance. London: *Journal of Transport Economics and Policy*, Vol. 9(2), 1975, 93–114.

2711 Al-Beldawi, A. H. *Modelling Travel Patterns and Attitudes Towards Intercity Transportation Systems for a Developing Country using Multivariate Techniques.* Bangor: University of North Wales (PhD Thesis), 1988. 226 pp.

2712 Al-Rabeh, Ala H. and **Selim, Shokri Z.** On the Modeling of Pedestrian Flow on the Jamarat Bridge. Baltimore, MD: *Transportation Science*, Vol. 25(4), November 1991, 257–263.

Develops a model for regulating pedestrian flow on to the Jamarat bridge which becomes congested during the Moslem pilgrimage season.

2713 Alastair Dick and Associates. *Regional Highway Traffic Model Project Review – Figures.* London: Department of Transport, 1978. 49 pp.

Collection of figures for the Regional Highway Traffic Model Project Review.

2714 Allen, Bruce W. and **Doi, Masayuki.** A Time Series Analysis of Monthly Ridership for an Urban Rail Rapid Transit Line. Amsterdam: *Transportation*, Vol. 13(3), 1986, 257–269.

Presents two time series regression models, one in linear form and the other in logarithmic form, to estimate the monthly ridership of a single urban rail rapid transit line.

2715 Anas, Alex. Statistical Properties of Mathematical Programming Models of Stochastic Network Equilibrium. Peace Dale, RI: *Journal of Regional Science*, Vol. 28(4), November 1988, 511–530.

An entropy-maximising model is proposed which over-estimates the travel-cost coefficient with much lower bias and much higher statistical efficiency. Finds that the use of observed entropy levels is undesirable and should be avoided since maximising entropy provides an unambiguously superior alternative.

2716 Anas, Alex. *Residential Location Markets and Urban Transportation: economic theory, econometrics, and policy analysis with discrete choice models.* New York: Academic Press, 1982. 263 pp.

Develops a theory of equilibrium in urban rental housing markets that includes within it the theory of urban commuting and residential location demand. Model is applied to the analysis and evaluation of public transportation finance policy and specific public transportation projects proposed for Chicago.

2717 Anas, Alex. The Estimation of Multinomial Logit Models of Joint Location and Travel Mode Choice from Aggregated Data. Illinois: *Journal of Regional Science*, Vol. 21(2), May 1981, 223–242.

Using small aggregation units of the Chicago SMSA, multinomial logit models of joint location and travel mode choice for downtown commuters are estimated. Concludes that the frequency distribution of spatial choices is remarkably robust with respect to alternative specifications of probabilistic choice models and that errors in estimated coefficients due to model specification are much more serious than errors due to aggregate estimation.

2718 Aoyama, Yoshitaka. A Historical Review of Transport and Land-Use Models in Japan. Oxford: *Transportation Research*, Vol. 23(1), 1989, 53–61.

Examines transport models; land-use models; concepts used in modelling land-use; and a view of modelling for the future.

2719 Ashton, H., Harrison, W. J., Jones, P. M. and **Pell, C.** Some Advances in Model Design Developed for the Practical Assessment of Road Pricing in Hong Kong. Oxford: Transportation Research, Vol. 20A(2), March 1987.

Describes the methods used in a study commissioned by the Hong Kong Government to assess the impacts of road pricing schemes in the territory.

2720 Atkins, Stephen T. The Crisis for Transportation Planning Modelling. London: *Transport Reviews*, Vol. 7(4), October–December 1987, 307–325.

Examines the performance of land-use transportation study techniques over the past ten years. The changing context and tasks for modelling are reviewed and the current role and application of such models considered.

2721 Bacon, Robert W. The Travel to Shop Behaviour of Consumers in Equilibrium Market Areas. London: *Journal of Transport Economics and Policy*, Vol. 22(3), September 1992, 283–298.

Constructs a model of shopping behaviour in which the frequency of shopping is endogenous. Identifies the size of an equilibrium market area for a set of consumers and derives theoretical expressions for the total number of trips to a shopping centre, the average distance travelled, the average number of trips per shopper and the average distance travelled to shop per period.

2722 Bacon, Robert W. A Model of Travelling to Shop with Congestion Costs. London: *Journal of Transport Economics and Policy*, Vol. 27(3), September 1993, 277–290.

Models the endogenous frequency of shopping in a linear town, for the case where the costs of travel are affected by the degree of congestion along the road to the centre caused by other households travelling to shop, and where the costs of parking are also affected by the degree of congestion in the available car parking.

2723 Bayliss, Brian. *Transport Policy Planning: an integrated analytical approach.* Washington, DC: The World Bank, 1992. 68 pp.

Describes a comprehensive transport model which is able to evaluate policy options. Appropriate examples and case studies are provided.

2724 Ben-Akiva, M. E. and **Ricard, M. G.** *A Disaggregate Travel Demand Model.* Farnborough: Saxon House, 1975. 163 pp.

Considers the development of behavioural urban travel models.

2725 Bevilacqua, G. L. *Parallel Processing Applied to Road-Traffic Modelling.* Manchester: University of Manchester Institute of Science and Technology (PhD Thesis), 1978.

2726 Borukhov, E. Diseconomies of Scale in Urban Transportation. Baltimore, MD: *Southern Economic Journal*, Vol. 38(1), July 1971, 79–82.

Presents a model of a city which consists of a housing industry with a Cobb Douglas production function, and a transportation industry with constant marginal costs. The model is explicitly solved for total population and total construction and transportation costs. Demonstrates that these costs increase faster than population and discusses the welfare implications of this phenomenon.

2727 Bovy, P. H. L., le Clercq, F., van Est, J. P. J. M. and **Jansen, G. R. M.** (eds). *New Developments in Modelling Travel Demand and Urban Systems: some results of recent Dutch research.* Farnborough: Saxon House, 1979. 403 pp.

Presents the result of Dutch research on the modelling of travel demand and urban systems.

2728 Boyce, David E., Chon, Kyung S. and **LeBlanc, Larry J.** Network Equilibrium Models of Urban Location and Travel Choices: a retrospective survey. Peace Dale, RI: *Journal of Regional Science*, Vol. 28(2), May 1988, 159–183.

Considers two principle formulations: the network equilibrium problem with variable travel demand, and the combined model of trip distribution and traffic assignment.

2729 Branston, D. M. *Models of Single Lane Traffic Flow.* London: University College London (PhD Thesis), 1977.

2730 Bremner, J. D. G. *A Trip Generation Model to Estimate Travel Demand in Ireland.* Dublin: Dublin Trinity College (MSc Thesis), 1982.

2731 Broughton, J. *The Validation of a Model for the Journey to Work.* TRRL Laboratory Report 1096. Crowthorne: Transport and Road Research Laboratory, 1983. 22 pp.

Describes the applications of a random utility model using data from the Tyne and Wear Household Survey 1975 to describe how average salaries at representative points are estimated from the income data.

2732 Bryson, M. *Road Junction Models.* Glasgow: University of Glasgow (MSc Thesis), 1978.

2733 Champernowne, A. F., Coelho, J. D. and **Williams, H. C. W. L.** Some Comments on Urban Travel Demand Analysis, Model Calibration and the Economic Evaluation of Transport Plans. London: *Journal of Transport Economics and Policy*, Vol. 10(3), September 1976, 267–285.

Compares two frameworks for the analysis of travel demand, incorporating constraints. Trip distribution models from each approach, Entropy Maximising and consumer surplus, are set in a common dual programming framework for purposes of calibration, demand analysis and assessment of user benefit.

2734 Chapman, Jeffrey; Haring, Joseph E. and **Slobko, Thomas.** The Impact of Alternative Transportation Systems on Urban Structure. London: *Journal of Urban Economics*, Vol. 3(1), January 1976, 14–30.

Extends a recent Von-Thunen type model of urban structure by Mills to include two competing forms of transportation, and then compares simulated representative American and European cities with respect to size, density and land rents.

2735 Cochrane, R. A. A Possible Economic Basis for the Gravity Model. London: *Journal of Transport Economics and Policy*, Vol. 9(1), January 1995, 34–49.

Presents a derivation of the gravity model for trip-distribution and relates it to general economic theory.

2736 Congdon, Peter. A Model for the Interaction of Migration and Commuting. Glasgow: *Urban Studies Journal*, Vol. 20(2), May 1983, 185–196.

Presents a simultaneous equations model for the interaction of migration with changes in commuting, employment and housing stocks.

2737 Cook, Peter; Lewis, Simon and **Minc, Marcelo.** Comprehensive Transportation Models: past, present and future. Westport, CT: Transportation Quarterly, Vol. 44(2), April 1990, 249–266.

Presents an overview of comprehensive transportation modelling; the types of use these models serve and their strengths and weaknesses. Identifies areas where there have been significant advances in modelling technology and where further advances are anticipated.

2738 Daly, A. J. and **Zachary, S.** *The Effect of Free Public Transport on the Journey to Work.* TRRL Supplementary Report 338. Crowthorne: Transport and Road Research Laboratory, 1977. 26 pp.

Employs linear logit models to examine the effect of the many different travel and socio-economic factors on mode choice between car and public transport for the journey to work and on single and multiple car ownership.

2739 Daor, E. S. *An Analytical Technique for Designing a Trip Generation Model, with Reference to London.* London: London School of Economics and Political Science (M.Phil Thesis), 1978.

2740 Demetsky, Michael J. and **Korf, Jerry L.** Modelling Park 'N Ride and Kiss 'N Ride as Submodal Choices. Amsterdam: *Transportation*, Vol. 8, 1979, 409–426.

Logit modelling methodology is applied to include transit access mode choices in conjunction with the automobile vs transit travel choice decision. Identifies the practical problems that arise when the choice set expands beyond two alternatives.

2741 Dow, P. D. C. *Models for Strategic Road Assignment.* Leeds: University of Leeds (PhD Thesis), 1977.

2742 Downes, J. D. and **Emmerson, P.** *Urban Transport Modelling with Fixed Travel Budgets: An evaluation of the UMOT process.* TRRL Supplementary Report 799. Crowthorne: Transport and Road Research Laboratory, 1983. 41 pp.

A transport model, Unified Mechanism of Travel, considers known regularities such as travel budgets. These considerations are expected to be transferable from town to town. Here it is compared to values observed in Reading.

2743 Drissi-Kaitouni, Omar. A Dynamic Traffic Assignment Model and a Solution Algorithm. Baltimore, MD: *Transportation Science*, Vol. 26(2), May 1992, 119–128.

Focuses on the modeling of the Dynamic Traffic Assignment Problem for predicting the flows of urban transportation networks, mainly at peak periods.

2744 Duarte, C. E. *A Model to Evaluate Public Transport Systems in Urban Areas.* Glasgow: University of Glasgow (PhD Thesis), 1980.

2745 Echenique, M. H., Flowerdew, A. D. J., Hunt, J. D., Mayo, T. R., Simmonds, D. C. and **Skidmore, I. J.** The MEPLAN Models of Bilbao, Leeds and Dortmund. London: *Transport Reviews*, Vol. 10(4), October–December 1990, 309–322.

Develops a trio of closely related land-use/transport interaction models using Marcial Echenique & Partners' software package MEPLAN, using models for the cities of Bilbao, Dortmond and Leeds, all calibrated using data drawn from earlier studies.

2746 Economic Research Centre: European Conference of Ministers of Transport. *Passenger Transport Demand in Urban Areas: methodology for analysing and forecasting.* Report of the Thirty-Second

Round Table on Transport Economics. Paris: Organisation for Economic Co-operation and Development, 1976. 82 pp.

Analysing or forecasting passenger transport demand in urban areas ultimately involves a model. Report provides a yardstick both for evaluating a model and also for classifying it according to the manner in which its designer has tried to make it operational.

2747 Edwards, S. L. and Gordon, I. R. Holiday Trip Generation. London: *Journal of Transport Economics and Policy*, Vol. 7(2), May 1973, 153–168.

Authors develop a gravity model for a holiday trip in Great Britain and apply it to major road improvements projected for the South West Region.

2748 Ferguson, D. C. Joint Products and Road Transport Rates in Transport Models. London: *Journal of Transport Economics and Policy*, Vol. 6(1), January 1972, 69–76.

Claims that location of economic activity is often considered on the basis of point trading models which show the cost of transport of products. Suggests that models are defective as they do not make specific allowance for backloading.

2749 Flynn, M. J. *Data Filtering and Modelling in Urban traffic Networks.* Glasgow: University of Strathclyde (MSc Thesis), 1980.

2750 Galbraith, Richard A. and Hensher, David A. Intra-Metropolitan Transferability of Mode Choice Models. London: *Journal of Transport Economics and Policy*, Vol. 16(1), January 1982, 7–29.

Considers whether the coefficients of mode choice models are transferable to areas other than that for which they were estimated.

2751 Gaudry, M. J. I. Dogit and Logit Models of Travel Mode Choice in Montreal. Toronto: *Canadian Journal of Economics*, Vol. 13(2), May 1980, 268–279.

Compares dogit and logit specifications of a mode choice model using Montreal data on transit trips and on car vehicle trips.

2752 Goodman, P. R. *An Investigation of Trip End Modelling Techniques.* Leeds: University of Leeds (M.Phil Thesis), 1975.

2753 Hall, Randolph W. Passenger Delay in a Rapid Transit Station. Baltimore, MD: *Transportation Science*, Vol. 21(4), November 1987, 279–292.

An analytical queuing model for predicting passenger delay in a busy rapid transit station is developed and tested.

2754 Harker, Patrick T. Private Market Participation in Urban Mass Transportation: application of computable equilibrium models of network competition. Baltimore, MD: *Transportation Science*, Vol. 22(2), May 1988, 96–111.

Presents the theory and application of a computable equilibrium model of urban mass transportation which is designed to address the issues of sustainability and distributional equity in the private market.

2755 Hayfield, C. P. and **Stoker, R. B.** The Geographical Stability of a Typical Trip Production Model: applications of national and local data in four urban areas. Amsterdam: *Transportation*, Vol. 7, 1978, 211–224.

Investigates the geographical stability of the trip production model by comparing the number of trips estimated by the model when using national rather than local data.

2756 Heggie, Ian G. Are Gravity and Interactance Models a Valid Technique for Planning Regional Transport Facilities? New York: *Operational Research Quarterly*, Vol. 20(1), 1969, 93–111.

Concludes that these models cannot yet be used for explaining existing or future traffic flows.

2757 Hensher, David A. and **Mannering, Fred L.** Hazard-Based Duration Models and their Application to Transport Analysis. London: *Transport Reviews*, Vol. 14(1), January–March 1994, 63–82.

Suggests that a number of transport-related phenomena deal with a time element that defines the duration until an event's occurrence. Claims that hazard-based duration models are an obvious choice for modelling such transport phenomena.

2758 Hensher, David A. and **Stopher, Peter R.** (eds). *Behavioural Travel Modelling.* London: Croom Helm, 1989. 861 pp.

Reports the findings of the Third International Conference on Behavioural Modelling, and demonstrates the progress that was made over a two-year period.

2759 Hensher, David A., Milthorpe, Frank W. and **Smith, Nariida C.** The Demand for Vehicle Use in the Urban Household Sector: theory and empirical evidence. London: *Journal of Transport Economics and Policy*, Vol. 24(2), May 1990, 119–138.

Model examines households with one, two, three, and four or more vehicles and examines elasticities of fuel and other costs that vary with distance travelled, and the possibility of transfer to use of another vehicle within the household.

2760 Holzapfel, Helmut. *Trip Relationships in Urban Areas.* Aldershot: Gower, 1986.

Examines the difficulties encountered by transport planners in determining trip relationships by means of distribution models.

2761 Huzayyin, A. S. *Importance of Accessibility in Trip Generation Modelling.* Leeds: University of Leeds (PhD Thesis), 1978.

2762 Izraeli, Oded and **McCarthy, Thomas R.** Variations in Travel Distance, Travel Time and Modal Choice among SMSAs. London: *Journal of Transport Economics and Policy,* Vol. 19(2), May 1985, 139–160.

Study adopts the monocentric model (modified to include urban subcentres) as the theoretical framework from which hypotheses regarding journey to work behaviour is tested.

2763 Jackson, R. L. and **Tunbridge, R. J.** *A Disaggregate Modelling Study of Modal Choice for the Journey to Work.* TRRL Laboratory Report 1097. Crowthorne: Transport and Road Research Laboratory, 1983. 28 pp.

Investigates factors likely to influence levels of demand for bus and car pooling.

2764 Jackson, R. L. and **Tunbridge, R. J.** *The Journey to Work: a study of drive-alone/car-pool choice.* TRRL Supplementary Report 815. Crowthorne: Transport and Road Research Laboratory, 1983. 19 pp.

Deploys a disaggregate binomial logit model and data from a travel-to-work survey of staff at the Atomic Energy Research Establishment as the first stage of a more generalised survey.

2765 Jansson, Kjell. Optimal Public Transport Price and Service Frequency. London: *Journal of Transport Economics and Policy,* Vol. 27(1), January 1993, 33–50.

Models optimal price and service frequency for urban, regional and interregional public transport.

2766 Jessop, Alan. *Decision and Forecasting Models: with transport applications.* New York: Ellis Horwood, 1990. 468 pp.

Demonstrates how a body of techniques inspired by Bayesian Decision Theory can be applied to problems of transport planning and management.

2767 Jovanis, Paul P., Koppelman, Frank S. and **Moore, Anthony J.**

Modeling the Choice of Work Schedule with Flexible Work Hours. Baltimore, MD: *Transportation Science*, Vol. 18(2), May 1984, 141–164.

Develops a behaviourally based structure, using utility maximisation concepts, to relate travel; family; workplace; and individual influences to the workers' choices of arrival times with flexitime.

2768 Kim, Tschangho John. *Advanced Transport and Spatial Systems Models: applications to Korea.* New York: Springer, 1990. 255 pp.

Provides an introduction to national development plans and planning issues in Korea which focuses on modelling procedures and the application of integrated models to the analysis of policy issues.

2769 Kirshner, Daniel and **Talvitie, Antti.** Specification, Transferability and the Effect of Data Outliers in Modeling the Choice of Mode in Urban Travel. Amsterdam: *Transportation*, Vol. 7, 1978, 311–331.

Examines three problems of importance to urban travel demand modelling using mutli-nominal logit models. First, the effect of data outliers on model coefficients; second the effect of model specification on coefficients and model explanatory power; and third, the transferability of model coefficients within the region, between regions and in time.

2770 Kondo, Katsunao and **Sasaki, Tsuna.** An Entropy-Maximising Distribution Model and its Application to a Land-Use Model. London: George Godwin, *International Forum Series*, Vol. 1, 1981, 59–72.

Focuses on the use of entropy models in the analysis of travel and spatial interation.

2771 Kutter, Eckhard. A Model for Individual Travel Behaviour. Harlow: *Urban Studies*, Vol. 10, 1973, 235–258.

2772 Langdon, M. G. and **Mitchell, C. G. B.** *Personal Travel in Towns: the development of models that reflect the real world.* TRRL Supplementary Report 369. Crowthorne: Transport and Road Research Laboratory, 1978. 29 pp.

Conventional and disaggregated models are examined and it is shown that accurate calibration is no guarantee of accurate predictive ability. Fundamental questions of the spatial and temporal stability of transport models are also discussed.

2773 Lardinois, Christian. Supply Models for Intercity Passenger Transport: a review. London: *Transport Reviews*, Vol. 7(2), April–June 1987, 119–143.

Review of supply models in the field of intercity passenger transport, together with an attempt to characterise these models with regard to normative and predictive approaches, and in relation to the full hierarchy of strategic, tactical and operational decision-making situations.

2774 Lee, Chi-Kang. *Implementation and Evaluation of Network Equilibrium Models of Urban Residential Location and Travel Choices.* Illinois: University of Illinois (PhD Thesis), 1987. 197 pp.

Focuses on questions of developing and evaluating network equilibrium models for combining urban residential location and travel choices.

2775 Lewis, Richard A. and **Widup, David P.** Deregulation and Rail-Truck Competition: evidence from a Translog Transport Demand Model for Assembled Automobiles. London: *Journal of Transport Economics and Policy*, Vol. 16(2), May 1982, 139–150.

2776 Littlechild, S. C. Myopic Investment Rules and Toll Charges in a Transport Network. London: *Journal of Transport Economics and Policy*, Vol. 7(2), May 1973, 194–204.

Develops a model and decides that under simple conditions a myopic investment rule is adequate for a road or a network if congestion tolls are applied.

2777 Louviere, Jordan J. Conjoint Analysis Modelling of State Preferences: a review of theory, methods, recent developments and external validity. London: *Journal of Transport Economics and Policy*, Vol. 22(1), January 1988, 93–120.

Discusses commonalities and differences among different conjoint analysis techniques, including the assumptions required to use the techniques and to simulate individuals' choices.

2778 Mackett, R. L. *The Impact of Transport Policy on the City.* TRRL Supplementary Report 821. Crowthorne: Transport and Road Research Laboratory, 1984. 35 pp.

Forecast of the impact of transport policy in an urban area using a computer simulation model: Leeds Integrated Land Use Model.

2779 Mackett, R. L. The Systematic Application of the LILT Model to Dortmund, Leeds and Tokyo. London: *Transport Reviews*, Vol. 10(4), October–December 1990, 323–338.

Applies the Leeds Integrated Land-Use Transport Model to three study areas, as part of the work of the International Study Group on Land-Use Transport Interaction.

2780 Mackett, R. L. A Model-Based Analysis of Transport and Land-

Use Policies for Tokyo. London: *Transport Reviews*, Vol. 11(1), January–March 1991, 1–18.

2781 Mackett, R. L. *The Impact of Transport Planning Policy on the City: a model-based approach applied to Leeds.* Leeds: University of Leeds (PhD Thesis), 1982.

2782 Mackett, R. L., Simmonds, D. C. and **Wegener, M.** One City, Three Models: comparison of land-use/transport policy simulation models for Dortmund. London: *Transport Reviews*, Vol. 11(2), April–June 1991, 107–129.

Reports on simulation experiments conducted by the International Study Group on Land-Use/Transport Interaction for the metropolitan region of Dortmund in the Federal Republic of Germany.

2783 Mackett, Roger L. The Relationship between Transport and the Viability of Central and Inner Urban Areas. London: *Journal of Transport Economics and Policy*, Vol. 14(3), September 1980, 267–294.

Deploys a computer model to analyse past trends and to forecast the effects of various possibilities for the city of Leeds.

2784 Madan, D. B. and **Groenhout, R.** Modelling Travel Mode Choice for the Sydney Work Trip. London: *Journal of Transport Economics and Policy*, Vol. 21(2), May 1987, 135–150.

A discrete choice model is constructed and estimated explaining the binary choice of private car vs public transport for travel to work in Sydney during the a.m. peak.

2785 Martin, P. H. and **Tunbridge, R. J.** *The Optimisation of Public Transport in Small Towns.* Crowthorne: Transport and Road Research Laboratory, 1977. 42 pp.

A study determining the optimum form of public transport in a particular Oxfordshire town was used to construct a demand model which demonstrates a close alignment with three different levels of public transport.

2786 McDonald, M. *Analytical Models of Traffic at Road Junctions and on Inter-Urban Transport Networks.* Southampton: University of Southampton (PhD Thesis), 1981. 536 pp.

2787 McFadden, D. The Measurement of Urban Travel Demand. Lausanne: *Journal of Public Economics*, Vol. 3(4), November 1974, 308–328.

Article develops models of travel behaviour that recognise the qualitative nature of individual travel choices and the concomitant nature of travel in other consumption activities. Forms of the models suitable for econometric analysis are developed.

2788 McGillivray, R. G. Binary Choice of Urban Transport Mode in the San Francisco Bay Region. Virginia: *Econometrica*, Vol. 40(5), September 1972, 827–848.

Analysis of mode choice for selected urban trips in the Bay Area is presented developing a restricted consumer choice model, where the mutually exclusive collectively exhaustive choice is between auto driver and transit passenger.

2789 Mendes, M. T. F. S. *The Implementation and Validation of Road-Traffic Models.* Manchester: University of Manchester Institute of Science and Technology (PhD Thesis), 1980.

2790 Meyer, J. R. (ed.). *Techniques of Transport Planning.* Vol. 2: systems analysis and simulation models. Washington, DC: Brookings Institution, 1971.

Describes the development of a large-scale computer macroeconomic transport simulation model, with submodels, for transportation planning, and an application to Colombia.

2791 Miller, Hugh Wilson Jr. *Urban Modeling Systems: dynamic properties and equilibrium tendencies.* Philadelphia, PA: University of Pennsylvania (PhD Thesis), 1987. 481 pp.

Focuses on the component parts of an urban model (for example the employment location model; the residential location models; and the urban transportation planning model), and the way in which they are combined into an operational whole.

2792 Moore, J. E. and **Seo, J. G.** Reverse Commutation in a Monocentric City. Peace Dale, RI: *Journal of Regional Science*, Vol. 31(3), August 1991, 291–310.

Deploys a general equilibrium multiperiod linear programming model of urban land use in order to identify reverse commutation as a rational response to economic change.

2793 Neto, I. U. *The Development and Testing of a Non-Recursive Aggregate Passenger Travel Demand Modelling Approach.* Bristol: Bristol University (PhD Thesis), 1988.

Develops and tests a non-recursive aggregate passenger travel demand modelling approach capable of substituting to advantage the recursive trip generation and trip distribution stages of the sequential passenger travel demand model.

2794 Nowlan, David M. Optimal Pricing of Urban Trips with Budget Restrictions and Distributional Concerns. London: *Journal of Transport Economics and Policy*, Vol. 27(3), September 1993, 253–276.

Urban transport is modelled as a set of services provided by an integrated transport sector, the objective of which is to set prices and to invest in service infrastructure so as to maximise a social welfare function over the community.

2795 Oldfield, R. H. *A Theoretical Model for Estimating the Effects of Fares, Traffic Restraint, and Bus Priority in Central London.* TRRL Laboratory Report 749. Crowthorne: Transport and Road Research Laboratory, 1977. 47 pp.

2796 Oppenheim, Norbert. A Combined, Equilibrium Model of Urban Personal Travel and Goods Movements. Baltimore, MD: *Transportation Science*, Vol. 27(2), May 1993, 161–173.

Proposes a combined model of urban personal travel and goods movements, in which commodity flows (for example retail goods movements) are generated by individual consumption in the conduct of a given urban activity (for example shopping).

2797 Oppenheim, Norbert. *Urban Travel Demand Modelling: from individual choices to general equilibrium.* New York: John Wiley and Sons, 1995. 480 pp.

Indicates how generalised network equilibrium may be rigorously forecast from the optimal travel choices of 'trip consumers' without the need to resort to heuristic procedures such as feedbacks. Models for optimal transportation supply decisions are integrated with the demand models.

2798 Organisation for Economic Co-operation and Development. *Transport Choices for Urban Passengers: measures and models.* Paris: Organisation for Economic Co-operation and Development, 1980. 121 pp.

2799 Orlandi, Alessandro. Transportation Engineering: a rationalised general model. London: George Godwin, *International Forum Series*, Vol. 1, 1981, 191–200.

2800 Ortuzar, J. de D. and **Willumsen, L. G.** *Modelling Transport.* 2nd ed. Chichester: John Wiley and Sons, 1994. 439 pp.

Presents a contemporary account of key transport modelling techniques and applications. Identifies methods of responding to current pressing transport planning issues and problems, reflecting radical innovations from which transport modelling techniques have benefited in recent years.

2801 Paulley, N. J. and **Webster, F. V.** Overview of an International Study to Compare Models and Evaluate Land-Use and Transport Policies. London: *Transport Reviews*, Vol. 11(3), July–September 1991, 197–222.

Describes the results obtained from Phase 2 of the International Study Group on Land-Use/Transport Interaction. Draws together the main findings of the study and comments on the performance of the models.

2802 Pines, David and **Sadka, Efraim.** Gasoline Prices, Welfare and Congestion Tolls. Oxford: *Scandinavian Journal of Economics*, Vol. 86(4), 1984, 440–451.

Effects of a gasoline price increase are examined using an urban model with traffic congestion.

2803 Planning and Transport Research and Computation Company. *Urban Traffic Models.* London: PTRC Education and Research Services, 1974. 243 pp.

2804 Putman, S. H. *Integrated Urban Models.* London: Pion, 1983. 332 pp.

2805 Richardson, A. J. Transport Planning and Modelling: a twenty year perspective. Victoria: *Australian Road Research*, Vol. 20(1), March 1990, 9–29.

Chronicles the major innovations in modelling techniques used to support transport planning activities throughout the 1970s and 1980s. It concentrates on those modelling techniques used to describe, explain, and predict demand for personal travel.

2806 Saccomanno, F. F. Transport Policy Analysis Through Site Value Transfer. London: *Journal of Transport Economics and Policy*, Vol. 14(2), May 1980, 169–184.

Empirical model of site value transfer for the residential sector, based on data from Toronto which employ an iterative algorithm that interrelates reductions in the following: commuting expenditures; changes in site value; land development adjustments; population employment allocation; and transport planning.

2807 Smith, D. J. *Transportation and Traffic Models: a critical review of current methodologies.* Glasgow: University of Glasgow (MSc Thesis), 1977.

2808 Southworth, F. A Disaggregated Trip Distribution Model with

Elastic Frequencies and Expenditures. London: *Journal of Transport Economics and Policy*, Vol. 13(1), May 1979, 209–224.

2809 Southworth, F. *The Calibration of Disaggregated Trip Distribution and Modal Split Models: some comparisons of macro and micro analytical approaches.* Leeds: University of Leeds (PhD Thesis), 1977.

2810 Stevens, Walter R. and **Supernak, Janusz.** Urban Transportation Modelling: the discussion continues. Amsterdam: *Transportation*, Vol. 14, 1987, 73–82.

2811 Taylor, Michael A. P. and **Young, William.** A Parking Model Hierarchy. Amsterdam: *Transportation*, Vol. 18, 1991, 37–58.
Outlines a hierarchy of microcomputer models and information systems that can investigate parking policy and study the 'level of services' provided by parking systems.

2812 Taylor, Michael A. P. and **Young, William.** A Review of Australian Traffic System Design Models. London: *Transport Reviews*, Vol. 8(1), January–March 1988, 19–38.
Reviews developments in techniques for modelling the impact of changes in the traffic system.

2813 Transnet. *Energy, Transport and the Environment.* London: Transnet, 1990. 112 pp.
Suggests that new models are required to understand the true energy and environmental costs of transport needs.

2814 Transport and Road Research Laboratory. *Traffic Modelling: 1991–1994.* Current topics in transport no. 85. Crowthorne: Transport and Road Research Laboratory, 1995. 41 pp.

2815 Underwood, J. R. *Comparative Assessment of Alternative Modal Split Models for Inter-City Travel.* Leeds: University of Leeds (PhD Thesis), 1977.

2816 Veraprasad, N. *Transport Costs and the Dynamics of Population Redistribution: two strategic models for the South-East.* Cranfield: Cranfield Institute of Technology (PhD Thesis), 1979.

2817 Vickerman, Roger. The Demand for Non-Work Travel. London: *Journal of Transport Economics and Policy*, Vol. 6(2), May 1972, 176–210.
Builds generation models for shopping; recreational; social and pleasure trips for each of four regions using national travel survey data.

2818 Viton, P. A. Equilibrium Short-Run Marginal-Cost Pricing of a Transportation Facility: the case of the San Francisco Bay Bridge. London: *Journal of Transport Economics and Policy*, Vol. 14(2), May 1980, 185–203.

Derives empirical estimates of the equilibrium peak period congestion tolls when no further investment in congestion-reduction capacity is possible; the facility is used by commuter modes and one mode of goods transport; and commuters choose between the two modes available. Model is calibrated using cost and demand data for commutation trips between San Francisco and the East Bay in California.

2819 Viton, Philip A. Privately-Provided Urban Transport Services: entry deterrence and welfare. London: *Journal of Transport Economics and Policy*, Vol. 16(1), January 1982, 85–94.

Estimates a simulation model to test the hypothesis that existing 'public utility' transit services serve to deter private-carrier entry.

2820 Wardman, Mark. A Comparison of Revealed Preference and Stated Preference Models of Travel Behaviour. London: *Journal of Transport Economics and Policy*, Vol. 22(1), January 1988, 71–92.

Contributes to the issue of the validity of using stated preference experiments by comparing the values of time derived from revealed preference and stated preference models of travel behaviour.

2821 Watling, D. *A Review of Models of Urban Traffic Networks.* Leeds: University of Leeds, Institute for Transport Studies, July 1991. 51 pp.

2822 Watling, David. Urban Traffic Network Models and Dynamic Driver Information Systems. London: *Transport Reviews*, Vol. 14(3), July–September 1994, 219–246.

2823 Willumsen, L. G. *An Entropy Maximising Model for Estimating Trip Matrices from Traffic Counts.* Leeds: University of Leeds (PhD Thesis), 1981.

2824 Zahavi, Yacov. The Measurement of Travel Demand and Mobility. London: George Godwin, *International Forum Series*, Vol. 1, 1981, 169–182.

Reports on some recent developments in urban transportation models initiated by the World Bank.

Simulation

2825 Al-Salman, H. S. T. *A Computer Simulation to Investigate Delay to Vehicles at a Signalised Highway T-Junction.* Bradford: University of Bradford (MSc Thesis), 1972.

2826 Bolland, J. D. *Simulation of a Bus Network Based on a Multipath Passenger Assignment Algorithm.* Leeds: University of Leeds (PhD Thesis), 1978.

2827 Bull, P. *Vehicle Detection at Pelican Pedestrian Crossings.* Sheffield: University of Sheffield (PhD Thesis), 1987.

Presents the results of a computer simulation study of the effects of the use of vehicle detection at Pelican pedestrian crossings.

2828 Calhau, J. A. P. *Simulation of Vehicle Queuing Situations.* Manchester: University of Manchester Institute of Science and Technology (MSc Thesis), 1970.

2829 Chin, H. C. *A Computer Simulation Model of Traffic Operation at Roundabouts.* Southampton: University of Southampton (PhD Thesis), 1983.

2830 Clapham, J. C. R. *The Combined Use of an Algorithmic Approach and Simulation to Minimize Traffic Signal Delays in a Network.* London: University College London (PhD Thesis), 1976.

2831 Collins, F. M. *Transport System Simulation.* Ireland: National University of Ireland (M.EngSc Thesis), 1971.

2832 Cooke, B. M. *Traffic Simulation: assessment and development.* Birmingham: University of Birmingham (MSc Thesis), 1971.

2833 Dewees, D. N. Urban Express Bus and Railroad Performance: some Toronto simulations. London: *Journal of Transport Economics and Policy,* Vol. 10(1), January 1976, 16–25.

Compares the relative performance of the traditional local transport modes with a proposed investment in a commuter railroad or in express bus operations.

2834 Gadd, S. C. L. *Cospartan Simulation of Road Traffic Networks: an assessment of accuracy.* Birmingham: University of Birmingham (MSc Thesis), 1970.

2835 Johnson, K. R. *A Driving Simulation Technique for the Investigation of Gap Acceptance Behaviour.* Newcastle Upon Tyne: University of Newcastle Upon Tyne (MSc Thesis), 1976.

2836 Leiser, David and Stern, Eliahu. Determinants of Subjective Time Estimates in Simulated Urban Driving. Oxford: *Transportation Research*, Vol. 22A(3), 1988, 175–182.

An urban driving simulator is used to generate a data base for calibrating and testing a casual path model for subjective time estimates.

2837 Poston, J. M. *Simulation of the Effect of Bus Priority Schemes at a Signalised Intersection.* Leicester: University of Leicester (MSc Thesis), 1971.

2838 Powner, E. T. *Some Aspects of the Digital Simulation of Multiple Traffic Intersections and Associated Flow Problems.* Manchester: University of Manchester Institute of Science and Technology (MSc Thesis), 1970.

2839 Ramsey, J. B. H. *The Simulation and Analysis of Traffic in Simple Road Networks.* Newcastle Upon Tyne: University of Newcastle Upon Tyne (MSc Thesis), 1971.

2840 Sherwood, C. P. K. *The Use of a Simulation Model to Test the Effect of a Dial-a-Bus System on Travel Patterns.* Newcastle Upon Tyne: University of Newcastle Upon Tyne (MSc Thesis), 1977.

2841 Shmanske, Stephen. A Simulation of Price Discriminating Tolls. London: *Journal of Transport Economics and Policy*, Vol. 23(3), September 1993, 225–236.

Uses computer simulation to compare uniform tolls on a congested facility against a price-discriminating toll collection scheme.

2842 Tranter, R. A. *Computer Graphics for Traffic Simulation.* Leicester: University of Leicester (MSc Thesis), 1971.

Temporal and spatial analysis

2843 Banister, David and Camara, Paulo. Spatial Inequalities in the Provision of Public Transport in Latin American Cities. London: *Transport Reviews*, Vol. 13(4), October–December 1993, 351–373.

2844 Beesley, M. E. and **Dalvi, M. Q.** Spatial Equilibrium and Journey to Work. London: *Journal of Transport Economics and Policy*, Vol. 8(3), September 1974, 197–222.

Observes that the length of the journey to work may depend on choice of residence from a fixed job site or on choice of job from a fixed residence. Considers the factors that influence both in South East England, and the effects on males and females separately.

2845 Berresford, M. R. *A Study of the Capacity of Merging Areas on Urban Motorways.* Salford: University of Salford (MSc Thesis), 1971.

2846 Botterill, R. and **Bowyer, D.** Monitoring Urban Spatial Dynamics. Amsterdam: *Transportation*, Vol. 14, 1988, 345–359.

Considers the progress which has been made in, and use of, procedures for monitoring urban transport spatial-related changes.

2847 Button, K. J. and **Gillingwater, D.** (eds). *Transport, Location and Spatial Policy.* Aldershot: Gower, 1983. 260 pp.

Offers a series of studies which examine the ways in which the decisions and structures in one sector, namely transport, have an impact on other sectors, especially cities and regions, and spatial policy in general.

2848 Chee Chung Tong; Hadi Baaj; Hani, S. and **Mahmassani, M.** Characterization and Evolution of Spatial Density Patterns in Urban Areas. Amsterdam: *Transportation*, Vol. 15(3), 1988, 233–256.

Examines the spatial patterns of population density, household automobile ownership and other socio-demographic variables that affect urban travel, as a function of distance from the central city core.

2849 Cochrane, R. Chaos Theory and Spatial Dynamics: a comment. London: *Journal of Transport Economics and Policy*, Vol. 26(2), May 1992, 197–201.

2850 Forrest, J. Spatial Aspects of Urban Social Travel. Harlow: *Urban Studies*, Vol. 11, 1974, 301–313.

Examines spatial patterns of vehicular trips for social purposes for an urban area in New Zealand; investigates the role of distance as a constraint on social interaction; and analyses relationships between levels of socio-economic status.

2851 Gillespie, A. E. *Transport and the Inner City.* Social Science Research Council, 1980. 79 pp.

Study of the problems of the inner-city in its temporal, spatial, socio-economic and policy context which looks at transport technology and change in inner city areas from a historical perspective.

2852 Hutchinson, Bruce G. and Said, Galal M. Spatial Differentiation, Transport Demands and Transport Model Design in Kuwait. London: *Transport Reviews*, Vol. 10(2), April–June 1990, 91–110.

2853 Jovanovic, Miomir. Urban Transport and Social Stratification. Yugoslavia: *Socioloski Pregled*, Vol. 20, 1986, 39–50.

Analyses the interdependency of urban transport and spatial segregation of populations. Claims that both developed and developing countries are experiencing a movement of the wealthy into cities and the poor into the suburbs.

2854 Lesley, L. J. S. *A Study of Public Transport in Relation to Urban Form.* Glasgow: University of Strathclyde (PhD Thesis), 1971.

2855 Mannering, Fred; Murakami, Elaine and Kim, Soon-Gwam. Temporal Stability of Travelers' Activity Choice and Home-Stay Duration: some empirical evidence. Dordrecht: *Transportation*, Vol. 21, 1994, 371–392.

Explores the temporal stability of activity type-choice models and models of travellers' home-stay duration.

2856 Starkie, D. N. M. *Traffic and Industry: a study of traffic generation and spatial interaction.* London: London School of Economics and Political Science, 1969. 71 pp.

Examines the relationship between commercial road traffic and the characteristics of the firms that generate the traffic. Uses a sample of firms from Medway towns.

2857 Vaughan, Rodney. *Urban Spatial Traffic Patterns.* London: Pion, 1987.

Provides an account of continuous models of urban travel.

2858 Vickerman, Roger W. Review Article: transport and spatial development in Europo. Oxford: *Journal of Common Market Studies*, Vol. 32(2), 1994, 249–256.

Review of six books covering the economic geography of transport in an endeavour to discover whether there is sufficient understanding of the processes involved to evolve a common transport policy.

2859 Vidakovic, Velibor. Analysing Transportation Problems through

Daily Life Patterns. London: George Godwin, *International Forum Series*, Vol. 1, 1981, 141–156.

Reports on a travel/activity research programme carried out in the Netherlands.

2860 Wheaton, W. C. Residential Decentralization, Land Rents and the Benefits of Urban Transportation Investment. Massachusetts: *American Economic Review*, Vol. 67(2), March 1977, 138–143.

Using a simple spatial model, expressions for the general equilibrium benefits of transportation improvements that incorporate changing spatial structure in addition to the direct savings to highway users are derived.

Time

2861 Bruzelius, Nils. *The Value of Travel Time Theory and Measurement.* London: Croom Helm, 1979.

Investigation into leisure travelling time within the framework of welfare economic theory.

2862 Coulter, John W. and **Schuler, Richard E.** The Effect of Socio-Economic Factors on the Value of Time in Commuting to Work. Amsterdam: *Transportation*, Vol. 7, 1978, 381–401.

2863 Dalvi, M. Q. and **Lee, N.** Variations in the Value of Travel Item: further analysis. London: *Manchester School of Economic and Social Studies*, Vol. 39(3), September 1971, 187–204.

Applies regression analysis to explain the considerable variation between individual commuters' valuations of travel time.

2864 Edmonds, Radcliff G. Jr. Travel Time Valuation through Hedonic Regression. Baltimore, MD: *Southern Economic Journal*, Vol. 50(1), July 1983, 83–98.

Presents linkage of residential location, Lancastrian consumer, and implicit market models to provide a theoretical basis for the use of hedonic regression in estimating some of the different values of travel time.

2865 European Conference of Ministers of Transport. *Value of Time.* ECMT Round Table 30. Paris: Organisation for Economic Cooperation and Development, 1976. 71 pp.

Report aimed at identifying and discussing a number of the problems associated with putting money value on time spent travelling.

2866 Forsyth, P. J. The Value of Time in an Economy with Taxation. London: *Journal of Transport Economics and Policy*, Vol. 14(3), September 1980, 337–361.

Argues that valuations of travel time for cost-benefit studies should not be based exclusively on individual values or on the wage rate, but should combine both, with allowance for taxation.

2867 Goodwin, P. B. Human Effort and the Value of Travel Time. London: *Journal of Transport Economics and Policy*, Vol. 10(1), January 1976, 3–15.

Considers various possible measures of 'effort' (factors additional to time and money which affect demand for travel).

2868 Gronau, Reuben. The Effect of Travelling Time on the Demand for Passenger Transportation. Chicago, IL: *Journal of Political Economy*, Vol. 78(2), 1970, 377–394.

2869 Guttman, Joel M. Uncertainty, the Value of Time, and Transport Policy. London: *Journal of Transport Economics and Policy*, Vol. 13(2), May 1979, 225–229.

Examines the effects of uncertainty in time costs for the commuter's journey to work.

2870 Guttman, Joel M. and **Menashe, Eliahu.** Uncertainty, Continuous Modal Split, and the Value of Travel Time in Israel. London: *Journal of Transport Economics and Policy*, Vol. 20(3), September 1986, 369–376.

Develops a car-bus modal split model from an Israeli sample.

2871 Hall, J. W., Matteson, J. H. and **Sawhill, R. B.** User Benefits in Economic Analysis of Metropolitan Freeway Construction. *Highway Research Record*, Vol. 31(4), 1970, 32–40.

2872 Heggie, Ian G. (ed.). *Modal Choice and the Value of Travel Time.* Oxford: Clarendon Press, 1976. 190 pp.

2873 Henley, Davis H., Levin, Irwin P., Louviere, Jordan J. and **Meyer, Robert J.** Changes in Perceived Travel Cost and Time for the Work Trip During a Period of Increasing Gasoline Costs. Amsterdam: *Transportation*, Vol. 10, 1981, 23–34.

Examines the relationship between actual and perceived values of cost and time for the work trip and how perceptions have changed over a period of dramatically increased travel costs.

2874 Hensher, David A. and **Truong, Truong P.** Valuation of Travel Time Savings: a direct experimental approach. London: *Journal of Transport Economics and Policy*, Vol. 19(3), September 1985, 237–262.

2875 Howe, J. D. G. F. Valuing Time Savings in Developing Countries. London: *Journal of Transport Economics and Policy*, Vol. 10(2), 1976, 113–125.

2876 Hyde, T. *Some Factors Affecting Journey-Times on Urban Roads.* London: University College London (PhD Thesis), 1981.

2877 Moreau, Agnes. Public Transport Waiting Times as Experienced by Customers. Brussels: *Public Transport International*, Vol. 41(3), 1992, 52–53.

Examines ways in which time is viewed through a study which considers whether customers sense the passing of time and whether customers tend to overestimate waiting time.

2878 Pells, S. R. *The Evaluation of Reductions in Travel Time Variability.* Leeds: University of Leeds (PhD Thesis), 1987.

Considers the extra time in commuters' schedules which is added for possible delays, time that could be used more productively in origin activities.

2879 Starkie, D. N. M. Modal Split and the Value of Time: a note on 'Idle-Time'. London: *Journal of Transport Economics and Policy*, Vol. 5(2), May 1971.

Considers that models used to determine modal choice have failed to recognise the value of time lost through schedule delays and the unpredictability of travel.

2880 Thomas, Simon. Non-working Time Savings in Developing Countries. London: *Journal of Transport Economics and Policy*, Vol. 13(3), September 1979, 335–337.

Claims that savings in non-working time, as well as savings in costs to car drivers, should be valued for both urban and inter-urban projects, but should be weighted by a distributional index.

2881 University of Leeds Transport Studies Institute and University of Oxford Transport Studies Group. *The Value of Travel Time Savings.* Berks: Policy Journals, 1987. 221 pp.

Extends the neo-classical model of consumer theory to include time dimension.

2882 Watson, Peter L. *The Value of Time: behavioural models of modal choice.* Lexington, MA: Lexington Books, 1974. 170 pp.

Vehicles

2883 Aldous, Alan. Electric Vehicles. London: *Transport*, Vol. 6, June 1985, 21–22.

Surveys the present and future for electric vehicles.

2884 Deluchi, Mark; Sperling, Daniel and **Wang, Quanlu.** Electric Vehicles: performance, life-cycle costs, emissions, and recharging requirements. Oxford: *Transportation Research*, Vol. 23(3), 1989, 255–278.

Provides a detailed evaluation of the performance, costs, environmental impacts, and recharging requirements of electric vehicles.

2885 Dufour, Christopher. CityRider: a combination of steel-wheel rail system and automated urban transit system. Brussels: *Public Transport International*, Vol. 44(3), 1995, 25–26.

Reviews 'CityRider', a driverless system designed for urban and suburban areas.

2886 Fletcher, Scott. APTA Conference in Charlotte Examines Future of the Transit Bus. California: *Metro*, Vol. 88(4), 1992, 46–47.

2887 Fox, Gerald D. *A Comparison of Some New Light Rail and Automated-Guideway Systems.* Paper presented at the National Conference on 'Light Rail Transit: new system successes at affordable prices'. Washington, DC: Transportation Research Board, National Research Council, 1989, 98–110.

Argues that although the new AGT systems represent a further advance in the development of urban transit technology, they may also contain the seeds of future problems.

2888 Franzen, Stig and **Parkes, Andrew M.** (eds). *Driving Future Vehicles.* London: Taylor and Francis, 1993. 458 pp.

A collection of articles from industry and academia concerned with the design of efficient, safe, and consumer acceptable vehicles.

2889 Garret, Ken. A World First for the UK Electric Van. London: *Transport*, Vol. 3, March/April 1982, 19–20.

Examines the development of Karrier Motors' traffic-compatible electric van.

2890 Hamilton, William. *Electric Automobiles: energy, environmental, and economic prospects for the future.* San Francisco: McGraw-Hill, 1980. 425 pp.

Considers the prospects and the advantages and disadvantages of electric cars.

2891 Hellewell, D. Scott. Electric Public Transport: hoping for a boost. London: *Transport*, Vol. 2, March/April 1981, 67–68.

Controller of operations and planning at South Yorkshire PTE discusses the operational implications of the wider electrification of public passenger transport in the United Kingdom.

2892 Irving, Jack H., with **Bernstein, Harry; Olson, C. L.** and **Buyan, Jon.** *Fundamentals of Personal Rapid Transit.* Lexington, MA: D. C. Heath, 1978.

Summarises the work on personal rapid transit carried out at the Aerospace Corporation between 1968 and 1976.

2893 Kurani, Kenneth S., Turrentine, Tom and **Sperling, Daniel.** Demand for Electric Vehicles in Hybrid Households: an exploratory analysis. Oxford: *Transport Policy*, Vol. 1(4), October 1994, 244–256.

The primary finding of this study indicate that consumers' perceived driving range needs are substantially lower than previous hypothetical stated preference studies conclude. Results provide evidence in favour of a viable market for battery operated electric vehicles with sixty to a hundred miles driving range.

2894 Kyle, Chester R. *Racing with the Sun: the 1990 World Solar Challenge.* Warrendale: Society of Automotive Engineers, 1991. 166 pp.

Chronicles the 1990 World Solar Challenge; a race from Darwin to Adelaide for solar powered cars.

2895 Leembruggen, L. R. Townmobile Electric City Transit System. London: George Godwin, *International Forum Series*, Vol. 2, 1981, 97–104.

Systems of electric passenger transport and their applications are described and compared with other modes.

2896 Lesley, Lewis. *Electrifying Urban Public Transport: application of new technologies.* Proceedings of Conference, 1983. Liverpool: Liverpool Polytechnic, 1984. 224 pp.

Collection of papers that consider the decline of urban public transport in Britain in the face of changing social and demographic patterns, and the growth in car ownership. Makes the case for the application of electrically based technologies which give environmental comfort and economic advantages over the traditional diesel double decker bus.

2897 Lones, Trevor. Brazilian Companies in Power Race. London: *Transport*, Vol. 1, November/December 1980, 51.

Report on the breakthrough of electrically powered cars in Brazil.

2898 Nutley, Stephen D. 'Unconventional Modes' of Transport in the United Kingdom: a review of types and the policy context. Oxford: *Transportation Research*, Vol. 22A(5), September 1988, 329–344.

Attempts to establish a definition of 'unconventional' modes of transport as an aid to classification and to clarify terminology.

2899 Nwagboso, Christopher O. (ed.). *Road Vehicle Automation.* London: Pentech Press, 1993. 309 pp.

Proceedings of the 1st international Conference on Road Vehicle Automation held at Vehicle Systems Research Centre, School of Engineering, Bolton Institute, Bolton in May 1993.

2900 Parkhurst, G. *Guided Urban Transport: land use and environmental impacts.* Oxford: Oxford University, Transport Studies Unit, 1992. 21 pp.

2901 Sperling, Daniel. *Future Drive: electric vehicles and sustainable transportation.* Washington, DC: Island Press, 1995. 175 pp.

Addresses the adverse energy and environmental consequences of increased travel, and analyses initiatives and strategies for creating a more environmentally benign system of transportation.

2902 Vijayakumar, S. Optimal vehicle size for road-based urban public transport in developing countries. London: *Transport Reviews*, Vol. 6(2), April–June 1986, 193–212.

2903 Womack, James P. The Real Electronic Vehicle Challenge: re-inventing an industry. Oxford: *Transport Policy*, Vol. 1(4), October 1994, 266–270.

Examines the prospects for electric vehicles.

17 Mobility

General

2904 Adams, John; Hillman, Mayer and **Whitelegg, John.** *One False Move: a study of children's independent mobility.* London: Policy Studies Institute, 1990. 187 pp.

Claims that the decline in road accidents involving children has come about because parents no longer allow their children to be exposed to the dangers of the road. This has resulted in parents spending more time escorting their children to school, thus adding to traffic congestion.

2905 Altshuler, Alan and **Rosenbloom, Sandra** (eds). *Equity Issues in Urban Transportation.* Lexington, MA: Lexington Books, 1980.

Argues that those without ready access to automobiles find themselves cut off from numerous destinations.

2906 Banister, David. *Transport Mobility and Deprivation in Inter-Urban areas: research findings and policy perspectives.* Reading: University of Reading, 1980. 61 pp.

Summarises a two year research project investigating patterns of mobility in areas separate from, but within the influence of, an urban area. Notes that a large proportion of non-urban Britain comes within this definition.

2907 Banister, David. *Transport Mobility and Deprivation in Inter-Urban Areas.* Hampshire: Teakfield, 1980. 200 pp.

Examines the nature of present travel behaviour and latent demand in communities separate from, but within the influence of, an urban area.

2908 Barton, Mark. School Is the Place to Learn. Peterborough: *Coach and Bus Week*, Issue 162, April 1995, 24–25.

Describes the organisation for the Yellow bus operation in Springfield, Massachusetts, and its provision of school transport for the city.

2909 Benaouda, M. *The Effect of Age and Sex on Travel Patterns.* Loughborough: University of Loughborough (MSc Thesis), 1978.

2910 Brog, Werner. Assessments of Mobility in Europe. Brussels: *Public Transport International*, Vol. 41(1), February 1992, 60–68.

Reports the results of a survey commissioned by the International Union of Public Transport to examine views in Europe as regards mobility. Observes that the principal problem common to all countries is car traffic. Article in English with French and German translations.

2911 Darker, John. Paris Triumphs over its Mobility Problems. London: *Transport*, Vol. 3, January/February 1982, 6–7.

Assesses the French approach to mobility in the Republic's capital city.

2912 Goodwin, P. B. Family Changes and Public Transport Use 1984–1987: a dynamic anlysis using panel data. Amsterdam: *Transportation*, Vol. 16(2), 1989, 121–154.

Examines changes in the nature of the family and the effect that has on the use of public transport and car ownership.

2913 Gordon, Peter; Kumar, Ajay and **Richardson, Harry W.** Beyond the Journey to Work. Oxford: *Transportation Research*, Vol. 22A(6), 1988, 419–426.

Analyses the Nationwide Personal Transportation Study surveys of 1977 and 1983–1984 which revealed a remarkable increase in non-work travel.

2914 Henderson, Irwin; Hillman, Mayer and **Whalley, Anne.** *Personal Mobility and Transport Policy.* London: Political and Economic Planning, 1973. 134 pp.

Considers basic mobility needs and methods of travel and reports on a survey which investigated the travel patterns of adults, teenagers and primary school children.

2915 Jones, S. R. *Accessibility and Public Transport Use.* TRRL Supplementary Report 832. Crowthorne: Transport and Road Research Laboratory, 1984. 19 pp.

Investigates the relationships between accessibility and travel behaviour. Considers a specific case in a large urban area using data from Tyne and Wear.

2916 Keller, Hartmut and **Muller, Wilfried.** Optimising School Bus Operation. London: George Godwin, *International Forum Series*, Vol. 2, 1981, 243–254.

Presents a review of existing algorithms applicable to the school bus problem and attempts to demonstrate the potential of the operations research approach to solve urban transport problems.

2917 Kunert, Uwe. Weekly Mobility of Life Cycle Groups. Dordrecht: *Transportation*, Vol. 21(3), 1994, 271–288.
Study of travel patterns of urban residents on seven consecutive days.

2918 Levine, Howard J. *Street Cars for Toronto Committee: a case study of Citizen Advocacy in transit planning.* Paper presented at the National Conference on 'Light Rail Transit: new system successes at affordable prices'. Washington, DC: Transportation Research Board, National Research Council, 1989, 190–198.
Examines Toronto Citizen's campaign to retain the city's streetcar system.

2919 Mensah, Joseph. Journey to Work and Job Search Characteristics of the Urban Poor. Dordrecht: *Transportation*, Vol. 22(1), 1995, 1–19.
Examines gender differences in commuting and job search patterns of the urban poor.

2920 Mowforth, M. R. N. *Accessibility to Employment in Selected Areas of London.* London: University College London (PhD Thesis), 1985.

2921 Owen, Wilfred. *Strategy for Mobility.* Washington, DC: Brookings Institution, 1964.
Classic account of the importance of urban transport in developing countries.

2922 Owen, Wilfred. *Transportation for Cities: the role of federal policy.* Washington, DC: Brookings Institution, 1976. 70 pp.
Examines the merits and shortcomings of federal programmes to improve mobility in metropolitan areas. Argues for a more innovative use of federal aid to deal with the related problems of transportation, energy and the environment.

2923 Pucher, John and Williams, Fred. Socioeconomic Characteristics of Urban Travellers. Westport, CT: *Transportation Quarterly*, Vol. 46(4), October 1992, 561–581.
Examines variations in income, race ethnicity, age and sex among users of different urban transportation modes.

2924 Rainbow, Roger and Tan, Henry. *Meeting the Demand for Mobility.* London: Group Public Affairs, Shell International Petroleum Company Ltd, 1993. 15 pp.

Examines the growing demand for mobility, particularly in relation to private car use and the environmental concerns associated with vehicle emissions, the structure of cities and the problems of urban congestion.

2925 Scottish Association for Public Transport. *Fares Please? Urban Public Transport – how to ease the mobility gap.* Glasgow: Scottish Consumer Council, 1981. 73 pp.

Examines who is using public transport and where it is being used in Scotland. Also looks at fares; reliability of public transport; and the effectiveness of financial support, and offers recommendations for reform.

2926 Shembesh, A. M. *A Study of Travel in Contemporary Tripoli, with Reference to the Problems of Mobility and Accessibility.* Glasgow: University of Strathclyde (MSc Thesis), 1981.

2927 Smith, Jose (ed.). *Transport and Welfare.* Salford: University of Salford, Transport Geography Study Group, 1994. 151 pp.

Covers a broad range of research detailing transport provision and people's quality of life which, combined, illustrate the importance of welfare issues in relation to transport geography.

2928 Thornthwaite, S. E. *The Effects of Legislative, Demographic and Social Changes in the Provision of School Transport Services by Local Education Authorities in the United Kingdom.* Newcastle upon Tyne: University of Newcastle upon Tyne (PhD Thesis), 1991.

Examines the long term demographic and social trends affecting the provision of school transport services by the Local Education Authorities and the institutional responses to these trends.

2929 Thornthwaite, Sian. *School Transport: the comprehensive guide.* TAS, 1994.

Provides a guide to British school transport operations.

2930 Ward, Colin. *Freedom to Go: after the motor age.* London: Freedom Press, 1991. 112 pp.

Examines the consequences of personal mobility and argues the case for alternatives to the automobile.

2931 Webster, F. V. Transport in Towns: some of the options. London: *Journal of Transport Economics and Policy*, Vol. 20(2), May 1986, 129–152.

Argues that deterioration in public transport causes hardship to those without access to a car, including some members of car-owning households.

2932 Workman, H. M. *Accessibility and Public Transport in Sheffield: case studies of police implementation.* Milton Keynes: Open University (PhD Thesis), 1986.

2933 Zehner, Robert B. *Access, Travel, and Transportation in New Communities.* Massachusetts: Ballinger Publishing, 1977. 219 pp.

Examines the demographic and community characteristics which determine travel behaviour and suggests changes in the design of towns might result in reduced travel and potential energy savings.

Community transport

2934 Adenji, A. Odutola and **Taylor, Addis C.** Services and Longevity of Paratransit Operation. Westport, CT: *Transportation Quarterly*, Vol. 44(1), January 1990, 151–162.

Attempts to develop a paratransit paradigm of variables that enhance paratransit success and longevity by examining the effect of policies and strategies on paratransit services.

2935 Bailey, J. M. *Voluntary and Social Services Transport in Birmingham, Redditch and Bromsgrove.* TRRL Supplementary Report 467. Crowthorne: Transport and Road Research Laboratory, 1979. 22 pp.

Reports on organisations running small vehicles to provide communal transport as a form of welfare. Operation of Social Services Department transport is also investigated.

2936 Banister, David; Taylor, John; Gretton, John; Harrison, Anthony and **O'Leary, Laura** (eds). Community Transport. In *Transport UK: an economic, social and policy audit.* Berks: Policy Journals, 1987, 27–35.

Examines the operation and funding of community transport including minibus schemes; dial-a-ride; community buses; and social car schemes.

2937 Bhatt, Ronald F., Kemp, Kiran U., Kirby, Ronald F., McGillivray, Robert G. and **Whol, Martin.** *Para-Transit: neglected options for urban mobility.* Washington, DC: The Urban Institute, 1975. 319 pp.

Examines the operation of the numerous forms of transportation which fall between private cars and public transport.

2938 Bryman, A., Gillingwater, D. and **Warrington, A. J.** *The Co-Ordination of Community Transport Resources: a case study of the* *minibus pooling scheme adminstered by Tower Hamlets community transport.* Loughborough: University of Loughborough, 1987. 85 pp.

A case study of the organisation and co-ordination of community transport resources.

2939 Cross, Charles. Right to Expense for School Journeys. London: *Local Government Chronicle*, No. 6581, October 1993, 13.

Debates whether Local Education Authorities could adopt a policy for the payment of school travelling expenses which discriminated against some children.

2940 Department of Transport. *A Guide to Community Transport.* London: HMSO, 1978. 60 pp.

States that community transport is about local people organising their own transport services using volunteer, unpaid drivers and offers simple practical advice and information on the operation of such services.

2941 European Conference of Ministers of Transport. *Paratransit.* ECMT Round Table 40. Paris: Organisation for Economic Co-operation and Development, 1978. 165 pp.

Examines a selection of transport modes, organisational procedures and services falling midway between two pre-eminent types of conventional transport, i.e. private cars and public transport services.

2942 Feibel, Charles Edward. *Paratransit and Urban Public Transport Policy in Low and Medium-Income Countries: a case study of Istanbul, Turkey.* Chapel Hill, NC: University of North Carolina (PhD Thesis), 1987.

Considers the efficiency and effectiveness of paratransit services as compared to publicly provided bus services and automobiles.

2943 Hillman, Mayer. Children, Transport and the Quality of Life. London: *Childright*, No. 107, 1994, 14–15.

Examines the restrictions imposed on children's freedom and opportunities for independent mobility by transport policies which promote the automobile.

2944 Marshall, D. *Community Transport: passenger need and the coordination of resources.* Nottingham: Nottingham Polytechnic (M.Phil Thesis), 1990.

Examines the concept of need in transport planning and the contribution that community transport service, through co-ordination, can make to meeting unmet transport needs.

2945 Nutley, Stephen D. *Unconventional and Community Transport in* *the United Kingdom.* New York: Gordon and Breach Science Publishers, 1990. 430 pp.

Classifies and describes the whole range of 'unconventional' and 'community' transport modes, reviewing their origins, distribution, social role and economic performance.

2946 Peiser, Richard B. Land Use Versus Road Network Design in Community Transport Cost Evaluation. Madison, WI: *Land Economics*, Vol. 60(1), February 1984, 95–109.

Evaluates the relative importance of land use location and road network design as they affect overall transportation costs within a community.

2947 Slevin, Roger (ed.). *Dial-a-Ride Symposium.* Cranfield: Cranfield Institue of Technology, 1974. 148 pp.

Collection of papers presented at the first British Dial-a-Ride Symposium in 1974 two weeks after the first major experiment in Dial-a-Ride started in Harlow.

2948 Southdown Motor Services. *The Cuckmere Community Bus Project.* Brighton: Southdown Motor Services, 1977. 20 pp.

Reports on the establishment and organisation of the 'Cuckmere Community Bus Project' using volunteer drivers from villages within a given area.

2949 Sutton, J. C. Transport Innovation and Passenger Needs: changing perspectives on the role of Dial-a-Ride systems. London: *Transport Reviews*, Vol. 7(2), April–June 1987, 167–182.

Reviews the changing role of Dial-a-Ride systems in the period 1969 to 1985 as a case study in transport innovation.

2950 Sutton, John. *Coordination and Social Policy.* Aldershot: Avebury, 1988. 213 pp.

Considers special services for those without access to the private car or conventional public transport. Including voluntary sector community transport and public sector social transport.

2951 Waling, H. G. The Haarlem Multibus. Brussels: *Public Transport International*, Vol. 43(1), January 1994, 38–39.

Disadvantaged

2952 Alexander, Jennifer and **Oxley, Philip.** *Disability and Mobility in London: a follow-up to the London Area Travel Survey.* Technical

Report 34. Crowthorne: Transport and Road Research Laboratory, 1994. 94 pp.

Describes the results of a survey of 2417 people identified in the London Area Travel Survey as having a disability or long-standing health problem that made travelling difficult.

2953 Alexander, Terry. *Travel Behaviour of the Elderly and Handicapped in Lawrence, Massachusetts and Allegheny County, Pennsylvania.* Berkeley, CA: University of California, 1988. 281 pp.

2954 Ashford, Norman; Bell, William G. and **Rich, Tom A.** (eds). *Mobility and Transport for Elderly and Handicapped Persons.* New York: Gordon and Breach Science Publishers, 1982. 383 pp.

Proceedings of a conference held in England in 1981.

2955 Automobile Association. *Mobility for All: disabled travellers and their needs.* Basingstoke: Automobile Association, 1992. 49 pp.

2956 Bailey, J. M. and **Layzell, A. D.** *Special Transport Services for Elderly and Disabled People.* Aldershot: Gower, 1983. 352 pp.

Discusses the managerial and organisational issues involved in providing a comprehensive set of special transport services.

2957 Begag, Azouz. The Social Effects of Immigrants' Spatial Mobility. Geneva: *International Migration*, Vol. 26(2), June 1988, 199–212.

Investigation into the North African immigrants in France including research on self-produced urban transport.

2958 Boda, John A. and **Kershaw, Robert E.** *Elderly and Handicapped Accessibility: the California ways.* Paper presented at the National Conference on 'Light Rail Transit: new system successes at affordable prices'. Washington, DC: Transportation Research Board, National Research Council, 1989, 147–162.

2959 Brooks, B. M., Ruffell-Smith, H. P. and **Ward, Joan S.** *An Investigation of Factors Affecting the Use of Buses by Both Elderly and Ambulant Disabled Persons.* Crowthorne: Transport and Road Research Laboratory, 1972, 109 pp.

2960 Cantilli, Edmund J. and **Falcocchio, John C.** *Transportation and the Disadvantaged.* Lexington, MA: D. C. Heath, 1974. 189 pp.

2961 Carpenter, John E. Accommodating Cognitive Disabilities in

Public Transport. Virginia: *Transportation Quarterly*, Vol. 48(1), Winter 1994, 45–54.

2962 Chadda, Himmat S. and **Noel, Errol C.** Consolidating Elderly and Handicapped Transportation Services. Westport, CT: *Transportation Quarterly*, Vol. 41(2), April 1987, 229–246.

2963 Chadjipadelis, T., Vougias, S. and **Zafiropoulos, C.** Transport and Social Discrimination: the case of Menemeni, Thessaloniki. London: *Transport Reviews*, Vol. 14(1), January–March 1994, 1–12.

Argues that transport improvements could be a useful tool to achieve a certain degree of social amelioration and a better quality of life.

2964 Cooke, Peter. Mobility: a consumer's view. Peterborough: *Coach and Bus Week*, Issue 177, July 1995, 24–25.

Gives a wheelchair user's opinion of a range of specialist vehicles for the disabled and aged on show at the 1995 Disability Roadshow.

2965 Desrosiers, J., Dumas, Y., Ioachim, I., Solomon, M. M. and **Villeneuve, D.** A Request Clustering Algorithm for Door-to-Door Handicapped Transportation. Baltimore, MD: *Transportation Science*, Vol. 29(1), February 1995, 63–78.

2966 Edwards, M., Fowkes, A. and **Gallon, C.** *Accidents Involving Visually Impaired People Using Public Transport or Walking*. Crowthorne: Transport and Road Research Laboratory, 1995. 77 pp.

2967 European Conference of Ministers of Transport. *Transport for People with Mobility Handicaps: public transport by bus.* Paris: Organisation for Economic Co-operation and Development, 1991. 116 pp.

Report of an international seminar examining the ways in which buses and bus services could be improved for people with mobility handicaps.

2968 European Conference of Ministers of Transport. *Transport for Disabled People: international comparisons of practice and policy with recommendations for change.* Paris: Organisation for Economic Co-operation and Development, 1986. 139 pp.

2969 European Conference of Ministers of Transport. *Transport for Disabled People: a review of the provisions and standards for journey planning and pedestrian access.* Paris: Organisation for Economic Co-operation and Development, 1991. 114 pp.

2970 European Conference of Ministers of Transport. *Transport for People with Mobility Handicaps: information and communication.* Paris: Organisation for Economic Co-operation and Development, 1991. 154 pp.

2971 Frye, Ann. Whose Handicap? London: *Transport,* Vol. 11, June 1990, 133–137.

Claims that over 12 per cent of the population in the United Kingdom have a disability and that providing mobility for them is a major problem.

2972 Greater London Association for Disabled People. *Transport in London for People with Disabilities: individual borough profiles.* London: Greater London Association for Disabled People, 1984.

A borough by borough report of the statutory transport provision available to the disabled together with details of cost; population; registered disabled people; number of vehicles; type and capacity and the provision supplied by the voluntary sector.

2973 Greater London Association for Disabled People. *Transport for People with Disabilities: patterns of use.* London: Greater London Association for Disabled People, 1984. 26 pp.

Claims that many disabled persons cannot use most of the common means of transportation, and that many more are restricted in their means of travel and in the frequency of journeys they make.

2974 Greater London Association for Disabled People. *Transport in London for People with Disabilities: existing provision.* London: Greater London Association for Disabled People, 1984.

Based on material collected from interviews with both statutory and voluntary transport agencies carried out in 1983 in all London boroughs and with organisations concerned with transportation such as London Transport, British Rail, the London Ambulance Service, taxi organisations, trades unions and many others.

2975 Heraty, Margaret. Tackling a Global Problem. London: *Transport,* Vol. 8, February 1987, 23–26.

Reports on initiatives in transport to assist people with reduced mobility or having a transport handicap.

2076 Heraty, Margaret and **Oxley, Philip R.** *Mobility for Disabled People in London.* Cranfield: Cranfield Institute of Technology, 1989. 35 pp.

Discusses the three main forms of public road transport available for use by disabled people in London: dial-a-ride, Mobility Bus and Taxicard. Examines the role of each of these services and what scope exists for future coordination.

2977 Hunter, David. Disabled Travellers Still Not Satisfied. London: *Transport*, Vol. 9, July/August 1988, 352–353.

2978 Jegede, Francis. *Transport for Elderly Persons: mobility survey of ten counties in England and Wales.* Derby: Department of Geography, University of Derby, 1993. 96 pp.

Examines the experiences of elderly people in their use of public transport in England and Wales and identifies the transport needs of the elderly according to personal circumstances and local conditions.

2979 Kikuchi, Shinya. Vehicle Routing and Scheduling Development for Transportation of Elderly and Handicapped. Westport, CT: *Transportation Quarterly*, Vol. 41(2), April 1987, 207–228.

2980 King, Joe Jr. Adequacy of Transportation in Minority Communities for Handicapped, Low Income and Elderly Groups. Westport, CT: *Transportation Quarterly*, Vol. 41(2), April 1987, 247–262.

Addresses the accessibility of transportation services for disabled, low income and elderly persons, using the Jackson, Mississippi metropolitan area as the case study.

2981 Mannion, R. *Transport Provision and Mobility Assistance for Disabled People: a consumer evaluation of planning and practice.* Manchester: University of Manchester Institute of Science and Technology (PhD Thesis), 1993.

Provides a consumer evaluation of transport provision and mobility assistance for disabled people, and explores a range of closely connected issues (both substantive and theoretical) relevant to such an undertaking.

2982 McConville, James and **Thompson, Andrew.** *The Growing Demand for Accessible Urban Transport: an analysis of the provision of services for the transport disadvantaged.* London: City of London Polytechnic, 1990. 27 pp.

Considers the demand for transport services from 'transport disabled' people, and the approach of the bus industry to the question in terms of research and policy making.

2983 Oxley, Philip R. and **Richards, Michael J.** A Review of the Personal Costs of Disability in Relation to Transport. Oxford: *Transport Policy*, Vol. 2(1), January 1995, 57–65.

Article claims that there is no firm evidence to support the generally stated hypothesis that personal expenditure by disabled people on transport is higher, because of their disability, than that of their able-bodied peers.

2984 Perrins, Christine and **Starrs, Margaret.** The Market for Public Transport: the poor and the transport disadvantaged. London: *Transport Reviews*, Vol. 9(1), January–March 1989, 59–74.

Examines the markets for public transport services in the context of the argument that public transport subsidies redistribute income to the less well-off and improve the mobility of the transport disadvantaged.

2985 Pfeiffer, David. MBTA Call-a-Lift Bus Program. Westport, CT: *Transportation Quarterly,* Vol. 45(2), April 1991, 243–258.

Discusses the use of accessible buses, which provide transportation to all citizens including disabled persons, by the Massachusetts Bay Transit Authority.

2986 Poernomosidhi, H. K. Powerwo. *The Impact of Paratransit on Urban Road Performance in the Third World.* Cardiff: University of Cardiff (PhD Thesis), 1992.

2987 Skelton, N. G. *An Investigation into the Travel of Elderly People in Urban Areas.* Newcastle Upon Tyne: University of Newcastle Upon Tyne (PhD Thesis), 1978.

2988 Southern, A. C. *Accessibility Indices and Linked Trips: a case study of the elderly.* Birmingham: Aston University (PhD Thesis), 1982.

2989 Tamo, Andre. Bus Accessible to Persons of Reduced Mobility Integrated into Scheduled Public Transport Services. Brussels: *Public Transport International*, Vol. 41(3), 1992, 42–43.

Study of the accessibility of buses to people with limited mobility. Article in English with French and German translations.

2990 Transport and Road Research Laboratory. *Private Transport for Elderly and Disabled People.* Crowthorne: Transport and Road Research Laboratory, 1992. 122 pp.

Proceedings of an international seminar held at TRRL in June 1991.

2991 Transport and Road Research Laboratory. *Transport for the Disabled and Elderly: 1991–1993.* Current topics in transport no. 22. Crowthorne: Transport and Road Research Laboratory, March 1993. 37 pp.

2992 World Bank. *Urban Transport: sector policy paper.* Washington, DC: The World Bank, 1975. 103 pp.

Argues that reduction of costly inefficiencies in transport can help the urban poor, promoting equity and cost efficiency.

2993 Yearsley, Ian. Mind the Gap! London: *Urban Transport International*, July/August 1988, 18–19.

Discusses access to light rail transit for wheelchair passengers.

Recreation and tourism

2994 Avery, J. Charles. *Transport for Tourism: a foreigners' perspective.* Cambridge, MA, 1994. 287 pp.

Examines how transport systems have been modified and marketed to encourage use by tourists.

2995 Billington, G. *Predicting Choice in Public Transport: a comparison of passenger attitudes and behaviour in the choice of bus service for urban shopping trips.* Leeds: University of Leeds (PhD Thesis), 1982.

2996 Halsall, D. A. *Transport for Recreation.* Lancaster: University of Lancaster, 1982. 231 pp.

2997 Kostyniuk, Lidia P. and **Recker, Wilfred W.** Factors Influencing Destination Choice for the Urban Grocery Shopping Trip. Amsterdam: *Transportation*, Vol. 7, 1978, 19–33.

2998 Page, Stephen. *Transport for Tourism.* London: Routledge, 1994. 202 pp.

Assesses the effects of tourist travel and the challenges it poses for transport planners, providers and policy makers in the 1990s.

2999 Pol, Louis; Ponzurick, Thomas G. and **Rakowski, James P.** Sporting Event Ridership: the forgotten public transit market. Oxford: *Transportation Research*, Vol. 20A(5), September 1986, 345–349.

Examines the planned consumer usage of public transit as a means of transportation to and from sporting events with the focal sporting event being professional football.

3000 Public Transport International. Sydney's Transport Strategy for the 2000 Olympics. Brussels: *Public Transport International*, Vol. 42(1), March–April 1993, 48–50.

3001 Public Transport International. State Transit: a key role in tourism. Brussels: *Public Transport International*, Vol. 42(1), March/April 1993, 44–46.

Claims that state transit plays a key role in tourism.

3002 White, Peter R. Use of Public Transport in Towns and Cities of Great Britain and Ireland. London: *Journal of Transport Economics and Policy*, Vol. 8(1), January 1974, 26–39.

Reviews the experience of municipal transport undertakings.

Women

3003 Ahmed, Rehana; Bashall, Ruth and **Torrance, Hilary.** *Free to Move: Women and Transport in Southwark: a report for the London borough of Southwark by the Campaign to Improve London's Transport and Research Unit.* London: Campaign to Improve London's Transport Research Unit, 1987. 186 pp.

3004 Allen, D. M. *Women's Safe Transport Survey.* Middlesbrough: Cleveland County Council, 1994. 15 pp.

3005 Almetair, A. N. *The Impact of Socio-Economic Change on Saudi Urban Transportation, Eastern Region: female transportation.* Durham: Durham University (PhD Thesis), 1988.

Examines the impact of socio-economic changes on Saudi urban transportation, with special reference to the urban transportation of women, particularly those in employment.

3006 Atkins, S. and **Lynch, G.** The Influence of Personal Security Fears on Women's Travel Patterns. Amsterdam: *Transportation*, Vol. 15(3), 1988, 257–277.

Investigates the influence that women's fears and apprehension about attack and harassment have on use of transport facilities.

3007 Davis, E. P. *Aspects of the Economics of Housewives' Travel.* Oxford: Oxford University (M.Phil Thesis), 1981.

3008 Fouracre, Philip and **Turner, Jeff.** Women and Transport in Developing Countries. London: *Transport Reviews*, Vol. 15(1), 1995, 77–96.

Examines the issue of women and transport in developing countries and attempts to assess how transport might contribute more positively to women's interests.

3009 GLC Women's Committee. *Methodology.* Women on the Move. Vol. 7. London: Greater London Council, 1986. 6 pp.

3010 GLC Women's Committee. *Detailed Results: Part 2: Black Afro-Caribbean and Asian Women.* Women on the Move. Vol. 5. London: Greater London Council, 1986. 8 pp.

3011 GLC Women's Committee. *Women with Disabilities.* Women on the Move. Vol. 9. London: Greater London Council, 1986. 15 pp.

3012 GLC Women's Committee. *Survey Results: safety, harassment and violence.* Women on the Move. Vol. 3. London: Greater London Council, 1986. 8 pp.

Details women's views on their own safety using material from a survey.

3013 GLC Women's Committee. *Detailed Results: Part 7: differences between women's needs.* Women on the Move. Vol. 4. London: Greater London Council, 1986. 27 pp.

3014 GLC Women's Committee. *Women on the Move.* GLC Survey on Women and Transport: 2. Survey Results: The Overall Findings. London: London Strategic Policy Unit, 1988. 16 pp.

Survey of women's transport needs, involving travel patterns, to work, shopping, other activities, escorting others; women's view of transport and safety and security.

3015 Grieco, Margaret. *At Christmas and on Rainy Days: gender, travel and transport in urban Accra.* Aldershot: Avebury, 1996. 200 pp.

Examines the transport hierarchy of urban Accra from a gender perspective. Claims that the majority of traders in Accra are female and that this produces a distinctive set of transport and travel needs. Considers the social organisation of traders and the strategies they use to meet their travel needs and thus ensure their household survival.

3016 Grieco, Margaret; Pickup, Laurie and **Whipp, Richard** (eds). *Gender, Transport and Employment: the impact of travel constraints.* Aldershot: Avebury, 1989. 236 pp.

Name Index

Subject Index